EDITED AND WITH AN
INTRODUCTION BY
MariJo Moore

Eating Fire, Tasting Blood

BREAKING THE GREAT SILENCE OF
THE AMERICAN INDIAN HOLOCAUST

RUNNING PRESS
PHILADELPHIA • LONDON

9 8 7 6 5 4 3 2
Digit on the right indicates the number of this printing

Copyright © 2006 by MariJo Moore

Library of Congress Cataloging-in-Publication Data is available.

ISBN-10: 1-56025-838-1
ISBN-13: 978-1-56025-838-4

Book design by Pauline Neuwirth, Neuwirth & Associates, Inc.

This book may be ordered by mail from the publisher.
Please include $2.50 for postage and handling.
But try your bookstore first!

Running Press Book Publishers
2300 Chestnut Street
Philadelphia, PA 19103–4371

Visit us on the web!
www.runningpress.com

For My Granddaughters

Zoey Makayla Jaynes and Emma Kate Jaynes

To Share with their Children and Grandchildren
and On and On and On—

CONTENTS

Permissions   ix

Introduction   *MariJo Moore*   xi

1: MANIFEST DESTINY: GREED DISGUISED AS GOD   xvii

A Flood of Tears and Blood: And Yet the
Pope Said Indians Had Souls   *Eduardo Galeano*   1

The Savages in the Mirror: Phantoms and
Fantasies in America   *Paula Gunn Allen*   16

The Name Is Half the Game: The Theft of "America"
and Indigenous Claims of Sovereignty   *Jack D. Forbes*   32

Indian Affairs: Hebrews 13:8   *Vine Deloria, Jr.*   52

2: SACRED RITES: SUPPRESSION AND SUBSISTENCE   63

Christian Civilization   *Ohiyesa (Charles Alexander Eastman)*   65

Colonial FasciNations: God Save the—Oh, Say,
Can You—Oh, Canada   *James Aronhiotas Stevens*   68

Speaking Out: Religious Rights and Imprisoned
American Indian Women   *Laura E. Donaldson*   74

"I Learned to Preach Pretty Well, and to Cuss, Too": Hopi
Acceptance and Rejection of Christianity at Sherman Institute,
1906–1928   *Matthew T. Sakiestewa Gilbert*   78

Remembering: Atop Polacca on First Mesa   *MariJo Moore*   96

3: PROPAGANDA: EXPOSURE AND SURVEILLANCE   105

Indian Nations and the American Holocausts   *Carter Revard*   107

Choctaw Legacy: How to Lose Your Country Twice in
  Fourteen Treaties   *Don L. Birchfield*   112

The Cherokee Nation: A Colonial Morality Play
  in Three Acts   *Steve Russell*   128

Weeds from the Under World: The Conquest of Tsenacomoco
  and Monascane   *Jay Hansford C. Vest*   146

Washita, a Slaughter, Not a Battle: A Cheyenne Survivor's
  Perspective   *Translated, edited, and annotated by*
  Eugene Blackbear, Sr., and Kimberly Roppolo   170

Nicaragua: "What's Ward Churchill Got Against You?"
  David Seals   182

4: MATRIARCHY: WHERE WERE/ARE THE WOMEN IN ALL OF THIS?   199

One Dress to Walk 800 Miles   *Pamela J. Kingfisher*   201

Fire   *Linda Hogan*   216

One Woman Can Make a Grand Difference
  Lela Northcross Wakely   228

Winyan Wakan (Sacred Woman)   *Mary Black Bonnet*   232

From Wasouk to Shoah and Back: A Mi'kmaq Honor Song
  Alice M. Azure   238

In Each Trace of Footstep: The Constant Song of SpiritMemory
  (For my mom, Janice Hernández)   *Inés Hernández-Ávila*   249

**5: AT THIS MOMENT: REVIVING THE SPACE BETWEEN
THEN AND WHEN?**   265

American Heritage   *Eric Gansworth*   267

Looking to the Past to Find the Future   *Yufna Soldier Wolf*   278

Resilience and Responsibility: Surviving the New Genocide
  Shaunna Oteka McCovey   287

Majesties Lost   *Alfred Young Man*   296

When the True Ending Began   *Joseph A. Dandurand*   305

So Our Children Will Know   *Clifford E. Trafzer*   315

6: REMEMBERING AND NEVER FORGETTING:

THE FIRESTORM IN BETWEEN   329

Performing Nation, Performing Identity: American Indian
Storytelling, Poetry, and Song in Practice *(Thoughts on
cultural survival in the wake of the new Indian Wars)*
   Carolyn Dunn and Cindi Alvitre   331

jumping through the hoops of history *(for columbus,
custer, sheridan, wayne, and all such heroes of yesteryear)*
   Suzan Shown Harjo   344

Long Time Gone Cradleboard Song   *Dawn Karima Pettigrew*   354

Japanese Gardens   *Joel Waters*   356

All My Ancestors Have Blisters on Their Toes   *Sara Sutler-Cohen*   358

Lady in Turtleneck   *Shirley Brozzo*   361

Invisibility Lessons #1 and #2   *Drucilla Mims Wall*   363

Giveaway *(In gratitude for all of it—theft, smallpox, relocation,
and denial.) Wi-do.*   *Kim Shuck*   365

I Dreamt the World Was Round   *Nakesha Bradley*   367

To Tell Our Side   *Rita Joe*   369

Apprenticed to Justice   *Kimberly Blaeser*   370

Finding Carrie: Reaffirming Identity through Blood, Beads,
and Bones   *Kathryn Lucci Cooper*   374

Contributors   386
About the Editor   397
Index   399

PERMISSIONS

INTRODUCTION

And one morning everything was burning
and one morning the fires
were shooting out of the earth
devouring beings,
and ever since then fire—
and ever since then blood.
—PABLO NERUDA

WE LIVE on a restless planet that is in a constant state of creation and destruction. A planet covered in countries with diseased souls who have forgotten they know the most important ingredient of the medicine needed to heal: Truth. For indigenous peoples, written history is concocted with lies that exacerbate our inability to be respected as an evolving race. Written history makes us more aware of the silenced truths concerning past and current deceit, theft, abuse, annoyance, decimation, murder, and racism toward our ancestors and ourselves. Eating fire, tasting blood—what does this imply? Eating the fire of the Indian holocaust, tasting the blood of truth. Of course, this is a painful venture, but many of us want these truths revealed. We want the silence broken.

I must admit this has been an extremely difficult book to edit, not only because of the contents but also because of the absolute timely necessity of the finished work. When John Oakes, Publisher at Thunder's Mouth Press, presented the idea to me, I was skeptical but determined. Would people be willing to search for the hidden truths, reveal what they knew, revisit the pain again? Would they be willing to step out and follow in the footsteps of Vine Deloria, Jr., Linda Hogan, Eduardo Galeano, and Paula Gunn Allen (whose brilliant essays concerning the subject matter are included)? When I approached divergent indigenous peoples, I was not surprised at the various answers:

"It won't be easy to write about how the government has pushed us together on reservations, forced us apart with bloodlines, and caused us to fight each other."

"How have we allowed these truths to stay hidden for so long?"

"I know what happened to my people and I don't want to write about this because it is too painful."

"Yes, I am willing to write the truth for posterity's sake and for the sake of my family."

"It won't be easy to put on paper."

"How can we cover it all in one anthology?"

"Thank goodness, an Indian editor who won't 'whitewash' our writings!"

"Yes, it is time."

Long before the idea of this book was born, my grandfather knew it would be written. He knew I would be the one who would make it happen: I would be the one who would agree to the task—both overwhelming and essential. He knew the timing would be right and what had to be told. He knew what obstacles I would face, would overcome, and whose words would be included. Maybe he didn't know the authors by name but he knew their spirits. Grandfather knew lots of things that were going to happen; he felt them. He knew I felt things, too. That is why, after over forty years, his spirit still comes around when I need him. To encourage, to chastise, to guide, to direct. After all, he is Indian. And he knows things.

When I was growing up in Tennessee the townspeople didn't take him seriously because he was Indian and because he was the town drunk. He only spoke his Cherokee language when inebriated, and that is when he told things he felt, things he intuited. Perhaps inside his contentious stupor of intoxication is where he felt the safest from the ridicule, from the harassment, from the misunderstandings. (No one wanted—or wants—to deal with a drunk Indian.) But he knew that I knew what he felt. He knew I believed, and he knew I would continue to believe that Indians have a right not only to be heard but also to be listened to, not only to be respected but to be acknowledged. And the only way to know Indians is to understand how Indians know themselves.

We know ourselves through our history. My grandfather was sure that at some point people would desire to know this history. Not the white-washed, academic-tainted, hypothetical, surmised, guesswork history, but history from our viewpoints—what we have been told and retold, what we have seen, what we have experienced. He knew that one day American Indians would have opportunities to tell the history of their ancestors, the history of the holocaust and the continuing residue. That some would rise above the written lies and seize the opportunity to break a great silence. This book is one of those opportunities—a sounding revelation, so to speak.

The writings in this anthology present perspectives of Indian history that should be incorporated into modern day history lessons. Blame is not a reliant contingent here. We all know of people, Indian and non-Indian, who have no souls. Who have and still are destroying the lives of others by making greed-based decisions that will affect untold thousands for many generations to come. Pointedly, the past repeating itself. But these collected writings are not by preying politicians, theologizing criminals, archeological theorists, or philosophizing poets; nor are they summations and ponderings from professing pundits. The resplendent significance of this anthology, which includes scholarly as well as personal writings, is from the source—indigenous peoples themselves. Their documentation includes familial and personal memories, photographs, heartfelt pain, gratitude, and proof of survival. These writers are intent on dispelling the ugly lies by presenting the uglier truths. This is the way of genetic ancestral healing. A process to help the wounded, wandering spirits find comfort in knowing there are those willing to tell the truth and to enlighten the spirits of those who will follow.

Of course, these writings do not speak for all indigenous peoples of North, Central, and South America, for all nations: What a ludicrous thought. There are many nations, numerous indigenous peoples, and countless diverse views on scores of various events. No one in this book represents the whole of his or her nation; they simply speak. This is *Indian speak* in its grandest form: painful, poignant, angry, didactic, intense, beautiful, and resolute. As you explore this anthology, no doubt the realization will come that several of these essays and poems "bleed over" into the subject matter presented in other chapters. This is an example of one of the idiographic ironies of history: one story bleeds into another and another, until finally the totality of realism is unstained.

On these pages native writers from diverse tribes reveal the immoral suppression of religious rites, the systematic slaughtering of innocent peoples, the attempted decimation of their cultures, broken treaties between the U.S. government and Indians, and misappropriation of funding, as well as the total annihilation of many Indian nations. These are writers whose lives are still very much entwined with the millions of people who were silenced due to murder, pandemics of diseases, greed, rape, pillage, threats, and so-called Christian Manifest Destiny.

Why write a book of this caliber? Why bring to focus horrors that have long passed, hopefully been forgotten, determinedly left out of history books, or covered over with false ceremonies honoring the dead? Because our historical truth is a fire that assiduously burns, a fire that demands recognition, a fire whose flames still scorch. In order to subsist in today's mêlée of war, injustice, economic deprivation, and senseless slaughter we need to be aware of what human beings have done to each other, and are still capable of doing. We need to know ourselves as well as we know our enemies.

To eat the fire of truth is to taste the blood of our existence. Once the silence is broken there is no quieting the soul. Perhaps one doesn't need a soul that grows if one continues to believe in the made-up history. For those who aspire to know the fiery truth, this book offers a plethora of blazing voices. Negation of the past does not make the world a better place. Negation of the past allows the perpetuation of racial genocide to continue, albeit in milder forms, but to continue never-theless. Why should anyone care? Because if one believes in a higher power, a God of any sort, a supreme being, or gods of all things, then one must know that somewhere deep inside we are all connected. What is done to one is done to all. Psychic conflicts are not individual matters. We owe it to our own well-being to understand what greed, manipulation, and restructuring can do to those who are in their paths. Historical silence can be a systemic killer. Listen to this silence and remember that what has happened to one has happened to all. The future is simply the past repeated unless it is understood.

As you walk out of your front door tomorrow morning, look to your left and to your right. Reach down and touch the earth, the concrete, the sidewalk, the flowers, whatever surrounds you. Indubitably you will be touching the layered coverings of the remains of indigenous peoples—not arrowheads, not broken pieces of pottery, but the very DNA of the first peoples of this continent.

If you take a stroll in Washington, D.C., you will be walking over the skeletons of the Conoy Indians, on whose main trading town, Naconch-tanke, the capital city was built. At the time of first contact with the Europeans the village was the home of Chief Patawomeke from which Potomac is derived. Today Naconchtanke survives only in its Latinized corruption, Anacostia, which is one of the subdivisions of Washington. Cultural geography clearly shows Indian names: Roanoke, Tallahassee, Poughkeepsie, Kansas, Dakota, Utah, and Oklahoma. Interestingly enough, although American Indians were often referred to as savages, Texas comes from the Caddoan word for friend or ally and Dakota has the same meaning in the Dakota language. There are a vast number of rivers with Indian names, including Mississippi, Ohio, Tennessee, Tal-lapoosa, Tallahatchie, and Catawba. And, of course, most of the major lakes—Ontario, Erie, Michigan, Tahoe, Shasta, and Winnebago—are all Indian words. Perhaps keeping the original names helped to salve the conscience of those who decided the fates of entire nations, as did con-vincing their greedy souls that the original inhabitants were not human beings worthy of equal acceptance. Nevertheless, this land was populated with an estimated 100 million original inhabitants before Columbus stumbled into what he deemed the Indies. After European contact that number began to dwindle dramatically, and continues to do so.

Who can speak for these dead lips? Who can offer rest to these wandering spirits? Who can attest to the still reverberating sounds in the wounds of this great silence? The indigenous people of today.

We know racism is still alive, discrimination is still a force to be reckoned with, and, in most areas, Indians are still considered second-class citizens looking through a glass ceiling at the arenas of politics and academia, as well as in the general work force.

It is not surprising to me that it is the eve of my nineteenth year of sobriety as I write this. Today I am a grandmother of two lovely, charming granddaughters, and I have an unshakable perception of how my grandfather sensed the future in me. His indomitable belief about life was that it is cyclical. And so it is. Thousands of us are still here, shouting out our existence—traditionally and momentarily. This we do for those who never had the opportunity to speak, and for those who will continue to search for the original truths.

For some, the Indian wars are over. Their advice? Accept what you have been dealt. Those of you who have per capita payments enjoy the monies, and all realize there are not enough of you to sway any congressional election. Perhaps the Indian wars are over, give or take a hundred or so ongoing battles.

MariJo Moore
In the mountains of western North Carolina
August 18, 2005

1

MANIFEST DESTINY:

GREED DISGUISED AS GOD

A FLOOD OF TEARS AND BLOOD:

AND YET THE POPE
SAID INDIANS HAD SOULS

EDUARDO GALEANO

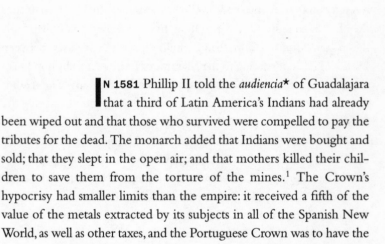

IN 1581 Phillip II told the *audiencia** of Guadalajara that a third of Latin America's Indians had already been wiped out and that those who survived were compelled to pay the tributes for the dead. The monarch added that Indians were bought and sold; that they slept in the open air; and that mothers killed their children to save them from the torture of the mines.[1] The Crown's hypocrisy had smaller limits than the empire: it received a fifth of the value of the metals extracted by its subjects in all of the Spanish New World, as well as other taxes, and the Portuguese Crown was to have the same arrangement in eighteenth-century Brazil. Latin American silver and gold—as Engels put it—penetrated like a corrosive acid through all the pores of Europe's moribund feudal society and, for the benefit of nascent mercantilist capitalism, the mining entrepreneurs turned Indians and black slaves into a teeming "external proletariat" of the European economy. Greco-Roman slavery was revived in a different world; to the plight of the Indians of the exterminated Latin American civilizations was added the ghastly fate of the blacks seized from African

---

* An *audiencia* was a judicial district as well as a judicial, administrative, and advisory body. In Mexico, it was the supreme court of administration and judgment. (Trans.)

villages to toil in Brazil and the Antilles. The colonial Latin American economy enjoyed the most highly concentrated labor force known up until that time, making possible the greatest concentration of wealth ever enjoyed by any civilization in world history.

THE PRICE of the tide of avarice, terror, and ferocity bearing down on these regions was Indian genocide: the best recent investigations credit pre-Columbian Mexico with a population of between 30 million and 37.5 million, and the Andean region is estimated to have possessed a similar number; Central America had between 10 million and 13 million. The Indians of the Americas totaled no less than 70 million when the foreign conquerors appeared on the horizon; a century and a half later they had been reduced to 3.5 million. In 1685 only 4,000 Indian families remained of the more than 2 million that had once lived between Lima and Paita, according to the Marquis of Barinas. Archbishop Liñán y Cisneros denied that the Indians had been annihilated: "The truth is that they are hiding out, "he said, "to avoid paying tribute, abusing the liberty which they enjoy and which they never had under the Incas."[2]

While metals flowed unceasingly from Latin American mines, equally unceasing were the orders from the Spanish court granting paper protection and dignity to the Indians whose killing labor sustained the kingdom. The fiction of legality protected the Indian; the reality of exploitation drained the blood from his body. From slavery to the encomienda of service, and from this to the encomienda of tribute and the grime of wages, variants in the Indian labor force's juridical condition made only superficial changes in the real situation. The Crown regarded the inhuman exploitation of Indian labor as so necessary that in 1601 Philip III, banning forced labor in the mines by decree, at the same time sent secret instructions ordering its continuation "in case that measure should reduce production."[3] Similarly, between 1616 and 1619, Governor Juan de Solórzano carried out a survey of work conditions in the Huancavelica mercury mines (directly exploited by the Crown, in distinction to the silver mines, which were in private hands): "The poison penetrated to the very marrow, debilitating all the members and causing a constant shaking, and the workers usually died within four years," he reported to the Council of the Indies and to the king. But in 1631 Philip IV ordered that the same system be continued and his successor Charles II later reaffirmed the decree.

In three centuries Potosí Cerro Rico consumed eight million lives. The Indians, including women and children, were torn from their agricultural communities and driven to the Cerro. Of every ten who went up into the freezing wilderness, seven never returned. Luis Capoche, an owner of mines and mills, wrote that "the roads were so covered with people that the whole kingdom seemed on the move." In their communities the Indians saw "many afflicted women returning without husbands and with many orphaned children" and they knew that "a thousand deaths and disasters" awaited them in the mines. The Spaniards scoured the countryside for hundreds of miles for labor. Many died on the way, before reaching Potosí, but it was the terrible work conditions in the mine that killed the most people. Soon after the mine began operating in 1550 the Dominican monk Domingo de Santo Tomás told the Council of the Indies that Potosí was a "mouth of hell" that swallowed Indians by the thousands by the year, and that rapacious mine owners treat them "like stray animals." Later, Fray Rodrigo de Loaysa said, "These poor Indians are like sardines in the sea. Just as other fish pursue the sardines to seize and devour them, so everyone in these lands pursues the wretched Indians." Chiefs of Indian communities had to replace the constantly dying mitayos with new men between eighteen and fifty years old. The huge stone-walled corral where Indians were assigned to mine and mill owners is now used by workers as a football ground. The mitayos' jail—a shapeless mass of ruins—can still be seen at the entrance to Potosí.

The Compilation of the Laws of the Indies abounds with decrees establishing the equal right of Indians and Spaniards to exploit the mines and expressly forbidding any infringement of Indian rights. Thus formal history—the dead letter of today that perpetuates the dead letter of the past—has nothing to complain about, but while Indian labor legislation was debated in endless documents and Spanish jurists displayed their talents in an explosion of ink the law in Latin America "was respected but not carried out." In practice, "the poor Indian is a coin with which one can get whatever one needs, as with gold and silver, and get it better," as Luis Capoche put it. Many people claimed mestizo status before the courts to avoid being sent to the mines and sold and resold in the market.

At the end of the eighteenth century, Concolorcorvo, who had Indian blood, denied his own people: "We do not dispute that the mines consume a considerable number of Indians, but this is not due to the work they do in the silver and mercury mines but to their dissolute way of life." The testimony of Capoche, who had many Indians in his service, is more enlightening. Freezing outdoor temperatures alternated with the infernal heat inside the Cerro. The Indians went into the depths "and it is common to bring them out dead or with broken heads and legs, and in the mills they are injured every day." The mitayos hacked out the metal with picks and then carried it up on their shoulders by the light of a candle. Outside the mine they propelled the heavy wooden shafts in the mill or melted the silver on a fire after grinding and washing it.

The *mita* labor system was a machine for crushing Indians. The process of using mercury to extract silver poisoned as many or more than did the toxic gases in the bowels of the earth. It made hair and teeth fall out and brought on uncontrollable trembling. The victims ended up dragging themselves through the street pleading for alms. At night, six thousand fires burned on the slopes of the Cerro and in these the silver was worked, taking advantage of the wind that the "glorious Saint Augustine" sent from the sky. Because of the smoke from the ovens there were no pastures or crops for a radius of twenty miles around Potosí and the fumes attacked men's bodies no less relentlessly.

Ideological justifications were never in short supply. The bleeding of the New World became an act of charity, an argument for the faith. With the guilt, a whole system of rationalizations for guilty consciences was devised. The Indians were used as beasts of burden because they could carry a greater weight than the delicate llama, and this proved that they were in fact beasts of burden. The viceroy of Mexico felt that there was no better remedy for their "natural wickedness" than work in the mines. Juan Ginés de Sepúlveda, a renowned Spanish theologian, argued that they deserved the treatment they got because their sins and idolatries were an offense to God. The Count de Buffon, a French naturalist, noted that Indians were cold and weak creatures in whom "no activity of the soul" could be observed. The Abbé De Paw invented a Latin America where degenerate Indians lived side by side with dogs that couldn't bark, cows that couldn't be eaten, and impotent camels. Voltaire's Latin America was inhabited by Indians who were lazy and stupid, pigs with navels on their backs, and bald and cowardly lions. Bacon, De Maistre, Montesquieu, Hume, and Bodin declined to recognize the "degraded men" of the New World as fellow humans. Hegel spoke of Latin America's physical and spiritual impotence and said the Indians died when Europe merely breathed on them.

In the seventeenth century Father Gregorio Garceia detected Semitic blood in the Indians because, like the Jews, "they are lazy, they do not believe in the miracles of Jesus Christ, and they are ungrateful to the Spaniards for all the good they have done them." At least this holy man did not deny that the Indians were descended from Adam and Eve: many theologians and thinkers had never been convinced by Pope Paul III's bull of 1537 declaring the Indians to be "true men." When Bartolomé de las Casas upset the Spanish court with his heated denunciations of the conquistadors' cruelty in 1557 a member of the Royal Council replied that Indians were too low in the human scale to be capable of receiving the faith. Las Casas dedicated his zealous life to defending the Indians against the excesses of the mine owners and encomenderos. He once remarked that the Indians preferred to go to hell to avoid meeting Christians.

Indians were assigned or given in encomienda to conquistadors and colonizers so that they could teach them the gospel. But since the Indians owed personal services and economic tribute to the enomenderos there was little time for setting them on the Christian path to salvation.

Indians were divided up along with lands given as royal grants, or were obtained by direct plunder: in reward for his services, Cortés received 23,000 vassals. After 1536, Indians were given in encomienda along with their descendants for the span of two lifetimes, those of the encomendero and of his immediate heir; after 1629 this was extended to three lifetimes, and after 1704, to four. In the eighteenth century the surviving Indians still assured many generations to come of a cozy life. Since their defeated gods persisted in Spanish memory, there were saintly rationalizations aplenty for the victors' profits from their toil; the Indians were pagans and deserved nothing better.

The past? Four hundred years after the papal bull, in September 1957, the highest court in Paraguay published a notice informing all the judges of the country that "the Indians, like other inhabitants of the republic, are human beings." And the Center for Anthropological Studies of the Catholic University of Asunción later carried out a revealing survey, both in the capital and in the countryside: eight out of ten Paraguayans think that "Indians are animals." In Caaguazú, Alto Paraná, and the Chaco, Indians are hunted down like wild beasts, sold at bargain prices, and exploited by a system of virtual slavery—yet almost all Paraguayans have Indian blood and Paraguayans tirelessly compose poems, songs, and speeches in homage to the "Guaraní soul."

The Militant Memory of Tupac Amaru

WHEN THE Spaniards invaded Latin America, the theocratic Inca empire was at its height, spreading over what we now call Peru, Bolivia, and Ecuador, taking in part of Colombia and Chile and reaching northern Argentina and the Brazilian jungle. The Aztec confederation had achieved a high level of efficiency in the Valley of Mexico, and in Yucatán and Central America the remarkable civilization of the Mayas, organized for work and war, persisted among the peoples who succeeded them.

These societies have left many testimonies to their greatness despite the long period of devastation: religious monuments built with more skill than the Egyptian pyramids, technically efficient constructions for the battle against nature, and art works showing indomitable talent. In the Lima museum there are hundreds of skulls that have undergone trepanning and the insertion of gold and silver plates by Inca surgeons. The Mayas were great astronomers who measured time and space with astonishing precision and discovered the value of the figure zero before any other people in history. The Aztecs' irrigation works and artificial islands dazzled Cortés—even though they were not made of gold.

The conquest shattered the foundations of these civilizations. The installation of a mining economy had direr consequences than the fire and sword of war. The mines required a great displacement of people that dislocated agricultural communities; they not only took countless lives through forced labor but also indirectly destroyed the collective farming system. The Indians were taken to the mines, forced to submit to the service of the encomenderos, and made to surrender for nothing the lands they had to leave or neglect. On the Pacific coast the Spaniards destroyed or let die out the enormous plantations of corn, yucca, kidney and white beans, peanuts, and sweet potato; the desert quickly devoured great tracts of land, which the Inca irrigation network had made abundant. Four and a half centuries after the conquest only rocks and briars remain where roads had once united an empire. Although the Incas' great public works were for the most part destroyed by time or the usurper's hand, one may still see across the Andean cordillera traces of the endless terraces that permitted—and still do—cultivation of the mountainsides. A U.S. technician estimated in 1936 that if the Inca terraces had been built by modern methods at 1936 wage rates they would have cost some $30,000 per acre.[4] In that empire which did not know the wheel, the horse, or iron, the terraces and aqueducts were made possible by prodigious organization and technical perfection achieved through wise distribution of labor, as well as by the religious force that ruled man's relation with the soil—which was sacred and thus always alive.

The Aztecs also responded in a remarkable way to nature's challenges. The surviving islands in the dried-up lake where Mexico City now rises on native ruins are known to tourists today as "floating gardens." The Aztecs created these because of the shortage of land in the place chosen for establishing Tenochtitlán. They moved large quantities of mud from the banks and shored up the new mud-islands between narrow

walls of reeds until tree roots gave them firmness. Between these excep-
tionally fertile islands flowed the canals and on them arose the great
Aztec capital, with its broad avenues, its austerely beautiful palaces, and
its stepped pyramids. Rising magically out of the lake, it was condemned to disappear under the assaults of foreign conquest. Mexico
took four centuries to regain the population of those times.

As Darcy Ribeiro puts it, the Indians were the fuel of the colonial
productive system. "It is almost certain," writes Sergio Bagú, "that
hundreds of Indian sculptors, architects, engineers, and astronomers were
sent into the mines along with the mass of slaves for the killing task of
getting out the ore. The technical ability of these people was of no interest to the colonial economy. They were treated as so many skilled
workers." Yet all traces of those broken cultures were not lost: hope of
the rebirth of a lost dignity sparked many Indian risings.

In 1781 Tupac Amaru laid siege to Cuzco. This mestizo chief, a direct
descendant of the Inca emperors, headed the broadest of messianic revolutionary movements. The rebellion broke out in Tinta province,
which had been almost depopulated by enforced service in the Cerro
Rico mines. Mounted on his white horse, Tupac Amaru entered the
plaza of Tungasuca and announced to the sound of drums and *pututus*
that he had condemned the royal Corregidor Antonio Juan de Arriaga
to the gallows and put an end to the Potosí mita. A few days later Tupac
issued a decree liberating the slaves. He abolished all taxes and forced
labor in all forms. The Indians rallied by the thousands to the forces of
the "father of all the poor and all the wretched and the helpless." He
moved against Cuzco at the head of his *guerilleros*, promising them that
all who died while under his orders in this war would return to life to
enjoy the happiness and wealth the invaders had wrested from them.
Victories and defeats followed. In the end, betrayed and captured by one
of his own chiefs, Tupac was handed over in chains to the royalists. The
Examiner Areche entered his cell to demand, in exchange for promises,
the names of his rebel accomplices. Tupac Amaru replied scornfully,
"There are no accomplices here other than you and I. You as oppressor, I as liberator, deserve to die."[5]

Tupac was tortured, along with his wife, his children, and his chief aides, in Cuzco's Plaza del Wacaypata. His tongue was cut out; his arms and legs were tied to four horses with the intention of quartering him, but his body would not break; he was finally beheaded at the foot of the gallows. His head was sent to Tinta, one arm to Tungasuca and the other to Carabaya, one leg to Santa Rosa and the other to Livitaca. The torso was burned and the ashes thrown in the Río Watanay. It was proposed that all his descendants be obliterated up to the fourth generation.

In 1802 a chief named Astorpilco, also a descendant of the Incas, was visited by Humboldt in Cajamarca, on the exact spot where his ancestor Atahualpa had first seen the conquistador Pizarro. The chief's son took the German scholar on a tour of the ruins of the town and the rubble of the old Inca palace and spoke as they walked of the fabulous treasures hidden beneath the dust and ashes. "Don't you sometimes feel like digging for the treasure to satisfy your needs?" Humboldt asked him. The youth replied, "No, we never feel like doing that. My father says it would be sinful. If we were to find the golden branches and fruits, the white people would hate us and do us harm."[6] The chief himself raised wheat in a small field, but that was not enough to save him from white covetousness. The usurpers, hungry for gold and silver and for slaves to work the mines, never hesitated to seize lands when their crops offered a tempting profit.

The plunder continued down the years and in 1969, when agrarian reform was announced in Peru, reports still appeared in the press of Indians from the broken mountain communities coming with flags unfurled to invade lands that had been robbed from them or their ancestors, and of the army driving them away with bullets. Nearly two centuries had to pass after Tupac Amaru's death before the nationalist general Juan Velasco Alvarado would take up and apply Tupac's resounding, never forgotten words: "*Campesino!* Your poverty shall no longer feed the master!"

Other heroes whose defeat was reversed by time were the Mexicans Miguel Hidalgo and José María Morelos. Hidalgo, who till the age of fifty was a peaceable rural priest, pealed the bells of the church of Dolores one fine day to summon the Indians to fight for their freedom:

"Will you stir yourselves to the task of recovering from the hated Spaniards the lands robbed from your ancestors three hundred years ago?" He raised the standard of the Indian Virgin of Guadalupe and before six weeks were out eighty thousand men were following him, armed with machetes, pikes, slings, and bows and arrows. The revolutionary priest put an end to tribute and divided up the lands of Guadalajara; he decreed freedom for the slaves and led his forces toward Mexico City. He was finally executed after a military defeat and is said to have left a testament of passionate repentance. The revolution soon found another leader, however, the priest José María Morelos: "You must regard as enemies all the rich, nobles, and high-ranking officials...." His movement—combining Indian insurgency and social revolution—came to control a large part of Mexico before he, too, was defeated and shot. As one U.S. senator wrote, the independence of Mexico six years later "turned out to be a typically Hispanic family affair between European and American–born members ... a political fight within the dominating social class."[7] The encomienda serf became a peon and the encomendero a hacienda owner.

For the Indians, No Resurrection at the End of Holy Week

MASTERS OF Indian *pongos*—domestic servants—were still offering them for hire in *La Paz* newspapers at the beginning of the twentieth century. Until the revolution of 1952 restored the forgotten right of dignity to Bolivian Indians, the pongo slept beside the dog, ate the leftovers of his dinner, and knelt when speaking to anyone with a white skin. Four-legged beasts of burden were scarce in the conquistadors' time and they used Indian backs to transport their baggage; even to this day Aymara and Quechua porters can be seen all over the Andean *altiplano* carrying loads for a crust of bread. Pneumoconiosis was Latin America's first occupational disease, and the lungs of today's Bolivian miner refuse to continue functioning at the age of thirty-five: the implacable silica dust impregnates his skin, cracks his face and hands, destroys his sense of smell and taste, hardens and kills his lungs.

Tourists love to photograph altiplano natives in their native costumes, unaware that Charles III imposed these at the end of the eighteenth century. The dresses that the Spaniards made Indian females wear were copied from the regional costumes of Estremaduran, Andalusian, and Basque peasant women, and the center-part hairstyle was imposed by Viceroy Toledo. The same was not true of the consumption of coca, which already existed in Inca times. But coca was then distributed in moderation; the Inca government had a monopoly on it and only permitted its use for ritual purposes or for those who worked in the mines. The Spaniards energetically stimulated its consumption. It was good business. In Potosí in the sixteenth century as much was spent on European clothes for the oppressors as on coca for the oppressed. In Cuzco four hundred Spanish merchants lived off the coca traffic; every year, 100,000 baskets with a million kilos of coca leaf entered the Potosí silver mines. The Church took a tax from the drug. The Inca historian Garcilaso de la Vega tells us in his *Comentarios Reales Que Tratan del Origen de los Incas* that the bishop, canons, and other Cuzco church dignitaries got most of their income from tithes on coca and that the transport and sale of the product enriched many Spaniards. For the few coins they received for their work the Indians bought coca leaf instead of food: chewing it, they could—at the price of shortening their lives— better endure the deadly tasks imposed on them. In addition to coca the Indians drank potent *aguardiente*, and their owners complained of the propagation of "maleficent vices." In twentieth-century Potosí the Indians still chew coca to kill hunger and themselves, and still burn their guts with pure alcohol—sterile forms of revenge for the condemned. Bolivian miners still call their wages mita as in olden days.

Exiled in their own land, condemned to an eternal exodus, Latin America's native peoples were pushed into the poorest areas—arid mountains, the middle of deserts—as the dominant civilization extended its frontiers. *The Indians have suffered, and continue to suffer, the curse of their own wealth; that is the drama of all Latin America.* When placer gold was discovered in Nicaragua's Río Bluefields, the Cara Indians were quickly expelled far from their riparian lands, and the same happened with the Indians in all the fertile valleys and rich-subsoil lands south of the Rio Grande. The massacres of Indians that began with Columbus never stopped. In Uruguay and Argentine Patagonia they were exterminated during the eighteenth century by troops that hunted them down and penned them in forests or in the desert so that they might not disturb the organized advance of cattle latifundia.* The Yaqui Indians of the Mexican state of Sonora were drowned in blood so that their lands, fertile and rich in minerals, could be sold without any unpleasantness to various U.S. capitalists. Survivors were deported to plantations in Yucatán, and the Yucatán peninsula became not only the cemetery of the Mayas who had been its owners but also of the Yaquis who came from afar: at the beginning of our century the fifty kings of henequen had more than a hundred thousand Indian slaves on their plantations. Despite the exceptional physical endurance of the strapping, handsome Yaquis, two-thirds of them died during the first year of slave labor. In our day, henequen can compete with synthetic fiber substitutes only because of the workers' abysmally low standard of living. Things have certainly changed, but not as much—at least for the natives of Yucatán—as some believe: "The living conditions of these workers are much like slave labor," says one contemporary authority.[8] On the Andean slopes near

---

* The last of the Charruas, who lived by raising bulls in the wild pampas of northern Uruguay, were betrayed in 1832 by President José Fructuoso Rivera. Removed from the bush that gave them protection, deprived of horses and arms by false promises of friendship, they were overwhelmed at a place called Boca del Tigre. "The bugles sounded the attack," wrote Eduardo Acevedo Díaz in La Época (August 19, 1890). "The horde churned about desperately, one after the other of its young braves falling like bulls pierced in the neck." Many chiefs were killed. The few Indians who could break through the circle of fire took vengeance soon afterward. Pursued by Rivera's brother, they laid an ambush and riddled him and his soldiers with spears. The chief Sepe "had the tip of his spear adorned with some tendons from the corpse." In Argentina Patagonia soldiers drew pay for each pair of testicles they brought in. David Viña's novel Los dueños de la tierra (1959) opens with an Indian hunt: "For killing was like raping someone. Something good. And it gave a man pleasure: you had to move fast, you could yell, you sweated and afterward you felt hungry...the intervals got longer between shots. Undoubtedly some straddled body remained in one of these coverts—an Indian body on its back with a blackish stain between its thighs...."

Bogotá the Indian peón still must give a day's work without pay to get the *hacendado's* permission to farm his own plot on moonlit nights. As René Dumont says, "This Indian's ancestors, answering to no man, used to once cultivate the rich soil of the ownerless plain. Now he works for nothing to gain the right to cultivate the poor slopes of the mountain."[9]

Not even Indians isolated in the depths of the forests are safe in our day. At the beginning of the twentieth century 230 tribes survived in Brazil; since then, over ninety have disappeared, erased from the planet by firearms and microbes. Violence and disease, the advance guard of civilization—for the Indian, contact with the white man continues to be contact with death. Every legal dispensation since 1537 meant to protect Brazil's Indians has been turned against them. Under every Brazilian constitution they are "the original and natural masters" of the land they occupy, but the richer that virgin land proves to be, the greater the threat hanging over their lives. Nature's very generosity makes them targets of plunder and crime. Indian hunting has become ferocious in recent years; the world's greatest forest, a huge tropical zone open to legend and adventure, has inspired a new "American dream." Men and business enterprises from the United States—a new procession of conquistadores—have poured into Amazonia as if it were another Far West. This U.S. invasion has inflamed the avarice of Brazilian adventurers as never before. The Indians die out leaving no trace and the land is sold for a few dollars to the new interested parties. Gold and other plentiful minerals, timber, and rubber, riches whose commercial value the Indians are not even aware of, recur in the reports of each of the few investigations that have been made. It is known that the Indians have been machine-gunned from helicopters and light airplanes and inoculated with smallpox virus, that dynamite had been tossed into their villages, and that they have been given gifts of sugar mixed with strychnine and salt mixed with arsenic. The director of the Indian Protection Services, named by the Castelo Branco dictatorship to clean up its administration, was himself accused, with proof, of committing forty-two different kinds of crimes against the Indians. That scandal broke in 1968.

Indian society in our time does not exist in a vacuum, outside the general framework for the Latin American economy. There are, it is true, Brazilian tribes still sealed within the jungle, altiplano communities totally isolated from the world, redoubts of barbarism on the Venezuelan frontier; but in general the Indians are incorporated into the system of production and the consumer market, even if indirectly. They participate in an economic and social order that assigns them the role of victim—the most exploited of the exploited. They buy and sell a good part of the few things they consume and produce, at the mercy of powerful and voracious intermediaries who charge much and pay little; they are day laborers on plantations, the cheapest work force, and soldiers in the mountains; they spend their days toiling for the world market or fighting for their conquerors. In countries like Guatemala, for example, they are at the center of national economic life: in a continuous annual cycle they leave their "sacred lands"—high lands where each small farm is the size of a corpse—to contribute two hundred thousand pairs of hands to the harvesting of coffee, cotton, and sugar in the lowlands. They are transported in trucks like cattle and it is not always need but sometimes liquor that makes them decide to go. The contractors provide a marimba band and plenty of *aguardiente* and when the Indian sobers up he is already in debt. He will pay it off laboring on hot and strange lands which—perhaps with a few centavos in his pocket, perhaps with tuberculosis or malaria—he will leave after a few months. The army collaborates efficiently in the task of convincing the reluctant. Expropriation of the Indians—usurpation of their lands and their labor—has gone hand in hand with racist attitudes which are in turn fed by the objective degradation of civilizations broken by the Conquest. The effects of the Conquest and the long ensuing period of humiliation left the cultural and social identity the Indians had achieved in fragments. Yet in Guatemala this pulverized identity is the only one that persists.* It

---

* The Maya-Quichés believed in a single god; practiced fasting, penitence, abstinence, and confession; and believed in the flood at the end of the world. Christianity thus brought them few novelties. Religious disintegration began with colonization. The Catholic religion assimilated a few magical and totemic aspects of the Maya religion in a vain attempt to submit to the Indian faith the conquistadors' ideology. The crushing of the original culture opened the way for syncretism.[10]

persists in tragedy. During Holy Week, processions of the heirs of the Mayas produce frightful exhibitions of collective masochism. They drag heavy crosses and participate in the flagellation of Jesus step by step along the interminable ascent to Golgotha; with howls of pain they turn his death and his burial into the cult of their own death and their own burial, the annihilation of the beautiful life of long ago. Only there is no Resurrection at the end of their Holy week.

1 John Collier, *The Indian of the Americas* (New York: W.W. Norton, 1947), p. 138.
2 Emilio Romero, *Historia económica del Perú* (Buenos Aires, 1941).
3 Enrique Finot, *Nueva historia de Bolivia* (Buenos Aires, 1946).
4 According to a member of the United States Soil Conservation Service, cited in Collier, *The Indians of the Americas*, p. 53.
5 David Valcárcel, *La rebellion de Túpac Amaru* (Mexico, 1947).
6 Alexander von Humboldt, *Ansichten der Natur* (*Aspects of Nature*), vol. II; quoted in Adolph Meyer-Abich et al., *Alejandro de Humboldt, 1769–1859* (Bad Godesberg, 1969).
7 Ernest Gruening, *Mexico and Its Heritage* (New York: Appleton-Century-Crofts, 1928), p. 38.
8 Arturo Bonilla Sánchez, "Un problema que se agrava: la subocupación rural," in *Neolatifundismo y explotación, se Emiliano Zapata a Anderson Clayton & Co.* (México, 1968).
9 René Dumont, *Lands Alive* (New York: Monthly Review Press, 1965), p. 10
10 "Don Volcán necesita carne humana bien tostadita," in Carlos Guzmán Boeckler and Jean-Loup Herbert, *Guatemala: una interpretación histórico-social* (México, 1970).

THE SAVAGES IN THE MIRROR:

PHANTOMS AND FANTASIES IN AMERICA

PAULA GUNN ALLEN

I

"THE SAVAGES"
As we rowed from our ships and set foot on the shore
In the still coves,
We met our images.

Our brazen images emerged from the mirrors of the world
Like yelling shadows,
So we searched our souls,

And in that hell and pit of everyman
Placed the location of their ruddy shapes.
We must be cruel to ourselves.

THE FIRST thing that they did after landing was to steal all the corn they could carry from a nearby Wampanoag village. The natives of that place had seen them coming and, having been previously treated to the visits of white men, had fled into the forest. The next day the Puritans came back; yesterday's haul had been too little, they felt, so they took what was left in the storage bins.

> They now had no friends to welcome them nor inns to entertain or refresh their weather-beaten bodies; no houses or much less towns to repair to, to seek for succor. . . . All things stand upon them with a weather-beaten face, and the whole country, full of woods and thickets, represented a wild and savage hue.
>
> —WILLIAM BRADFORD

There was a Wampanoag village that had been emptied by previous contact with the Europeans; the inhabitants had died of some disease the years before. These poor, "weather-beaten bodies" repaired thereto and made themselves at home. The village that succored them was one filled with houses covered by elm bark of generous size, walled around by a "stockade" fence, which thus nicely separated from home that which they most feared: woods and thickets that, to their minds, represented a wild and savage face.

It is strange that accounts of early American experience overlook the presence of other human communities—a negligible presence, we are led to believe, all but gone right after the first Thanksgiving dinner. Despite American folklore that is all too often offered to children and adults alike as "fact," there were thousands upon thousands of people living in settled, agricultural communities along the Atlantic seaboard. And it was these societies—or, one may fairly say, this civilization—from which the colonials drew the strength, courage, and concepts upon which to base both their revolutions against England and, much later, Spain and to devise a form of nationhood that recognized the equal rights of all adult citizens, male and female, "high born" or "common," to have a voice in their own governance. And though it took them well over a century, from 1776 to 1947, eventually they recognized their founding ideals in law. "The shot heard round the world," as the American Revolution of 1776 was termed by pundits and philosophers of the eighteenth and nineteenth centuries, was fired from an Algonquin and Haudenoshonee gun.

Whoever the first Americans were, they weren't the Puritans, whose idea of social organization was to lock all citizens within the palisades, whip and chain people to stockades or to wagons or horses from which they were dragged out of town, or to banish them, alone, to the wilderness for in any way disagreeing with the "town fathers," who were the sole recognized authorities. Thus, it is strangest of all that "our images" were suitable mirrors of being, while we were, and still are, not allowed to be there at all.

I have sat through more hours of American history and American literature than I care to contemplate, and seldom was the word "Indian" (even that misshapen idol) mentioned. "With all due respect, ma'am," ever the courtly professional expert of white supremacy, "Indians never had an effect on America at all." (America's a self-made Marlborough man, ma'am.)

Did you know that the Cherokee tipped the balance of Spanish power that gave the South Atlantic coast to the English?

That the Haudenoshonee ("Iroquois") dominated the power struggle among France, England, and Spain for over two hundred years?

That the Chickasaw platoons who ran missions for Andrew Jackson during the War of 1812 were the reason for the victory of the United States over England?

I didn't.

I spent twenty-two years in school, and I didn't know that.

Nor in all those years was I ever given this moving speech to memorize. Delivered by Ta-ha-yu-ta (Logan), the lone survivor of his community and family during the French and Indian war. This bit of eloquence was featured in the McGuffy Reader and used for several generations in American public schools as exemplary oratory.

I appeal to any white man to say, if he ever entered Logan's cabin hungry, and he gave him not meat; if ever he came cold and naked, and he clothed him not. During the course of the last long and bloody war, Logan remained idle in his cabin, an advocate of peace. Such was my love for the whites, that my countrymen pointed as they passed, and I said, "Logan is a friend of the white man." I had even thought to have lived with you but for the injuries of one man. Colonel Cresap the last spring, in cold blood and unprovoked, murdered all of the relations of Logan, not even sparing my women and children. There runs not a drop of my blood in the veins of any living creature. This called on me my revenge. I have sought it; I have killed many; I have fully glutted my vengeance. For my country, I rejoiced at the beams of peace. But do not harbor a thought that this is the joy of *fear*. Logan never felt fear. He will not turn on his heel to save his life. Who is there to mourn for Logan? Not one!

—Ta-Ha-Yu-Ta [Logan], Iroquois

The French and Indian war was fought in the mid-1700s, before the founding of the Republic. The Puritans, historically deemed the nation's forefathers, had come ashore not two centuries before. But they were not the first Europeans to colonize what is now the United States. New Mexico was colonized long before Plymouth. Why was the Puritan colony designated the earliest American settlement? Why do chronological history or literature books start with the Puritans? In terms of the present boundaries of the United States, the Southwest was entered first and more or less subdued. Then Florida. Then New England and New France. Then California, Navajoland/Apache. Then the Plains. But American history marches ever westward, from the northern Atlantic coast of the United Sates to California. Let us ever be mindful that this particular history speaks English. But that it does so is accidental. English was made the national language by one vote over German because a cart carrying two delegates to the Continental Congress meeting on the issue broke down. Those two delegates, who were prepared to cast their votes for the German language missed the meeting. These instances of historians' oversights can be explained, of course. Europeans didn't invade, conquer, and "settle" America; Yale and Harvard—with barely perceptible assists from Andover, William and Mary, Dartmouth, and Princeton—did. There is more than a grain of truth in this explanation, but there is another, more intriguing, one: America has amnesia.

The American myth, for some reason, depends on an "empty" continent for its glory and for its meaningfulness to Americans. The Adam who names the beasts and the birds, who tends God's garden, wasn't to be beat out of his place, dethroned as "Firstborn of God" by Spaniards, Dutchmen, Frenchmen, or, heaven forbid, savages.

> *President Jackson asked,*
> *What good man would prefer a forested country ranged with savages*
> *To our extensive republic studded with cities*
> *With all the improvements art can devise or industry execute?*

The question that has haunted me for several years now is: What did they see when they saw their images emerge "from the mirror of the world"? People don't develop amnesia for the love of forgetfulness—or do they? Certainly, there is a passion for memory loss in American thought. Thoreau speaks with indignation of the grip of history on the free growth of the (civilized) soul. "One generation abandons the enterprises of another like stranded vessels," he said. And his construction is not unique to himself or to Americans. He was aware of the Aztec ceremonial renewal of all possessions every fifty-two years (but probably not of its meaning as renewal). He confused history with bondage, perhaps because the history of Europeans was the history of the bondage of others as well as themselves.

> *Then through the underbrush we cut our hopes*
> *Forest after forest to within*
> *The inner hush where Mississippi flows*
> *And were in ambush as the very source,*
> *Scalped to the cortex. Yet bought them off*
> *It was an act of love to seek their salvation.*

The mind is a curious instrument—that of a culture no less so than that of a person—and its existential messages are more profoundly illuminating than its protestations. This amazing trick of memory loss is such a case. It might tell us why America is ambivalent at best, schizoid, even schizophrenic, at worst. For how can one immediately experience the present without regard to the shaping presence of the past? Yet Americans have been, at least in the expressions of their artists and scholars, profoundly present-oriented and idea- or fantasy-centered. Their past has fascinated them, in a made-up form, but the real past is denied as though it is too painful—too opposed to the fantasy, the dream, the bespoken.

> *Pastor Smiley inquired,*
> *What good man would allow his sins or his neighbors'*
> *To put on human dress and run in the wilds*
> *To leap out on innocent occasions?*

Is that what they saw—their ideal of sin personified?

It is fairly clear that the European transplants did not see "Indians." It is possible that they did, as Josephine Miles (whose poem I've been quoting) suggests, see themselves. Certainly this connection is borne out by the curious scholarly amnesia regarding the tribes who, contrary to popular American opinion, covered this continent as "the waves of a wind-ruffled sea cover its shell-paved floor," to quote Sealth (Seattle). Until recently, American figures have estimated the entire contact population of the tribes to be around 450,000. The numbers now estimated are around ten million, and this figure is rising. Some maverick researchers have put it as high as fifty or sixty million (present in what is now the United States).

I suppose if I saw myself as murdering, one way or another, several million people and hundreds of cultures, I'd long to forget my past, too.

> *President Jackson asked,*
> *What good man would prefer a forested country ranged with savages*

To our extensive republic studded with cities
With all the improvements art can devise or industry execute?

"The only good Indian is dead," they said; now that the Indian is presumed dead, he gets better and better all the time. The "Indian" can be interjected into the American dream, transformed, dehumanized, a sentimentalized sentinel of America's ideal of virtue. Nobody loves a drunk Indian because a drunk Indian is real, alive, and not at all ideal. The "Indian" was one with nature, they say; and who can be more "one with nature" than a corpse?

Miss Benedict proposed,
The partial era of enlightenment in which we live,
Brings Dionysus to the mesa and the cottonwood grove,
And floats Apollo to the barrows of the civic group
To ratify entreaties and to harp on hope.

Americans may be the world champion forgetters. Yet their story has a strange logic of its own, and that logic is solidly based on the unconscious motives that propelled the actions and the rhetoric in the first place. And America has cultural amnesia, at least with regard to the Tribes. He, "American Adam," is born innocent, purer than Christ, having neither mother nor (legitimate) father. Yet all that is born on earth has parents: why is it so important that America pretend to be different in this respect, to reject her commonality with all things? The mother, the land, is forgotten and denied, but the father, Europe, is not forgotten so much as attacked, as in a Freudian Oedipal drama, conquered over and over, a recurrent bad dream.

The question, whether one generation of men has a right to bind another, seems never to have started on this our side of the water. Yet it is a question of such consequence as not only to merit decision, but place, also, among the fundamental principles of government.

—THOMAS JEFFERSON, 1789

The mother: Indian, earth, and nature (seen as one thing, according to Brandon in *The Last Americans*) were submerged into "the infinite pool of the unconscious," hopefully never to be recovered. Perhaps this is Oedipal also, Frank Waters tells us in *Pumpkin Seed Point*—that the Indian represents the lost unconscious that Americans must reclaim and redeem.

It was an act of love to seek their salvation.

The eternal Mother is forever forbidden to man, the story goes. The gulf between the Mother and son is enormous and widening. And this is the schizophrenic split: Americans are forever forbidden to love the source of their being and thus, it follows, their being itself. Since Mother can't be loved, her falsified image—a grotesque fantasy—must be forever conquered and possessed. However violent the fantasization process, violence is a necessary component of the repression. But Indians won't be fantasized and erased; they endure in spite of everything. History persists as well, but the fantasy is out of control, threatened with exposure (and annihilation) by ever-present reality—another recurrent nightmare.

II

THE AMERICANS separated themselves from their paternal heritage, or so they believed. They removed their maternal heritage from sight and embarked on the expediencies of treaty, fraud, murder, mass enslavement, duplicity, starvation, infection—deliberate as well as accidental—whipping, torture, and removal. They needed land, it is said. They were greedy, it is said.

But to my mind, neither need nor greed can explain the genocide. Neither can explain the raging destruction of the earth. Neither can explain the single-minded, horrifying assault on the tribes as tribal entities, long after Indian presence was reduced to nostalgic memory, long after Indians could possibly be a military or economic threat, so long after that even today the assault continues. What obscure drive causes this single-minded pursuit of destruction?

America, the lonely hero, sprung full-blown out of the mind of God. The moral condition. The righteous imperative. Without father or mother, alone, divided, singular, driven to destroy all that speaks of cooperation, sharing, communality. The Puritans' own communes couldn't last a single generation. I am told that "thirty years is a long time for a Utopia to last." (In America, I silently add. Other utopias have lasted millennia. But they weren't based on the idea that a single individual was more than God.) It seems that Americans, loving loneliness best of all freedoms, die from it. Perhaps the central truth of early colonial experience in New England was the enormity of their sense of isolation. Far from all that was familiar, the colonials learned, perforce, to view alienation as rugged individualism, making it their defining virtue. Isolation and self-referencing became "self reliance," providing the basic theme for American civilization for the ensuing two centuries.

The loneliness of exploration was—and remains—a compelling idea for Americans. The lone hero still wanders, determined and self-assured, however lost, across the pages of America. Ronald Reagan in the forties and Robert Redford in the seventies flicker in their autistic heroism across the projected screens of American life. The Great American Cowboy is cheered for his self-reliance; the most hated American is the one who accepts society's help through a welfare allotment. And it isn't a matter of virtue in the Protestant sense that creates this peculiarity. It is not that taking care of oneself is a virtue. It is that the hero is, above all things, lonely and happy in his estrangement from all bonds that bind and cling, depend and shape. Andrew Jackson was idolized for his singular determination to let no considerations of social need or wish, of moral or legal *noblesse oblige*, interfere with his isolated, splendid determination.

In America, law substitutes for custom. In America, society substitutes for love of family, comrade, village, or tribe. *Walden* is the self-proclaimed triumph of the isolated superior individual. Alone with nature—not in it, not of it. One can be with it as a scholar is with a book, but as an observer, not a creative participant.

Indians are called primitive and savage not because they commit atrocities; everyone commits atrocities one way or another. Indians are designated primitive because they place the good of the group and the good of the earth before that of the self. Mexicans are denigrated not because they speak with an accent, not because they take siestas, not because they routed American heroes at the Alamo, not because they have what Americans want—a larger share of North America—but because they think *sangre* is more important than reason, that *la familia* is more important than fame. The community is the greatest threat to the American Individual Ethic; and it is the community that must be punished and destroyed. Not because Americans take much conscious notice of community, but because community is what a human being must have to be human in any sense, and community is what Americans deny themselves—in the name of progress, in the name of growth. In the name of Freedom. In the name of the Hero.

A person can't cherish glorious loneliness from within a community. So most women, as keepers of community, are also despised. Remember "Momism?" Women are a constant reminder of the lonely male's need to belong to others so that he can belong to himself. And it was the natural and necessary belonging of the Native Americans that so infuriated the Americans, so much so that those men who are America's greatest heroes rose to commit mass murder of the tribes. The difference between Native Americans and Americans, William Brandon says in *The Last of the Americans*, is that belonging is most important to the Indians, while belongings are most important to the whites. But what are belongings but a badge of isolation, a mountain of clutter that walls one off from those around? Thoreau revealed the most about himself (and his admirers) by saying that he felt the name "Walden" was originally "walled in." He was most taken by the idea that Walden (or White) Pond had no apparent source for its water and no outlet. Entire unto itself. A very moist desert dependent on nothing. Caused by nothing. Surrounded by smooth, regular stones. A wall to keep its pristine clarity, its perfect isolation. Secure.

It is not so strange that everyman-American hates and fears communism. The very word strikes at the root of the American way and at the heart of the American sickness. A communist is one who must depend on others. A communist is one who must cooperate. A communist is one who must share.

And it is no wonder that the American scholar is believed to live in an "ivory tower"; that utopians invariably take themselves off to splendid isolation from the contamination of others; that Americans are obsessed with privacy and the terror of infectious disease; that America's proudest document is entitled the Declaration of Independence.

I have always wondered why Americans never cooperate on anything, why even a corporation, a company of many persons, is defined as a "legal individual." I begin to see why. Strange that Dionysus is relegated to the "mesa and the cottonwood grove" and Apollo to "the barrows of the civic group, "neither of which is considered American by rugged-individual Americans. Today, Dionysus is dying of thirst on the mesas and in the withering cottonwood grove, while Apollo is on his way to outer space. They cut off Dionysus's water supply and sent Apollo to the moon. Both are thus beyond the reach of encounter or confrontation. All that is left for America to deal with, to find itself with, are myths and mirrors and shadowy reflections that twist in on themselves and on time and space so much that truth—the truth about America's past and America's identity—can never be found, never be affirmed or renewed. And in this way, everything becomes relative—nothing related instead of the other way around, which is the only way we can remain sane.

> *Reading today this manual of wisdom,*
> *In the still coves*
> *We meet our images*
>
> *And, in ambush at the very source,*
> *Would buy them off. It is an act of love*
> *To seek their salvation.*

It is not that Americans are lonely that matters here, but that Americans cherish loneliness disguised as solitude as though it were a wife. They take that wife to their breasts and cleave to her with the determined clutch of catatonia. They will not let her go. They protect her with all the ferocious murderousness of a jealousy-crazed lover and will kill anything that threatens to tear their loneliness away.

It occurs to me that governments are instituted among men to keep them apart. And so is capitalism and its fodder, money. So are "nuclear" families—highly mobile, of course. And so is progress—the touchstone of corporatism, of the nation, and of every American's life. It occurs to me that the melting pot never worked because it was not intended to work, and that schools and other institutions are designed to teach and reinforce the principle that group experiences are painful, antihuman, and demoralizing, just as the infants in George Orwell's *1984* were taught through pain to fear music and flowers. Loneliness, the beloved of the American Hero, is a coiling, clinging snake. It is strangling the life out of the people, of the families around us, life killed by the murderous creation of our own minds. Yet it is seductive, hypnotic in its murderous intent, because, however fiercely loved, solitude is not really possible in this world, after all.

> And when the last red man shall have perished and the memory of my tribe shall have become a myth among the white men, these shores will swarm with the invisible dead of my tribe, and when your children's children think themselves alone in the field, the store, the shop, upon the highway, or in the silence of the pathless woods, they will not be alone. In all the earth there is no place dedicated to solitude. At night when the streets of your cities and villages are silent and you think them deserted, they will throng with the returning hosts that once filled them and still love this beautiful land. The white man will never be alone.
>
> —Sealth

Why is it essential that the American be self-reliant, community-less— without a place to belong, a past to remember, a beginning in the roots of time, a heritage that could give them a meaningful place in the living circle that is life on this earth? Americans have an overwhelming and all-consuming need to be different. Do we cling to loneliness because nothing can be so peculiar as this monstrous affair with isolation?

Professor Roy Harvey Pearce quoted,
These savages are outlandish Tartars and Cain's children,
Though someone reported once, "They do not withhold assent
From the truth set forth in a credible manner."
Is it possible?

III

IN 2006, as in 1976 when this essay was first published, Americans can no longer afford the masochistic love of loneliness. The problems that confront us cannot be solved by a lone hero riding into town, a "law unto himself." No *one* can save us, but we must learn how to save ourselves—*all* of ourselves. We cannot do it unless we have models of community. America needs to become a tribe.

In our history we have pursued a consistent policy of exterminating Indians; that guilt rests as heavily as would matricide. Just as with those Indians, America has relentlessly destroyed the earth and earth's creatures. Indians, nature, earth, all of these are America's mother who must be denied. The alone and lonely hero must be more than god; he must be entire unto himself—"walled-in." But the destruction wrought by individual initiative necessarily haunts us now, because everywhere we look we see death: past, present, and future. And death is what America has fled for over five hundred years.

There is something that can be done; there is a way around the destruction, but it requires giving up America's real love—loneliness. This time, America can't do it herself. She needs models for community; for a rational place for femininity in the community; for ways to integrate diverse lifestyles and ethnic values into the national community; for regaining deteriorating neighborhoods; for ways to handle

"deviance" so that the deviant can be allowed to continue as a participant in the community's life and so that most deviance just won't
occur. America needs child-rearing models and models for communities that integrate and support families in their economic, interpersonal,
and child-rearing tasks. America needs a guide to the overhauling of
institutions so that they can foster persons and communities instead of
dividing and destroying them. America needs to find ways to preserve
identity that do not result in destruction of the community: an individual
who has no home, no *place*, is not a human being but a prey of every
vagrant whim and demagoguery. Humans cannot exist in isolation; if
they try, they go insane. America needs to learn ways to preserve the
individual's sense of identity, and the nation's, in a pluralistic, culturally
diverse society. America needs to resolve the leadership problems (crisis, say some); to learn how to live in balance and harmony with the loving environment; to learn creative, participatory ways of meeting the
challenges of survival and technology instead of destructive, apathetic
reactions toward them.

America needs a way to understand how society and community can
function harmoniously and how a person can fit meaningfully into the
massive body of this century's life. Above all, America needs a tradition
that is relevant to the continent and the life upon it. America needs a sense
of history, a sense of America's place in eternal time, a way to use history as renewal, not as denial. To do this, America must absolve herself
of the historic guilt toward her predecessors and heal the split in her soul.

> *One party to the purchase*
> *Receipts the purchase price and hands us back*
> *His token of negotiation which redeems:*
> *We Cannibals must help these Christians.*

America has a ready way to find those models so desperately needed,
assuming America intends to solve the equation. To do this, though,
American scholars and officials have to stop looking at the American
Indians as "primitives" or "curios." They will have to give up the

concept of Indians as mirrors of idealizations and projections of imagined sinfulness and see us instead as peoples who know how to resolve the problems all of America faces. The tribes today and throughout history provide brilliant and solid models that America could learn from and build on. Instead of treating the tribes as "problems," America should relate to us as a potentially creative force in American life.

Most Native Americans see themselves as necessarily a part of America. Red and white have been through over five hundred years of experience together; whether that experience was good or bad, it has been bonding. As for the partners in an American marriage, that bond has been born of pain, fantasy, love, and shared grief as much as of horror and death, punishment and guilt. Native America has lived through every attempt at conquest and annihilation and knows that the human spirit is, in the last analysis, unconquerable. That knowledge alone, given in blood, written all over this continent in agony, can free Americans from their fear of annihilation if Americans are willing to share the agony and redemption with Native Americans.

For thousands and thousands of years the tribes faced the problems of community and survival, growth and freedom, and solved them; the only problem they could not solve was America's passion for isolation—that ambivalence, that destructiveness, that "craziness," those policies, and that contempt. Above all, the contempt, for—make no mistake—however benevolent America's patronage has been, it was always patronage; it is still patronage. Indians don't need that patronage, they need respect. They need to work together with greater America to resolve that last dilemma, which cannot be resolved without cooperation.

It is easy to say *how* America can solve the cruel problems that face us, but it is impossible to say that she *will*, for ever since white men came here, they were torn. On the one hand, they loved freedom, and the Native Americans helped them in that love, supported them, taught them what freedom means. But on the other hand, the immigrants hated freedom, feared it, feared to make the adjustments and sacrifices and immolations of self that freedom requires. They thought that the isolated self was the badge of strength and glory; they didn't see that a free being is free as a member of a universe of member beings, and they feared that perception as they feared the Devil and death. So in their terror and conflict they tried to enslave all that was free-thinking, perhaps to compromise between that love and that fear, that attraction toward freedom and that repulsion from what it entails. But they could never enslave the Indians. They had to resort to destruction in the attempt, as they had to destroy their own emblem, Eagle—as they destroyed Buffalo, Wolf, Whale and as they are presently determined to destroy Coyote and Mountain Lion. And failing in that destruction of native peoples, because they finally couldn't bring themselves to do it, nothing was left but to deny the Tribes' existence, meaning, and way of life.

But suppose they finally succeed; suppose all the free creatures are finally exterminated—dead or changed beyond all recognition; suppose all this Turtle Island is reduced to a wasteland of dead waters and dead plants and dead mountains. Will America have finally succeeded in realizing her dearest dream? For then America will be alone, with only death and terror for comfort and companionship.

We have finally reached that place: the seeds of destruction and the seeds of life have reached their season of harvest. Whether the one or the other is given to the people to eat depends in part on which seed grows hardiest in the soil that is America. It's reaping time; now we see how well we have sown.

THE NAME IS HALF THE GAME:

THE THEFT OF "AMERICA" AND
INDIGENOUS CLAIMS OF SOVEREIGNTY

JACK D. FORBES

SOVEREIGNTY AS a concept is derived from the Latin "super" (or "above") and fundamentally has denoted a political unit or governing authority asserting that its status is higher than that of any other entities within a given physical or social space. The concept has also been extended to entire peoples, especially whenever a democratic form of political life has been developed. Still further, the idea of sovereignty has been divided into a series of hierarchical layers in which some sort of "above-ness" is allowed to drift downward in a descending order of political levels, as within political unions such as Helvetia, the United States of America, and the European Union.

Historically, countless groups of people, organized in a wide variety of ways, have sought to preserve self-government or autonomy (self-law-making), often in the face of challenges from other political entities. The most common form of traditional self-government has probably exsisted in the village, local community, band, or city. Many First Americans, for example, have capped their governing pyramid at the city or community level, relations above that level being essentially conducted as a form of diplomacy (confederations, alliances, friendships, etc.). Ancient cities such as Cahokia, Yellow Jacket, Snaketown, Chan Chan, and Oraibi, among many others, come to mind.[1]

But autonomy not only requires being above other competing political formations it also normally requires physical space, that is to say, a land or territory identified with the group and usually bearing the name of the group. Thus the ancient Tyreans possessed Tyre, the Romans possessed Rome, the Athenians had Athens, and the Persians had Persia. In fact, one can argue that the possession of the name of the place that one claims as one's own is virtually essential to the assertion of sovereignty, since, at heart, one's existence as a people—as a polis—is defined by possession of a given, named space. Can one imagine a German state without a Germany?

Imperialism and colonialism have often attempted to interfere with the autonomy of weaker political units, sometimes by wholesale substitution of names. The British Island was once known as Alba (or Albion) during the days when Celtic-speaking groups dominated it. The Angles and Saxons who invaded and conquered a good part of it eventually selected the name England, a name derived from the Engels (or Angles), even as the Frankish conquerors of Gaul imposed the name Frankreich (softened later to France).

In recent centuries Europeans have invaded the other continents: America, Africa, Asia, and Australia. In southern Africa the Dutch invaders appropriated the name "African" for their own European language and called themselves "Africans" while giving non-land-based names to the true Africans. Did this facilitate their appropriation of the indigenous nation's lands? Did it coincide with the eventual denial of sovereignty to most indigenous political units?

Perhaps the most pertinent example for American Indians consists in the efforts of Zionist Jewish settlers in Palestine to appropriate the bulk of that land and to transform it into a Jewish-dominant state. In the course of doing so, many Israelis have adopted the strategy of never referring to the Palestinians by the latter name, the name of the land. Instead, they refer to them as "Arabs," and the implication is that they are roamers and invaders who came to Palestine from elsewhere or who belong to an alien Arab land of some kind. The fact that Palestine has never been vacant—and that the Palestinians are clearly descended from the people who were already there at the time of the Arab/Islamic conquest—is intended to be wiped out by the fact that the present Palestinians speak Arabic rather than the Aramaic (Syriac) and Greek of their pre-600 ancestors.

European writers in Europe, as I shall illustrate, generally decided to refer to Native Americans as Americans, although also using other terms on occasion. As colonialism emerged, the terms used for the American inhabitants often assumed a decidedly pejorative form, especially as used by colonial settlers and adventurers. British and French writers involved in the direct invasion of America seem to have preferred "savage" as an appellation but also continued the Spanish use of "Indian."

Part of the process of European invasion was to impose European names and nicknames upon America. Thus the Powhatan-Renape people's name for their land, Attan-Akamik (Our Own Land-Place), was replaced by "Virginia," a name that allowed the English to domesticate a bit of American territory, as it were. This process was repeated almost everywhere, although in some cases a native name was captured and transformed into a domesticated European use.

In any case, part of the Europeans' strategy appears to have been to refer to the American inhabitants by terms that denied ownership of a named land, or that implied that only "savages" were present. And savages are not only unlikely to possess any sovereignty that needs respecting but also are commonly seen as "roamers." Samuel Adams Drake, in his *The Making of the Great West* (1901), asserted that:

> Beyond their regular villages, which could be moved at a few hours' warning, the Indians of this [Missouri] valley had no fixed habitations, but *roamed the wide, treeless prairies in savage freedom, like wandering Arabs*. . . . [emphasis added].[2]

The combination of "roaming" and "savage" is quite important. Such concepts connected the Americans with European ideas about the supposedly mythical savages of Europe, who were "wild" people living in the forests with animals and who possessed no named territories or recognized sovereignty. In 1851 Commissioner of Indian Affairs Luke Lea said that "on the general subject of the civilization of the Indians, many . . . opinions have been put forth; but . . . like the race to which they relate, they are too wild to be of much utility. . . ." Lea advocated "their concentration, their domestication, and their ultimate incorporation," thus totally denying any self-government or land-based rights.

Numerous Bureau of Indian Affairs (BIA) officials from at least 1859 onward echoed the denial of political rights for First American nations. One commissioner asserted pointedly that white expansionism "will not permit the lands which are required for cultivation to be surrendered to savage tribes. . . . they should be "regarded as wards. . . ."[3]

Clearly, then, the colonial-settler leadership sought to deny the original Americans any connection with a named land or territory; but by using non-land-based terms such as Indians, savages, wild people, redskins, hunters, roamers, etc., they sought to undercut or deny any territorial sovereignty. It is significant that Native Americans were not only denied the name of Americans but were also denied such names as New Mexicans, Texans, Nebraskans, Kansans, Californians, and so on. Such terms were always reserved for white newcomers or, in New Mexico, for Spanish-speaking persons viewed as at least being semicivilized. Even when territories were given native names, such as Dakota, only white persons became real Dakotans.

The name America, which has been pushed back into geologic time by geologists, paleontologists, and archaeologists, is variously derived from a Native American word (such as Amerrique, Amaraque, or Maraca) or from the first name of Amerigo Vespucci. Regardless of origin it became the undisputed name of the continent in the early 1500s and has continued as the hemisphere's name to this day, albeit with an s sometimes added because of the existence of North America, Central America, South America, and Mesoamerica as regions of the hemisphere. Sometimes also, perhaps, the s is added to emphasize the existence of cultural and political divisions, such as Latin America,

Ibero-America, Luso-America, Franco-America, Indo-America, Anglo-America, and so on.

Until recently, the name America was firmly attached to the continent as a whole and virtually all older encyclopedias and dictionaries refer unequivocally to the hemisphere as America. My British encyclopedia of circa 1875 vintage has a picture of the entire continent labeled "America," and the article on the same deals with the hemisphere as a whole. Not only that, but the term "American" is used for the "native races" without any hyphens or qualifications. For example, the author states:

> Our object in this article is to take a comprehensive survey of the American continent. . . . it has yielded some of the oldest known remains of man . . . and it has afforded evidences of a civilized era, which may even have preceded that of Western Europe. . . . The American continent is four times as large as Europe. . . . The American race is distinguished by the form of the skull. . . . The color of the Americans . . . is more uniform than that of the inhabitants of Asia and Africa. . . . Of all the groups of American languages, the various dialects of the Algonquin stock furnish the most inviting field for the philologist.[4]

The name America indisputably belonged to the entire hemisphere, for the Spanish as well as the British. For example, in 1812 the geographical work of Antonio de Alcedo (1787) was translated and published in English, in which it states, "AMERICA, the Indies, or the New World, one of the four parts of the Universe, and the largest." It goes on to note that "America is also watered by the largest rivers in the universe; such are those of the Amazonas, Orinoco, Magdalena, Atrato, La Plata . . ." and so on. Alcedo also noted the existence of the "Republic of North America or the United States."[5] The editor, G. A. Thompson, continued to refer to the entire continent or hemisphere as America in additions he made to the text.[6]

One of the early history books I was given as a child was a four-volume set entitled *The Great Republic by the Master Historians,* a work of 1897 republished in 1902. Although a history of the United States, it set the stage by looking first at all of America. The very first chapter was entitled "On the Origin of the Americans," which was a selection from Hubert H. Bancroft's *Native Races of the Pacific States*, written a decade earlier and dealing exclusively with Americans of pre-Columbian ancestry. The editors noted that:

> The written history of America begins with the year 1492.... Yet there pertains to the preceding period a considerable variety of interesting material of a semi-historical character.... This literature is in no proper sense American history, yet it is all we know of the existence of man upon this continent during the ages preceding the close of the fifteenth century.... it cannot be ignored in any work on the history of the American continent.[7]

Bancroft in his selection refers to the native races as the "Americans" and very clearly refers to the entire continent as America.[8] The editors, in turn, summarize Bancroft's findings by noting that "none of the theorists have succeeded in proving that the Americans were of Old-World origin" and concur with Bancroft's conclusion that "no one at the present day can tell the origin of the Americans."[9] Subsequently, *The Great Republic* goes on to deal with the Chinese voyage of Hwui Shin to the Kingdom of Fu Sang or Mexico and with the Northmen's voyages to Newfoundland and Greenland. Then a chapter on the "Aborigines of America" by Charles Morris makes absolutely clear that America was the entire continent. Morris also notes that:

> The American languages approach in type those of northern Asia.... The same may be said of the American features. Yet if the Americans and Mongolians were originally of the same race, as seems not improbable, their separation must have taken place at a remote period....[10]

The next chapters have to do with Columbus in Europe and then with "the Discovery of America by Columbus." Since Columbus never reached the United States, it is quite clear that the continent is the America in question.

During the latter part of the nineteenth century it was apparently quite common for some scholars to refer to the Native Americans as simply Americans. Daniel G. Brinton in 1891 wrote in his book *The American Race* that:

> The American race was that which was found occupying the whole of the New World. . . . Its members are popularly known as "Indians," or "American Indians," because Columbus thought that the western islands . . . were part of India. . . . To the ethnographer, however, they are the only "Americans," and their race is the "American Race."[11]

I have reviewed early usage of the term American and have found numerous examples where European authors referred to the indigenous people of the continent by that name, from the sixteenth century to the very end of the nineteenth century and even beyond.[12] I will not review that evidence here, except to cite the eighteenth-century Prussian philosopher Immanuel Kant, who divided humankind into Europeans, Asians, Africans, and Americans, the latter being indigenous Americans only. He states:

> The race of the American [*das Volk der Amerikaner*] cannot be educated. It has no motivating force, for it lacks affect and passion. They are not in love, thus they are also not afraid. They hardly speak, do not caress each other, care about nothing and are lazy. . . . The race of the Negroes, one could say, is completely the opposite of the Americans [*den Amerikanern*]; they are full of affect and passion, very lively, talkative and vain. . . .[13]

Clearly Professor Kant did not know how to gather objective evidence. Still, he simply echoes the usage of most other academic writers of the period in regarding the Americans as being the autochthonous people of America. This usage was often echoed by popular writers, as in a schoolbook of 1831 from Connecticut, which has a page devoted to "The Original American."[14] A recent edition of *Webster's New Collegiate Dictionary* defines the noun "American" as: "1. an Indian of No. America or So. America, 2: a native or inhabitant of No. America or So. America, 3: a citizen of the United States." Thus even our modern dictionary makers, or at least some of them, continue the usage of past centuries.[15] In a similar vein, the Jesuit scholar John Francis Bannon, in his *History of the Americas* (1952, 1963) refers repeatedly to the Native Americans as Americans in his initial chapter, "The Americas before Columbus":

> It is difficult . . . to say why the progenitors of the American race came to the lands of the Americas. . . . If the Americans came from Asia . . . by what route . . . ? When did the Americans come? . . . It is highly probable that the first Americans came in successive migratory waves. . . .

Bannon also attempts to refer to the British colonists and their successors as Anglo-Americans, aware as he is of the presence of many other nationalities in America, north and south. The indigenous Americans are called "native Americans" on occasion, in contrast to Anglo-Americans.[16]

British subjects, as well as other Europeans who were born in America, often were puzzled about how to refer to themselves in the colonial period. Some began to use the term North American to distinguish themselves, while on occasion they were called Americans by British writers in a strictly geographic sense. A runaway slave advertisement of 1763 refers to "his Majesty's Gaols in North America."[17] In a similar manner, John Quincy Adams writes about the "Independence of North America" (1821), the "North American continent," (1821), "our proper dominion to be the continent of North America" (1819), and that the United States should annex Spanish territories and extend to the South Sea (Pacific) "until Europe shall find it a settled geographical element that the United States and North America are identical" (1819), and refers to the USA as "the North-American Union" and as "North America."

Adams and James Monroe were very clear that America referred to the entire hemisphere and that "the American hemisphere" (1823, 1826, etc.) included two continents, North America and South America. Although on rare occasion Adams referred to the United States as America, he also commonly used American to name all of the republics of the hemisphere and both continents, as in "these American nations," "the American continents," the "new American republics" (1826), and "the American nations" (1822). Adams refers also to the British activities on "the Northwest coast of America" and says "that AMERICA has a set of primary interests which have none or a remote relation to Europe," the latter in his message of 1826 to the House of Representatives and both being clear references to the hemisphere as America.

In President James Monroe's annual message of December 2, 1823, in which he promulgated the Monroe Doctrine, he states that "the American continents . . . are henceforth not to be considered as subjects for future colonization by any European powers. . . ." and he also refers to America as "this hemisphere." Thus it is very certain that in the days of Adams and Monroe the leading men of the United States were not trying to insist on any kind of exclusive possession of the terms America or American. Quite the contrary, it would seem. And this usage is still reflected in the Pan-American Union and the Organization of American States, both of which include most of the republics of the American hemisphere.[18]

During the same period, Alexis de Tocqueville spent 1831 in the United States and wrote up his findings by 1835. He seems to have found himself in a quandary as to how to use the term America, on occasion using it in reference to both the continent, and the United States. He often uses Anglo-American as well as American to refer to U.S. citizens born in North America, and European for those born in Europe. American Union is used for the United States, while British America also appears. The term American is always used so as to directly exclude "Negroes," as in "... Americans of the South, who do not admit that the Negroes can ever be commingled with themselves. ..." Neither are Indians Americans, except in a reference to ancient times. De Tocqueville imbibed the spirit of Anglo-American imperialism and destiny, as when he states that "The Americans of the United States ... their offspring will cover almost the whole of North America; the continent that they inhabit is their dominion, and it cannot escape them."[19]

Unfortunately, Anglo-American racism and nationalism gradually led to still more extreme forms of appropriation of the continent's name. Struggling against this were some native writers, such as Luther Standing Bear, who wrote President Franklin Roosevelt in 1933 as follows: "Today the children of our public schools are taught more of the history, heroes, legends, and sagas of the old world than of the land of their birth while they are furnished with little material on the people and institutions that are truly American."

Standing Bear wanted American Indian history to be taught in the schools. He hoped that "were the world to realize a new evaluation of the native American justice would naturally follow in the wake of enlightenment."[20]

Tragically, however, a new and pernicious viewpoint was being promoted by some white scholars, a viewpoint that essentially excluded non-Europeans from American-ness, in addition to appropriating the continent's name. Allow me to cite a few examples from texts, which angered me when I was a student. John D. Hicks, in his *A Short History of American Democracy* (1949) pontificated that "It is well to remember that American Society is definitely European in origin. The western world before Columbus produced no great civilization of its own, and such remnants of the Indian way of life as endured were always inconsequential in comparison with the heritage that came from across the seas."[21]

In the same vein, Avery Craven and Walter Johnson in their *The United States, Experiment in Democracy* (1952) state that "the history of the American people may be divided roughly into three periods. The first is the colonial period, in which different European groups . . . were adjusting themselves to one another and to the American environment. . . ."[22]

Virtually all other texts of the period were similar in that the concepts of American people, American society, and American culture were used in such a manner as to exclude all persons of First American, African, Asian, and other non-European ancestry. This often led to blatant stupidity, as when Richard Hofstadter, William Miller, and Daniel Aaron, in their *The United States: The History of a Republic* (1957), not only commenced with the usual European background, but went on to state that ". . . it is a full three hundred and fifty years since the first permanent settlement was made, at Jamestown, Virginia, on the territory that was to become the United States."

With this assertion, the authors dismissed Oraibi, Walpi, Acoma, Taos (all of them pre-1300), St. Augustine (1565), and Santa Fe (1598). But this dismissal of non-British activity and persons is not a result of mere chance but a product of a mind-set that excludes original Americans, Africans, Spaniards, and so on from being Americans and from being part of the ethnic group to which the authors owe their allegiance and devotion. In 1961 Richard N. Current, T. Harry Williams, and Frank Freidel begin their *American History: A Survey* with this clear assertion: "The story of the American people is fairly short if it be dated from the first enduring English settlement, at Jamestown in 1607. . . . But, of course, the American story actually begins in Europe."[23] Thomas A. Bailey, in his *The American Pageant* (1956), makes it all crystal clear when he tells us that:

> The American people . . . owe a genuine debt to the Indian. . . . He added immeasurably to our pioneering difficulties, but above all he helped to make us a tough and resourceful people. A substantial part of the American pageant could be written in terms of a relentless, three-hundred-year campaign against the Indians— one of the decisive campaigns of world history.

So here we have Professor Bailey letting us know that *he* belongs to "the

American people" but that the "Indian" does not, and that the latter was "*our*" enemy for 300 years![24]

In 1958 another historian, Daniel J. Boorstin, in his *The Americans: The Colonial Experience,* begins by telling us that "America began as a sobering experience. The colonies were a disproving ground for utopias. ...A new civilization was being born less out of plans and purposes than out of the unsettlement, which the New World brought to the ways of the Old."

He goes on to say that John Winthrop, while preaching to fellow passengers en route for America, "struck the key-note of American history." Thus we see that Boorstin views America not as a landmass or a geographical region at all, but rather as an "experience" or process that belongs to, and begins exclusively with, white Europeans. "American history" seemingly begins with a seaborne Puritan preacher and not with thirty thousand years of the continent's past!

Boorstin also remarks that "...in America the idea of equality had a self-evident meaning all its own. Of course, American facts would also limit American ideals; where the 'facts of life' in America seemed to deny equality (as in the case of the Negro or the Indian), many good Americans felt strong doubts." Clearly, African-Americans and Native Americans were not Americans, much less "good Americans," to Boorstin and they obviously possessed no "American ideals."[25]

In 1955 and 1966 professors Carl Bode, Leon Howard, and Louis B. Wright edited three volumes entitled *American Literature.* The first volume, *The 17th and 18th Centuries,* was touted as an "invaluable guide to the major poets, writers, orators and historians of our culture," but it unabashedly begins with European writers such as John Smith and includes not a single Native American orator or writer, nor any traditional native literature. Not a single item from the Spanish or French or Dutch colonies is included, thus revealing in a very clear manner that American literature of the period belongs to British colonials, even those whose stay in America was transitory. Thus "American" equals "Anglo-American," with the one exception of Jean de Crèvecoeur, whose stay was brief indeed but who is given a score of pages.[26]

In 1964 Robert Clifton Whittemore possessed the audacity to author a book entitled *Makers of the American Mind,* wherein it is made abundantly certain that the "American mind" (whatever that is) is wholly white and totally male. Not a single female or non-European graces Whittemore's pages, a reflection of a racism and sexism so deeply ingrained as to suggest that large sectors of the white intelligentsia, north and south, were physically and psychologically incapable of looking at North America from a multiracial, bi-gender perspective.[27] Whittemore, like many other white authors, is kind enough to include Europeans or European-born persons as "American thinkers." He says, " I count as American any thinker whose major works were written in, and reflect the spirit of, this country, or whose influence is essentially American." That could not, of course, include William Apess, W. E. B. DuBois, Eleanor Roosevelt, or Zora Neale Hurston.

Let us pause here and again emphasize what has happened: the name America has been stolen from the continent or hemisphere and has been appropriated for use as the name of a particular country, the United States. Ah, but wait, that is not the actual story, because in fact "America" does not refer to the United States of America as the specific geographic entity or country that we see today, but rather to an ever-expanding experiment and zone that happens to be controlled by British North Americans who have rebelled against Britain. "America," then, is treated as a metaphor, a metaphor for whiteness, for English-speaking people, for Anglo-Americans, and even for their colonial ancestors.

And this is the weirdest thing of all. The concept of "American" is pushed back by modern white writers to refer to the British colonists not only before they rebel against Britain but before they even land in North America! On shipboard they are already "Americans." But bear in mind that those British colonists "unfortunate" enough to land in New Brunswick, Nova Scotia, Newfoundland, Bermuda, Bahamas, Barbados, Jamaica, etc., are not "Americans," because their descendants chose to stay attached to the king.

Thus "future United States-ness," if you will, is what is really involved here, not the fact of being resident in North America or its nearby islands. But even that is not correct, for brown and black persons, and their mixed progeny by and large, are not to be allowed to be "Americans" by most of our white writers; only English-speaking Europeans and those other Europeans who have intermixed with them are to be so honored. It also seems highly unlikely that these same writers would speak of German, Dutch, Swedish, French, Swiss, and Spanish arrivals as Americans, whether on shipboard or as new arrivals. They would have to become Anglicized first and even that might not confer American status upon their arriving ancestors, it would seem. So we are dealing with a very narrow Anglo-British appropriation of America.

The appropriation of America constitutes a key element in the form of white supremacy that emerges in the area of the United States, even as the later appropriation of "Canada" by Anglo-Canadians has become a key aspect of white supremacy there, and as the appropriation of "Mexico," "Peru," "Chile," etc., by white or light-skinned elites has formed essential parts of white supremacy in Latin America. Stealing the name of a land, as noted, is certainly a vital part of conquest and the development of a strategy of domination and predation toward the native inhabitants.

As a consequence of the equaling of America with Anglo-American areas of control and, for the most part, with Caucasian English-speakers, an "ideal" or "real" American has been constructed. This American, in the Anglo-American discourse, has always been Caucasian and English-speaking, but in the period before the mid-twentieth century he or she was also a Protestant and preferably blonde with blue eyes. After the growth of the Roman Catholic population, and with the help of many Bing Crosby movies, Catholics were able to become acceptable if of the right color. More recently, Jews, Eastern Orthodox, and even southern Europeans with darker skins have become marginally or partially acceptable, especially in urbanized regions of the country.

But it is still my judgment that Native Americans, African-Americans, Mexican-Americans, and Puerto Ricans, among others, are often not really seen as "American," per se. Our border patrol knows that brown Americans have a "foreign" and "illegal" look. Our police know that black and brown Americans have a "criminal" look, and so on. In many Anglo-American's minds, they themselves are the only authentic, unhyphenated Americans. All others, including First Americans, are not readily described simply as Americans, but must be mentally hyphenated (Latino, for example is not verbally hyphenated but it is functionally treated as a hyphenation, and the same is true for Indian, Asian, Black.

I recently saw a hate flyer circulated in New York against the Oneida people, in which "Indians" were clearly denied status as Americans. But it is not only extremist groups that attempt to restrict the term to selected white persons. The University of Nebraska Press, in its book catalog for the end of 2000, has text that describes *The Shaping of American Ethnography* by Barry Alan Joyce, including a reference to the biases of scientists:

> . . . the Americans on the expedition filtered their observations of the indigenous peoples through the lens . . . as shaped by the American experience. The native peoples were classified according to the prevailing American perceptions of Native Americans as "wild" and African-American slaves as "docile. . . ." By applying American images of savagery to world cultures, American scientists helped to construct the foundation for an American racial *weltanschauung* that contributed to the implementation of manifest destiny and laid the ideological foundations for American expansion and imperialism. . . .

I cannot argue with the thrust of the above text, but it clearly excludes Native Americans from being Americans and gives the latter identity exclusively to white persons.[28] In a somewhat similar vein, the anthropologist Richard O. Clemmer, in his 1995 book on the Hopi, states:

> Even though Americans and American culture have framed Hopis' contacts with non-Indians in the Twentieth Century,

Americans and their culture did not intrude upon a "pristine" . . .
situation. . . . Americans constituted the fourth major . . . force that
had entered the Hopi realms. . . . The Spaniards were the first,
Navajos the second and Mormons the third. While it could be
argued that Mormons are merely a variety of Americans, in fact,
the Mormons saw themselves as armed with a distinctly different
set of values . . . from those of the Americans. . . .

The above is interesting in its suggestion that the Latter-day Saints were
not Americans, revealing, I think, a rather narrow conception of the way
in which the term American is used. But I am primarily desirous of
stressing that for Clemmer, Hopi and Navajo peoples are not American.[29] This reminds me of an early article of mine (written 1956–60,
published 1963) in which I suggested that the Hopi were surely as
American as the Pilgrims. This brought an indignant retort and rejection from the editor of the *Historian*, as I recall.[30] So things haven't
changed all that much in some forty years!

In any event, I would suggest that to be seen as an American, in the
current racist white supremacy mode, one must (1) speak English,
preferably without an accent; (2) never speak any other language in a
public situation; (3) be Caucasian or light-complexioned; (4) have wavy,
curly, or straightish hair; (5) exhibit a prescribed range of mannerisms,
body attitudes, ways of walking, and expressions of speech that are
within the range used by Anglo-Americans in various regions; and (6)
possess a first name used by Anglo-Americans.

Since America is being defined as a process belonging exclusively to
Anglo-Americans, one cannot belong fully to that process unless one
conforms to Anglo-American norms. This is very hard for original pre-
Columbian Americans, whether of U.S., Mexican, or other origin,
because they not only usually look distinctive but have languages and
cultures that make them almost certain to be different. This helps to
explain why some non-Anglos strive desperately to Anglicize and to
destroy all vestiges of their non-Anglo heritage and languages, as they
hope thereby to render themselves acceptable to the dominators of the

society. Of course, a great deal of self-hate, loss of family memory, alienation, and confusion often results, along with some cases of notable success where such persons become the protégés, or even spokespeople, for
right-wing white movements.

On the other hand, if we view the United States as a geographical
country, with a fixed territorial shape rather than as a racialized process,
we would discover rich regional cultures, each with its own wonderful
and distinct history, yet all a part of the whole. Thus we would cherish
French-speaking Louisiana, Spanish-speaking Florida, the Southwest,
Native American language areas, and so forth. But no! Instead we see
movements to destroy French, Spanish, Asian, and American languages.
We see hatred directed toward cultures that are beautiful and that run
deeply into the soil of our country, and we see efforts to destroy these
cultures. We witness constant efforts to deny value to those who look
different from the Anglo "normal," as on nightly television and in the
movie theater.

Should we not see the insanity of trying to destroy the only truly
American languages and cultures we have, those of Native nations and
Mexicans and others of indigenous stock? Isn't this derangement
derived, in part, from the convoluted way our dominant population
looks at what constitutes America and American? Or is it that the
Anglo-Americans, being such recent conquerors of the western United
States, Hawaii, and Alaska, still feel threatened by the existence of that
other America, that ancient America, that hemispheric America, which
still eludes them because of their very recentness?

Indeed, I saw the glow of eager excitement in the face of a white
female television commentator while she discussed the possibility that
Kennewick Man might have been white, that white people might have
been among the ancient Americans (ignoring the fact that his descendants would all be found among brown Native Americans, as well as the
fact that his skin color will forever be unknown). The excitement over
Kennewick was an illumination for all of us, revealing the almost
pathetic eagerness of some Anglo-Americans for a one-up on the
antiquity of their predecessors on this continent.[31]

The struggle over the name America really has to do with possession, with who has the right to possess and to dominate the land and who has the right to possess and to dominate the story of the land, its history, its character, and its future. Part of this story has to do with the very important question of whether the First Americans are to be viewed as being central to the American story, or as peripheral to it, and whether they are to be viewed as organic possessors of the land with embedded rights of sovereignty and autonomy.

I think we have seen how the racialization of America has had a great impact on the persistence of racial and ethnic discrimination. It is a very serious business when one is denied the status of being an American, when one is pushed to the periphery of history as an obstacle, or when one is always highlighted as a problem for those otherwise well-meaning Anglo-Americans who cannot understand why native tribes should be able to operate casinos and run governments independent of control by states, cities, and counties, and who are always demanding to be separate!

---

1 Jack D. Forbes, "The Urban Tradition Among Native Americans," in *American Indians and the Urban Experience,* Susan Lobo and Kurt Peters, eds. (Walnut Creek, CA: Altamira, 2001), pp. 5–25.

2 Samuel Adams Drake, *The Making of the Great West,* as cited in Jack D. Forbes, *The Indian in America's Past* (Englewood Cliffs: Prentice Hall, 1965), p. 212.

3 Forbes, *The Indian In America's Past*, pp. 105, 108, 113.

4 Charles Maclaren, "America" (c. 1875), reprinted in *Werner Encyclopedia* (Akron: Werner Company, 1909), I: pp. 587–604.

5 Antonio de Alcedo, *The Geographical and Historical Dictionary of America and the West Indies,* trans. and ed. G. A. Thompson (London: Carpenter, 1812), I: pp. 42–3.

6 *Ibid.,* p. 44.

7 *The Great Republic by the Master Historians,* ed. Charles Morris and Oliver H.G. Leigh (New York: Belcher, 1902), I:9–10.

8 Hubert H. Bancroft, "On the Origin of the Americans," in *Ibid.,* I: p. 12.

9 *Ibid.*, I: p. 17.

10 Charles Morris, "The Aborigines of America," in *Ibid.,* I: p. 29.

11 Daniel G. Brinton, *The American Race* (Philadelphia: McKay, 1901) pp. 17–18.

12 Jack D. Forbes, "How Europeans Have Stolen America," *The Guardian* (London), August 24, 1987, p. 19; "What Do We Mean by America and

Americans," *News From Indian Country,* VIII (12) Late June 1994, p. 16; and "Who Are the Americans," *Akwesasne Notes,* 8 (5) Mid-Winter 1976, pp. 37–8. See also "Who Are the Native Americans?" (c. 1961) Native American Movement pamphlet, in the Jack D. Forbes Manuscript Collection, Shields Library, University of California, Davis, category F-15.

13 Emmanuel Chukwudi Eze, "The Color of Reason: The Idea of "Race" in Kant's Anthropology," in Emmanuel Chukwudi Eze, ed., *Postcolonial African Philosophy: a Critical Reader* (Oxford: Blackwell, 1997) pp. 115–118, 135. Note that Kant refers to Tahitians as "Indians," (p. 127).

14 *Secondary Lessons or the Improved Reader,* by a "Friend of Youth" (New Haven, 1831), p. 89.

15 *Webster's New Collegiate Dictionary* (Springfield: Merriam, 1981) p. 36.

16 John Francis Bannon, *History of the Americas* (New York: McGraw-Hill, 1963) Vol. I, pp. 19–21, 296–7.

17 "Eighteenth Century Slave Advertisements," *Journal of Negro History,* p. 200.

18 Walter Lafeber, ed., *John Quincy Adams and American Continental Empire* (Chicago: Quadrangle, 1965) pp. 36, 37, 43, 44, 48, 90, 91, 110, 112, 113, 120, 121, 124, 134, 135, 136.

19 Tocqueville, Alexis de, *Democracy in America,* ed. by Phillips Bradley (new York: Vintage, 1957) I, pp. 23, 27, 29, 384, 387, 395–7, 406, 420.

20 Letter of Luther Standing Bear, May 2, 1933, copy from Bureau of Indian Affairs correspondence files, National Archives.

21 John D. Hicks, *A Short History of American Democracy* (Boston, 1949) p. 1.

22 Avery Craven and Walter Johnson, *The United States, Experiment in Democracy* (New York, 1952) pp. xi, xvii, 17.

23 Richard Hofstadter, William Miller, and Daniel Aaron, *The United States: The History of a Republic* (Englewood Cliffs: Prentice-Hall, 1957) pp. v–vi, 1, 20–22; and Richard N. Current, T. Harry Williams, and Frank Freidel, *American History: A Survey* (New York, 1961) pp. 3, 343.

24 Thomas A. Bailey, *The American Pageant* (Boston, 1956) pp. 571. See Jack D. Forbes, "The Historian and the Indian: Racial Bias in American History," *The Americas: Academy of American Franciscan History* XIX (4), April 1963, pp. 356–7, for other examples.

25 Daniel J. Boorstin, *The Americans: the Colonial Experience* (New York: Vintage, 1958) pp. 1, 3, 158.

26 Carl Bode, Leon Howard, and Louis B. Wright, *American Literature: the 17th and 18th Centuries* (New York: Washington Square, 1966) cover page and table of contents.

27 Robert Clifton Whittemore, *Makers of the American Mind* (New York: Morrow, 1964) table of contents, and xii.

28 University of Nebraska Press catalog, December 2000, p. 24.

29 Richard O. Clemmer, *Roads in the Sky: the Hopi Indians in a Century of Change* (Boulder: Westview, 1995) p. 27.

30 See Forbes, "The Historian and the Indian," *op. cit.*, pp. 350, 358.
31 For analyses of one-sided historical works, see Jack D. Forbes, "The Historian and the Indian: Racial Bias in American History," *The Americas* (Academy of American Franciscan History) XIX (4) April 1963; Jack D. Forbes, "Frontiers in American History," *Journal of the West* I (1), July 1962; Jack D. Forbes, "The Indian in the West: Challenge for Historians," *Arizona and the West* I (3) Autumn 1959; and Jack D. Forbes, "Racial Bias in Gold Rush History," *The Masterkey*, 33 (1), January–March 1959.

INDIAN AFFAIRS:

HEBREWS 13:8

VINE DELORIA, JR.

"**W**HENEVER AN Indian reservation has on it good land, or timber, or minerals," the Commissioner of Indian Affairs stated in his Annual Report for 1876, "the cupidity of the white man is excited, and a constant struggle is inaugurated to dispossess the Indian, in which the avarice and determination of the white men usually prevails."

Thirteen decades later we discover that, while times have changed considerably, ideas about Indians have remained more constant than the Rock of Ages. The feeling still remains that somehow there is a magic key to unlock the aboriginal psyche and that whoever finds this mysterious key can, within a reasonable time, create from the aboriginal inhabitants a type of person that has rarely been seen during the ages of man's existence.

One can only wonder at the profound inability of the white man to comprehend two factors of human existence that remain in many ways the most important factors of his social existence. These two factors are law and culture. While we all flippantly convince ourselves that we understand law and culture and the manner in which they appear to describe the interworkings of groups of people, a glance at the past two centuries' events and present attitudes should be sufficient to indicate to us that, far from understanding either law or culture, the white man has continued to base his comprehension of society upon what he would like to believe men *should* be rather than what they are.

The predominant—one might say overriding—concern of the influential whites of the nineteenth century was somehow to place the savage tribes on the evolutionary railroad track to civilization. Without examining the popular folklore of social evolutionary theories, whites assumed that nations of people followed inexorable rules of development. Arriving at national consciousness in a hunting state, the embryo nation was supposed to pass eventually to an agricultural state and then gradually evolve into a modern urban society. This process was believed to be part of God's divine plan, and American history was perverted to explain the process. Whether the present collective amnesia that blocks recognition of America's violent past developed during the closing years of the nineteenth century is irrelevant compared with the obvious beliefs, found in the writings of the past that things had happened in a certain way, perhaps revealing a divine plan for America.

The pity of the thinkers of the nineteenth century was that they refused to analyze their ideology in logical terms or to expend great amounts of energy observing history to validate the corollaries of their central doctrine. As we glance at the suggestions of such men as Carl Schurz and their view of the divinity of agriculture, and compare the actual performance of the federal government and the American people during the succeeding years, we shall find that the credibility gap is not a phenomenon of recent times. It has been the constant hidden factor at work crushing the possibilities of finding a peaceful and just solution to the problems of American Indians. It exists today in massive doses because it has prospered for over five centuries of the white man's existence on the continent and is just reaching natural fruition.

From what we can discern of the articles of the nineteenth century, they argued that agriculture was the next step in civilizing the Indian. Thus, the theory went, the Indian reservations should be broken into farming plots and tribal assets should be divided among the tribal members. With the injection of the magical properties of private property, the individual Indians would raise their heads and their sights beyond the limited horizon that hemmed in their tribal existence. The debate, if any existed, was whether the magic of private property could work on the savage psyche. Could Indians be saved, or were they to be exterminated like the buffalo? The debate was hardly above that of a savage mentality even if carried on by people with neckties and high-button shoes.

A glance behind the rhetoric of the time would be astounding even today. In ideological terms the debate was over the feasibility of making the Indian perform the evolutionary feat of leaping from hunting to agriculture in one generation. In practical terms the whites of the western states, cattlemen for the most part, wanted Indian lands. The allotment of the reservations and settlement of surplus lands would allow the sharper whites to gain large ranches for their cattle operations through their manipulation of the Homestead Act (1862). In forcing Indians to evolve from a hunting to an agricultural state, federal policy allowed the lower-class whites to continue in their slothful pastoral pursuits. The evolutionary theory did not withstand even a surface analysis of its validity.

Allotment appeared to be inevitable, and the leading exponent of the policy, Senator Henry Dawes of Massachusetts, finally saw his version of the legislation passed in 1887. The act gave policy direction to the president, but it was interpreted by the executive branch as an immediate mandate to allot all tribes, not simply those who applied for allotment. Hurried "agreements" were forced on some of the tribes while exotic inducements were dangled before others; soon most of the tribes of the West had become witting or unwitting victims of the policy.

To indicate how devastating the allotment process was to the tribal land estates, one need only view some of the figures of allotments and "surplus" lands that were reported by the Commissioner of Indian Affairs in 1891 and 1892. The Iowa tribe, for example, at the end of 1891, held 8,658 acres in allotted status and the government had purchased 207,174 acres of "surplus" lands from them—a loss of 90.8

percent of the tribe's landholdings. The Cheyenne and Arapaho tribes of Oklahoma had 529,682 acres left and had sold 3,500,562 acres of "surplus" lands—a loss of 81.5 percent of their lands. It should have been apparent, had anyone cared to understand, that allotment was a contemporary way to strip the tribes of their physical assets by ostensibly legal means.

Had the federal government maintained even a consistent program of allotment many of the tribes might actually have made the evolutionary leap forward that the reformers seemed to visualize. The Allotment Act had hardly been passed, however, when it was amended, and this amendment may have been the single most detrimental act the federal government ever perpetrated on Indians. In 1891 the General Allotment Act was changed so that Indian allotments could be leased out to non-Indians under the supervision of the Bureau of Indian Affairs.

The leasing amendment was not wholly without justification. Many Indians were very old and, having been forced to take allotments in their old age, were incapable of farming their lands. Indian children were given smaller allotments of land according to the provisions of the allotment acts that affected the different reservations. Generally they received forty acres—a tract insufficient for anything other than token acknowledgment that they were tribal members at the time the lands were divided. Giving allotments to children conflicted with the federal policy of bundling them off to government boarding schools early in life, and questions arose concerning the beneficial use of their lands during their school years.

The change of the allotment law was thus intended to meet these problems and the Bureau of Indian Affairs agents were given wide discretion to lease Indian lands through the development of a federal "trust" over the lands, which grew out of the twenty-five-year period of restriction on alienation that attached itself to the new allotments. From this innocent beginning, the present theory of federal trusteeship over Indian lands developed. But the trouble with vesting absolute discretionary powers in the Indian agents was that few of them were honest enough to consider the best interests of the Indians. Many were tied into the local pressure groups that sought long-term leasing on those Indian lands that they had been unable to gain through settlement laws. Very shortly, leasing was seen as a modern means of taking Indian lands.

In the northern plains, where allotment had created thousands of small tracts, the large ranching and farming combines began moving onto Indian lands. In 1916, for example, on the 2-million-acre Pine Ridge Indian Reservation in South Dakota, only forty acres of land were leased to a non-Indian. A year later nearly 80 percent of the land was leased to white cattlemen. Other reservations experienced the same phenomenon but at lesser rates of conquest. The net result of the leasing policy was to reduce the Indians to absentee landlords whose only purpose in life was to frequent the agency town, drinking and idle, waiting for their lease checks. Allotment, then, was an effort to force Indians to become white farmers; leasing was a convenient loophole to enable them to survive without understanding the cultural change that would have enabled them to prosper.

The great social experiment of the nineteenth century became a systematic exploitation of people during the twentieth century. For no sooner had the frontier been declared officially closed by Frederick Jackson Turner than people forgot about the thousands of Indians huddled on the desert reservations of the West. Nostalgia for the frontier overwhelmed public consciousness and dime novels and the new motion pictures created a West that never was but which everyone *thought* existed. The proper operation of federal laws depended on the continued glare of public understanding and opinion on the actions of the bureaucracy; when Indians were finally submerged as living people and replaced by their fictional counterparts, the bureaucracy moved in and snuffed out all signs of resistance.

Commissioner Francis Leupp, writing in his book, *The Indian and His Problem* (1910), declared, "The Indian problem has now reached a stage where its solution is almost wholly a matter of administration. Mere sentiment has spent its day; the moral questions involved have pretty well settled themselves. What is most needed from this time forth is the guidance of affairs by an independent mind, active sympathies free from mawkishness, an elastic patience and a steady hand." If America had not settled the problems of the world, it had at least solved a troublesome and perennial situation with the American Indians.

In the mind of Francis Leupp the solution might have been merely administrative, but the overweening ego of the white man failed to comprehend that such administration had not been a hallmark of present or previous behavior by the federal government. That administrative actions were decisive did not mean that they were moral, proper, or even efficient. Few people thought to inquire behind the actions of the government to determine if goals and results coincided.

It was by some strange intervention of fate that the Indian communities, beaten down with myriad rules and regulations, were placed on the road to cultural recovery. In 1913 a minor case involving the sale of liquor to the Pueblo Indians of New Mexico reached the Supreme Court. The question at issue was whether or not the Pueblos were so far under federal protection as to bar them from drinking. Sandoval, the defendant after whom the case was named, maintained that they were. The Supreme Court maintained they weren't. Not only that, the court found that the Pueblos had always been subject to the paramount power of Congress, and the implications of this decision suddenly dawned on everyone. The titles to thousands of acres of land that had been taken from the Pueblos by one method or another over the past century were voidable.

From 1913 until 1924 the Pueblo lands controversy raged in the Southwest. The Indians organized as the All Pueblo Council to meet the challenge head-on. It was the first time since 1688, when they had thrown the Spanish out of the New Mexico area, that a concerted effort was made by the Indians. The philanthropic groups that had so plagued Indians a generation before rose to the defense of the Pueblos. Under the able leadership of John Collier a coalition of groups spearheaded by the General Federation of Women's Clubs pushed aside the ranchers and farmers who had gathered under the leadership of New Mexico Senator Bursum and carried the day.

The Pueblo Lands Act set up procedures whereby the white intruders on Indian lands would have to prove their titles to the lands they claimed. The Pueblos were given a special attorney to handle their cases, and over a ten-year period several thousand squatters were expelled from the Pueblo lands. It was a rare instance of laws being used to defend Indian rights to land and communal existence rather than to despoil them.

The fight to protect the Pueblo lands must certainly stand as the turning point in the history of Indian Affairs. For the first time, Indians were considered to have rights that could be protected in court. The Cherokees had gone to the Supreme Court to defend their treaty rights in the 1870s with no relief. Again in the 1870s the Indian citizen John Elk had sued to gain the voting franchise without success. Indians had somehow survived a century of disenfranchisement without the ordinary forms of legal protection; in the Pueblo case, law was used for the first time to extend, if only by implication, the rights of Indians everywhere.

Collier emerged from the land confrontation as the strong man in the field of Indian Affairs. He spent the remainder of the 1920s needling both Congress and the administration for better conditions for Indians. Having become entranced by the Navajo and Pueblo lifestyle and religions, Collier devoted his energies to rebuilding the Indian cultural base and extending the land base on which the people conducted those ceremonies and lived the life that Collier loved and admired.

With the election of Franklin Roosevelt and the entrance of the New Deal ideologies into American life, Collier became the Commissioner of Indian Affairs. A report done half a decade earlier, by Lewis Meriam, on the administration of Indian Affairs, provided Collier with sufficient documentation and ammunition to drive through the Congress a completely new idea of Indian relationships with the federal government. In 1934 Congress passed the Indian Reorganization Act (IRA), which provided for formally organized and recognized governments for the reservations. Although the final version of the act was not what Collier had conceived, it was a giant step forward in the development of the Indian communities. Collier accepted what he could get and began to build on it.

The past generation has been dominated in one way or another by the work of John Collier. During the 1950s the tribes and Congress fought a bitter battle over the policy of terminating the tribes from federal supervision, services, and responsibilities. The first move by Congress was an effort to repeal the provisions of the IRA in order to cripple the ability of the tribes to fight back. Fortunately, the tribal governments had developed sufficient knowledge about the workings of the federal government to turn back the congressional challenge quickly. Collier's hunch about the continuing struggle between the tribes and the United States paid great dividends when put to test in the 1950s.

When the War on Poverty was declared, the Indian communities were in an ideal position to exploit the provisions of the legislation. Tribal governments were eligible for grants on the same basis as cities and counties and nearly every tribe had an extensive program developed within a year of the passage of the legislation. Many even admitted non-Indians to their programs in those areas where conservatives dominated local white governments and refused to apply for funds for the poverty war. On the whole, it was the ready-made status of tribal governments that enabled Indians to gain many advantages denied to other minority groups during the expansion of social programs in the 1960s.

The mere expansion of programs and opportunities created problems that even John Collier had been unable to foresee. The tribal governments set up under the Indian Reorganization Act were designed for depression conditions. In those days tribal income was exceedingly small; federal programs, even with the expansive nature of the New Deal, were miniscule, and none provided for direct funding of administrative costs to the tribes themselves. Thus the governments of the reservations resembled student governments in the large colleges rather than municipal governments with the ability to expand and contract according to the conditions that existed.

By the late 1960s the problem with the tribal governments was becoming apparent. Times and peoples had changed, but the tribal governments were burdened with an extensive and cumbersome process of amending their constitutions; consequently, few had done so. The intangible results of the poverty programs were often to raise the question of Indian identity to a crisis situation. People were being hired partly on the basis of their tribal membership and partly on the basis of their education and professional skills. The two factors seemed to work toward a common middle ground in which the problem of what it meant to be an Indian was the central question.

With the rise of Indian activism in a number of forms, this central question, avoided by both Indians and whites since the days of Carl Schurz, dominated the emotional consciousness of Indians without finding an intellectual context in which it could relate to the modern world. People knew that they were Indians and tried to develop pride in the fact of their existence, but the pride too often expressed itself in antiwhite sentiments, not in a reflection of the basic Indian values that had enabled the tribes to exist during a century of oppression.

In the operations of the poverty programs there was a great deal of wasteful expenditure of moneys. Rather than call the culprit to account to the Indian community for his misdeeds, Indians too often regarded the maladministration of programs as another attack against whites; they refused to call the Indian administrator to account because he would be punished by white-dominated courts and administrative proceedings.

The result for the Indian communities was that, instead of regaining the integrity that had been their chief characteristic in former years, the whole system of belief and faith in tribal institutions was so undermined that people began to call for the abolition of tribal governments. The final act of this tragic drama was, of course, the confrontation at Wounded Knee. People of equally sincere beliefs saw the Wounded Knee incident as the beginning of a new era of Indian involvement and the end of an era of inept radicalism during which Indian activists draped themselves in black clothing in order to make a name for themselves.

One would have to conclude that the process of assimilation has created a partial creature that in many ways can never again be made into a whole being. The integrity of law was never very strong when applied to Indians and, with the leasing amendment to the General Allotment Act, Congress virtually abdicated its responsibility for Indians and allowed the anonymous and inept bureaucrats to take final control over them. The struggles of the succeeding years, while spectacular in some respects and disastrous in others, have been simply the events that could have been expected when central issues were avoided or approached obliquely.

The central issue has been that of culture and civilization. How does one determine the relative value, worth, and reality of culture? What factors are considered in weighing the values by which men live? Does an expanding technology give to one group of people a divine right to force on another group of people behavior patterns, values, laws, and concepts that are foreign to them? What factors finally determine how we understand civilization as it appears among people?

Jefferson Davis remarked, "Surely the equitable or humane conclusion would be that it were better the white man, with his larger means and higher intelligence, should have been assigned to the region where artificial appliances were necessary to secure the irrigation which would render the land productive, and science would be available to combat the ravages of destructive insects." The question, then, of mortality, civilization, and culture has been raised previously without creating any great impact.

William Justin Harsha noted that "Law has always availed to settle and civilize society." One can trace throughout the past two centuries the absence of any integrity of the law when applied to Indians. It has been, rather, if one reflects on the events that have been reviewed, a curious mixture of sociological theories masquerading as legal concepts that has dominated Indian affairs. The recent disturbances in Indian Country have shown simply one thing—Indians are presently repeating the mistakes of the white man by attempting to force law to perform precisely those acrobatics that the whites of the 1880s and 1890s asked it to do.

In reflecting, therefore, on the foibles and follies of the past in the field of Indian Affairs and the learned expressions by policy makers of both red and white heritage, the most profound lesson we can manage is that history teaches nothing and men learn little from generation to generation. If within one generation a few people come to know themselves or to understand the nature of man's experience, it may be a major achievement. But the mixture of thought and emotion that has passed for Indian Affairs has done little for either red men or white men. While white men now own the continent, they are miserable—victims of pathological fears that they will lose their ill-gained wealth—and in the process of destroying the world. Indians have learned little except that they do not understand what has happened to them and have lost their ability to articulate what that means.

Whether such conflict, when it has occurred in other nations in other ages, can be satisfactorily resolved seems to depend in large measure on an innate sense of proportion—a historical tradition that we have conveniently labeled our sense of justice. It is the tragedy of our present situation that we cannot find even this sense of propriety, and we are unique among people of all ages in this inability to perceive values by which we can live. It would seem that Indians and whites were somehow destined to be each other's victims in unique and profound ways. Perhaps that is what we ultimately must live with.

2

SACRED RITES:

SUPPRESSION AND
SUBSISTENCE

CHRISTIAN CIVILIZATION

OHIYESA (CHARLES ALEXANDER EASTMAN)

IN TIME we came to recognize that the drunkards and licentious among white men, with whom we too frequently came in contact, were condemned by the white man's religion as well, and must not be held to discredit it. But it was not so easy to overlook or to excuse national bad faith. When distinguished emissaries from the Father at Washington, some of them ministers of the Gospel and even bishops, came to the Indian nations, and pledged to us in solemn treaty the national honor, with prayer and mention of their God; and when such treaties, so made, were promptly and shamelessly broken, is it strange that the action should arouse not only anger, but contempt?

The historians of the white race admit that the Indian was never the first to repudiate his oath.

I confess I have wondered much that Christianity is not practiced by the very people who vouch for that wonderful conception of exemplary living. It appears that they are anxious to pass on their religion to all other races, but keep very little of it for themselves. I have not yet seen the meek inherit the earth, or the peacemakers receive high honor.

It is my personal belief, after thirty-five years' experience of it, that there is no such thing as Christian civilization. I believe that Christianity and modern civilization are opposed and irreconcilable, and that the spirit of Christianity and of our ancient religion is essentially the same.

Lament For a Lost Vision

LONG BEFORE I ever heard of Christ or saw a white man, I had learned the essence of morality.

With the help of dear Nature herself, my grandmother taught me things simple but of mighty import.

I knew God. I perceived what goodness is. I saw and loved what is really beautiful. Civilization has not taught me anything better!

As a child, I understood how to give. I have forgotten that grace since I became civilized. I lived the natural life, whereas I now live the artificial.

Any pretty pebble was valuable to me then, every growing tree an object of reverence. Now I worship with the white man before a painted landscape whose value is estimated in dollars!

In this manner is the Indian rebuilt, as the natural rocks are ground to powder and made into artificial blocks, which may be built into the walls of modern society.

The Gift of My People

I AM an Indian; and while I have learned much from civilization, I have never lost my Indian sense of right and justice.

When I reduce civilization to its most basic terms, it becomes a system of life based on trade. Each man stakes his powers, the product of his labor, his social, political, and religious standing against his neighbor's. To gain what? To gain control over his fellow workers, and the results of their labor.

Is there not something worthy of perpetuation in our Indian spirit of democracy, where Earth, our mother, was free to all, and no one sought to impoverish or enslave his neighbor? Where the good things of Earth were not ours to hold against our brothers and sisters, but were ours to use and enjoy together with them, and with whom it was our privilege to share?

Indeed, our contribution to our nation and the world is not to be measured in the material realm. Our greatest contribution has been spiritual and philosophical. Silently, by example only, in wordless patience, we have held stoutly to our native vision of personal faithfulness to duty and devotion to a trust. We have neither advertised our faithfulness nor made capital of our honor.

But again and again we have proved our worth as citizens of this country by our constancy in the face of hardship and death. Prejudice and racial injustice have been no excuse for our breaking our word. This simplicity and fairness has cost us dear. It has cost us our land and our freedom, had even led to the extinction of our race as a separate and unique people.

But as an ideal we live, and will live, not only in the splendor of our past, the poetry of our legends and art, not only in the interfusion of our blood with yours and in our faithful adherence to the ideals of American citizenship, but also in the living heart of the nation.

COLONIAL FASCINATIONS: GOD SAVE THE—OH, SAY, CAN YOU—OH, CANADA

JAMES ARONHIOTAS STEVENS

IN **1779** the Town Destroyer, aka first president George Washington, decided—enough of the Haudenosaunee. The six tribes were troublesome and only the Oneida and the Tuscaroras were siding with American colonists. In the early summer Washington devised a plan to be carried out by New Hampshire's John Sullivan and Enoch Poor, New Jersey's General William Maxwell, Pennsylvania's Edward Hand, and New York's James Clinton, and their approximately forty-five hundred men. Sullivan was to begin moving from Easton, Pennsylvania, up the Susquehanna River Valley, while Clinton's men would march westward from the Mohawk River Valley, then down the upper Susquehanna River, meeting Sullivan's troops in Tioga. The militia was ordered to burn every village and destroy every field along the way, allowing for no peace treaties till "the total ruin of their settlements was effected." Washington outlined the goals for this march as "total destruction and devastation." He wrote, "Our future security will rest on the terror inflicted on them," a precursor to the, "[We'll] smoke them out of their caves, to get them running so we can get them" mentality that we are so familiar with under the current presidency.

Loyalty to the British Tories, due to promises of equal postwar national status for the Iroquois, as well as Chief Joseph Brant's (Thayendanegea) loyalties to his friend and brother-in law, Sir William Johnson, enraged the colonists. Bloody raids led by the Tory Raiders and natives, like the infamous battle at Wyoming, Pennsylvania, on July 3, 1778, precipitated President Washington's plan for Iroquois decimation. Hunger had been an ever-present threat to the Iroquois due to long harsh winters and short growing seasons and Washington believed that chopping down our orchards, torching great fields of ripe corn and vegetables, and burning all buildings along the routes were sure to destroy us.

Sullivan and Clinton experienced many setbacks in June of 1779 due to lack of supplies, lack of support, and unfulfilled promises from Pennsylvania to send volunteer militia. By July a new factor was added to the plan. Colonel Daniel Broadhead would lead troops and pro-American natives up the Allegheny River from Fort Pitt with the goal of joining up with Clinton and Sullivan. August found Clinton and his men camped at the south end of Lake Otsego, where they had dammed the lake. They would later break this dam, riding 220 flatboats on the resulting crest to join Sullivan at Tioga on August 19. The resulting flood destroyed Indian cornfields and Clinton's troops burned three Tuscarora villages, among others, below the important Indian trade town of Oquaga. Accounts say that the natives viewed this unnatural flood as a predestined apocalyptic sign, though this may be white conjecture similar to the return of Quetzalcoatl.

The rejoining of Clinton's and Sullivan's troops would culminate in the battle of Newtown on August 29 against a combined force of Brant's Indians and Tory rangers. The battle was over shortly, as an Indian scout for Sullivan spotted the loyalists lying in ambush on a ridge. Sullivan sprayed his enemies with shrapnel and the loyalists broke formation rather quickly, surrendering the battlefield to the American troops, who outnumbered them three to one. It took the celebrating Americans a full day to destroy 150 acres of the Iroquois' most excellent corn and the village of Newtown. Brant, Butler, and Johnson regrouped on the other side of the Genesee River, but a second battle never took place.

The original delay in this genocidal campaign allowed the colonial troops an added benefit. By mid-August the cornfields and vegetable gardens were at their most productive and the blow to the food supply would be devastating, leading not only to starvation but also to a strain on the supplies of the British at Fort Niagara, who would now be forced to feed the survivors that straggled into camp for the winter. This campaign of nearly forty-five hundred American men had destroyed or razed twenty-eight of the approximately thirty Iroquois villages between Ohio, Lake Erie, and the Mohawk River. Two villages remained untouched. As a final thrust at the Iroquois, Sullivan ordered the Mohawk's "lower castle" burned and its people taken prisoner. They had been farming peacefully among white families, but now their farms and lands were to be confiscated and turned over to settlers.

In spite of this Washington-planned genocide, skirmishes and raids were fought across Iroquoia by the surviving and reviving Haudenosaunee for four more years. In 1784, with the Indian loyalists still willing to fight, the Treaty of Fort Stanwix was signed between the United States and Great Britain, and the Six Nations Reserve in Canada was granted by the Crown to the survivors of Brant's loyalist Iroquois. The original Haldimand Grant promised a stretch of land six miles wide on either side, from the source of the Grand River in Ontario to the mouth of the river on Lake Erie, but by 1793 British Governor John Simcoe was forcing cession of much of the land. Chief Brant also sold a great deal more of the land between 1798 and 1834 in order to provide for his people. By 1847 the Six Nations Reserve had taken its present dimension of 20,000 hectares, centered around the small village of Ohsweken.

This is the history of the people of my grandfather, Earl Burnham. My *Totah's* (grandmother's) relations would have been relatively safe in the Adirondacks and north, as the terrain prohibited Sullivan and Clinton from their burning and pillaging. Besides, the Jesuits had earlier been successful in Christianizing Mohawks along the Saint Lawrence. These early Catholic Mohawks were called Tarbells, and my Totah's great-grandmother, born in 1835, was enrolled as Louise Oronhioken Curly-head Tarbell, attesting to her conversion.

My grandfather's people however, would be removed to Canada, where the strong hand of the British Crown would continue to reshape their way of life. In 1785 an Anglican church was built called Her Majesty's Chapel of the Mohawks. The first chapel built to honor Queen Anne had been built in 1712 at Fort Hunter, New York, after a group of Mohawks had been to England to pledge their loyalty and to request that a chapel be built back home. The Queen gave a Bible, a set of communion silver, and prayer books. During the American Revolution the silver service was buried and when recovered it was divided between the Mohawks of the Six Nations and Tyendanaga Reserves. This communion service was still in use when I visited as a child. The chapel is the final resting place of Chief Joseph Brant and his son.

In 1831 The New England Company, a Britain-based protestant mission, built the Mohawk Institute in Brantford, Ontario, once Brant's Ford till the removal of his people to a place farther south on the Grand River. This school, known popularly as "The Mush Hole," was responsible for much of the loss of Iroquois culture. My great-grandfather, James Burnham, was sent to this school with his brother Phillip, never to know his own language, or even to be certain of his family name. This school was the demise of many young people, both physically and culturally.

Currently the Woodland Cultural Centre, it is a museum and resource center and, ironically, it helps to teach the Iroquois culture it once sought to destroy. I went there with my grandfather on a trip back to "the bush," to buy some cornbread before my schooling took me out West. We toured the grounds and he told me horror stories of beatings and escapes and other things not to forget. We also went to the chapel and to see family graves; we drove to the longhouse, to Mohawk poet E. Pauline Johnson's home at Chiefswood, to Smith's pottery, and to Aunt Mary Montour's old farmhouse. Now, as my grandfather has just passed, not yet three weeks ago, I reflect on that trip fondly. He had even let me drive the Bonneville.

After having spent years in New Mexico and Kansas, there is a great pride for me in returning to Iroquoia. Reminders of the strength and, to borrow Ojibway scholar Gerald Vizenor's term, survivance of my people, constantly surround me. When I drive up north to Niagara County to visit my mother or grandparents, I am following the Ongiara Trail along the Niagara River, past the portage. Not one mile from where I grew up is the castle and grounds at Fort Niagara where my cousins and I would climb over the stone wall, bypass the south redoubt, sneak along the walls past the trading post and the hotshot furnace, and successfully slip into the castle. We would joke that this is how our ancestors had done it. Once inside, we'd choose a bedroom for ourselves and pretend that we lived in the castle. Occasionally we'd scare ourselves into hearing the headless ghost of the well, who (of course) had lost his head to another soldier in an argument over a *beautiful Indian princess.*

At the time, I didn't know my history as well. I didn't know of President Washington's scorched earth campaign to erase my people from the face of the earth. I didn't know yet to listen in that castle for the murmur of Chief Joseph Brant's negotiations with the British to provide for his people. I hadn't yet imagined the miles of burned cornfields and trampled gourds, the flooding of the upper Susquehanna, and the bloodied prisoners. I hadn't pictured the survivors making their way through subzero snowstorms to Niagara's far-western post in search of food. Above the entrance to the castle is a blue crest that reads *Porte des Cinq Nations.* On the daily tours it is explained that this is the gate where the five original Iroquois tribes could enter for friendly trade. It is not explained that through this gate the multitudes of starving Mohawks, Senecas, Cayugas, and Onondagas passed, to remind Colonel Guy Johnson of his promises for their well-being.

Recently I drove out to Hartwick College in Oneonta, New York, to do a poetry reading. I drove through German Flats and Painted Post, where an old post marked in red the number of people killed in a Seneca battle, past the Newtown Battlefield, and up the Susquehanna to the site of Oquaga (now a campsite). When I arrived at my reading, I opened with three poems in Mohawk, letting the language fill the room and pour from the windows and doors, feeling a great sense of pride knowing that these *Kanienkehaka* words belonged there. After the reading, a Cherokee/Huron friend and fellow poet led me to the library to look at the land purchase agreement that John Hartwick made with the Mohawks, an agreement never to be fulfilled. We joked that our historically unconventional alliance of two, a Mohawk and a Huron, should reclaim this college.

On the way back I passed Tioga and drove along the Chemung River; at Newtown I stopped to read a historical plaque where I saw Clinton and Sullivan's names. At the other end of Route 17, closer to my home, I crossed the Allegheny River, now dammed by Kinzua Dam, with the Cornplanter Reservation and Quaker school beneath the murky waters of the lake as well as beneath the murky waters of history. I imagined breaking the dam and riding the crest down the Allegheny to flood out Colonel Broadhead and his troops. Sad, that these men's names remain, passing for the history of New York State, while our own names were so often lost or had English ones tacked on.

My grandfather's mother, Ida Anderson, carried the family name of her grandfather, who when orphaned moved in with his sister and adopted her husband's name. My grandfather's father, James Burnham, when orphaned with his siblings, Phillip, Margaret, and Melinda, was adopted by a Burnham family, sometimes recorded as Burnum, while records show the children's original name as Burning. Whatever the names were, they were not our names. Our names are known by the land around us, by our mothers and grandmothers, to call us when they need us ... *Oronhiokon, Tekaniatarekwen, Konarathakwas, Katsitsa'waks, Aronhiotas* ... and we are here. We still answer.

This essay is dedicated to the memory of my grandfather,
Earl Timothy Burnham
(1914–2005)

SPEAKING OUT:

RELIGIOUS RIGHTS AND IMPRISONED AMERICAN INDIAN WOMEN

LAURA E. DONALDSON

I N 2004 a Muskogee (Creek) friend of mine visited the Central Oklahoma Correctional Facility for Women, a for-profit prison built by the Corrections Corporation of America (CCA) and managed by Dominion Correctional Services (DCS). The purpose of this visit was not only to gather information that she could use to contest the building of similar prisons in Oklahoma but also to visit a group of Native Hawaiians who had recently been transferred to the Central Oklahoma facility. Two persons accompanied my friend, who is an ordained minister, on this visit: a staff member from the United Church of Christ's Council on Racial and Ethnic Minorities, and a Native Hawaiian leader starting a restorative justice program on his ancestral islands. When the visitors called out to the imprisoned Hawaiian women in their indigenous language many of them burst into tears. They described how agonizing it was that the prison staff addressed them only in English. For these women both chanting and hearing their Native Hawaiian tongue constituted an indispensable element of *aloha*, a spiritual principle similar to the biblical concept of *shalom*. As Haunani Kay Trask has noted, aloha is often translated simply as "love," but it is a love inflected by a "profoundly Hawaiian sense that is, again, familial and genealogical. . . . The significance and meaning of aloha underscores the centrality of the Hawaiian language, or "olelo," to the culture."[1] The prison's failure to meet this need consequently denied these prisoners' religious rights.

The Hawaiian women's access to their spiritual traditions are further complicated by several factors. First, prison substance abuse programs require participants to be segregated from the general population. When the group's primary chanter entered Central Oklahoma's substance abuse program all the Hawaiian women suffered spiritual deprivation.[2] Second, chaplains—and especially the predominantly conservative Christians staffing for-profit prisons—are unable (and often unwilling) to provide culturally appropriate programming for American Indian or Alaskan/Hawaiian Native women incarcerated far from home. Even when near to home, prisons often refuse to hire Indian spiritual leaders to perform ceremonies for their female inmates. In Montana, for example, former governor Stan Stephens dismissed a plan to hire native religious leaders and counselors by stating that he would only implement it if tribes in the state assisted in the financing.[3] Salish scholar Luana Ross notes the neocolonial racism in this perspective, since the governor did not approach white communities and ask them to finance white counselors for the white prisoners in the Montana system (p. 140).

The Supreme Court has ruled in *Cruz v. Beto,* 405 U.S. 319 (1972) that the Texas prison system could not deny a male Buddhist inmate "a reasonable opportunity of pursuing his faith comparable to the opportunity afforded fellow prisoners who adhere to conventional religious precepts. . . ." The gains from *Cruz* remain divided along gender lines, however: although native men have had some success in forcing prisons to build sweat lodges and hire native counselors, the spiritual needs of native women have remained unnoticed and unheard. For them, the Supreme Court's 1972 ruling and the American Indian Religious Freedom Act of 1978 have had very little impact. In the few instances where female native prisoners have won concessions from prison administrations they are hampered by hostile and stereotypical understandings of their spiritual traditions. For example, Catherine (Cedar Woman), an inmate at the Montana state prison for women, recounts that both the institution's nurse and a guard tried to convince her to have an unnecessary hysterectomy and "let go" of her Native beliefs: "To hell with your traditions and beliefs!" the nurse screamed. "This is a medical issue."[4]

Such distorted perspectives also extend to the use of sweetgrass and sage for "smudging," which is a crucial religious practice that uses the smoke from these materials for purification and prayer. Some non-native staff and inmates mistakenly consider sage and sweetgrass to be drugs; others classify native spiritual traditions as "recreation" undeserving of the consideration accorded to conventional religious beliefs. Nor are prisons alone in this regard. Boston University threatened to evict a native student from his dorm room because he burned sage and sweetgrass while he prayed. They claimed that his smudging violated the school's ban on candles and incense in the dormitories, and an administrator subsequently told him that the chapel was the most obvious location for prayer and worship.[5] This failure to understand the nature of native spirituality, whether it occurs in prisons or universities, has not only resulted in the unconstitutional denial of religious rights to American Indians but also caused irreparable harm to some of society's most vulnerable members. Without access to their traditions, many native women become even more susceptible to the endemic violence and bitterness of the prison environment. They themselves assert that spirituality, and not tranquilizers or Euro-American counseling, is the answer both to surviving "prisonization" and to achieving well-being.[6]

All we who are scholars and activists concerned with human rights must raise our voices in support of religious rights for incarcerated native women. Through our teaching, research, and cultural work we must protest the noncompliance of most state and federal prison systems with judicial and legislative mandates affirming the right of prisoners to practice diverse spiritual traditions. We must also protest the role of for-profit prisons in which prisoners become commodities that are shipped to facilities thousands of miles away from their families, communities, and religious resources. These women have desperately fought for survivance in a cell some have described as a coffin, in a prison they call a grave-stone, and amongst themselves as the walking dead.[7] Let us support their struggle by demanding that the sounds of aloha resound throughout the halls of the Central Oklahoma Correctional Facility for Women and, indeed, throughout the entirety of the U.S. justice system.

1 From *A Native Daughter: Colonialism & Sovereignty in Hawaii* (Monroe, Maine: Common Courage Press, 1993): p. 187.
2 When she returned to the main prison population, the Hawaiian women were allowed to do some chanting in the evening.
3 Luana Ross, *Inventing the Savage: the Social Construction of Native American Criminality* (Austin, Texas: University of Texas Press, 1998): p. 140.
4 Luana Ross, "Punishing Institutions: The Story of Catherine (Cedar Woman)," in *Native American Voices: A Reader*, ed. Susan Lobo and Steve Talbot (New York: Longman, 1998): p. 415.
5 See DaShanne Stokes, "Sage, Sweetgrass and the First Amendment," *The Chronicle of Higher Education,* May 18, 2001: p. B16.
6 Ross 1998, p. 141.
7 From an interview with a First Nations woman conducted by Fran Sugar, as quoted in Ross 1998, p. 139.

"I LEARNED TO PREACH PRETTY WELL, AND TO CUSS, TOO":

HOPI ACCEPTANCE AND REJECTION OF CHRISTIANITY AT SHERMAN INSTITUTE, 1906–1928

MATTHEW T. SAKIESTEWA GILBERT

IN THE early twentieth century the United States government sought to destroy native cultures by forcing Indian people across North America to attend on- and off-reservation boarding schools.[1] Government officials, along with public opinion of the day, viewed Indians as uneducated "savages" who desperately needed to be saved from their "uncivilized" and "devil-like" ways. In order to civilize the Indians, the government constructed boarding schools and demanded that Indian pupils attend whether they wanted to or not. Often, in spite of parent and student disapproval, government officials forced Indian pupils to leave their families and homes for schools such as Carlisle Indian School, Phoenix Indian School, and Sherman Institute, an off-reservation boarding school in Riverside, California.

In November 1906, shortly after an internal Hopi division known as the Oraibi Split,[2] government officials forced my great-grandfather, Victor Sakiestewa, and several other Hopis[3] to leave their homes in northeastern Arizona to attend Sherman Institute.[4] Born and raised in the village of Oraibi, the oldest inhabited village in North America, Victor came to Sherman with little knowledge of life in California. Unfamiliar with his new surroundings, he embarked on an adventure that took him well beyond the mesas of the Hopi Reservation. At Sherman, school officials instructed him in arithmetic and language. He learned to play musical instruments such as the clarinet and gained valuable skills as a plumber, a trade he used later on in life. Victor also participated in Christian activities yet, at the same time, his Hopi culture remained intact. This is the story of Hopi students such as my great-grandfather, who accepted, rejected, and adapted Christianity at Sherman Institute and, in doing so, preserved Hopi culture for generations of Hopi pupils to come. Nonnative historians writing on this subject might be tempted to portray the Hopi pupils as victims; Hopis, however, like many other Indian people, demonstrated resilience, agency, and determination to overcome the opposition they experienced at off-reservation boarding schools. These are just a few of the reasons Hopi culture remains so alive and vibrant today.

Government Policy

IN THE early twentieth century government officials routinely exposed American Indian pupils to Christian teachings and values at numerous off-reservation Indian boarding schools scattered throughout the United States. Christian instruction served as an evangelistic tool for Protestant and Catholic clergy located at the schools, and it also played a significant role in the government's overall assimilation of Indian people to become "good" American citizens. Although off-reservation Indian boarding schools largely existed to train Indian students in industrial trades, school officials forced Indian pupils to attend Christian gatherings, pray Christian prayers, and adopt, at least for a time, a cultural worldview based on Christianity.

At Sherman Institute school officials incorporated the Christian faith in the school's curriculum, music instruction, and various activities held on and off the school campus. Among those in attendance at Sherman, the Hopi pupils accounted for a significant number of Indian students who experienced first hand the government's attempt to assimilate Indians through Christianity. While some Hopi students accepted the religious lessons and principles taught at the school, others rejected Christianity and refused to abandon or adapt their traditional Hopi beliefs for the white man's religion. In essence, Christianity at Sherman served a twofold purpose for the Hopi students. School officials used Christianity to assimilate Hopi pupils into white society, and the government also wanted Hopis to take Christianity home with them in order convert their families who remained on the reservation.

A Christian Foundation

HOPI KNOWLEDGE of Christianity did not begin at Sherman Institute. Like many other Indian students who attended off-reservation boarding schools in the early twentieth century, Christianity for them had already been established in Indian communities across North America. For more than a hundred years Protestant, Mormon, and Catholic missionaries attempted to convert Hopis to their respective religions. When Catholic missionaries first brought Christianity to the Hopi people in the sixteenth century some welcomed them, while others despised the priests and in 1680 forced the Catholic church off Hopi land. In *Pages From Hopi History* (1974), historian Harry C. James correctly observed that "[t]here developed" such a "distrust [and] hatred of everything Spanish" that it "permeated Hopi thinking down through the centuries."[5]

Unlike the Catholics, whose cruel treatment of the Hopi resulted in few converts, the Mormons had a more effective approach with the Hopi people. In *Me and Mine* (1969), Louise Udall recounted Helen Sekaquaptewa's opinion of the Mormons as "different and separate from other whites."[6] According to Sekaquaptewa, the Mormons "were friendly and did not look down at the Indians. They were industrious and would share their food" with Hopis. Sekaquaptewa also noted that when the Hopi were invited into "their homes" they were welcomed and the Mormons ate with them. "They do not give [the Hopi] food on a plate to eat outside like dogs."[7]

Prior to their attendance at Sherman Institute no early twentieth-century Christian directly influenced the Hopis more than Reverend Heinrich R. Voth. Born in Russia in 1855, Voth, a Christian Mennonite, ministered to the Hopi from 1893 to 1902. Shortly before he arrived, Peter Stauffer, a fellow Mennonite and government mechanic, informed Voth that the Hopis needed "more than the white man's clothing, houses and education," they needed the "Gospel of Jesus Christ."[8] Voth realized that, for Christian purposes, providing the Hopis with food, clothing and education only met the obvious needs of the Hopi people. However, regardless of Voth's fluency in the Hopi language and understanding of Hopi culture, his evangelistic efforts did not produce any immediate Hopi conversions. In *Rethinking Hopi Ethnography* (1998), Peter Whiteley noted that in "his seven years as [a] missionary" to the Hopi, Voth did not secure one Hopi convert.[9]

The absence of Hopi conversions should not be perceived as a complete Mennonite failure. The Mennonites required all converts to make a public profession of faith of baptism by immersion. Unless a missionary baptized an individual, he or she would not be considered a genuine convert. In the early twentieth century, some Hopis believed in the Christian God, but did not make a public confession of faith before their families or village leaders. In spite of the Mennonite's understanding of "genuine converts," a small handful of Hopis participated in Christian services and actively attended church. Many of those who attended Voth's church were Hopi children who eventually enrolled as students at Sherman Institute.

Polingaysi Qoyawayma, a Hopi pupil from Oraibi who came to Sherman in 1906, knew Voth personally and took part in his ministry at Oraibi before she went to school in Riverside. In her autobiography, *No Turning Back* (1964), Polingaysi recalled that as a young girl she enjoyed "attending religious services" led by Voth and the Mennonites, "for she loved to sing."[10] The Mennonites taught Polingaysi and the other Hopi children many religious songs. More important from the missionaries' perspective the Mennonites used the songs and stories to introduce the Hopi to the Bible and the Christian faith. The religious foundation Voth and the Mennonites laid, particularly with the Oraibi children, carried on with the Hopi pupils to Sherman Institute.

Voth's ministry with the Hopi people did not exist without its share of Hopi critics. In his autobiography, *Sun Chief* (1942), Don C. Talayesva, a Hopi pupil from Oraibi who came to Sherman Institute in 1906, recalled that when Voth and the "Christians came to Oraibi and preached Jesus in the plaza where the Katcinas danced," the "old people paid no attention" but the children "were told to accept any gifts and clothing."[11] Don recalled that Voth "never preached Christ" to him alone, but always talked about Christ to the Hopis in a group. Voth told Don and the other Hopi children that Jesus Christ was their Savior who suffered for their sins. To demonstrate the power of the Christian God, Voth told the Hopis to "ask Jesus for whatever" they wanted and that he would give it to them. For Don, oranges and "candy looked pretty good" to him, so he prayed for these just as Voth had instructed him to do. But when Don finished praying and "looked up into the sky," Jesus did not "throw anything down" to him.[12]

Don's reluctance and distrust in the Christian faith existed long before he arrived at Sherman. When he prayed for oranges and candy and did not receive any, Voth told Don that the Hopi gods he believed in "were no good." But instead of listening to Voth, Don sought the counsel of the "old people," who "pointed out" that "when the Katcinas danced in the plaza it often rained."[13] "Even as a child . . . the old ones" taught Don "that the missionaries had no business condemning [their] gods," for doing so "might cause droughts and famine." Don's opinion of Christianity transferred with him to Sherman Institute, where other missionaries tried to convince him to abandon Hopi beliefs for the white man's religion.

Government Chrisitan Agenda

THE GOVERNMENT created off-reservation Indian boarding schools in order to destroy Indian cultures and further the ideals and values of white Protestant America. Christianity was only one of many tools the government used to accomplish these goals. In this regard, off-reservation Indian boarding schools did not operate solely as secular institutions, nor did they did function entirely as religious ones. Unlike Catholic Indian boarding schools, such as St. Boniface in Banning, California, government schools merged Christianity with Indian education in order to create Indian citizens. According to the government and the popular thought of the day, the hoped-for Indian citizen would no longer think, talk, or behave like an Indian. The government realized that Indian people would not permanently change unless the government, through the institution of Indian boarding schools, stripped the Indians of their native religion and replaced it with the Christian faith.

For Protestant and Catholic missionaries the primary objective in sharing the Christian gospel with the Hopi centered on an internal spiritual transformation of the soul. In addition to this transformation, missionaries throughout Hopi history used Christianity to destroy Hopi culture, which fell more in line with the government's use of Christianity with the Hopi and other Indian people. The necessity to include Christianity in the overall objective for Indian education largely stemmed from the government's desire to create Indian students who would reflect a Protestant America. In the early twentieth century, philanthropists who financially supported American Indian education gained much of their "moral energy" from religious reformers who wanted America to consist primarily of Christian citizens. In *Education For Extinction*, David Wallace Adams keenly observed that philanthropists did not simply want to "snatch the Indians' soul from a hellish fate," they adamantly believed that Indian citizenship would not exist apart from Christian conversion.[14]

At Sherman Institute, the religious and educational policies primarily came from Commissioner of Indian Affairs Francis E. Leupp. In a nine-page letter to B. B. Custer, superintendent of the Indian school in Albuquerque, New Mexico, Leupp outlined his policy regarding the use of Christianity in federal Indian boarding schools.[15] Leupp told Custer that he had "grown up in the old-fashioned notion" that the American government stood for "all religious faiths" and that the "separation

of Church and State" was "the chief tenet" in the United States' "patriotic creed." Leupp further argued that "any school system conducted at
the public expense ought either to eliminate all religions" or "adopt one
which will be as nearly universal as it can possibly be made."[16]

Leupp admitted to Custer that had he established the first Indian
school system he would have "cut it wholly free, as far as the Government's share in the training of the children was concerned, from any and
all ecclesiastical connections."[17] While this may have been Leupp's personal conviction, he made it clear to Custer that he did not intend to
"abolish religion from the schools, but merely confine the school's
own teaching, as far as its spiritual phases were concerned, to good
morals."[18] Consequently, Indian boarding schools throughout the United
States, including Sherman Institute, adapted Commissioner Leupp's
policy in their use of Christianity.

Although Sherman Institute did not provide students with specifics
courses on religious subjects, such as theology taught at Catholic Indian
boarding schools, school officials required Indian pupils to participate
in Christian activities held on and off the school campus. The government intended for students to learn about Jesus Christ, Christian doctrine, and the Bible. Christian activities at Sherman included weekly
Bible studies for both boys and girls and weekly chapel services located
in the school's auditorium. In accordance with the government's Indian
education Christian policy, Leupp advocated that all "dogmatic religion"
be left to "missionary bodies" that would have the "freest access" to
Indian pupils (Ibid).[19] Leupp insisted that officials at the school incor-
porate Christian principles in daily academic instruction. However, in
areas such as evangelistic preaching and in-depth Bible study, he allowed
Protestant and Catholic clergy to have full reign.

At the insistence of Leupp, school officials at Sherman limited
Christianity in the classroom to universal moral values, which included
"virtues of kindness," "self control of passions; charitableness of judgment and gentleness of speech and action." Leupp further encouraged
school officials to enforce the Christian principles of "cleanliness of
body and mind; honesty and unselfishness" and all "elements of human

conduct which [made] for better relations between fellow men."[20] Although not exclusively Protestant ideals, the virtues taught at the school generally reflected the teachings of all major Christian denominational faiths in the United States at the time.

At no point in the early twentieth century did the federal government allow non-Christian religious groups—Jews, Muslims, Buddhist, and Native American Church—to work among students at Indian boarding schools. Religious principles and values "expressed and encouraged" at Sherman Institute mirrored those of the Christian faith. Few, if any, pupils at Sherman would have chosen the Jewish or Muslim faith as their primary religion. In each of the Hopi school applications from 1902 to 1928, every Hopi student checked "Protestant" as their preferred religious persuasion. The Hopi's only other option would have been to check "Catholic," as school officials did not theoretically allow "Native religion" at the school.

Christianity at Sherman

IN MAY 1909 the *Sherman Bulletin*, a student-written school newspaper, included a short article that reflected the overall Christian tenor of the school. The article noted that "[i]f the world is ever to be conquered for Christ it will be by every one doing his own work, filling his own sphere, holding his own part, and saying to Jesus, 'Jesus, what wilt that have me to do?'"[21] At Sherman Institute Christianity had a greater, world objective. According to school and religious leaders, the world primarily meant other Indian people living on the reservation. In this regard, Sherman Institute trained Indian pupils in Christianity to conquer their fellow Indians for Christ. Consequently, for Hopi pupils, school officials wanted them to return to the reservation as mechanics, plumbers, housewives and Protestant missionaries. In any case, regardless of their occupations on the reservation, school officials wanted Hopis and other students to spread Christ and teach the Gospels.

The government's Christian "world" objective was clearly evident in a sermon given by Don Talayesva at a YMCA meeting at the school. When Don and two other Hopi pupils, Adolph Hoye and Harry McClain, attended the gathering, the association leaders expected them to stand on their "feet and testify for Jesus Christ." At some point during his three years at Sherman Institute, Don "prepared a little sermon" that he willingly recited if called upon to give a testimony. The sermon he wrote and memorized is a telling commentary on how officials used Christianity at the school. "Well, my partners," the sermon went, "I am asked to speak a few words for Jesus. I am glad that I came to Sherman and learned to read and cipher. Now I discover that Jesus was a good writer. So I am thankful that Uncle Sam taught me to read in order that I may understand the Scriptures and take my steps along God's road. When I get a clear understanding of the Gospel I shall return home and preach it to my people in darkness. I will teach them all about Jesus Christ, the Heavenly Father, and the Holy Ghost.'"[22] In the second half of Don's sermon, he beseeched his friends to "pray to God" for "understanding." Don told his audience that when God provided understanding, they "will be ready for Jesus to come" and be taken "up to heaven." Don told a group of YMCA boys: "I don't want any of my friends to be thrown into the lake of hell fire, where there is suffering and sorrow forever. Amen."[23]

Don's sermon was exactly what school officials and religious leaders wanted to hear from a Hopi pupil. Don's appreciation for the education he received at Sherman and the connection he saw between learning to read and understanding Scripture surely won him favor in the eyes of YMCA leaders and Sherman's administration. And his words played well with the general public. What is perhaps most significant in Don's sermon, however, is his apparent eagerness to return home and preach the Gospel to the Hopi people. A few years before, while living on the reservation, Don had serious doubts about the Christian faith. In light of Don's sermon, one may be tempted to conclude that Don had experienced Christian conversion. But Don's profession of faith did not make him a genuine convert. In fact, when he returned home, he became a Sun Chief[24] and actively participated in Hopi ceremonies.

Two Christian Organizations

THE YOUNG Men's Christian Association (YMCA) and the Young Women's Christian Association (YWCA) held important roles at Sherman Institute and other off-reservation Indian boarding schools. At Sherman the two Christian organizations held weekly Bible studies and met regularly on campus for Christian fellowship. Pastors from local churches or important men from the greater Riverside area often gave inspirational talks to the boys in the YMCA. In March 1907, the Honorable C. E. Rumsey, "one of Southern California's prominent and busy men," led the YMCA Bible study. Some of the students at the school noted that Rumsey "wields a strong influence for good, and Sherman appreciates his efforts."[25] At times the YMCA called on medical professionals, such as Dr. William W. Roblee, to speak on both medical and religious issues. In May 1907 Roblee spoke to a group of forty-six Indian students, some of them Hopi, on health issues that specifically related to boys "under fourteen."[26]

Although the exact subject matter of the meeting is uncertain, the YMCA had previously published short pamphlets on masturbation and distributed them to the Indian boys at the school. Since Dr. Roblee worked in the medical profession and served in a leadership role in the YMCA he may have, at some point, spoken to the boys about this particular subject. Don Talayesva recalled in his autobiography that the YMCA pamphlet told the pupils that masturbation "ruined a boy's health and caused him to go insane."[27] Fear tactics, such as the ones used in the masturbation pamphlet, were all too common with the YMCA.

The girls in the YWCA also had a growing Bible study on campus. At the same time Dr. Roblee spoke to the boys on practical health issues, Alice Marmon and Mrs. Hall, wife of Superintendent Harwood Hall, facilitated a talk on "Covetousness or [P]etty Jealousy" to the YWCA girls.[28] Those in attendance noted that the meeting was "very helpful" and commented on how Mrs. Hall never failed "to enthuse and help the girls."[29] In April 1907 several YWCA girls, along with their leader, Sadie Asquabe, spoke on "Our School Work and Our Religion," or "Weekday

Practice of Sunday Preaching."[30] How religion practically affected the Indian pupil's school life became a common theme for Christian messages at Sherman Institute. In "Our School Work and Our Religion" the message emphasized that a "girl's religion, if genuine, will show in her daily deportment as well as in her industrial and class work."[31]

In 1914 Francis E. Leupp observed that the YMCA and YWCA had become an "important feature of missionary work among the pupils in the various government schools and among the returned students on the Indian reservations."[32] Leupp further commented that students who returned "from schools such as Carlisle and Hampton to the comparative isolation and limitations of tribal life, [were] not only subject to temptations incident to both heredity and environment," but to great "differences in the changes and modes of life." In Leupp's opinion, the YMCA and YWCA had become a godsend to Indian students in need of "friendly sympathy" upon returning to the reservation.[33]

Hopi Involvement and Rejection

AT OFF-RESERVATION Indian boarding schools Indian students participated in Christian activities for various reasons. Although school officials at Sherman encouraged students to join Christian organizations, the amount of student involvement varied by each pupil. Some of the students found the social environment appealing, while others attended the meetings because their friends attended. Both the YMCA and YWCA meetings often included food and musical entertainment, which likely encouraged Indian pupil attendance. In addition to the social and material reasons for the Hopi attendance at the meetings, some Hopi pupils, like Polingaysi Qoyawayma, had a genuine interest in the Christian faith and eagerly participated in various Christian organizations at the school.

School officials at Sherman did not force the Hopi, or any other Indian pupil, to become "born again" Christians. Simply attending Christian services did not automatically mean that an Indian pupil became a committed follower of the Christian faith. Some Hopi pupils attended Christian services because school officials forced them to do so. Others attended meetings such as the YMCA out of mere curiosity. Meetings also provided students with an opportunity to socialize with other pupils, which broke up the regular routine of the school week. Don Talayseva recounts in his autobiography that, in order for him to join the YMCA, religious leaders required him to sign his name on a dotted line, which demonstrated his "allegiance" to the Christian faith. Like many other Indian pupils, Don did not understand the implications of signing his name. However, shortly thereafter he attended Bible study every Thursday night and received prizes for learning the names of each book in the Bible. Don even memorized passages of Scripture, which helped him to win a Bible of his own.[34]

Although Don attended Christian gatherings at the school, his loyalty to Jesus Christ and the Christian faith lacked serious commitment. In several occasions throughout his autobiography, Don revealed that he had sex with numerous girls at the school, which included a Navajo pupil named Dezba from Crystal, New Mexico.[35] In addition to premarital sex, Don clearly demonstrated inconsistent behavior with Christianity in his language. In *Sun Chief*, Don commented that he "learned to preach" and "cuss" "pretty well." Since the "Hopi language [had] no cuss words in it," the new vocabulary Don learned at school allowed Don to express himself as he had never done before. Don further noted that "even the Y.M.C.A. and the Catholic boys cussed like hell." While at first the constant cussing made him "tired," once he "got into the habit" he became used to it. From then on, whenever he "wanted anything," he would say, "Give me that God-damn thing."[36] When Don returned to Oraibi in 1909 he eagerly returned to the Hopi way and committed himself once again to Hopi religion. Unlike Polingaysi Qoyawayma, Don despised Christianity and wanted nothing to do with the white man's morals, culture, and values. In spite of his three-year attendance at Sherman Institute, Don remained, in many ways, untouched by white society.

Taking Christianity Home

SCHOOL OFFICIALS never intended Christianity to remain at the school when the Indian pupil returned to the reservation. In addition to their new industrial skills and familiarity with English grammar, officials expected Indian pupils to take the Christian Gospel home with them in order to witness to those who remained in spiritual "darkness." Returning home and sharing the Gospel with others therefore became a gauge by which genuine Hopi conversion could be determined. While some Hopi pupils, such as Don Talayesva, participated in Christian organization at Sherman, it became clear that once they returned to the reservation, they renounced the Christian faith altogether. Other Hopis returned home with a greater appreciation of the white man's world and a genuine love for Jesus Christ.

Effie Sachowengsie, a Hopi pupil from Oraibi who attended Sherman from 1906 to 1909, represents one of several students who took Christianity back to the reservation. Known at the school for her ability to bake, Effie noted on a 1911 Record of Graduates and Returned Students form that the "interest" of "her life" was "Jesus Christ." "So happy in Him," Effie told Superintendent Conser and other school officials that she had been involved in the Lord's "work every day" since she left Sherman Institute.[37] In a letter to an unknown individual, Effie wrote that she was "still laboring for the Lord." She commented that the "harvest is [plentiful], but the worker[s] are few," and concluded her correspondence by asking for prayer for "more workers."

Shortly after Effie returned home from Sherman in 1909, she found work as a cook at the Mission to the Navajo and Other Indian Tribes station in Tolchaco, Arizona. In May 1911 Effie received a letter from Conser, in which Conser invited her to attend the school's annual commencement ceremony. When Effie responded to Conser's letter, she informed the superintendent that she would not be able to attend the commencement since the "Lord's work" was in "great need" of her at Tolchaco.[38] Although likely disappointed that Effie could not participate in the commencement, Conser surely understood and valued the Christian work of Effie.

Louise Talas, a Hopi pupil from the village of Moencopi, Arizona, also participated in various Christian activities at Sherman. Baptized into the Presbyterian Christian Union in 1918, Louise engaged in religious leadership roles while a student at the school. In November 1920 Louise led a YWCA Bible study and delivered a message titled "How I Should Treat the Bible."[39] Those who attended the meeting commented that Louise's subject matter "was very interesting." When Louise returned to the reservation in 1924, she eventually found work in Los Angeles as a nurse in a Methodist hospital in 1929,[40] and eventually found employment as a nurse at Sherman Institute in 1931.[41]

When some of the Hopi pupils returned home with Christianity, their new faith and appreciation of the white man's ways unsurprisingly created serious tensions with their families. The most well-known example of this is found in Polingaysi Qoyawayma's *No Turning Back*. Polingaysi's stay at Sherman Institute had a profound impact on her as a Hopi woman. When she returned to Oraibi in 1910, she struggled to live in the world of her Hopi parents. For the young woman, the Hopi way lost its appeal as she experienced the white man's world in a way that would have been impossible had she remained on the reservation. Although Polingaysi loved her family, "she did not relish the idea of going home to stay." At Sherman, Polingaysi had "made many new friends" and "learned the white man's way of living and liked it."[42]

Even though Polingaysi changed while a student at Sherman Institute, her parents did not. Polingaysi, like other Hopi pupils, experienced a different life away from home. Whether the Hopi pupils had a positive or negative experience at school, their time at Sherman undoubtedly changed their opinion of life on the reservation. Within minutes after Polingaysi arrived at her home in Oraibi, she scolded her parents for not having the commodities she learned to appreciate at school: "Why haven't you bought the white man's beds to sleep on? And a table? You should not be eating on the floor as the Old Ones did." Polingaysi reminded her parents that as "a little girl," she "did not mind sleeping on the floor and eating from a single bowl in which everyone dipped." But she was "used to another way of living now," and did not intend to live as she once had.[43] Polingaysi's words grieved her parents and, not long after her arrival home, she rejected all Hopi superstitions entirely and publicly professed Christianity before the Oraibi people. Having been exposed to Christianity at the school, Christian missionaries at Oraibi encouraged Polingaysi to rid herself of Hopi religion and convinced her that taking part in the traditional Katchina dances was "Devil worship."

Conclusion

HOPI CHRISTIAN involvement at Sherman Institute existed in several forms and had various layers of meaning. Just as at other Indian boarding schools at the time, some Hopi pupils came to Sherman as genuine and committed Christians. Others had some familiarity of the Christian faith as a result of the work by Protestant missionaries or day school teachers prior to their attendance at the school. When the Hopi pupils arrived at Sherman, school officials automatically expected or assumed that the new group of students wanted a Christian education. But whether they desired an education based on Christian principles or not, the government still forced it upon them.

It is uncertain how much the Hopi students, or their parents, fully realized the government's agenda in using Christianity as a tool to destroy their culture. It would be difficult for the Hopis to fathom that a faith based on "love," would ever view their culture as "evil," "wicked," or of the "Devil." While some of the Hopis returned home and witnessed to their "pagan" families, others demonstrated an even greater distrust of the white man, which only strengthened their commitment to the Hopi way. Still other Hopis, such as my great-grandfather Victor, accepted and adapted Christianity to fit with life on the Hopi Reservation. Rather than growing bitter toward the government for its past wrongs against the Hopi people, he used the education he received at Sherman to better serve his family and Hopi community. Later on in life he made certain that his children attended school, not to encourage or endorse the destructive influences of the government but as a way to preserve their culture.

Note:
"I Learned to Preach Pretty Well, and to Cuss, Too" is part of a larger study known as "The Sherman Project: A History of Hopi Student Involvement at Sherman Institute, 1902–2005." The Sherman Project is conducted with the cooperation and involvement of the Hopi Cultural Preservation Office (Kykotsmovi, Arizona), the Sherman Indian Museum (Riverside, California), and the University of California, Riverside.

1   Clifford E. Trafzer. *As Long as the Grass Shall Grow and Rivers Flow.* (Fort Worth, TX: Harcourt College Publishers, 2000), p. 289.

2   The Oraibi Split took place on September 8, 1906. This Hopi division involved two broad issues: Christianity and government-run education.

3   The government forced nearly seventy-one Hopi pupils from Oraibi to attend Sherman in November 1906.

4   I have written more on this subject in a forthcoming article titled "'The Hopi Followers': Chief Tawaquaptewa and Hopi Student Advancement at Sherman Institute, 1906–1909," *Journal of American Indian Education*, Fall 2005, vol. 44, no. 2.

5   Harry C. James. *Pages from Hopi History*, 8th edition. (Tucson, AZ: The University of Arizona Press, 1994), p. 55.

6   Louise Udall. *Me and Mine: The Life Story of Helen Sekaquaptewa*, 9th edition. (Tucson, AZ: University of Arizona Press, 1991), p. 238.

7   Ibid.

8   James, *Pages from Hopi History*, p. 148.

9   Peter M. Whiteley. *Rethinking Hopi Ethnography*. (Washington, D.C.: Smithsonian Institution Press, 1998), p. 145.

10 Polingaysi Qoyawayma, as told to Vada F. Carlson. *No Turning Back: A Hopi Indian Woman's Struggle to Live in Two Worlds*, 8th edition. (Albuquerque, NM: University of New Mexico Press, 1992), p. 14.

11 Don C. Talayesva. *Sun Chief: Autobiography of a Hopi Indian*. (New Haven: Yale University Press, 1942), p. 41.

12 Ibid.

13 Ibid.

14 David Wallace Adams. *Education for Extinction: American Indians and the Boarding School Experience, 1875, 1928*. (Lawrence, KS: University of Kansas Press, 1995), p. 23.

15 Francis E. Leupp to Mr. Custer, September 21, 1905, Box 55, RG-75:
 Records of the Bureau of Indian Affairs (BIA), Sherman Institute, Records of
 the Superintendent, Letters and Telegrams from the Commissioner, National
 Archives and Records Administration (NARA), Laguna Niguel, California
 (Pacific Branch). Documents secured from Leleua Loupe, "Sherman Indian
 Institute Research Guide, 1893–1910," vol. 3: 1906, Sherman Indian
 Museum, Riverside, California, Winter 2003. Hereafter referred to as: SIIRG,
 Leleua Loupe.

16 Ibid.

17 Ibid.

18 Ibid.

19 Ibid.

20 Ibid.

21 *The Sherman Bulletin* (Hereafter "TSB"). The Sherman Indian Museum,
 Riverside, California, May 5, 1909, p. 3.

22 Talayesva. *Sun Chief*. pp. 116, 117.

23 Ibid, p. 117.

24 "Sun Chief" is the leader of the Sun Clan.

25 TSB, March 6, 1907, p. 2.

26 TSB, April 24, 1907, p. 4.

27 Talayesva. *Sun Chief*. p. 117.

28 TSB, April 10, 1907, p. 3.

29 Ibid.

30 TSB, May 1, 1907, p. 3.

31 Ibid.

32 Francis E. Leupp. *In Red Man's Land*. (New York: Fleming H. Revell Company, 1914), p. 156.

33 Ibid, 157.

34 Talayesva. *Sun Chief*. p. 116.

35 Ibid., p. 114.

36 Ibid., p. 117.

37 Effie Sachowengsie, "Sachowengsie, Effie," Record of Graduates and
 Returned Students, March 25, 1911, Box 315, RG-75, BIA, Sherman Indian
 High School Student Case Files, NARA, Laguna Niguel, California (Pacific
 Branch).

38 Effie Sachowengsie to Frank Conser, "Sachowengsie, Effie," 1911, Box 315,
 RG-75, BIA, Sherman Indian High School Student Case Files, NARA,
 Laguna Niguel, California (Pacific Branch).

39 TSB, November 5, 1920, p. 3.

40 F. D. Hall to Conser, "Talas, Louise," March 18, 1929, Box 351, RG-75, BIA,
 Sherman Indian High School Student Case Files, NARA, Laguna Niguel,
 California (Pacific Branch).

41 Commissioner to Conser, "Talas, Louise," May 26, 1931, Box 351, RG-75,
    BIA, Sherman Indian High School Student Case Files, NARA, Laguna
    Niguel, California (Pacific Branch).

42 Qoyawayma. *No Turning Back.* p. 67.

43 Ibid., p. 69.

REMEMBERING:

ATOP POLACCA ON FIRST MESA

MARIJO MOORE

SOME THINGS are hidden in the immensity of the Arizona desert. Others are forever reappearing. As I walk across the burning sands, I feel traces of lightning that wove itself into this mesa hundreds of celebrations ago. Traces that scratch open my vision in preparation for a remarkable mystery. The hot wind sprays dust in my face, spits into my heart prayers floating in the ether for eons, and I intuitively know I will never be the same.

Today, spirits will materialize in answer to ritualistic prayers. Spirits will sing, drum, and dance. The Katsinam are coming.

It is Summer Solstice, and I am a visitor on First Mesa on the Hopi Reservation in Arizona, invited by the Sinquah family to observe an age-old ceremony closed to non-Indians.

Consisting of approximately four thousand square miles of arid plateaus and desert, Hopi land encompasses various dwellings, which cling to the rocky cliffs of First, Second, and Third Mesas. First Mesa, barren of trees, juts out over the village of Polacca. The sky is close, turquoise, and beautiful. The mesa is colored only by sand; there is not one blade of green grass. Even the houses are sand-colored.

"Sometimes, you focus on the black highway just to ease your eyes," Dale Sinquah tells me as we drive up the winding mountain road. The parched earth of the desert floor is cracked open in places, showing even more dryness beneath. Yet looking down from the six-hundred-foot high mesa, I see tiny brown patches that are fields of blue corn. To my eyes, used to acres of lush green cornfields growing in a rainy Southeastern climate, seeing corn grow in this parched desert is truly a miracle.

The industrious and spiritual Hopi have managed to survive in the dry, barren desert for thousands of years. Although modern conveniences have made their way into the villages, Hopi traditions have survived. The Hopi language is still spoken fluently, baskets are still woven from yucca plants, and celebratory traditions still have precedence. Katsinam— spirit beings who represent all aspects of universal life and live on the snowcapped San Francisco Mountains in the Cochina Forest—still come in colorful ceremony to pray for rain and abundance as they sing, not just for the survival of the Hopi but also for the entire world.

Traces of lightning in the sand burning feet, scratching eyes
wind spraying dust, spitting awareness
prayers bringing in respected spirits
young men on flat rooftops, standing
women with colorful shawls, sitting
children, dark and beautiful, watching

rose embroidered on loincloth of dancing Katsinam
clouds, a lizard, the sun
Katsinam dancing dancing Katsinam embodying the world
the entire lost, lonely world

somewhere, far away from this plaza, children are crying
women are hurting, men are dying
all will eventually feel the prayers of dancing Katsinam Katsinam
    dancing

their guttural singing tearing at my throat
splitting open my soul
taking me to a place so deep inside the sky
I may never go there again
mesmerized by movements, dreamed awake by colors
I fall deeper and deeper inside myself
than I have ever dared visit before

Young men, serious and observant, line the flat tops of the ancient stone houses. Women, reverent in their colorful shawls, sit in rows of chairs on the plaza. Children with dark, beautiful faces wait with ancestral anticipation for the sine qua non.

A slow, steady drumbeat begins to reverberate inside my heart as the plaza becomes filled with drumming, movement, and color. The Katsinam are here. Singing and dancing.

This dance, like all American Indian dances, is not a form of mindless amusement but a form of praise, a way to experience interconnectedness through motion. The art of dancing was part of life for American Indians before the conception of art ever existed. American Indian dances are beautiful metaphors for celebrating life to the fullest. Music and dance are representatives of the full range of life for us American Indians. They are integral fuels that have always fed the fires of honor and traditions. Dance is a necessary spiritual action requiring dedication and a devout sense of reverence. To dance is to pray, to pray is to heal, to heal is to give, to give is to live, to live is to dance.

Katsinam dancing dancing Katsinam are lined inside of me
celebrating not explaining celebrating the mysteries
of all interconnectedness
knowing not hoping knowing all the people need their prayers
small chosen rocks rattling inside gourds
bringing visions of cool life-giving rains
my skin erupting letting go cold chills
quickly vanishing in the hot, dry desert

Am I seeing what I am seeing?

dancing Katsinam Katsinam dancing circle never closing
eagle feathers dripping from turquoise mouths
lush green juniper surrounding singing throats
movements . . . gourd rattles raise upward meeting lowered faces
heads turning left
bows and arrows lowered heads following
two right steps in one place now one left now turn and repeat
singing always singing

Symbolism is more than just imagined reality to American Indians. Symbols represent spiritual reality where thought and feeling, storyteller and story, spirit and creation, are considered the same. One need only watch a true artisan at work carving a ceremonial pipe from stone to see how ancestral spirits are present during creation. And there is no doubt evoked ancestral spirits are here within this plaza today, manifested in these otherworldly colorful beings.

Watching the Katsinam dance, my senses heighten as cultural chants mix with swishing rain sounds falling from gourd rattles and fill the air. Haunting, mystical sounds transport my spirit to the place inside myself where deep wounds lie hidden, and I ache for a simpler existence. The drum—its round form representing the shape of the sacred universe— emits a strong, steady heartbeat that entrances my mind, and I become one with all. Agile and full of purpose, the sacred, fruitful dance chills my soul. I am alive.

I sit in awe of this celebratory vision and poetry births itself inside my spirit. Poetry has been the medium of mystics, prophets, and healers for thousands of years. For me, poetry is proof of the mystery living inside me; it is reality scratching at the surface of my soul; it is my true connection to the whole. Poetry is ceremony woven from the voices of the old ones, intuition, dreams, and visions. The poems that find me are gifts from Spirit through me to others.

In the belief system of American Indians, this quintessential Spirit is

known by many names and has many voices. These voices often pen-
etrate our spoiled, scarred psyches and force thoughts to materialize,
expressing themselves in creative forms—song, dance, music, art, and literature. These creations provide us a sense of interconnection, a sense
of being. They give us proof of what we all seem to crave the most: love
and hope.

Why love and hope? Is love respect or is it the other side of indifference? Is it something that can be captured, bottled, sold to the highest bidder? Has love, like the words "sacred," "holy," and "respect"
become meaningless from overuse? And what about the word "hope"?
What is hope? Why do we need hope? What have we forgotten? What
have we lost touch with? I firmly believe most people have lost touch
with the land, thus they have lost touch with themselves.

To American Indians, ceremony is a necessary act to obtain or regain
balance with the earth. It is the highest form of giving back to the earth
so that she can replenish her supply for humankind. The purpose of ceremony is to integrate, to unite one with all of humankind and creation
as well as the realm of the ancestors. Consciousness is raised and the idea
of individuality shed. Ceremony brings into balance all there is.

Though each ceremony has its own special purpose, which varies
from nation to nation, all ceremony provides deep illumination and the
realization there is no separation from anything or anyone.

Poetry, song, art, music, and dance can help us understand this relationship, and often provide spiritual healings. Only in isolation can
spiritual sicknesses exist; therefore, to heal, one must recognize a one-
ness with the universe.

The Cherokee story "How the Plants Gave Us Medicine" tells of a
time when humans lived peacefully with the animals, were in total com-
munication with them, and always asked the permission of the animal
for its life before taking it. But when the people began to lose respect
for the animals and began hunting for sport, they needlessly killed animals and destroyed the balance of the forests. Because the people forgot the importance of ceremony, the animals began to inflict diseases and

infirmities upon them. The plant world, in sympathy for the people, gave their medicines as cures for the diseases. Now this plant world is being destroyed. Since the beginning of the nineteenth century medical science has turned its back on nature. The aspect of Spirit participating in one's healing is quickly pushed aside in favor of synthetic drugs and quick-fix therapies.

The Hopi call this *Koyaanisqatsi*, "Life out of balance; crazy life; life disintegrating; a state of life that calls for another way of living." Is life out of balance? How else can one explain the continuing destruction of the world's original forests? And the poisoning of waters, the widening hole in the ozone, the thousands of dollars spent on the excavating of bones to be examined, while the problems of modern-day people continue to be ignored? What about individual lives? Are they out of balance? What about the continuing racist hate crimes, the bitter stings of discrimination and stereotyping? The rising number of suicides every year (especially among youth), the ever-present damage caused by alcoholism and drug abuse, children being born addicted and with fetal alcohol ayndrome, and on and on? How have we lost this important contact with our inner selves? How have we lost our connecting responsibility to each other and to the land? What have we put in the place of ceremony?

Ceremony is often shunned in favor of organized society and religion, in favor of shortcuts to spirituality, in favor of ignoring one's inner call by listening to the outer calls demanding more and more material gain. Ceremony is passed over in favor of defining instead of celebrating one's existence. In other words, we are cut off from our inner selves, from the place where we can experience spiritual connection with all that exists. Shunning ceremony can cause all of life to become out of balance.

But today, atop Polacca on First Mesa, white clouds are beginning to loom in the turquoise sky, adding their celestial contribution to the celebration of the Great Mystery. And the Katsinam, poetry in motion surrounded by an aura of ceremonial certainty, dance on, singing and praying. Praying for balance to be restored to all.

reminding the arid earth roots of ancestral corn
are resting in its ancient belly
corn meal yellowed on chests
corn meal leaving women's hands
landing on the sacredness
the blessed ageless ceremonial sacredness of
dancing Katsinam Katsinam dancing
turtle-shells speaking jingling bells answering fox tails swinging
head Katsinam directing white-haired priest circling

all the people silent
I believe my heart explodes I believe my spirit takes flight
I believe my mind is touched as never before
and maybe as never again
Mudhead Katsina drumming stopping changing positions
drumming dancing turning
singing praying moaning

ho'oooooteeeee ho'te ho'te

Katsinam dancing, dancing Katsinam
dancing for all the people
dancing for all the world
stopping
leaving a changed silence
returning to the dark kiva
to pray and prepare to dance again.

The Hopi, like all American Indians, are not without factional problems. As their ancestors in the emergence stories, modern-day Hopi are still in disagreement concerning maintaining traditional beliefs or embracing progressiveness, which includes acceptance of non-Hopi ways. But today, ancestral spirits are here, dancing, singing, and praying. There is the collective acceptance of tradition.

I, like all the observers, am silent. Pausing in the space between knowledge and understanding. The space between wounding and healing. The space between hope and acceptance. I hear the haunting, guttural prayer-song and the accompanying sound of the slow mesmerizing drum beat. The Katsinam dance two right steps in one place, one left, turn, and then repeat. These synchronized movements remind me that all is really one. That we are really a part of the all. This is truly a ceremonial celebration, truly a prayer in motion.

The human element is almost totally disregarded as the entire physical universe is recognized, revered, and celebrated. There is no attempt at explaining the universe, only at celebrating its existence. There is no cathedral, church, or temple isolating the Creator, only natural surroundings. There is no collection plate; the people give their respect and full attention. There is no preacher ranting and raving about heaven or hell, no laying on of hands, no manipulation by guilt, no Sunday-best clothing. No tarot card readings, no channeling of the archangel Michael. No one seeking an Indian name, performing a vision quest, or ingesting peyote. There is no competitive dancing, no war whoops, no clapping. Only a changed silence as the Katsinam finish their dance and head back to the darkness of the kiva, to pray and prepare to dance again.

Rainer Maria Rilke wrote, "Teaching means: to ask of each person what he feels closest to in silence." As a writer, I am a teacher. And as a teacher, I am continually learning. Witnessing the metaphorical beauty of the Katsinam returning to the source of creation has deepened my silence. As I drive across the changing desert to Phoenix to catch a flight back to North Carolina, I ask myself what I feel closest to in silence.

And I hear a voice, a silvery voice wrapped in secrets of red and purple, telling me to go deep, deep inside myself. Deep to the deepest part where the light lies in the center of the darkness—that it will be here I will find the celebration of who I am, why I exist, where I come from, and where I am going. And in this celebration I will find the explanation that requires no explaining, the knowledge that requires no knowing, the answer that requires no questioning. Then I would understand, and then I would not understand, and then it would not matter.

What so many of us long to know and often guess about the universe and its mystical workings, the traditional Hopi know and respect. The most important realization is to celebrate and acknowledge the Great Mystery, not try and explain. What I have experienced is pure faith. A faith that obviously exists because, after all, the Hopi still have rain and their corn still grows in the arid desert.

3

PROPAGANDA:
EXPOSURE AND
SURVEILLANCE

INDIAN NATIONS AND THE AMERICAN HOLOCAUSTS

CARTER REVARD

WHAT SEEMS to matter most is the great silence, the denial of any holocaust.

The United States, like every other nation I know of, is a nation built on genocide, an empire whose capital building foundations rest on the skeletons of American Indians (like the Romans' capital building said to be set on the skeleton of Remus, the murdered brother of Romulus, who founded Rome). We are a culture whose schools only gingerly touch and mostly ignore the actual history of the nation, the empire, the culture, so far as those might include detailed reference to the Indian nations deliberately destroyed and still "undiscovered," even though every year a new set of missionaries is sent to the reservations to report on the people there. Historians are only beginning to include accounts of the Indian nations who lived on this continent as taking part in the shaping of the European colonies and the colossal new Ameropean empire that grew out of those.

It seems that any empire must construct a legendary history of itself in which the other nations that were killed and feasted upon were somehow participants, not mere victims of rape but happy members of its harems, not extinguished cultures but mistaken resisters of higher civilization. The *Aeneid* is one model for such a legendary history, but every U.S. history book presents us with comparable uses of legend and suppression and slanting. Long before the Romans became the dominant Indo-European tribal confederacy, however, the various other invading Indo-European nations, most of whom the Romans subjugated and usually wiped out (Gauls, for instance), had themselves already extinguished many nations and cultures. The Basques are perhaps the only remnant of those cultures who still have a language left among them (the Etruscans, for instance, do not), and the Basques are still kept from resurgent nationhood by the remaining Imperial Guards of Spain.

I think that the Indians of our surviving nations, like Jews, should never forget, but it seems harder to persuade citizens of the United States to remember or acknowledge the American Holocausts of which our nations are survivors, because to remember them is to confront skeletons in the American empire's own closet. It is one thing to believe Hitler and Stalin were monsters. It is quite another to view the American presidents, from Washington onward, as following agendas that provided models not only for the British Empire (in South Africa, explicitly evoked; in India and elsewhere, less directly) but also for the Third Reich (Hitler cited South Africa and the U.S. examples as models) and for Stalin's Soviet Empire—the "evil empire," as Reagan famously called it. No nation wants to see itself as having a criminal past, as Germans realized very sharply after World War II. Every nation has its true stories of heroism, of virtue, of a great and brave people achieving its free and full nationhood. No nation wants to admit the dark side of its ascent to power and wealth.

It may be that a better procedure for Indian peoples, better than achieving only a Museum of the American Holocausts, would be to try and insist that the majority culture should be shown and asked to admit the positive achievements of American Indian Nations, as well as to confront the negatives presented in standard accounts. By analogy, it might be that along with a Holocaust Museum for Jews in Washington, D.C., there should be a celebratory museum in which the courage, brilliance, decency, and incredible achievements of Jewish people in the history of these United States would be displayed; achievements that show this tiny minority to have been perhaps the greatest overall contributors to what is good in our national history and the culture. There has been, in the past half century or so, a really useful and reasonably successful effort to show that Black is Beautiful, to bring out the contributions of blacks to American history and culture. Similarly, for American Indians it is good to have some record in the National Museum of the American Indian of our positive achievements—yet there should also be a full record of the dark side, which Americans are still denying or belittling—in other words, facts of the American Holocaust.

I saw a review article on the National Museum of the American Indian not long ago (in 2004, I think) in the *New York Times* by a writer who (it seemed to me) sniffed at those who try, in the NMAI, to show some of the achievements of American Indians. The reviewer actually seemed to take offense at efforts by Indians to show the positives. I was—and am still—incensed by his sneering and by all such patronizing snobs. They are harmful and they also show more of their own ignorance of American history, and Indian nations within that history, than they realize. Reading his comments on the NMAI was like reading a sneering opera review by someone who shows himself both tone deaf and musically illiterate. Yet when that same reviewer, not so long afterward, went over to London and reviewed a performance there of Schiller's play, *Don Carlos,* he showed intelligence, perceptiveness, literary and theatrical knowledge, and sense. Seeing this, I found it all the more exasperating that he had carped at the NMAI's record of achievements by American Indians.

As it happens, I am writing these words in London, where lately I saw a splendid production of another play by Schiller, *Mary Stuart,* and the theatre critics are rejoicing that it is finally possible to "bring back" the achievements of a great German playwright whose work, because of the infamy of the Third Reich, has been little presented in England since 1945. I have also just gone to reasonably good performances of Shakespeare's *Henry the Fourth,* both Part One and Part Two, whose brilliance and continual relevance to political events from 1595 to 2005 and beyond are almost unbelievable. We can recognize that relevance immediately, when we hear the opening lines of Part One—spoken by Henry the Fourth, who has attained the throne by what he will later admit to his son were "indirect and crooked ways." In this first speech Henry tells his courtiers that he hopes to end the civil war and insurgencies at home by leading an army to Jerusalem so that all the English factions can fight a common foe, the Muslims, in Palestine, "to chase these pagans in those holy fields," as he puts it. Later, in *Henry the Fourth, Part Two,* as Henry lies dying, he will advise his son, Prince Hal, to do likewise—start a foreign war in order to divert English rebels and consolidate his royal control of the nation. I hope viewers will reflect, as they see these literary achievements of an English playwright, on the startling relevance of this play to the American election of 2000, by which George W. Bush assumed the presidency through indirect and crooked ways, and on the "crusade" upon which the American people have since been led in the name of national unity.

By the same token, I would love to have, in a Museum of the American Holocausts, a section devoted to some of the great recorded ceremonies of American Indian peoples, with attention to the continuing relevance of those ceremonies. For instance, I would like to see the long, elaborate, and very beautiful Pawnee ceremony of the Hako presented in the museum, so that for visitors this Peacemaking, Brother-making Ceremony, this "Singing the Calumet," could once more be made visible, so Americans could see that before the Europeans arrived Indian nations were not merely wild groups of warring savages, but had good ways of bringing together different factions, tribes, and nations in peace and brotherhood. I would also like to see an exhibit devoted to the Osage Naming Ceremony, which was recorded and preserved in two different versions (one each from two different clans) by Francis La Flesche in the early 1900s—and in this presentation I would especially want the visitors to notice a brief passage in which La Flesche asked which of the two versions was correct, in a section where they differed somewhat. It is the answer given by an Osage elder to La Flesche's question that I would want visitors to hear: "They are both right!"

I would want that to be heard, because I think it is no less relevant than the plays of Shakespeare or Schiller to the widespread wars and sectarian murders and tortures still going on in the twenty-first century, as well as to those reported in the Old Testament books of Judges, Samuel, and Kings, to those narrated in the New Testament, and to those described by the historian Josephus. When we look back on the several thousand years of sectarian slaughter, the torments of the Inquisition, the Reformation and Counter-Reformation, the dreadful history of the Thirty Years War (it requires a Jonathan Swift to summarize European history in these matters)—surely it would not have been a bad thing if the Osage elder's words had been the guiding ones for European priests and statesmen. I would like for some of the achievements of such elders to be made visible in any Museum of the Holocausts, never to be forgotten so long as there are humans to remember them.

CHOCTAW LEGACY:

HOW TO LOSE YOUR COUNTRY
TWICE IN FOURTEEN TREATIES

DON L. BIRCHFIELD

NOT LONG after the end of the American Revolution, on January 3, 1786, the infant United
States—consisting of thirteen loosely confederated states located entirely
east of the Appalachian Mountains, largely on the Atlantic seaboard itself
but loudly claiming sovereignty over Indian land all the way to the Mississippi River—formally made the acquaintance of the far distant
Choctaw Nation, in "Treaty with the Choctaw, 1786."[1]

The Choctaw Nation, located deep in the interior of the continent
in the Lower Mississippi River Valley, was a great distance from even the
nearest American frontier settlement and was in no sense under any kind
of American control. But it was part of American ambitions under the
doctrine of "discovery."[2]

In 1786 the Choctaw people, much like the three million Americans,
were loosely organized as a confederation. That Choctaw confederation
of three distinctly different divisions (*Okla Falaya*—Long People, *Okla
Tannap*—People of the Opposite Side, and *Okla Hannali*—Sixtowns
People) consisted of about 15,000 to 20,000 Choctaws, living in more
than one hundred largely autonomous towns. The great majority of
those towns were situated along the upper watersheds of the streams in

present-day east central Mississippi.[3] The isolation of those towns in those upper watersheds was apparently a survival strategy to escape the contagions of European disease that had spread along the river-bottom trading paths in the region.

Choctaws, premier agriculturalists, were descended from people who had been cultivating corn for about three thousand years. Their immediate ancestors, highly complex, large populations of river bottom, agricultural, Temple Mound civilizations, had been devastated by those European diseases during what ethnologists call the black hole of Indian history—those unrecorded, chaotic, and deadly decades following the abrupt onset of the holocaust, with the arrival of the lethal Spanish expedition of Hernando de Soto in the region in the late 1530s and the train of European pestilence left in its wake, which may have killed as much as 90 percent of the pre-holocaust Indian population.[4]

Eighteenth-century Choctaws were a nation of survivors. They were highly skilled farmers who supplemented their diet by hunting an abundance of deer and other game in their river bottoms and by harvesting their extensive forest resources, which they carefully managed by the controlled burning of underbrush.[5]

By 1786 the Choctaws had survived the ambitions of both the French and the British. But the Spanish were still a dangerous presence in the Southeast, and there was no guarantee that the French or the British would not return. The Americans represented an opportunity for the Choctaws to enter into an alliance with a new people, a people who were loudly proclaiming how different they were from the European colonial powers.

In 1786, for the first Choctaw treaty with that new American nation, negotiated at Hopewell in South Carolina, the Choctaws granted the United States an exclusive right to regulate Choctaw trade (Article VIII) in exchange for a commitment of protection by the United States (Article II). The Choctaws agreed to admit American traders into the Choctaw Nation (Article IX) and to allow them three tracts of land, six square miles each, to build trading posts (Article III). If any citizen of the United States attempted to settle on Choctaw land, that person would forfeit the protection of the United States "and the Indians may punish him or not as they please" (Article IV). The boundary of the Choctaw Nation was reaffirmed, as it had been established earlier by the Choctaws and the British (Article III).[6]

In that treaty, the Choctaws made a good bargain for themselves, an arrangement that is known in international law as a *protectorate*.[7] The sincerity of the American treaty commissioners was encouraging and virtually all of the terms of the treaty had been freely offered by the Americans as expressions of the will of Congress to have relations with Indian nations grounded in mutual respect and fairness, under the direction of the U.S. national government.[8] It was a good start, one that held a lot of promise for the future.

But the southern states, in the years after 1786, would refuse to abide by the Hopewell treaties the United States negotiated that winter with the Choctaws, Cherokees, and Chickasaws (nearly identical treaties),[9] and would sabotage the attempt of the U.S. government to honor its commitments under those treaties. The southern states would also refuse to abide by the U.S. Constitution, which would shortly be written and ratified and which would make the regulation of commerce with Indian nations the exclusive province of the U.S. national government (Article II, Section 8). The southern states would also refuse to abide by decisions of the U.S. Supreme Court regarding Indians, with a devastating impact upon the Supreme Court that continues to this day.

The U.S. federal government would not be willing to go to war with those southern states over any of those issues, as it would in the 1860s over the issue of slavery. Instead, with the election of Andrew Jackson to the presidency in 1828, the U.S. government would conspire with state governments to suppress the rule of law on the North American continent.

The Choctaw, Chickasaw, and Cherokee nations would have to await the day, which is still at some indefinite point in the future, when the treaties their nations negotiated with the United States at Hopewell will be honored by the American people. How much longer they might have to wait is an open question. But they are ancient peoples, and the holocaust is a comparatively contemporary event, only five centuries old and far from having run its course, with many centuries remaining before the drama is likely to have played itself out. For the short run of history, however, for the brief period of the next two centuries after 1786, matters turned decidedly grim for the Choctaws.

Fifteen years after that first Choctaw treaty at Hopewell, in the second Choctaw treaty—"Treaty with the Choctaw, 1801"—the United States sought and received permission from the Choctaws to build a wagon road through the Choctaw country.[10] On that wagon road Americans poured into the region in such great numbers that on January 10, 1817, the United States Congress admitted Mississippi to the United States as the twentieth state.

Thirty years after granting the right of way for that wagon road, in the aftermath of the ninth Choctaw treaty—"Treaty with the Choctaw, 1830,"[11]—the Choctaws found themselves on that road, being herded toward a new homeland hundreds of miles away west of the Mississippi River, having been dispossessed by the American people of all that they had ever owned east of that river.

Choctaws became the first Indian nation forced to travel the infamous "Trail of Tears" under the provisions of the Indian Removal Act of 1830. That genocidal event, conducted by the United States in two brutal winter migrations in 1831–32 and 1832–33 and a final autumn removal in 1833, killed twenty-five hundred Choctaws (approximately one out of every seven of their population).[12]

The conditions were appalling. At times, torrential winter rains forced some of them to wade through waist-deep water. At other times, barefoot Choctaws were forced to huddle around open fires in freezing temperatures with nothing but a blanket for protection from snowfall as deep as five inches. Others encountered devastating cholera epidemics. Weakened and exhausted, ill-provisioned and easy victims to disease, they continued to die in great numbers after their arrival in the West.[13]

There are six things regarding the callousness and duplicity of that event that are particularly noteworthy and that might be sobering for contemporary Americans to contemplate:

(1) The removal of the Choctaws was an act of betrayal by the American people of its own loyal military ally.

It was Choctaws, under the vigorous leadership of Pushmataha, who dashed Tecumseh's dreams of bringing the southern Indian nations into Tecumseh's pan-Indian military alliance in the War of 1812, the last war on the North American continent in which Indian military power still mattered.[14]

During the War of 1812, Pushmataha was commissioned a brigadier general in the United States Army, as he led between six hundred and eight hundred Choctaw troops in support of the U.S. Army in Alabama against Tecumseh's Red Stick faction of the Creeks at the Battle of Horseshoe Bend and the Battle of Etowah, and against the British in the Pensacola campaign in Florida and at the Battle of New Orleans in Louisiana.[15]

When the war was over the profoundly grateful Mississippi territorial legislature awarded Pushmataha an annuity of fifty dollars a year for five years and presented him with a fifty-dollar "rifle gun."[16]

Upon the death of Pushmataha in 1824 in Washington, D.C., Senator John Randolph of Virginia eulogized his life on the floor of the United States Congress on behalf of a sincerely grateful American people. Pushmataha was accorded the rare honor of burial in the Congressional Cemetery, with General Andrew Jackson himself leading his impressive military funeral procession. The procession stretched for a mile through the streets of the nation's capital—a capital, one might recall, that had been burned to the ground by the British in the War of 1812, as the infant American republic had barely escaped having its life snuffed out in that war, a war in which Pushmataha and the Choctaws had played such a prominent role. At the time of his death, Pushmataha was arguably the Indian most beloved by the American people in all of American history up to that time.[17]

Today, Pushmataha is virtually unheard of and the Choctaws are virtually unknown in American popular culture, undoubtedly because— for their loyalty to the United States, for their sacrifice of having shed their Choctaw blood on the battlefields on behalf of the United States—

the Choctaws were rewarded with the horrors of the Trail of Tears. American historians haven't quite figured out how to put the right kind of spin on that.

(2) The United States required the Choctaws to pay the entire expense of their removal. Choctaws were forced to finance their removal by allowing the United States to sell all of their remaining Choctaw land in Mississippi (10,423,130 acres)[18] to whites by the terms of Article XVIII of the removal treaty.[19]

The United States received $8,095,614.89 for the sale of the Choctaw land in Mississippi and spent $5,097,367.50 on the removal of the Choctaws, leaving a balance due to the Choctaws of almost three million dollars. But the United States refused to pay even that money to the Choctaws.[20]

Choctaws were forced to hire a long succession of lawyers who attempted to collect the money from the U.S. government. It took decades, requiring further treaty negotiations in 1855 (in the thirteenth Choctaw treaty, Articles 11 and 12 of "Treaty with the Choctaw, 1855"), arbitration by the U.S. Senate in 1859, Congressional legislation in 1881 referring the matter to the Court of Claims, and, finally, a U.S. Supreme Court decision in 1886. In 1888, the United States finally paid the nearly three million dollars to the Choctaws—sort of. By then the monumental expenses the Choctaws had incurred in trying to collect the money, including the decades of attorneys' fees, consumed almost all of it.[21]

(3) Despite the fact that it was the Choctaws who were being forced to pay for their own removal, the United States decided that the ill-provisioned conditions of near starvation and lethal exposure to bitter cold of the first winter migrations had been too expensive. The United States fired the independent contractors who had conducted the removals during the first winter and whose incompetence, internal feuding, and chaotic lack of coordination between the removal parties had directly contributed to the appalling number of deaths.

The U.S. Army was placed in charge in order to save money. And save money the army did. It decided to save the expense of hauling the

Choctaws in wagons. The remaining thousands of Choctaws would walk the entire distance, in violation of Article XVI of the removal treaty: "In wagons . . . the U.S. agree to move the Indians to their new homes. . . ."[22] With the U.S. Army in charge, the human misery and loss of life exceeded even that of the first winter removals.[23]

(4) By the explicit terms of Article XIV of the removal treaty, Choctaws not desiring to remove to the West had the option of registering with the U.S. agent, becoming citizens of the United States, and being granted title to their farms in Mississippi (including one full section of land, 640 acres, for each head of a family, plus 320 acres of adjoining land for each unmarried child over ten years of age and 160 acres for each child under ten), with a guarantee that "Persons who claim under this article shall not lose the privilege of a Choctaw citizen."[24]

Thousands of Choctaws attempted to exercise that option. The American agent in charge of that registration, William Ward, with the support of his U.S. government superiors, simply refused to honor that provision of the treaty, allowing only a token number of Choctaws to register. To their shock and disbelief, thousands of Choctaws who had not planned to remove and who had consented to the removal treaty only because it offered them that option, were suddenly forced to remove.[25]

(5) Choctaws received no land whatsoever in the West for surrendering their remaining 10,423,130 acres in Mississippi. Choctaws already owned the land in the West that they were removed to. They had purchased it from the United States a decade earlier in the seventh treaty, "Treaty with the Choctaw, 1820,"[26] as modified by the eighth treaty, "Treaty with the Choctaw, 1825."[27] To acquire that land in the West in 1820 the Choctaws had exchanged approximately five million acres of their Mississippi land (which was subsequently divided into nine Mississippi counties).[28]

(6) Choctaws tried their best to learn from their early exposure to what would turn out to be the salient features of the American national character. When forced by the United States to enter into the removal treaty in 1830 the primary leverage the United States used was its

claim that it was helpless to keep the state of Mississippi from extending its laws over the Choctaws, which the state of Mississippi had
claimed to have done in January, 1830.[29]

The claim was knowingly facetious, yet that calculated deception on
the part of the presidential administration of Andrew Jackson is embodied in the Choctaw removal treaty. The preamble of "Treaty with the
Choctaw, 1830," states:

> Whereas the General Assembly of the State of Mississippi has
> extended the laws of said state to persons and property within the
> chartered limits of the same, and the President of the United States
> has said that he cannot protect the Choctaw people from the oper-
> ation of these laws; Now therefore that the Choctaws may live
> under their own laws in peace with the United States and the State
> of Mississippi they have determined to sell their land east of the
> Mississippi and have accordingly agreed to the following articles
> of treaty. . . ."[30]

Two years after the Choctaw removal treaty, a U.S. Supreme Court
decision in 1832, *Worcester v. Georgia*,[31] would confirm that state laws
could not be extended to Indian nations when the state of Georgia and
Andrew Jackson's U.S. government would try to use that same deception to remove the Cherokees. But the *Worcester* decision would break
the back of the Supreme Court. The decision would have stopped the
removal of the Cherokees. But President Andrew Jackson and the state
of Georgia simply refused to abide by the rule of law. They ignored the
Supreme Court, which found itself helpless to enforce its decision.[32]
The Supreme Court would never again attempt to intervene in the illegal taking of Indian land. The Court would choose to try to preserve
its own survival as an institution, rather than attempt to uphold the rule
of law, fatally crippling the Supreme Court forever.

The only thing the Choctaws secured for themselves in the 1830
removal treaty (other than a few token annuities for the support of
schools and other governmental functions) was a guarantee from the

American people that the extension of state laws over the Choctaws would never happen again. They secured that guarantee at the cost of ten million acres of some of the richest agricultural land in the world, at the cost of suffering the brutality of their removal, which devastated virtually every family in the nation with the death of loved ones, and at the cost of bitter disillusionment at being betrayed by their military ally and protector.

That guarantee is embodied in Article IV of "Treaty with the Choctaw, 1830." It consists of eighty-three words in plain English, plain enough that any American school child could comprehend it, if it were allowed to be taught in the American schools, plain enough that all the other nations of the world can comprehend it:

> The Government and people of the United States are hereby obliged to secure to the said Choctaw Nation of Red People the jurisdiction and government of all the persons and property that may be within their limits west, so that no Territory or state shall ever have a right to pass laws for the government of the Choctaw Nation of Red People and their descendants; and that no part of the land granted them shall ever be embraced in any Territory or State. . . .[33]

Those eighty-three words are not taught by the illegal state of Oklahoma in its school system. Oklahoma history is depicted as a celebration of a wonderful frontier spirit, while conveniently leaving out details such as Article IV of "Treaty with the Choctaw, 1830."

That wonderful frontier spirit came railroading into the Choctaw Nation in the West by the terms of the fourteenth and final Choctaw treaty, "Treaty with the Choctaw and Chickasaw, 1866," in which the Choctaws were forced by the United States to allow the construction of railroads through their nation.[34] Much like the access afforded by the wagon road in 1801 in Mississippi, whites poured into the Choctaw country in the West on those railroads in such great numbers that before the end of the nineteenth century those illegal intruders outnumbered Choctaws in their own country, where they began clamoring for American statehood and clamoring for the extinction of the Choctaw Nation.[35]

Article 7 of "Treaty with the Choctaw and Chickasaw, 1855" states that ". . . all persons, with their property, who are not by birth, adoption, or otherwise citizens or members of either the Choctaw or Chickasaw tribe, and all persons, not being citizens or members of either tribe, found within their limits, shall be considered intruders, and be removed from, and kept out of the same, by the United States agent, assisted if necessary by the military. . . ."[36]

In 1907 those intruders got their wish, when the illegal state of Oklahoma was created by the United States Congress, in violation of Article IV of "Treaty with the Choctaw, 1830," when the Congress caved in to the pressure from its constituents, betraying the Choctaw people for the second time. Choctaws, and all other members of the so-called Five Civilized Tribes (Cherokees, Creeks, Seminoles, Chickasaws, and Choctaws) in "Indian Territory" (now approximately the eastern half of the illegal state of Oklahoma) were forced to accept the individual allotment of farms and were declared to be Oklahoma citizens. The tribal estate (ownership of land in common) was thus broken up and the Indian nations were declared to be dissolved.[37]

The justices of the Supreme Court of the United States turned tail and ran, mindful of what had happened to the Supreme Court the last time it tried to intervene in the illegal taking of Indian land, in 1832 in *Worcester v. Georgia*. They ran so far and so fast they abdicated any further meaningful role in the United States government when the Court declared, in 1903 in *Lone Wolf v. Hitchcock*, that the U.S. Congress has plenary (full) power over Indians, that the Congress can unilaterally abrogate any clause of any Indian treaty whenever it chooses to do so and that the lower courts cannot intervene—basing all of that upon the pretext that Indian affairs were a "political" matter.[38]

That voluntary vassalage of the Supreme Court to the U.S. Congress has left the Supreme Court ruling on nothing regarding Indians except for interpreting legislation passed by the Supreme Court's masters in the

U.S. Congress and for matters regarding Indian treaties that the Congress has not yet voided, creating an illusion that the Court still has some meaningful role in the government. In reality, in 1903 the Supreme Court removed the judicial branch from the checks and balances of the U.S. governmental system, which reconstituted that system as one that now consists of only legislative and executive branches, both popularly elected. On the issues of Indian land and Indian sovereignty the American experiment of trying to create a republic based on democratic principles failed, confirming the worst fears of native peoples that the American Revolution succeeded in doing nothing more than turning loose a renegade nation on the face of the earth, one with no respect for the rule of law.

The people of the illegal state of Oklahoma wasted little time illegally separating the Indians of the former Indian Territory from their allotments. Much of that was accomplished by court fraud in one of the largest and most pervasive criminal conspiracies in the history of the United States, one that involved the commission of felonies by many people throughout the Oklahoma legal establishment—including lawyers, judges, and some the most prominent politicians of the time. The catalyst for the most feverish court fraud was the discovery of rich oil fields underlying many of those Indian allotments.[39]

The scale of the court fraud was so monumental that the lightly populated Federal District Court for the Eastern District of Oklahoma was the second busiest federal district court in the United States, second only to the District of Manhattan in New York City.[40]

Throughout most of the twentieth century the United States attempted to maintain the legal fiction that the Choctaw Nation no longer existed. In the mid-1970s the United States Congress, red-faced with embarrassment at how the violent confrontations with the American Indian Movement had brought international media attention to the desperate poverty of Indians throughout the continent, finally allowed the Choctaws to adopt a new constitution and form a government again for the first time in seven decades.

In 1975, in explaining to the world why it was passing the Indian

Self-Determination and Educational Assistance Act (Public Law 93-638), the U.S. Congress declared that "The Congress . . . finds . . . (2) the Indian people will never surrender their desire to control their relationships both among themselves and with non-Indian governments, organizations, and persons."[41]

In the thirty years since then, the Choctaw Nation has rapidly expanded its operations, assuming responsibility for many programs from the Bureau of Indian Affairs, including administration of the Indian hospital at Talihina. It has created revenue-generating tribal enterprises, including casino gaming, for which it has had to fight the illegal state of Oklahoma every step of the way, in attempting to address the appalling poverty that has afflicted the landless nation ever since that once-prosperous civilization of farmers was descended upon by that wonderful frontier spirit. By August 2005, the membership of the Choctaw Nation stood at 171,389, making it one of the largest Indian nations on the North American continent.[42]

But the illegal state of Oklahoma still claims the Choctaws' land and still claims a right to meddle in the affairs of the Choctaw people—in the tradition of the antebellum southern states—creating an uneasy coexistence between two quasi sovereigns (the Choctaw Nation and the illegal state of Oklahoma) as Oklahomans struggle to comprehend the long-range implications of having failed to extinguish the Indian nations.

Choctaws and other Indian nations are a long way from reasserting sovereignty over their land and dismantling the illegal state of Oklahoma. But Choctaws are also a long way from being the dying and disappearing people the Americans portrayed them to be little more than a century ago.

In the long run, a renegade American nation might finally see the benefits for everyone if everyone lives under the rule of law, and the Choctaw Nation might achieve the protectorate relationship that was established by "Treaty with the Choctaw, 1786" and again by "Treaty with the Choctaw, 1830" and live in friendship with its American neighbors—secure in its own land, under its own laws. That's what the

American people committed themselves to—twice—and it would be one of the biggest steps they might take toward restoring their credibility with the other nations of the world.

1 "Treaty with the Choctaw, 1786," Charles J. Kappler, editor and compiler, *Indian Affairs: Laws and Treaties,* Vol. II, Treaties (Washington, D.C.: U.S. Government Printing Office, 1905), pp. 11–14 (hereinafter Kappler, Treaties). Kappler's compilation of the U.S. Indian treaties is the standard printed version of the treaties; all of the treaties in Kappler's Vol. II, Treaties, are available online at an Oklahoma State University Library Web site; the Choctaw treaties are found most easily by accessing the index under *C,* and scrolling down to "Choctaw," http://digital.library.okstate.edu/kappler/.

2 The doctrine of discovery is a doctrine of religious bias, which proclaimed that Indians were not capable of ownership of their land because they were not Christians. In 1823, in Johnson and Graham's *Lessee v. William M'Intosh* 21 U.S. 543, 5 L.Ed. 681, 8 Wheat. 543, the U.S. Supreme Court declared that the foundation of the U.S. claim to sovereignty over Indian land is the doctrine of discovery, thereby grounding that claim upon the quicksand of religious prejudice. It remains the law of the land in the United States to this day and is the reason why the U.S. claim to sovereignty over Indian land cannot be challenged in U.S. courts. Very little of U.S. history regarding Indians can be comprehended without an understanding of the deep religious prejudice that has pervaded virtually every aspect of it. The full text of the *M'Intosh* decision is available online http://www.utulsa.edu/law/classes/rice/USSCT_Cases/JOHNSON_V_MCINTOSH_1823.HTM; for a detailed discussion of the discovery doctrine, tracing its roots to Medieval legal thought, see Robert A. Williams, Jr., *The American Indian in Western Legal Thought: The Discourses of Conquest* (New York: Oxford University Press, 1990); see also David E. Wilkins, *American Indian Sovereignty and the U.S. Supreme Court: The Masking of Justice* (Austin: University of Texas Press, 1997), pp. 27–35.

3 Peter H. Wood, "The Changing Population of the Colonial South: An Overview by Race and Region, 1685–1790," in Peter H. Wood, Gregory A. Waselkov, and M. Thomas Hatley, editors, *Powhatan's Mantle: Indians in the Colonial Southeast* (Lincoln: University of Nebraska Press, 1989), pp. 68–72; Angie Debo, *The Rise and Fall of the Choctaw Republic* (Norman: University of Oklahoma Press, 1934, 1961 revised edition), pp. 1, 28; Muriel H. Wright, *A Guide to the Indian Tribes of Oklahoma* (Norman: University of Oklahoma Press, 1951), pp. 98–101.

4 Robert J. Conley, *The Cherokee Nation: A History* (Albuquerque: University of New Mexico Press, 2005), p. 18; Patricia Galloway, *Choctaw Genesis: 1500–1700* (Lincoln: University of Nebraska Press, 1995), pp. 5, 128–143.

5 Richard White, *The Roots of Dependency: Subsistence, Environment, and Social Change among the Choctaws, Pawnees, and Navajos* (Lincoln: University of Nebraska Press, 1983), pp. 16–33.

6 "Treaty with the Choctaw, 1786," Kappler, Treaties, Vol. II, 11–14 (available online, see Note 1). Much nonsense has been published by historians, who had no legal training, purporting to interpret this treaty and other Indian treaties. Those historians have been unaware that, as a rule of law, the specific language of an Indian treaty does not prevail over what the Indians were told orally that they were agreeing to. The minutes of the council for this Choctaw treaty are in the Draper Manuscripts, 14 U pp. 56-92. For a brief report on this treaty negotiation, placing it within the context of the other Indian treaties the U.S. negotiated at Hopewell, see Francis Paul Prucha, *American Indian Treaties: The History of a Political Anomaly* (Berkeley: University of California Press, 1994), pp. 62–63. The "canons of construction" of Indian treaties have been enunciated by U.S. courts many times. Professor Ronald N. Satz gives a concise summary of those canons of construction: "1. treaties must be liberally construed to favor Indians; 2. ambiguous expressions in treaties must be resolved in favor of the Indians; 3. treaties must be construed as the Indians would have understood them at the time they were negotiated; and 4. treaty rights legally enforceable against the United States should not be extinguished by mere implication, but rather explicit action must be taken and 'clear and plain' language used to abrogate them." See Ronald N. Satz, *Chippewa Treaty Rights: The Reserved Rights of Wisconsin's Chippewa Indians in Historical Perspective* (Wisconsin Academy of Sciences, Arts and Letters, 1991), p. 91. Those canons of construction were designed to protect Indians from fraud, because the treaties were being written in English, a foreign language to them. For a recent U.S. Federal Circuit Court enunciation and application of the canons of construction, see *Lac Courte Oreilles Band of Lake Superior Chippewa Indians v. Wisconsin* 700 F.2d 341 (7th Cir. 1983), known as the *Voigt* decision and the *LCO I* decision. It is also available in law school case books, such as Robert N. Clinton, Nell Jessup Newton, and Monroe E. Price, editors, *American Indian Law: Cases and Materials,* 3rd ed. (Charlottesville, Virginia: The Michie Company, 1991), pp. 844–845 for "Canons of Construction Pertinent to Indian Law."

7 See Sharon O'Brien, *American Indian Tribal Governments* (Norman: University of Oklahoma Press, 1989), pp. 58, 257–259.

8 Benjamin Hawkins and Andrew Pickens to Charles Thompson, December 30, 1785, *American State Papers, II Indian Affairs,* Vol. I, p. 49; Benjamin Hawkins, Andrew Pickens, and Joseph Martin to John Hancock, January 4, 1786, *American State Papers, II Indian Affairs*, Vol. 1, pp. 49–50. The *American State Papers* are available online http://memory.loc.gov/ammem/amlaw/lwsp.html.

9 Compare "Treaty with the Cherokee, 1785," and "Treaty with the Chickasaw, 1786," with "Treaty with the Choctaw, 1786," in Kappler, Treaties, Vol. II

(available online, see Note 1). The Cherokee treaty was negotiated just before the Choctaws arrived at Hopewell, and the Chickasaw treaty was negotiated at Hopewell directly after the Choctaw treaty. See also Prucha, *American Indian Treaties,* pp. 59–63.

10 "Treaty with the Choctaw, 1801," Kappler, Treaties, Vol. II, pp. 56–58.

11 "Treaty with the Choctaw, 1830," Kappler, Treaties, Vol. II, pp. 310–319.

12 Angie Debo, *Rise and Fall of the Choctaw Republic,* p. 56; H. Glenn Jordan, "Choctaw Colonization in Oklahoma," in *America's Exiles: Indian Colonization in Oklahoma,* edited by Arrell Morgan Gibson (Oklahoma City: Oklahoma Historical Society, 1976), pp. 16–33; Arthur H. DeRosier, Jr., *The Removal of the Choctaw Indians* (Knoxville: University of Tennessee Press, 1970), pp. 129–164.

13 Jordan, "Indian Colonization in Oklahoma," p. 31; Grant Foreman, Indian Removal (Norman: University of Oklahoma Press, 1953 edition, originally published in 1932), pp. 98–99; Wright, *A Guide to the Indian Tribes of Oklahoma,* p. 104.

14 H. B. Cushman, *History of the Choctaw, Chickasaw, and Natchez Indians,* edited by Angie Debo (New York: Russell & Russell, 1962, first published 1899), pp. 242–263; a detailed account of the face-to-face debates between Tecumseh and Pushmataha in the Choctaw country in the fall of 1811 can be found online in ch. III "Tecumseh Among the Chickasaws and Choctaws" of Halbert and Ball, "The Creek War of 1813 and 1814," http://www.marcies alaskaweb.com/creekwar.htm; for an account of those debates from Tecumseh's perspective, see Allan W. Eckert, *A Sorrow in Our Heart: The Life of Tecumseh* (New York: Konecky & Konecky, 1992).

15 Cushman, H*istory of the Choctaw, Chickasaw, and Natchez Indians,* pp. 63, 238, 260–262, 266–67; Debo, *Rise and Fall of the Choctaw Republic,* pp. 40–41; Jesse O. McKee and Jon A. Schlenker, *The Choctaws: Cultural Evolution of A Native American Tribe* (Jackson: University Press of Mississippi, 1980), p. 54.

16 "Resolution From State Capitol, Mississippi," *Chronicles of Oklahoma* 6, no. 3 (December 1928), pp. 481–482.

17 DeRosier, *Removal of the Choctaw Indians,* pp. 82–83; McKee and Schlenker, The Choctaws, pp. 58–59; "Pushmatahaw," James Grant Wilson, John Fiske, and Stanley L. Klos, eds,, *Appleton's Cyclopedia of American Biography* (New York: D. Appleton and Company, 1887–1889 and 1999), available online, http://famousamericans.net/choctawchiefpushmatahaw/; for the most detailed account of Pushmataha's role in Choctaw history and U.S. history, see his definitive biography by Anna Lewis, *Chief Pushmataha, American Patriot: The Story of the Choctaws' Struggle for Surviva*l (New York: Exposition Press, 1960).

18 Jordan, *Indian Colonization in Oklahoma,* p. 22.

19 Article XVIII, "Treaty with the Choctaw, 1830," Kappler, Treaties, Vol. II, p. 314.

20 Jordan, *Indian Colonization in Oklahoma*, p. 31.

21 Debo, *Rise and Fall of the Choctaw Republic,* pp. 203–211.

22 Article XVI, "Treaty with the Choctaw, 1830," Kappler, Treaties, Vol. II, p. 313.

23 Jordan, *Indian Colonization in Oklahoma,* p. 30.

24 Article XIV "Treaty with the Choctaw, 1830," Kappler, Treaties, Vol. II, p. 313.

25 Jordan, *Indian Colonization in Oklahoma*, p. 23.

26 "Treaty with the Choctaw, 1820," Kappler, Treaties, Vol. II, pp. 191–195.

27 "Treaty with the Choctaw, 1825," Kappler, Treaties, Vol. II, pp. 211–214.

28 Debo, *Rise and Fall of the Choctaw Republic,* 49; Ruth Tenison West, "Pushmataha's Travels," Chronicles of Oklahoma, Vol. XXXVII, No. 2 (Summer 1959), p. 162.

29 Jordan, *Indian Colonization in Oklahoma*, pp. 20–21.

30 Preamble, "Treaty with the Choctaw, 1830," Kappler, Treaties, Vol. II, pp. 310–311.

31 *Worcester v. Georgia*, 31 U.S. 515 (1832).

32 For a discussion of *Worcester v. Georgia* within its historical legal context, see Clinton, Newton, and Price, *American Indian Law,* pp. 2–33.

33 Article IV, "Treaty with the Choctaw, 1830," Kappler, Treaties, Vol. II, p. 311.

34 "Treaty with the Choctaw and Chickasaw, 1866," Kappler, Treaties, Vol. II, pp. 918–931.

35 Debo, *Rise and Fall of the Choctaw Republic*, pp. 245–290.

36 Article 7, "Treaty with the Choctaw and Chickasaw, 1855," Kappler, Treaties, Vol. II, p. 708.

37 Debo, *Rise and Fall of the Choctaw Republic*, pp. 269–290.

38 *Lone Wolf v. Hitchcock* 187 U.S. 553 (1903); for a detailed discussion of the Lone Wolf decision within its historical context, see Blue Clark, *Lone Wolf v Hitchcock: Treaty Rights and Indian Law at the End of the Nineteenth Century* (Lincoln: University of Nebraska Press, 1994); see also, Wilkins, *American Indian Sovereignty and the U.S. Supreme Court,* pp. 105–117.

39 Angie Debo, *And Still the Waters Run: The Betrayal of the Five Civilized Tribes* (Princeton University Press, 1940), pp. 86–88, 286–287, 305–313.

40 "Indians, Outlaws, and Angie Debo," PBS video, produced for *The American Experience* by Barbara Abrash and Martha Sandlin, 1988.

41 Indian Self-Determination and Educational Assistance Act (Public Law 93–638), available online, http://edworkforce.house.gov/publications/eseacomp/indseled.pdf).

42 Bishinik, Official Publication of the Choctaw Nation of Oklahoma, August 2005, p. 1.

THE CHEROKEE NATION:

A COLONIAL MORALITY PLAY IN THREE ACTS

STEVE RUSSELL

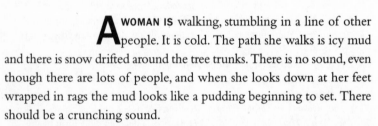

A WOMAN IS walking, stumbling in a line of other people. It is cold. The path she walks is icy mud and there is snow drifted around the tree trunks. There is no sound, even though there are lots of people, and when she looks down at her feet wrapped in rags the mud looks like a pudding beginning to set. There should be a crunching sound.

The woman falls and she thinks a snowdrift beside the path looks like a soft downy pillow. She is sleepy. There is no sensation of cold. She closes her eyes.

She wakes with a sharp pain in her side. A man is standing over her, a soldier. He has poked her in the side with the barrel of a rifle. He shouts something and menaces her with the rifle, but there is still no sound. She climbs laboriously to her knees and then to her feet and stumbles back into the line.

Sometimes I watch this scene from above, sometimes from up or down the trail. Sometimes I am the woman and sometimes the soldier. The other people are many but faceless.

When I am the soldier, I feel no hatred. I move with a dispassionate efficiency, but with no more feeling than my grandmother had toward the chicken when she wrung its neck for Sunday dinner.

It was many years later and after many visions of this scene that I learned how my family got to Indian Territory, now called Oklahoma. They could have been Old Settlers, who moved to Arkansas to escape colonial expansion, clashed with the Osage, and wound up in Oklahoma. They could have been survivors of Duwali's band, massacred in Texas and chased north. They could have been members of the Treaty Party, who made the trek early and as volunteers to escape the justice of the Blood Law.

No, my great-great-great grandmother walked what the perpetrators have come to call the Trail of Tears, a loose translation from the Cherokee. It was even after learning that, and after getting a law degree, that I learned how the Trail of Tears came in defiance of a United States Supreme Court ruling that the removal of the Cherokee people to Indian Territory was without legal authority. "John Marshall has made his decision," President Andrew Jackson is rumored to have said of the chief justice, "now let him enforce it!"

So it was that a people who were wealthier and better educated than their white neighbors were rounded up at gunpoint and force-marched through a winter for which they had not been allowed to prepare. So it was that the wife of Chief John Ross died in Arkansas after, the story goes, giving up her blanket to another. So it was that a third—or was it "only" a fourth?—of our nation perished and that I was born in Oklahoma. If I am linked with that history as certainly as I am linked to the United States, what does it matter to how I walk in the world?

The late historian John Higham defined "ethnicity" as a sense of community based on shared historical memories. That's ours. I cannot remember when I learned of the Trail of Tears. Oklahoma public schools mentioned it in, if memory serves, the eighth grade, but I feel that I have always known about it. The Trail of Tears was a factual backdrop of being Cherokee, like the story of Quatie Ross giving up her blanket. We, the tribal descendants scattered in Indian Territory (now Oklahoma), learn that the Trail of Tears is part of our identity, but it is best to keep quiet about it. Is it in return for this favor that Oklahoma calls itself "Indian America?"

INDIAN AMERICA

Oklahoma of Rogers and Hammerstein
and green growing lilacs
hard by red dirt roads and paintless outhouses,

Oklahoma of Will Rogers the Paint Clan Cherokee
with the friendly grin
and wit like a straight edge razor,

Oklahoma of the Deep Fork bottom
and papershell pecans,
whiskered catfish,
3.2 beer and holy rollers,

Oklahoma of Friday night football,
rodeo cowboys,
and niggertown Saturday night,

Oklahoma of bootlegger pints
and small town vandals,
Indian art,
Indian clothing,
Indian food,
Indian Indians in Indian America
where an Indian can be anything

except alive.

Take out a map of Oklahoma and look at the place names. It's a lesson in the difficulty of expressing native languages in English and, if you track down the names, in the history of the peoples removed to Indian Territory when it was the continent's largest reservation. If you don't run down the history, then Pushmataha is a county, Tenkiller is a lake, and Tahlequah is a city. Of course, even the places where lots of full-bloods live to this day don't necessarily have Indian names. There's nothing recognizably Cherokee about Jay and Vian and Kenwood. Well, there is if you live nearby. But being Indian in Oklahoma, as in most of the United States, is a constant tension between caricature and invisibility.

HOW TO SUCCEED AS AN INDIAN POET

Don't say "hunger."
Write of the plump red strawberries
grown by Cherokees
in the Cookson Hills,
rather than rodents fried in lard,
garnished with herbs from the bar ditch,
government commodities on the side.

Don't say "homeless."
Write of the red wildflowers and stark beauty
of the Black Hills in South Dakota
rather than the gutted mobile homes and appliance cartons
on the Pine Ridge Reservation.

Don't say "disease."
Tell us of the red sand
slipping through the hand
of a Navajo medicine man
rather than reminding us
that hantavirus is spread by rats.

Don't say "genocide."
Tell us of Red Cloud and Rolling Thunder,
Crazy Horse and Tecumseh,
safe dead Indians
—Pontiac as a hood ornament—
rather than reminding us
of a Cheyenne child at Sand Creek

exploding like an overripe watermelon,
red within and red without,
from the business end
of a .50 caliber Sharps.

Do tell,
do write,
O wise and noble red man,
Native American shaman,
share your hard-won wisdom
—-but not too much of it.

Cherokee history might logically be divided into three periods of great prosperity, each interrupted by the European colonists. The first period was before Europeans "discovered" us. It is part of the burden of being Cherokee to say that we hunted and gathered but we were not hunter-gatherers. We lived in wooden houses, not tipis, and our government was more a confederation of towns than a nation. We had agricultural surplus, which meant that we could support thinkers and artists. Cherokee was spoken everywhere from what is now West Virginia down to Northern Florida and over to Kentucky and Alabama. Notice I said that Cherokee was spoken—not that everyone in those territories was Cherokee. We were a prosperous people and trading was common. The beginning of the end of that first period of prosperity was 1539, when Hernando deSoto began his *entrada*. DeSoto was not the first Spaniard to spread European diseases and values in the Southeast, but he was the first one to touch Cherokees with death—in hindsight, an omen.

In time, the gold seekers gave way to traders, and our ancestors learned they were not as prosperous as they had thought. They "needed" European trade goods. Metal tools and cloth and guns. In the trading centers near the coast, Cherokees were early on decimated by smallpox, but adapted to the trade culture to the extent that we actually managed to hunt the white-tailed deer nearly to extinction. This is absurd both because the white-tailed deer is an adaptable and prolific breeder and

because our traditions told that we could not kill a deer without asking the deer's pardon. Our traditions quickly took a backseat to our
wants—which were easier to identify then than they are today.

WHAT INDIANS WANT

"What do you want?"
The Question comes
with and without good will
but it comes.

"Acknowledgment of our history here!" says my Indian sister Ruth
 Soucy.

"Denazification!" says the faux Indian
Ward Churchill.

These things and more,
and they will cost you dear!
More than giving the country back,
much, much more.

I think of the German civilians forced to file through the death camps
 at the point of American guns,
how the civilians tried to turn away
but our GIs grimly insisted
and the German townspeople
stood there and cried, more
naked than the stacks of
naked Jewish corpses,
stripped of deniability.

Once you stand there
naked,
stripped of innocence,

bereft of "Indian depredations,"
without casinos or tax exemptions or smoke shops—
without myth or trivia,

when you stand there
naked as my hunger,
when you know the price
of taking a deer
without the deer's permission,

then we can talk.

When deerskins didn't buy the things we had been taught to want, we ceded land. And ceded land. And ceded land. In 1785, in 1791, in 1798, in 1804, in 1805, in 1806, in 1816, in 1817, in 1819, we ceded land. Let us not discuss fraud or the broken promises that kept bringing us back to the table where our interests would be carved to fit imperial ambitions. Let's follow the fortunes of my ancestors.

Some Cherokees had accepted western lands in return for land cessions in 1817. From early in the nineteenth century, Cherokees moved west in groups of varying size seeking that which would never be found in North America—a space beyond colonial expansion.

The Cherokees who stayed formed a constitutional government in 1827. Missionaries had infested the nation for some time, with mixed results. They brought patriarchy to a society where women had been equal to men in council. But they also brought education and, with Sequoyah's invention of the Cherokee syllabary, the Cherokees achieved virtually complete literacy. The missionaries brought printing presses, and the Cherokee Nation had not only a higher literacy rate but also more books and newspapers than the white people of Georgia who coveted still more land cessions.

Intermarriage with white people was widespread and, at first, not a social problem. Cherokees had no concept of race and the child of a

Cherokee woman was always a Cherokee, with a clan identity inherited from the mother. Fathers in Cherokee society could be white men without disruption because most of the socialization and discipline of children was the duty of the eldest male sibling of the mother or other clan representative. Most early intermarriage was white men and Cherokee women, since the colonists had come for the most part without women.

Later there would be folks like my Cherokee father, who married a white woman and produced me. We would be, in tradition, clanless and therefore without legal standing as Cherokees. The Tribal Council recognized us as Cherokee citizens in 1825.

BLOOD QUANTUM
Marry for love, squaw man.
Marry for love, clanless mother.

> *But have a care, Tsalagi,*
> *for the thin red line, thinning to gray.*

> > *The Keetoowahs want a fourth.*
> > *The Eastern Band, like the marrow bank, wants a sixteenth.*

> *So have a care, Tsalagi,*
> *for the thin red line, thinning to gray.*

There is strength in numbers but also gray gone oblivion.

Landless, clanless, without medicine or meaning,

tourist tipis and model names on trucks,

here we remember proud people

> *who married for love.*

As our land disappeared into white hands and our clan customs became diluted, we still prospered in the economic sense. We even adopted the white custom of chattel slavery, an ironic turn for a people the British had at first tried to enslave! To stop the bleeding of our land base, we passed the Blood Law. It became a capital crime for a Cherokee to sign a document purporting to cede any more Cherokee lands.

In 1835, in spite of the Cherokee Blood Law, the bogus Treaty of New Echota ceded all Cherokee land east of the Mississippi in return for a reservation in Indian Territory. On September 28, 1836, Chief John Ross wrote to Congress: "We are overwhelmed! Our hearts are sickened, our utterance is paralyzed, when we reflect on the condition in which we are placed, by the audacious practices of unprincipled men. . . .

The instrument in question is not the act of our Nation; we are not parties to its covenants; it has not received the sanction of our people. The makers of it sustain no office nor appointment in our Nation. . . ." Ross's spirited defense of Cherokee rights in Washington came within one vote of preventing ratification of the Treaty of New Echota, but ratified it was. From behind this legal fig leaf, President Andrew Jackson dispatched soldiers to remove the Cherokees, beginning the central horror of our tribal identity and the end of our second period of prosperity. The land in Indian Territory, of course, did not turn out to be completely worthless.

THE YEAR THEY DRILLED FOR OIL

Ten months before the lease was up
they brought in the drilling rig.

The driller's shack took the bean field.

Joe tried to put in some lettuce around the edges
but those big tires don't know
lettuce from Bermuda.

There was not enough Bermuda left to graze the cow,
so Joe's kids learned to get milk in bottles.

The hole killed one of the roots on Joe's pear tree.
It didn't die, but there were no pears that year.

The noise from the rig disturbed the chickens
and they quit laying.

One morning we found the beehive empty,
and we all helped put up the honey in jars,
not knowing when there would be more.

The pond down below the well got salty and all of Joe's catfish died at
   once.

We were afraid to eat the fish, but Joe said we could use them to
   fertilize the corn.
The corn came that year
in small ears
with tiny hard kernels
that did not gush juice
across the table
when bitten.

Only the melons
seemed to ignore the drilling,
but when the fruit came
it tasted salty, like chemicals.

The blackberry bushes along the fence line
were coated with dirt,
and the berries had to be washed with care
but we got a few pies.

The man from the oil company came to see Joe in the last month of the lease and said the rig would have to leave soon.

Joe, a six foot Muscogee who called himself "Red Stick Creek," started to cry.

Not understanding, the oil man offered to stay and bring in the well if Joe would extend the lease on terms a bit more favorable to the company. He said the core samples looked "very promising."

Joe declined.

I heard the oilman tell another as they walked away that Joe had missed a chance "better than nothing."

"These Indians," he said, "just do not understand how to use land."

Next year, the pear crop was small, but it came early.

The Cherokee Nation rebuilt in Indian Territory. Some Cherokees in North Carolina hid out from the soldiers, disappeared into the mountains. They would become what is today the Eastern Band of Cherokees, and their history is as marked by the Removal as is that of other Cherokees. Hiding out for years in the wilderness is, in its way, just as significant as a forced march at gunpoint. Before the Eastern Band was able to come out of hiding the Cherokee government had built the first school for women west of the Mississippi.

More schools followed, and the printing presses hummed once again. Cherokee farmers broke the soil; craftsmen flourished. Hard work prevailed once again and the prospect of mineral wealth on tribal lands promised a bright future. For a third time, the Cherokee Nation prospered. Two more intrusions of colonial politics destroyed that prosperity.

First, the Civil War and the slavery question ripped apart the nation.

Cherokees fought on both sides and had we been white people that might have meant an enhanced political position no matter which side won. Since we were Indians that meant we would be punished no matter which side won. This economic catastrophe is something we might have surmounted but for the crowning blow: allotment.

Early colonial literature describing the Cherokees pointed out two of our customs that were particularly unsavory from the European point of view—women's social equality and common landholding. A Cherokee woman could hold political office and a Cherokee farmer could fence whatever part of the commons he was able to keep in crops.

In Oklahoma, women's equality was long gone. Cherokee women had not signed treaties with the colonists and as the clans lost power patriarchy came to people who had been matrilineal and matrilocal. However, the tribe still held land subject to its own rules for usufruct. Henry Dawes set out to change all that and, not so incidentally, open up "surplus" land for white settlement. "Surplus" was whatever was left after each Cherokee man, woman, and child got approximately 160 acres to be held (or not, as it turned out) individually.

After litigation failed to stop allotment there was widespread civil disobedience in Indian Territory. U.S. Marshals had to be called in to accomplish allotment over the resistance organized by the Cherokee Redbird Smith and the Muscogee Chitto Harjo.

CHITTO HARJO
Crazy Snake said: "Don't sign!"
  Indians signed.

Crazy Snake said: "Hold the white man to his word!" ★
  Indians took what they could get.

Crazy Snake refused his allotment. They put him in a cage.

★ "He told me that as long as the sun shone and the sky is up yonder this agreement will be kept. He said as long as the sun rises it shall last; as long as the waters run it shall last; as long as grass grows it shall last. That is what he said, and we believed it."

*(Indian justice under white rule required only a whipping post and a
gallows: whipping and death, pain and the end of pain. A couple of
cells to sober up drunks—but no living in a cage.)*

*They put Crazy Snake in a cage. Almost everybody signed, and the
Muscogee Reservation disappeared.*

Leaving historians to examine the transaction and ask:

Who was crazy?

Who was a snake?

On the Dawes Rolls, the list of Cherokees who received allotments,
I can see my grandfather, my great-grandfather, and numerous collat-
eral relatives. Most of them got plots near Bartlesville, Oklahoma, the
city that Phillips Petroleum owned and operated. Of course, by the time
the oil was produced my family, like most Cherokees, had been snook-
ered out of their allotments. My father's part in the oil boom was as a
roughneck, and his family had followed the jobs across the border from
the Cherokee Nation to Bristow, which was in the Creek Nation. And
Indian nations were untaught history to white Oklahomans.

WHAT I LEARNED AND DIDN'T LEARN
AT THE BRISTOW, OKLAHOMA,
HISTORICAL SOCIETY MUSEUM

I

Peanuts grow without dirty hands.

Oil wells drill themselves.

*Oklahoma was empty land, settled by people in neckties who were
served by invisible cooks and waitresses.*

*Slavery and Jim Crow left no mark in the red dirt of Oklahoma. The
Historical Society removed the "Colored" restrooms and water foun-
tain to be certain of that.*

*Oklahoma was a land without Negroes, Indians, roughnecks, drunks,
whores. . . .*

*A land where crops and goods appeared and swell people traded among
themselves between church services on Sunday and Wednesday and
football games on Friday.*

It was such a perfect place—no wonder I had to leave.

II

When Gene Autry worked at the Frisco Depot

The Frisco Depot had four restrooms and two water fountains

When Gene Autry worked at the Frisco Depot

Henry Dawes had so recently stolen the Muscogee Nation

that the owners still smoldered and sought out the

bootleggers

When Gene Autry worked at the Frisco Depot

Halliburton was North of town

Bristow was peanut farms and oil wells

Gene Autry went to Hollywood

Halliburton to Iraq

The peanuts moved to Georgia

Not likely to come back

Money changers tell the Temple's story

of Gene Autry at the Frisco Depot

Negroes who knew their place

An oil patch without roughnecks

Peanuts grown without hands in the red dirt

Steak houses where dishes washed themselves

White bankers and bosses in ties and suits with golden watch fobs

Smugly tread on Muscogee bones.

The current Cherokee Chief, Chad Smith, declares that the lesson of our history is that Cherokees "survive, adapt, prosper, and excel." He is right about our history, but it's fair to wonder how many times a people can have prosperity snatched away. Those of us who manage to achieve a college education are fascinated by the histories of other Indian nations and how they so often revolve around some central horror like the Trail of Tears. We come to wonder who we are. We were supposed to die out, plainly, but we did not. And we sometimes compare our stories to those of Europeans, modern stories that give us neologisms like "ethnic cleansing" and "genocide."

BOSQUE REDONDO:
HOMAGE TO YEVGENY YEVTUSHENKO

Over Bosque Redondo
there is a new memorial.
Stones from Dinetah on the rolling flat near the brackish river.

> *Today I'm as ancient in years as the Diné people.*
It seems to me at this moment—
> *I am Diné.*
Instead of The Trail Where We Cried,
> *The Long Walk.*
Instead of Tsa-la-gi,
> *Diné.*

Oh, how you taught us our assigned station!

You taught us well!

Even today, the ladies with parasols
> *point with scorn at drunken Indians outside Gallup bars,*
> *point as they daintily avoid the New Mexico sun and search*
> *between the bars for old pawn treasures,*
> *point as another 'skin, pawn money drunk up, is chucked into the*
> *street.*
> *point at the present without seeing the past, recent past:*
> > *"Red niggers!"*
> > *"The only good Indians I ever saw were dead."*
> > *"Don't play with the Indians, dear."*

Oh, my American people!
> *I know the melting pot is your guiding metaphor.*
> *But those with unclean hands—stained with the blood of people*
> *who will not melt—besmirch your own clean name:*
> > *the "Indian fighters" and their great battles, their Washitas*

and Sand Creeks, reputations written with the blood of women and
children and old men,
>   the missionaries who broke our connections and took our souls
in exchange for names in Spanish and English,
>   the Indian agents who stole us blind in both the buying and
the selling,
>   the politicians who say we're extinguished, distant history and
garbled fiction, Squanto and Tonto.

The goodness of my native land I know.
But an Indian child, frail as a twig in April, trembles before your
>   schools.
I want just that we should see each other—as we are.

>   Here we were forbidden the sacred journey to the four corners
of Dinetah. How can I show you the rocky spire where Spider
Woman gave the gift of weaving to the Diné? If I cannot, how will
you know a Navajo rug?

Over Bosque Redondo only rustling wild grasses move.
The trees watch sternly
>   like judges arrayed.
Here silence itself cries aloud—
>   I remove my hat
and feel I am gradually going gray.
This is no place to take a child to play
until she is ready to hear the story
spoken by this land. When is that, I wonder.

And I myself
>   am like an endless soundless cry,
over these thousands of buried ones.
Each one
>   of these murdered elders
>   am I.

I
        am each of their murdered
                        sons and daughters.
Nothing within me will ever forget this
that nothing outside me dares to remember.

Let the drums thunder their might
when will be buried for eternity
the earth's last racist White.

Native blood my veins runs through
but Scottish blood and Irish too
as proof that love crosses between us.

Let the hatred that birthed this place of fear
and the Starving Diné Clan
sink into this sterile soil.

Let the tourists who come upon this ground
that grew nothing but pain
mourn the lives represented by these stones from Dinetah
and come away free, resolved to answer
those who question pedigree:

I am a true American!

WEEDS FROM THE UNDER WORLD:

THE CONQUEST OF TSENACOMOCO AND MONASCANE

JAY HANSFORD C. VEST

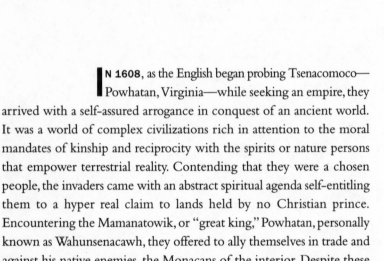

IN 1608, as the English began probing Tsenacomoco—
Powhatan, Virginia—while seeking an empire, they
arrived with a self-assured arrogance in conquest of an ancient world.
It was a world of complex civilizations rich in attention to the moral
mandates of kinship and reciprocity with the spirits or nature persons
that empower terrestrial reality. Contending that they were a chosen
people, the invaders came with an abstract spiritual agenda self-entitling
them to a hyper real claim to lands held by no Christian prince.
Encountering the Mamanatowik, or "great king," Powhatan, personally
known as Wahunsenacawh, they offered to ally themselves in trade and
against his native enemies, the Monacans of the interior. Despite these
foreign overtures, the paramount chief appears to have smelled a rat and
he bluntly replied, "Many do inform me your coming hither is not for
trade but to invade my people and possess my country." These Tassantassas, or foreigners, nonetheless attempted to persuade him that they
came in peace, but upon seeing their armaments the Mamanatowik
offered that they should leave their weapons in their barge saying, "We
being all friends and forever Powhatans."[1]

As an uneasy peace began to break Powhatan informed the faithless invaders: "Having seen the death of all my people thrice … I know the difference of peace and war better than any in my country." Earlier, he had heard from the Nansemond that these Tassantassas intended to "destroy my country."[2] In an earlier encounter while probing the interior along the Rappahannock River, this view of conquest was aptly ascertained in the words of a captive Mannahock man, Ammoroleck, of the Monacan confederacy, who informed the aliens that he had heard that they "came from under the world to take their world from them."[3] In this manner, the natives of Tsenacomoco and Monascane were met by the Tassantassas, or English invaders; thus began the ensuing conquest and genocidal holocaust that accompanied the English in conquering the Virginia Indians.

In the land now referenced as Virginia there were two great native confederacies drawn along linguistic affiliations. Inhabiting the tidewater region that begins along the fall line where the rivers break out onto the coastal plain there was the Algonquian Powhatan confederacy that included thirty-three nations. Notwithstanding this great nation, there were amid these people an independent Algonquian people, the Chikahominies. Known as "the densely populated land" or "our place," Tsenacomoco was exclusively an Algonquian province. Adjacent to it in the west there lie the piedmont rolling hills, mountain uplands, and valley provinces extending into present-day West Virginia. Called Monascane, these lands were home to the Monacan confederacy and its three great alliances. These included the Mannahoacs in the north to the Potomac River, the Nahyssans in the south extending into Carolina, and the Monacans in the center reaching into West Virginia. Collectively, these were the earth people who inhabited Monascane. While there was also an Iroquoian presence along the border fringes of contemporary Virginia, with the Meherrin and Nottoway in the east and the Cherokee in the southwest, I have chosen to omit these natives from the scope of this essay.

At the outset of the English arrival, the Monacans and the Powhatans were traditional enemies. However, with the duplicity and aggressive character of the Tassantassas, a peace was secured between these native nations by 1612, or within four years of the colonial invasion. In the scope and character of European conquest and colonialism the effect upon the native nations in Virginia was much the same in wasting and destroying the indigenous peoples. Before exploring these impacts and their history, however, there is need to give definition to the native holocaust experience.

During the past two years, while writing a paper addressing the Conquest of the Americas as an allegory depicted in the film, *The Mission*, I encountered some resistance from one of the anonymous referees of my essay.[4] This scholarly critic seemed to dismiss the notion of a systematic conquest of the Americas, passing it off as an inadvertent disease-based disaster. He or she wrote:

> Genocide is a term that was introduced to describe the systematic attempt on the part of Nazi Germany to exterminate all the Jewish people. Subsequently, the term has been extended to refer to the conscious attempt to kill the entire population of any ethnic group. It is true that large numbers of natives died in the process of contact, many of them due to disease and many more due to conditions of slavery as well as warfare. But, it is not clear to me that death by disease, which accounts for the largest numbers of deaths, is evidence of a widely accepted strategy to wipe out the native populations of the Americas.[5]

Obviously with "scholar-friends" like this one, associated with one of our leading native-centered academic publications and pedagogy, and doubtlessly employed at an American institution of higher learning, it is unlikely that we surviving natives need enemies. Indeed, we have plenty of "friends" to assure us into perpetituity with their goodwill.[6]

In order to appreciate the systematic nature of the Conquest and subsequent holocaust, however, it is worthwhile to review and consider the initial European observations. Following landfall in the Americas and his initial notices of the natives, Columbus wrote: "They should be good and intelligent servants, for I see that they say very quickly everything that is said to them; and I believe that they would become Christians very easily, for it seemed to me that they had no religion."[7] Columbus' remarks manifest a conclusion that has dominated Western intellectual attitudes and governmental actions toward native peoples throughout world history. Historian Frederick Turner has characterized the Columbian impact on Native America as "the Western Spirit against the wilderness"; "the coming of European civilization to the wildernesses of the world is a spiritual story. To me it is the story of a civilization that had substituted history for myth as a way of understanding life. It was precisely this substitution that enabled Europeans to explore the most remote places of the globe, to colonize them, and to impose their values on the native populations."[8]

Initiating the Conquest, the Spanish were brutal in their application of colonial and papal decrees upon the aboriginals. "It was the Spaniards," according to Lewis Hanke, "who first realized the necessity to work out Christian laws to govern their relations with the Indians they encountered."[9] Speculation concerning the origin of American Indians and questions as to whether they were men or savage beasts plagued Spanish and European authorities as they initiated the Conquest. The invasion of the Americas was foreshadowed by the accumulated events and experiences that grew out of Christian expansion in Europe. Fueling a savagism dogma, notions of the "wild man" abounded in the literal and noncontextual reading of European and Middle Eastern mythologies.[10] As a result, Spanish captains pursued the Conquest while fully expecting to encounter monsters and mythical beings such as giants, pygmies, dragons, griffins, white-haired boys, bearded ladies, human beings adorned with tails, headless creatures with eyes in their stomachs or breasts, and other fabulous folk characters. These were the savage or monstrous races of men that filled the pages of the bestiaries and captured the popular imagination during the Middle Ages.[11]

Although the Papal Donation of 1493 had declared Indians to be men, Pope Alexander VI, with the advice of the Archbishop of Seville, decreed that the Indians should serve the Spaniards and that this vassalage was in accordance with law, human and divine. Armed with their folk bestiaries and fertile imaginations, the Spaniards felt justified in the Conquest, and this policy was later rationalized in the Great Debate at Valladolid, 1550–1551, when Aristotle's Theory of Natural Slavery was applied to American Indians. Aristotle had held that some men born of inferior race were natural slaves and that they constituted a condition of "animate possession" when held by a superior race. It was this authority that gave the Spaniards rights of natural lordship and permanent superiority over the American aboriginals.[12]

Preceding the Great Debate (1550–1551) in November 1505, King Ferdinand asserted the state's sovereignty over the Americas when referencing the 1493 Papal Donation and declaring himself to be the "perpetual administrator by apostolic authority." To this effort on June 6, 1511, Ferdinand charged Diego Columbus that the Indians be baptized and instructed in "Our holy Catholic faith, for this is the principal foundation upon which we have based our conquest of these regions."[13] The papal bulls of Alexander VI and Julius II, moreover, conferred special authority upon the Spanish Crown granting greater power for the direct administration of church affairs in the Americas. Hanke observed that "the acceptance by the crown of the obligation to provide for the Christianization of the Indian led to a theory of empire and colonial policy in which ecclesiastics, who had always been imparted in royal councils, became trusted advisors to the crown and to the Council of the Indies, the principal administrative body for ruling America" (2, 27). Despite treaties, laws, rules and requirements designed by the state's ecclesiastical advisors, the Conquest in its wanton brutality and waste challenged the moral authority of Christendom. As a result, there emerged a struggle for moral justice that championed Christian precepts in the relations between peoples. Hanke comments, "This attempt became basically a spirited defense of the rights of the Indians, which rested on two of the most fundamental assumptions a Christian can make: namely, that all men are equal before God, and that a Christian has a responsibility for the welfare of his brothers no matter how alien or lowly they may be" (1).

The exploitation and depletion of native populations following

Columbus's penetration of the Americas is, nevertheless, vividly depicted in Bartolomé de las Casas' *Apologética Historia*. On the island of Española (modern Haiti and the Dominican Republic) alone, Las Casas estimates that between 1494 and 1508 nearly eight million souls perished—slain in war, sent to Castile as slaves, or consumed in the mines and at other labor. In summation, historian Kirkpatrick Sale noted that "Spanish surveys of Española taken in 1508, 1510, 1514, and 1518 all show the same rough picture, of a population then *under 100,000* and declining precipitously. The most detailed census, the *repartimiento* of 1514, listed just under 22,000 adults that after official revision was expanded to 27,800. Noting a reduction rate at 99 percent, Sale emphatically states the facts of this genocide: '*from 8 million to 28,000 in just over twenty years.*' "[14] Astonished at this death and destruction of the aboriginals, Las Casas soberly remarked, "Who of those born in future centuries will believe this? I myself who am writing this and saw it and know most about it can hardly believe that such was possible."[15] In fact, by 1542 Las Casas, who was there at the time, reported that only two hundred Tainos remained on Española, and these were probably the last natives surviving anywhere in the islands.[16] Projected across the Americas in incidents one after another, this wanton destruction of human life—the Conquest, as we know it—constitutes the greatest episode of genocide in world history. Among the natives of Tsenacomoco and Monascane, the holocaust took three forms. These included first, colonization with disease, war and massacre; second, the advent of internecine tribal warfare encouraged by European displacement and trade policies; and third, institutional racism in apartheid segregation and sterilization. In the explication of these matters, there is ample evidence of Powhatan and Monacan holocaust history that remains in place and effective in the contemporary policies of the United States. Recalling Powhatan's remark that he had thrice seen the death of his people and that the Tassantassas's arrival was intended to destroy his country, we may begin our explication of native holocaust history in Tsenacomoco and Monascane.

In popular accounts of the Conquest of Tsenacomoco, it is commonly believed that in 1607 two vastly alien and unknown cultures were encountering each other for the first time. In fact, the English declared the land virgin, as in Virginia. Such historically naive accounts have generated much fiction and they give no hint of the manifold evidence of an aggressive European invasion and colonization prior to 1607. Evidence, nevertheless, bears out Powhatan's remark concerning three or so prior encounters with the deadly Tssantassa assault.

The earliest foreign intruder with Tsenacomoco was apparently Giovanni da Verazzano, who in 1524 sailed past the Virginia Capes into Chesapeake Bay.[17] While there is no record of contact with the Real People, Powhatans, it is known that in earlier encounters in the south Verazzano did engage natives in personal contact. A 1546 storm subsequently forced an English ship into a "very good bay" in "the land of La Florida in 37°," in the account of a cabin boy that was given to the Spanish in 1559.[18] While anchored in the bay, "over thirty canoes in each of which were fifteen to twenty persons" came along side the ship seeking trade. Given that the thirty-seventh parallel runs through the entrance of Chesapeake Bay, this encounter may have been among the first within Tsenacomoco. At any rate, these initial encounters both present possibilities of introducing the first viral disease pathogens within the Powhatan community. Initial encounters between the virus-free native communities and the virus-infected Europeans have historically led to significant pathological outbreaks that are known to severely reduce an indigenous population. In fact, anthropologists have estimated that the effects of initial viral outbreaks among "virgin" native communities result in a survival rate of one member in twelve. It is, therefore, probable that "the densely populated land" Tsenacomoco was significantly depleted when the English arrived in 1607 and that their observations of a Powhatan confederacy of less than five thousand inhabitants is a woefully inadequate estimate of the precontact population.

Occurring between 1559 and 1560, there is the first documented encounter between Europeans and the Powhatan nation. In this case, a Powhatan Indian, while visiting south in the Carolina sound region, was picked up and taken to the Spanish West Indies. Called Paquinquineo, his Spanish captors baptized him with the name of his sponsor, Don Luis de Velasco.[19] Speculation regarding the identity of Paquinquineo has suggested that he was the father of Wahunsenacawh, Powhatan, or perhaps the same person as Opechancanough.[20] Educated among the Dominicans in Mexico, Don Luis was sent in 1566 with two friars and thirty soldiers to locate a mission among his people. When he failed to find the Virginia Capes,[21] he returned to Cuba and was later sent out with eight Jesuits in 1570 to found the mission. On 10 September 1570, they landed at College Creek, five miles east of Jamestown Island. Crossing the peninsula, they reached the York River at either Kings or Queens Creek and there settled in among the Paspaheghs, or perhaps the Chikahominies, with their mission. Don Luis subsequently left the priests, returning to his native people, but when the missionaries' supplies ran out they sought him out in early February 1571. Loyal to his people, however, Paquinquineo chose to eliminate the Jesuits.[22] Later, a Spanish relief ship arrived and the captain became suspicious when he could not find the priests. However, one young novice, Alonso de Lara, did survive. Following his return to the Spanish, Paquinquineo feared reprisal; in August 1572 it arrived under the command of the governor of Cuba. The punitive expedition took many natives captive while attacking the Chikahominies.

Beginning in 1584, the ill-fated ventures at Roanoke sponsored by Sir Walter Raleigh were subsequently located on the fringe of Tsenacomoco. Bound in hostility, these colonies failed while leaving several members to their fate. In the scope of these activities, the Spanish sailed again into Chesapeake Bay in 1588 as far north as the Potomac River, where they seized an Indian youth and carried him away. Taken to Santo Domingo, he converted to Christianity and died shortly thereafter from smallpox.[23] When the third or, later, "lost" colony arrived again at Roanoke and failed, the refugees were in 1587 taken northward, perhaps among the Chesapeakes, who were later thought to have been conquered by the Powhatans before 1607.[24] In each of these encounters, the natives of Tsenacomoco were again exposed to deadly viral pathogens, which may have again reduced their numbers such as Powhatan described. As a result, the 1607 Jamestown expedition entered a Tsenacomoco greatly impacted and reduced by Spanish and English incursions. A standing holocaust brought on by disease and punitive campaigns was historically well-founded when Powhatan informed John Smith of the threefold death of his people.

As the English invaders arrived at Jamestown in 1607, the Powhatans were experiencing a severe drought, thereby reducing their agricultural production. The English, however, were not well-provisioned and Captain John Smith, with his companions, was very aggressive, demanding corn at gunpoint from the Powhatans. It is, perhaps, from this perspective that it became common in the pictographic language of the Real People to represent the English as a swan belching fire. Herein the white-skin English evidence a simile of association in using their fire-belching weapons with the appearance of an aggressive swan. During the ensuing years from 1607 to 1622 there was a war of attrition as the English continued to rob the Powhatans of their corn and expanded their squatting on native lands. The Real People were incrementally pushed off their better agricultural land as the English claimed it for their tobacco plantations. As this invasion persisted and intensified, the Real People had no choice but to strike back in the great assault of 1622, so Opechancanough organized a systematic attack on Good Friday, March 22, seeking to extinguish the invaders and drive them from Tsenacomoco. Betrayed in the assault by sympathetic tribespeople, a small number of the Tassantassas survived. These were soon reinforced with arrivals from England, and the native uprising was used as a propaganda ploy to justify a systematic war of annihilation upon the Powhatans. In the reprisals, entire tribes were wiped out, with the survivors of one, at least, being sent to the West Indies as slaves. Afterward the Real People were forced into increasingly smaller enclaves and made aliens within their own lands. When in 1644 an aged Opechancanough renewed another "great assault," the Real People were so decimated that they were confined to small reservations, which could neither sustain their traditional way of life nor secure their future as a people in their own homeland.

Meanwhile, in Monascane during the early seventeenth century, the Monacan people were under fire from an aggressive and expanding

Iroquois confederacy. Mooney informs us that until 1670 these Monacan tribes had been "little disturbed by whites," although they were given to much shifting about due to "the wars waged against them by the Iroquois."[25] Initial contacts with colonial explorers and the Monacans, including the Nahyssans, Yesang or Tutelo, Saponi, and Occaneechi, began in the 1670s with the German physician-explorer, John Lederer, as well as the trade-oriented Batts and Fallam expedition. It was apparent, however, that independent Indian traders had already made commercial and social inroads among the central Virginia tribes. In fact, the rebel Nathaniel Bacon fell upon the Occaneechi and nearly wiped them out, despite their standing as tributary Indians protected by treaty.

By the time of Bacon's Rebellion in 1676, the Monacan tribes had begun to ally themselves together in close association near their Occaneechi confederates on a series of islands in the present Roanoke River near contemporary Clarksville, Virginia. Prompted to this defensive strategy by their implacable enemies from the north, the Iroquois, the Monacans were forced to seek security in treaty alliance with the Virginia colony. By 1685 Iroquois raids directed at the Tuteloes in Virginia triggered the colonial governor of Virginia, Lord Howard of Effingham, to treat with the Haudenosaunee at Albany. The Iroquois had been harassing the Tuteloes, who were under the supervision and protection of Virginia, with the intent of driving them "into the Covenant Chain as direct tributaries of the Five Nations rather than through the intermediation of Virginia." Lord Howard's treaty concluded with a pledge from the Iroquois to stay behind the mountains and beyond the Virginia settlements, however, the Haudenosaunee "demanded that the Virginians send one of their allied tribes to become an Iroquois tributary." While Lord Howard assumed he had secured the League's agreement to halt their wars upon the Virginia tribal tributaries, including the Tuteloes, it was by no means settled and the Iroquois continued to raid the Tuteloes.

The Monacan, nevertheless, received their share of massacres from the English. Initially, as Captain Newport captured Amorololeck, the English promised in alliance with the Powhatans to make war on the

Monacans. The extent of this early assault is not known but later, following a treaty with the Powhatans in 1646, it included the Monacans.

There is evidence that the Monacans of Mowhemcho suffered a cruel
reprisal from local landowners near the falls of the James. In this regard,
Francis Louis Michel records:

> About thirty years ago they still dwelt there. But when they
> inflicted some injury upon the Christians, Colonel Bornn, who
> is still alive and who was then living on the frontier, namely at
> Falensgrig [Falling Creek], as soon as he heard of this ravage,
> mounted at once his company (he was then captain) and attacked
> the Indians boldly (who had promised obedience but had not kept
> it). He soon overcame them after some resistance and put all of
> them to the sword, without sparing anyone. He also destroyed their
> settlement and whatever they owned. For this service the then
> King of England granted him the whole district between his land
> and this place, which extends twenty-five miles in length and
> eighteen miles in width. Those Indians who were not at home or
> escaped, still camp during the summer not far from their former
> home.[26]

In all likelihood, the Monacans did not bring about the attack upon the
Falling Creek colonials; however, the Iroquois were known to commit
depredations upon the Monacan and frontier communities during this
period. In fact, "Shurenough, King of the Monacans," was a signatory
of the 1677 treaty of the Middle Plantation,[27] thereby indicating that
the tribe was a tributary under the protection of the colony. This
account of the massacre of the Monacan tribe, however, may explain
why no Monacans were mentioned in the Fort Christanna treaty negotiations or other subsequent documents.[28] It may also suggest that the
Monacan proper survived in association with the Huguenots, but isolated from the Saponi at Fort Christanna. Although Michel made no
effort to record a census of the Monacans during his stay among the
Huguenots, it was reported about twenty-five years earlier that the

Monacan proper could muster thirty bowmen. With a ratio of three family members per bowman, this suggests that there were about one hundred twenty Monacans in the early 1670s.

In accordance with the frontier policy of Virginia Governor Alexander Spotswood, the Monacan tribes agreed in 1714 by treaty to occupy and possess the Fort Christanna Reservation near present-day Lawrenceville, Virginia. A mutual protection compact, the 1714 treaty provided for a reservation of six miles square, a palisaded fort with cannons and a group of armed rangers for defense, and a school for Indian children, as well as a governing factor commanding the post and administrating Indian affairs under the authority of the Virginia Indian Company.[29] Continuing their depredations against the Monacans, the Iroquois in 1777 launched an attack upon a visiting delegation of Catawba leaders who were camped outside the fort as invited guests of the Virginia government.[30] While Iroquois raiding parties continued to boldly march home through the colonial settlements of Virginia in 1719, Spotswood began negotiation with the governors of Pennsylvania and New York seeking a means to secure peace with the Haudenosaunee. As his concerns increased, Spotswood communicated his fears regarding these "Northern Indians" to the Virginia executive council, declaring that the Iroquois were "threatening to come in greater Numbers to Fall upon the English of the Colony and so cutt off and destroy the Sapponie Indians."[31] Governor Spotswood accordingly petitioned the New York government and the Haudenosaunee for a conference designed to secure a lasting peace.

In September 1722, during the treaty conference at Albany, the Iroquois revealed their bitter hatred towards the Monacan tribes: "Though there is among you," they replied to the Virginians, "a nation, the Todirichones, against whom we have had so inveterate an enmity that we thought it could only be extinguished by their total extirpation, yet, since you desire it, we are willing to receive them into this peace, and to forget all the past."[32] Even afterwards, in 1729 when renewing the covenant of 1685 with Virginia and Maryland, the Iroquois deputies presented a wampum belt to Governor Spotswood "in token of their friendship, and blandly requested permission to exterminate the Totero [Tutelo]."[33] Indeed, Mooney concluded, "The great overmastering fact in the history of the Siouan tribes of the east is that of their destruction by the Iroquois."[34]

Although several tribal segments or bands, including members of the Tutelo, Saponi, and Occaneechi, joined the Iroquois in the Haudenosaunee confederation, aboriginal Monacans nonetheless appear to have returned from Fort Christanna to the central Blue Ridge region of Rockbridge and Amherst Counties circa 1740. A connection to the Fort Christanna Saponi Reservation is clearly evident in this Orange County history of the "last Saponey Indians"[35] and those 1740s era Indians of Rockbridge and Amherst Counties, as well as today's Monacan Indian Nation.[36]

In the interval of Monacan absence, however, colonial opportunists, as well as the Cherokee and Shawnee nations, began entering Monascane, claiming it for themselves. The Shawnee, in particular, began to raid the English frontier settlements during the French and Indian war. By this time, the surviving Monacans amid the central Blue Ridge were all but forgotten. Their history and identity as the Earth People was maliciously obscured by the institutional racism and apartheid segregation enforced in Virginia.

Writing in 1785 Thomas Jefferson commented, "An inhuman practice once prevailed in this country of making slaves of the Indians."[37] In a manuscript note, Jefferson, furthermore, declared, "This practice commenced with the Spaniards with the first discovery of America."[38] Although Jefferson took no further notice of this institutional slavery as applied to American Indians, there is a well-precedenced history that included his beloved state of Virginia.

While Jefferson's observations may have been a matter of selective perception characteristic of his times, the failure of subsequent writers to give consideration to this history is less forgivable. As oppressed minorities, particularly, African-Americans began to struggle for their civil rights and overthrow apartheid segregation in the South; little thought was given to the historical survivance of American Indians in the region. After all, in the minds of most Americans, those southern Indians had been removed to the West and those remaining were at best "tri-racial isolates" and not "real" Indians. Reflecting, however, Jefferson's observation of more than a century before, ethno historian Irving Hallowell wrote in 1963, "in the colonial period of our history some Indians shared the status of slaves with Negroes."[39]

European enslavement of American Indians began with Christopher Columbus, who in 1494 sent more than five hundred Indians to Spain and the slave market.[40] After enslaving the natives of Espanola for exploitation in Spanish gold mines, great mortality was experienced among captives, leading slavers to raid the Bahamas and Florida in the early 1500s. American Indians, accordingly, were consigned to slavery in the West Indies concurrently with the first African slaves who were introduced there between 1501 and 1503.[41] During the 1520s, Lucas Vásquez de Ayllón took over one hundred fifty eastern Siouan Indians as slaves from the Cape Fear River area.[42]

There are several accounts of Indian enslavement in Virginia. For instance, as the "Old Dominion" began asserting its colonial institutions in the early 1600s, the practice of educating Indian children at the College of William and Mary became a ruse for officials to sell the children as slaves.[43] Following the 1644 Powhatan uprising and the Treaty of October 1646, Indian prisoners were kept by the English and made into servants.[44] Despite an act of 1660 in Virginia that "Indians [were] not to be sold as slaves,"[45] it later became legal during Bacon's Rebellion to enslave tributary Indians who had committed acts such as fighting, or who were deemed hostile by the English.[46] In fact, following a May 1676 attack upon the Occaneechi, the Virginia General Assembly passed laws "declaring all Indians who deserted their towns or harbored hostile Indians to be enemies, and any Indians captured in 'war' were to be slaves."[47] By 1682 the Assembly "declared all servants who were not Christians at time of purchase, as well as all Indians sold by 'neighboring Indians or any other' people, to be slaves."[48]

The proprietors of Colonial South Carolina identified Indian enslavement in that colony writing: "Mr. Maurice Matthews & Mr.

James Moore have most Contemptuously disobeyed our order about sending away Indians & have contrived most unjust warrs [sic] upon the Indians in order to the getting of Slaves & were Contriving new warrs for that purpose.[49] Matthews and Moore were associates within a group of powerful Carolina planters known as the Goose Creek men who were notorious for their incitement of tribal allies to war upon neighboring natives whom they captured and sold as slaves.[50] The South Carolina colonist Dr. Henry Woodward reports in 1674 to Lord Shaftsbury "trade was opened from St. Giles' plantation for 'deare skins, furrs and *young Indian slaves.*' "[51] Emphasis is given to Woodward's account in the following year (1675) when "a Chisca (Yuchi) woman ... escaped from slavery in Carolina" to the Spanish Apalache in Florida.[52] While the Carolinians engaged in limited Indian wars prior to 1680, there were a series of clashes, which "developed the notorious traffic in Indian slaves, in which South Carolina achieved a bad eminence among the English colonies."[53] In 1680 the colonial Proprietors charged that the powerful Charles Town slave dealers made the Westo [Indian] war for the purposes of selling Indian slaves in the West Indies.[54] Following this precedent, the Carolinians regularly encouraged and conducted Indian slave raids against tribes, as diverse and far away as the "Winyahs from the North Carolina border, Appomatox from Virginia, Cherokee from the mountains, and Chatot from the Gulf of Mexico."[55] Expanding this commerce in Indian slaves, the Carolinians encouraged intertribal warfare, which was "extraordinarily wasteful in its effects, and led to rapid penetration of the interior."[56] Noting the 1690–1700 war with the Choctaw, Vernon Crane writes "that the ultimate aim of the English was to exhaust them by wars in order to seize their lands and send them all slaves into distant countries."[57]

Indian slavery was also practiced for the Carolina domestic economy. In a 1704 raid upon the Apalachees, Moore boasted of returning with four thousand captive Indian women and children slaves for the colony.[58] Crane further notes that traffic in Indian slaves spread to other colonies and the West Indies. While many southern Indian slaves were shipped off to New England[59] and the West Indies, southern plantations remained rich with enslaved natives. Crane notes, for example, "In 1708, when the total population of South Carolina was 9,580, including 2,900 Negroes, there were 1,400 Indian slaves held in the province."[60] Although not peculiar to South Carolina, Indian slavery reached greater proportions there than in any other English colony. Following the Tuscarora war in 1711, at least seventy-five of these North Carolina and Virginia Iroquoian peoples were brought to South Carolina as slaves.[61] Available records reveal that a minimum of 5,500 Indians were enslaved in the Carolinas.[62] Although Indian groups survived in the South,[63] those who remained as slaves, however, melted into the black population.[64] Charles Royce, furthermore, notes "systematic slave hunts had nearly exterminated the aboriginal occupants of the Carolinas before anybody had thought them sufficient importance to ask who they were, how they lived, or what were their beliefs and opinions."[65]

While many Carolina Siouans were sold onto plantations within their original homelands, others were sold as captives into West India bondage.[66] Actually, as early as 1638 the Massachusetts English had deported many of the conquered Pequots to the Bermudas as slaves.[67] Transportation of Indian slaves to the West Indies included captured Kussoe Indians during the war of 1671–1674.[68] In fact, six hundred householders on Jamaica reported holding fifty-one Indian slaves between the years 1670 and 1700.[69] Governor Cabrera of St. Augustine expressed his grief over Indian enslavement and the slave trade with Barbados.[70] Decreed by the Barbados governing council, it was announced in 1636 that "*Negroes* and *Indians* that come here to be sold, should serve for life. . . ."[71] Not to be outdone, the Virginia English decreed that all Nanzaticos aged twelve years and older were to be sold in servitude in the West Indies and as a result an entire Powhatan tribal group was eliminated from Virginia and enslaved in Antiqua.[72]

Another factor contributing to the disassociation of American Indian identity in the south was the racial integrity codes that were legally binding in the region. Governor William Gooch promised "the better government of Negroes, Mulattoes, and Indians," with a 1724 Virginia law that deprived men in those categories of their political franchise. As early as 1705 the Virginia Assembly decreed, "The child of an Indian and the child, grandchild, or great-grand child of a negro shall be deemed, accounted, held and taken to be a mullato." The legislative intention was clearly to include Indians among the colony's colored population, thereby creating a biracial—white and colored—society.[73] Politically exclusive of Native Americans, southern colonies began legislating Indians into oblivion. In 1712 South Carolina followed Virginia with apartheid legislation, which North Carolina also affirmed in 1712 and 1741.[74] A century later the Virginia General Assembly passed a law in 1823 stating, "Be it enacted and declared, and it is hereby enacted and declared, That the child of an Indian and the child, or great-grandchild of a Negro shall be deemed, accounted, held and taken to be a mulatto."[75] In this pre-Civil War period, anyone declared black or mulatto was subject to severe civil depravation, including enslavement. Later, with the Virginia Racial Integrity Law of 1924, the state continued to acknowledge only two races—white and black. This law reads in part:

> It shall be unlawful for any white person in this State to marry save a white person, or a person with no other admixture of blood than white or American Indian. For the purpose of this act, the term "white person" shall apply only to the person who has no trace whatsoever of any blood other than Caucasian; but persons who have one-sixteenth or less of the blood of an American Indian. . . .[76]

The product of Dr. W. A. Plecker, registrar of the State Bureau of Vital Statistics, this statute outlawed Indians in Virginia. Plecker had decided that no Native Americans remained in Virginia and he determined to legislate those claiming to be Indians out of existence. Plecker systematically altered Indian birth, death, and marriage certificates to read "colored" or "Negro." Thus, at this time no one could claim a Native American racial heritage, and if they attempted to do so they were labeled mulatto or black by the state.[77]

Addressing the apartheid history of Virginia and the South is never an easy matter. On the one hand, one seeks to identify the racist's indicators, such as the term mulatto, as a means of affirming native ancestry, while on the other hand, one must be sensitive to the slight of African-Americans. As Helen Rountree explains, natives were forced into the "colored" status, thereby making them a "third race" in a "biracial state."[78] Rountree, moreover, writes:

> People of dark complexion claimed that their "suspicious" ancestor had been an Indian, sufficiently far back, and they were then classed as whites. Plecker and his associates were outraged at this; it did not seem to occur to them that the menial jobs and second-rate schools and hospitals set aside for "colored" people were enough to make anybody pass for white who could.[79]

As chief of the state's vital statistics bureau, Plecker was methodical when classifying Indians. He drew, furthermore, upon the 1823 racial code classifications to discredit Indian descendants under the authority of the 1924 Racial Integrity Act that he pushed through the Virginia legislature. As Rountree explains, "If the Indians category was a way station to whiteness, it had to be eliminated, or at least discredited. This meant proving that all people in Virginia who claimed to be Indian were actually of African ancestry and therefore colored."[80] During this apartheid segregation era, no one could claim a Native American tribal/racial/ethnic heritage under the color of Virginia law lest they be disenfranchised of their constitutional liberties and civil rights. These racial integrity laws remained in force until 1969, when they were repealed by the Virginia General Assembly as a result of the Supreme Court ruling in *Loving v. Virginia*.[81] Common throughout the South for over three centuries,[82] these laws made it possible to disassociate tribal and native identity from those surviving Native Americans in the region based upon erroneous biracial apartheid proscriptions.

In conclusion, the Powhatan and Monacan natives of Tsenacomoco and Monascane have suffered the weeds of the underworld in a holocaust of invasion, disease, war, and apartheid segregation. Through the systematic erasure of identity, these natives continue to suffer the indignities of a government that refuses to recognize and acknowledge their lawful standing and treaty rights as sovereign nations. Collectively in scope and application throughout the Americas, the Conquest has no match within world history.

1 John Smith, *A Map of Virginia* [with historical section compiled from various texts by William Simmond]. In *The Complete Works of Captain John Smoth (1580–1631)*. Edited by Philip L. Barbour, 3 vols. (Chapel Hill: University of North Carolina Press, 1986), 274; Smith, *The General Historie of Virginia, New England, and the Summer Isles, 1624*. In *The Complete Works of Captain John Smith (1580–1631)*. Edited by Philip L. Barbour, 3 vols. (Chapel Hill: University of North Carolina Press, 1986), pp. 199–200; also see Helen C. Rountree, *Pocahontas, Powhatan, Opechancanough: Three Indian Lives Changed by Jamestown* (Charlottesville: University of Virginia Press, 2005) pp. 120–121.

2 Smith, *Map of Virginia*, p. 274; and Smith, *General History*, pp. 199–200; and Rountree, *Three Lives*, pp. 120–121.

3 Smith, *General History*, p. 175; and Rountree, *Three Lives*, p. 111.

4 Jay Hansford C. Vest, "The Jesuit Republic and Brother Care in *The Mission*: An Allegory of the Conquest," *American Indian Culture and Research Journal*, 29:3 (2005), 33 pp.

5 Anonymous referee, comments upon draft manuscript, Vest, "*The Mission*: An Allegory of the Conquest," as reviewed by the *American Indian Culture and Research Journal* (April 21, 2005); in publication, see Vest, "Jesuit Republic."

6 By *Conquest*, I am conferring a status on the events—explorations, wars, missions, and diseases—that were collectively used by colonial Europeans to dispose of the indigenous inhabitants of the Americas. Given that this engagement is a macro event in world history, I have chosen to capitalize the term *Conquest*, as referenced to Native America. Although disease was a major factor in the depopulation of the Native Americans (see Alfred W. Crosby, Jr., *The Columbian Exchange: Biological and Cultural Consequences of 1492* [Westport, CT: Greenwood Press, 1972]; Alfred W. Crosby, *Ecological Imperialism: The Biological Expansion of Europe, 900–1900* [New York: Cambridge University Press, 1986]), the deliberate manner in which natives were enslaved, killed in war, and dispossessed of their aboriginal homelands illustrates an imperial Conquest. See, e. g., Frederick Turner, *Beyond Geography: The Western Spirit against the Wilderness* (New York: Viking, 1980); Tzvetan Todorov, *The Conquest of America: The Question of the Other* (New York: Harper and Row, 1982); Kirkpatrick Sale, *The Conquest of Paradise: Christopher*

Columbus and the Columbian Legacy (New York: Knopf, 1990), among many others; in a more polemical vein see Ward Churchill, *A Little Matter of Genocide: Holocaust and Denial in the Americas, 1492 to the Present* (San Francisco: City Lights Books, 1997), as well as a capsule summary of the Conquest in Colin S. Calloway, *First Peoples: A Documentary Survey of American Indian History*, 2nd ed. (Boston: St. Martin's, 2004), pp. 69–92.

7 Christopher Columbus, *The Dario of Christopher Columbus: First Voyage to America, 1492–1493*, abstracted by Fray Bartolomé de las Casas, transcribed into English, with notes and concordances of Spanish by Oliver Dunn and James B. Kelly, Jr. (Norman: University of Oklahoma Press, 1989), pp. 67–69.

8 Turner, *Beyond Geography*, p. xi.

9 Lewis Hanke, *Aristotle and the American Indians: A Study in Race Prejudice in the Modern World* (Bloomington: Indiana University Press, 1959), p. 2.

10 Roy Harvey Pearce, *Savagism and Civilization: A Study of the Indian and the American Mind* (Berkeley: University of California Press, 1953, 1988); and Richard Bernheimer, *Wild Men in the Middle Ages: A Study in Art, Sentiment, and Demonology* (Cambridge, MA: Harvard University Press, 1952).

11 Hanke, *Aristotle and the American Indians*, pp. 3–4.

12 Ibid., pp. 44–61.

13 Lewis Hanke, *The Spanish Struggle for Justice in the Conquest of America* (Philadelphia: University of Pennsylvania Press, 1949), p. 26. Subsequent quotations from this source in this paragraph are cited parenthetically in the text.

14 Sale, *The Conquest of Paradise*, p. 161, original emphasis.

15 Las Casas quoted in Carl Ortwin Sauer, *The Early Spanish Main* (Berkeley: University of California Press, 1966), pp. 68, 155–56.

16 Sale, *The Conquest of America*, p. 161.

17 Lawrence C. Wroth, *The Voyages of Giovanni da Verazzano, 1524–1528* (New Haven: Yale University Press, 1970), pp. 82–83, 90.

18 Clifford M. Lewis and Albert J. Loomie, *The Spanish Jesuit Mission in Virginia, 1570–1572* (Chapel Hill: University of North Carolina Press, 1953), p. 13; also David Beers Quinn, *England and the Discovery of America, 1481–1620* (New York: Knopf, 1974), p. 190.

19 Carl Bridenbaugh, *Jamestown 1544–1699* (New York: Oxford University Press, 1981); Lewis and Loomie, *Spanish Jesuit Mission in Virginia*, pp. 15–17.

20 Rogers Dey Whichard, *The History of Lower Tidewater Virginia*, 2 vols. (New York: Lewis Historical Publishing Company, 1959), I: pp. 49–51; Bridenbaugh, *Jamestown 1544–1699*.

21 Lewis and Loomie, *Spanish Jesuit Mission in Virginia*, pp. 18, 24.

22 Ibid., p. 44; Quinn, *England and the Discovery of America*, p. 209.

23 Lewis and Loomie, *Spanish Jesuit Mission in Virginia*, p. 56.

24 Quinn, *England and the Discovery of America*, pp. 345–353; and Helen C. Rountree, *Pocahontas's People: The Powhatan Indians of Virginia Through Four Centuries* (Norman: University of Oklahoma Press, 1990), p. 21.

25 James Mooney, *The Siouan Tribes of the East*, U. S. Bureau of American Ethnology, Bulletin 22, Smithsonian Institution (1894; Washington, D.C.: U. S. Government Printing Office, 1984), p. 51.

26 Francis Louis Michel, "Report of the Journey from Berne, Switzerland to Virginia, October 2, 1701–December 1, 1702," Translated and edited by Professor Wm. J. Hinke, PhD, *Virginia Magazine of History and Biography*, 24:1 (January, 1916), pp. 1–43 and 24: 2 (April, 1916), pp. 113–141, and 24: III (1916), pp. 275–303.

27 "Treaty between Virginia and the Indians, 1677," *Virginia Magazine of History and Biography*, 14: 3 (Jan. 1907), pp. 289–297.

28 "Treaty of Peace between Virginia and the Saponies, Stuckanoes, Occoneechees, and Totteros, Feb. 27, 1713 [14]," (Washington, D.C.: Library of Congress) CO5/1316: pp. 619–627; and "Treaty with the Sapponie Indians, concluded at Williamsburg, the 27th February, 1713," as referenced in the Public Record Office, Journal of the Commissioners for Trade and Plantations from February 1708–9 to March 1714–5 (London: His Majesty's Stationary Office, 1925), p. 528.

29 "Treaty of Peace between Virginia and the Saponies," pp. 619–27; "Treaty with the Saponie Indians," p. 528. See also Mooney, *Siouan Tribes*, p. 26, who concluded: "Thenceforth, accounts were heard of Nahyssan, Saponi, Totera, Occaneechi, and others, consolidated afterward in a single body at the frontier, Fort Christanna, and thereafter known collectively as Saponi or Tutelo."

30 H. R. McIllwanie, ed., *Executive Journal of the Council of Colonial Virginia* (Richmond: Virginia State Library, 1928), 3: pp. 450–52, referencing the August 1717 attack upon the Catawba Indians outside Fort Christanna perpetrated by the Iroquois who declared that they did not know these people, the Catawba, were friends of the English.

31 McIllwanie, ed., *Executive Journal*, 2: pp. 507–9.

32 O'Callaghan, *New York Historical Collections* [NYHC], 6: p. 660, in Horatio Hale, "The Tutelo Tribe and Language," *Proceedings of the American Philosophical Society* 21, no. 114 (1883), p. 5.

33 Leonidas Dodson, *Alexander Spotswood: Governor of Colonial Virginia, 1710–1722* (1932; reprint, New York: AMS Press, 1969), p. 105.

34 Mooney, *Siouan Tribes*, p. 14.

35 Dr. A. G. Grinnan, "The Last Indians in Orange County, Virginia," *Virginia Historical Magazine*, 3: pp. 189–190.

36 Jay Hansford C. Vest, "The Buzzard Rock: Saponi-Monacan Traditions from Hico, Virginia," *Lynch's Ferry: A Local History Journal*, 5:1 (Spring/Summer 1992), pp. 26–31; Vest, "From Bobtail to Brer Rabbit: Native American Influences upon Uncle Remus," *American Indian Quarterly*, 24:1 (Winter 2000), pp. 19–43; and in supplying direct evidence of the link with Fort Christanna, see Vest, "From Nansemond to Monacan: The Legacy of the Pochick-Nansemond among the Bear Mountain Monacan," *American Indian Quarterly*, 27: 3&4 (Summer & Fall 2003), pp. 781–806; Vest, "The Origins of the Johns

Surname: A Monacan Ethnogenesis," *Quarterly Bulletin*, Archeological Society of Virginia, 60:1 (March 2005), pp. 1–14; Vest, "The Lynchburg Tobacco Trade and the 19th Century Monacan Economy: Oral Traditions from the Blue Ridge at Hico—the Buzzard Rock," *Lynch's Ferry: A Local History Journal*, (Spring/Summer 2005) pp. 34–39; Vest, "Further Considerations in the Ethnogenesis of the Monacan Indian Nation: The Saponi Origins of Selected Families," *Quarterly Bulletin*, Archeological Society of Virginia, 60:3 (September 2005), pp. 133–149; Vest, "Opechancanough and the Monacans: The Legend of Trader Hughes and Princess Nicketti Reconsidered," *Quarterly Bulletin*, Archeological Society of Virginia, 60:4 (December 2005), pp. 198–215; Vest, "The Monacan Nation as Lost Tribes: The Origins of the Indians of the Central Blue Ridge Virginia and the Lynchburg Tobacco Trade," *Crossroads: A Southern Culture Annual*, forthcoming (December 2005), 38 pp.; Vest, "Monacans and Huguenots: Monacans and Huguenots: Manakin Town and the Ethnogenesis of the Monacan Nation," *Quarterly Bulletin*, Archeological Society of Virginia, forthcoming, 61:1, 34 pp.; Vest, "The Travels of Francis Louis Michel and the Ethnohistory of the Monacan Nation," *Crossroads: A Southern Culture Annual*, in review (2005), 35 pp.; and Vest, "The Adventures of John Lederer among the Monacan: Explorations and Oral Traditions," in presentation, 1st Annual Southeast Indian Studies Conference (Pembroke, University of North Carolina, April 2005), 10 pp.; see also, Vest, "An Odyssey among the Iroquois: A History of Tutelo Relations in New York," *American Indian Quarterly*, 29: 1 & 2 (July 2005), pp. 124–155; Vest, "A Tutelo Inquiry: The Ethnohistory of Chief Samuel John's Correspondence with Dr. Frank G. Speck," *American Indian Culture and Research Journal*, forthcoming (2005), 28 pp.; and Vest, "A Tutelo Heritage: An Ethnoliterary Assessment of Chief Samuel Johns' Correspondence with Dr. Frank G. Speck," *Canadian Journal of Native Studies*, in review (2005), 32 pp.

37 Thomas Jefferson *Notes on the State of Virginia* [1785]. Edited and with an Introduction & Notes by William Peden (Chapel Hill: University of North Carolina Press, 1982), p. 61.

38 Jefferson, *Notes on Virginia*, 61, fn. 89 where editor Peden references "Ms note by TJ. See Herrera. Amer. Vesp., Ed. note. Antonio de Herrera y Tordesillas (1559–1625), Spanish Historian, author of *Historia General de los Hechos de los Castelanos en las Islas y Tierra Firme del Mar Oceano* (Madrid, 1601–15, 4 vols.).

39 A. Irving Hallowell, "American Indians, White and Black: The Phenomenon of Transculturalization," Current *Anthropology*, 4(1963): p. 522.

40 Donald Grinde, Jr., "Native American Slavery in the Southern Colonies," The *Indian Historian*, 10: 2 (1977), p. 38.

41 A. F. Chamberlain, "African and American: The Contact of Negro and Indian," *Science*, 17: 419 (1891), p. 85.

42 J. Leitch Wright, Jr., *The Only Land They Knew: The Tragic Story of the American Indians in the Old South* (New York: The Free Press, 1981), 103–104.

43 Rountree, *Pocahontas's People*, p. 168.

44 Ibid, p. 87.
45 Charles C. Royce, *Indian Land Cessions in the United States,* Smithsonian Institution, Bureau of American Ethnology, Annual Report, 1896–97, pt. 2 (Washington, D.C.: U. S. Government Printing Office, 1899), p. 567.
46 Rountree, *Pocahontas's People*, 139. Enslavement of Indians by the English is further discussed by Almon Wheeler Lauber, *Indian Slavery in Colonial Times within the Present Limits of the United States* [1913] (New York: AMS press, 1969). pp. 105–117.
47 Ibid., pp. 97–98.
48 Ibid., p. 139.
49 Quoted in Amy Ellen Friedlander, "Indian Slavery in Proprietary South Carolina," M. A. *Thesis* (Atlanta: Department of History, Emory University, 1975), p. 19.
50 Wright, *The Only Land*, pp. 102–125, discusses these colonials.
51 Vernon W. Crane, *The Southern Frontier 1670–1732,* [1929] (Westport, CN: Greenwood Press, 1977), pp. 16–17, emphasis added.
52 Ibid., p. 17.
53 Ibid., pp. 17–18.
54 Ibid., p. 19.
55 Ibid., p. 21.
56 Ibid., p. 23.
57 Ibid., p. 68.
58 Wright, *The Only Land*, p. 114.
59 Ibid., p. 114, it should be noted that "In the early eighteenth century the Boston News Letter printed frequent advertisements of runaway Carolina Indians," thereby promoting sale of the Indians as Slaves in New England.
60 Ibid., pp. 112–113.
61 Friedlander, *Indian Slavery*, p. 37.
62 Robert William Snell, "Indian Slavery in Colonial South Carolina, 1671–1795," *Dissertation* (Tuscaloosa: University of Alabama, 1972), p. 3.
63 See William Harlen Gilbert, Jr., "Surviving Groups of the Eastern United States," *Annual Report of the Smithsonian Institution* (Washington, D.C.: U. S. Government Printing Office, 1948), 419 where surviving *Monacan* groups from whom I am descendent are reported in Rockbridge and Amherst Counties, Virginia.
64 Friedlander, *Indian Slavery*, p. 80.
65 Royce, *Land Cessions*, p. 630.
66 Ibid., p. 631.
67 Friedlander, *Indian Slavery,* p. 37.
68 Chamberlain, "African and American," p. 86.
69 Friedlander, *Indian Slavery*, p. 8.
70 Ibid., pp. 29–30.

71 Alden T. Vaughn, *Roots of American Racism* (New York: Oxford University Press, 1995), p. 157.

72 Rountree, *Pocahontas's People*, p. 121.

73 Helen C. Rountree, "The Indians of Virginia: A Third Race in a Biracial State" in *Southeastern Indians Since the Removal Era*. Edited by Walter L. Williams (Athens: The University of Georgia Press, 1979), pp. 27–48.

74 Vaughn, *Roots of American Racism*, pp. 17–19.

75 William Waller Henning, *The Statutes at Large* (Philadelphia: Thomas De Silver, 1823), IV: p. 252.

76 "The Virginia Racial Integrity Law," No. 5, *Acts and Resolutions of the General Assembly of the State of Virginia*, (Davis Bottom, Superintendent of Public Printers, Richmond, 1924), p. 535.

77 Peter W. Houck, M.D., *Indian Island in Amherst County* (Lynchburg Historical Research Co., Lynchburg, 1984), pp. 72–73; see also Paul T. Murray, "Who is an Indian? Who is a Negro? Virginia Indians in the World War II Draft," *The Virginia Magazine of History and Biography*, 95: 2 (April 1987), pp. 215–231; and Susan Greenbaum, "What's in a label? Identity Problems of Southern Indian Tribes," *The Journal of Ethnic Studies*, 19: 2 (1991), pp. 107–126. For a thorough discussion of this matter see J. David Smith, *The Eugenic Assault on America: Scenes in Red, White and Black* (Fairfax, VA: George Mason University Press, 1993).

78 Rountree, "Indians of Virginia," pp. 27–48.

79 Ibid., 41.

80 Ibid.

81 *Loving v. Virginia*, 388 U. S. 1 (1967); see also Lombardo, "Miscegenation, Eugenics, and Racism: Historical Footnotes to *Loving v. Virginia*," *University of California, Davis Law Journal*, 21 (1988), p. 421 for a discussion of these circumstances in Virginia history.

82 Cf. Charles M. Hudson, *The Catawba Indians* (Athens: University of Georgia Press, 1970), pp. 69–71 where he identifies the bi-racial problems generated by Black Codes in South Carolina; see also David Duncan Wallace, *South Carolina: A Short History, 1540–1948* (Chapel Hill: University of North Carolina Press, 1951), pp. 569–590, 632; William H. Gilbert, Jr., "Memorandum Concerning the Characteristics of the Larger Mixed-Blood Racial Islands of the Eastern United States," *Social Forces*, 24 (1946), pp. 438–447; Gilbert, "Surviving Indian Groups of the Eastern United States," pp. 407–438; Brewton Berry, "The Mestizos of South Carolina," *American Journal of Sociology*, 51 (1945), pp. 34–41; Berry, *Almost White* (New York: Macmillan Company, 1963).

WASHITA, A SLAUGHTER, NOT A BATTLE:

A CHEYENNE SURVIVOR'S PERSPECTIVE

TRANSLATED, EDITED, AND
ANNOTATED BY EUGENE BLACKBEAR, SR.,
AND KIMBERLY ROPPOLO

AFTER THE *massacre at Sand Creek on November 29, 1864, public dismay at the brutality Chivington and his men displayed toward the Cheyenne led to the formation of a Peace Commission. This, in turn led to the Medicine Lodge Creek Treaty of 1867, under which the Cheyenne and other Southern Plains tribes were assigned reservations in Indian Territory. They were promised homes, agricultural supplies, farmland, and annual payments of blankets, food, and clothing. Some young men, unable to accept these terms as fair considering the circumstances, continued to raid in Kansas. General Philip H. Sheridan planned a winter campaign in retaliation, in which he promised to cripple the Indians at their weakest time, when their horses were thin and weak, when they themselves were merely trying to survive the months of bitter cold on the Plains. Black Kettle, who had already been attacked at Sand Creek under both a U.S. and a white flag, tried to appeal to General William Hazen at Fort Cobb for peace, tried to seek protection for his people inside the fort; however, Custer was the only one with authority to grant that, and he was away. Though his wife and others tried to get Black Kettle to relocate their camp nearer to larger encampments of Cheyennes and other tribes, Black Kettle simply did not believe that Sheridan would order an attack without counseling for peace. After the attack on Washita, Custer smoked a pipe with*

Cheyenne Chiefs, promising never to attack Cheyenne women and children again, knowing that his own life would be forfeit if he broke this solemn oath. Six years later, when Custer attacked Cheyennes and Sioux at the Battle of the Little Bighorn, it was a direct result of his broken promise that he was killed.[1]

With eight hundred soldiers based at Fort Supply, Custer attacked Black Kettle's encampment at dawn, having set up outside the small camp of fifty-one lodges just after midnight on November 27. Custer claimed there were a hundred Cheyennes killed; Cheyenne accounts differ on this number. Army records show that only twenty-one soldiers died, most from Major Joel Elliott's detachment, which encountered Cheyenne warriors coming to the aid of Black Kettle.[2] *Custer had over eight hundred Cheyenne horses killed following the massacre of the people. As well, fifty Cheyennes, mostly women and children, were taken captive.*[3] *The translation that follows is an excerpt from a book-length work we have in progress regarding Cheyenne stories and ways. In this translation, Andrew Bird Chief, son of the Bird Chief in this story, first spends some time telling the requirements for a Cheyenne chieftainship. Craig Womack, in* Red on Red, *suggests that part of the problem with the way the oral traditions of various tribes have been recorded is that they have been taken out of context and depoliticized (57–59). In an attempt to record a more traditional context for this story we have preserved this chieftain section that precedes the story of the genocidal attack. Its very inclusion fights back against the long ongoing genocide of Cheyenne people, by encouraging the preservation of cultural values through the words of this elder, cultural values that Loretta Fowler in* Tribal Sovereignty and the Historical Imagination: Cheyenne-Arapaho Politics *shows are in danger of being lost today (220–25). Moreover, we have utilized English that reflects the structure of the Cheyenne, maintaining the rhetorical devices as closely as possible, while adding in what is implied in Cheyenne when necessary for understanding by mainstream readers. We see this, too, as an act of sovereignty and resistance.*

NOW, YOU young men, listen to what I have to say. I listened, when I was young. That is how I know what I have learned today. I am going to tell you. Listen to what I have to tell you. Now, you listen, I have become a Chief. I listened to Chiefs; how they become a Chief, listen to how they become a Chief, a Cheyenne Chief, a *real Chief*.[4] I watched my father[5] initiated into Chieftainship, and this is what he was told. Now, he had become a Chief, my father, Bird Chief, that's how he had become a Cheyenne Warrior Chief. He laid down his life for his people. And that's how we became Chiefs under him, how we got our positions through him. Broken Hand, that's how he became a Chief, when he took up for the Tsis-tsis-tas and Suhtai.[6] That Crow Old Man,[7] one of my grandfathers, that's how he earned the right, too, to be Chief. He was willing to lay down his life, him and Broken Hand. Now the selection of Chiefs for Chieftainship, now, you young men, listen. You look for a person that has common sense, good sense, when you look for a Chief, that is thinking good and right, a well-respected man. Now that is the way you qualify for these Chieftain positions. Now, you young men, you listen to these ways, these qualifications. Now that's the way the selections are made. Now my father, he done the same thing, and they were being driven by soldiers, they were running from soldiers, and this old man, he was young, he got off his horse, and he was going to stop and fight them guys so the rest of the people could get away. Now he told his people, "I'm going to hold off these guys, you get away. I'm going to hold them off as long as I can." He told his people to run away. After he let them people escape, then he got on his horse, and he ran toward the enemy. And for a while he killed a lot of them people, the soldiers, and then he disappeared, he must have got killed. And that's how we were told about him, what he done, how he earned that right, to be a Warrior Chief. And that's where we earned that right to be a Warrior Chief, he earned it for us. And that is why I am telling you these things. You children, listen.

Now listen, that's how men become Chiefs. They are selected. You have to be very careful in this selection. You have to be very careful. You have to live up to these things. You have to have pity and love for your people. Now, you young men, young and old, listen. That's how we put these Chiefs in these positions. They have to earn the right to become a Cheyenne Chief. Now at this time, these Chiefs today, they are over-riding their Chieftain position. They were supposed to be selected for

ten years at a time. Each Cheyenne Chief is supposed to select someone to take his place. If that kind of selection is not done, then the four
main principal Chiefs select the other forty Chiefs of the forty-four.[8]
Now, that's how you earn these high positions, the Warrior Chiefs.
When you earn these positions, it is good when you qualify for these
positions. You earn these ways. Follow them in a good way. Don't be
afraid to give away things, when you are selected and afraid. Things will
always come back to you. The only thing that is hard to get again is *life*.
That's the main thing in life, our *lives*. You always get things back again.
Now, what I have just told you, there is going to be nobody else who
will come around and tell you these things. How to become a Cheyenne
Chief. Now that's all I am going to tell you for now. Now that is the way
selections are made. There will be nobody else who will tell you that.
So you remember what I have told you.

These things are just a reminder. These Chiefs, their job is to talk, to
remind people any time there is a gathering, to be good to one another,
help each other, work together, show pity to each other. It is a Chieftain's job to remind people of that. Now following these things, what I
have told you, it is a Chief's job to remind people to live a good way
of life, and that is what I am telling you today. Now, no matter how
young a Chief might be, if he is talking, and he has a Chieftain position, you have to respect him, you have to listen to what he is trying to
tell you, to live in a good way, his people. Today, we are poor people. We
are trying to follow these ways. And these young men today, they qualify for these positions, they are trying to take up these leadership positions. Be sure and always pity your poor people. I'm going to tell you,
taking this pipe, this oath, is kind of hard. Taking an oath pipe is very
strong. Now, what I am telling you, it is very hard, and I wish you young
men would take it as advice, what I told you. Taking this pipe is a difficult thing, this pipe. Some of you might not live up to that. Now I am
going to tell you the purpose of this pipe. Now, the highest one, I've
done told you guys about it. My father, Bird Chief, how he got down
off his horse and laid down his life. That is the highest one. Now when
somebody takes that pipe, the oath, he is supposed to give his wife away

even if someone comes and asks for his wife. That is what is hard. Now I wish you would go around that, by not taking the pipe, so you won't have to give your wives up. You know, we love these women. It is hard, nowadays, to give up your wife. Now, don't take that pipe in that manner, and you can still become a Chief and be a good Chief, live up to it. Now, if you took an oath, and somebody came and asked for your wife, then you would try to think of a way out, and there would be no way out, and you would hurt yourself.[9] That's what I am telling you this morning. My ancestors, my fathers, they have been Chiefs since 1895.[10] Then, when my father became a Chief, I had some horses, eight or nine horses to give away. I'm telling you this morning, that's how you think about how to select a person; you think of them highly, that's how you select a Chief, respectability. Right there, when somebody is selected, he will have giveaways, and he will give away, and then there are some, even if they don't have anything to give away, go ahead, it's all right. Sometimes it's like that, we're poor. Even if he doesn't have anything to give away, go ahead and make him a Chief. Respect him like that anyway.

Now, that's the way you follow that Chieftainship. Try to follow it to the best of your ability. Now, that's why I am reminding you of these things. The old people, who used to say these things, are not around today. Look around; we've got a pitiful life. All of those old people are all gone. And you look around today, that's where we are—we're pitiful. Now, from this time on, you clans, Chiefs, and all these other clans, pity one another, work together as a Cheyenne tribe. And this drinking, it makes you do bad things, it makes people crazy. They get into fights. They hurt each other, they kill each other, and that's where a murderer comes from.[11] And that is how we have this Chieftainship; our father earned it for us. Even though we never have done what he did, he still earned it for us. We became Chiefs. Now that's the way menfolks, not only Cheyenne Chiefs, are supposed to do. We are supposed to take up for our kinfolks, our women, we are supposed to do that as men and as Cheyenne Chiefs. That is how we are supposed to live as Cheyennes. Right now, talk good to one another, say good things, and as I look around, there are some things that are not too good in Cheyenne ways. Right now, things are pretty rough, pretty hard times. Now, you young men, try to listen to what I am saying today, what I am telling you. Try to take care of these Chieftain positions in a good way. Live them, and carry them on in a good way. Love one another. And as Chiefs, love one another in a respectful way. You clans, all get along, love one another, respect one another. Don't be mad at each other. Do not be jealous of one another. Now, that's what I am telling now. My grandfather, Whirlwind Coming, he got some money from the government for what they did to us Cheyennes when they attacked us unfairly at other times. Now this is about all I am going to say at this time. Take care of your Chieftain positions. That's about all I am going to say this morning. Even if you don't get anything, go ahead and talk, talk good, and make people respect one another and say nice things to people. That's about all I am going to say this morning.

Now I am going to talk about Black Kettle at this time, this morning. Now, children, listen to me real good, listen to me closely, I am going to tell you the story of how Black Kettle was attacked and destroyed. The Suhtai were destroyed at Washita. Now, early in the morning, I guess it was snowing. Now, this man they call Custer, Long Hair, he attacked them early in the morning. Black Kettle, they got pushed back. Now, Broken Hand was taking up for his people. The women and kids were trying to run. And they (these warriors) were starting to defend them when the attack began. Old Blind Bear Man and Broken Hand, they were protecting the women and the kids when these soldiers attacked, and another man, he ran off and left his family, and these guys came along and took up for that family as well. Right there, some of these people ran up toward the Arapaho camp, up the creek, and there were Kiowas camping down the creek the other way as well. These men, they took some women and children up the creek to that Arapaho camp for safety. There were no Arapahos in our camp. And these women and kids were crying, when they took them to safety. Then the men went back to fight the enemy, and Broken Hand got killed. And Broken Hand, before he was killed, he shot a bunch of them soldiers and captured their horses. Then he rode against the other soldiers, that's when he got killed. Now, that's the story of Black Kettle. My father, Bird Chief, he was there, too. Later that day, my father would be shot by Custer. Then another grandfather of mine, Crow Old Man, he done the same thing as Broken Hand. He killed a bunch of soldiers off their horses. After that, he captured their horses. Later that day, he rode in against the enemy and was killed. Now, after Crow Old Man began fighting, Arapaho warriors came from up the creek where they were camped, after the women and children had run there, and they were moving these soldiers back, running them away. My father gathered up the women and kids and told them, "We ran the soldiers off. Come on. Come down this way where we other Cheyennes are camping down there." Them women were getting up, and some of their feet were really cold. They almost had frozen their feet off. Some of them also went to the Arapaho camp. The Arapahos gave them some food and some clothing. My father was standing there. Black Kettle went across with his two wives, and Custer shot Black Kettle. I saw it with my own eyes. Now I know the rest of this story, too, is true. It was told to me by people who were there. Now all you children, always remember these stories. The way it was told, that's the way I am telling it, that way, the truth. My grandfather, Crow Old Man and Bird Chief, my father, they ran off those soldiers. They would have all been killed, wiped away, the Suhtai, but these warriors came in and rescued them, Crow Old Man and Bird Chief. That's the story of Black Kettle.

The survivors went to the Arapaho camp for help. And the Arapahos really treated them good. All them women and kids left and went to the other Cheyenne camp. The Arapahos gave them some clothing and some food. That's where the Suhtai were demolished, at Black Kettle's camp. Most of them were killed. That's the story of how Bird Chief, my father, was killed in that battle, that is how the story was given to me. That is how Spotted Wolf also became a Chief. I was named after my father, Bird Chief. That's where the Suhtai were killed, most of them, that morning. Broken Hand was my grandfather. That's the way the story goes. The Suhtai, none of them would run away from each other, they were in a bunch, that's why they got killed. Now that's why they ruined themselves. They wanted some food,[12] and that's how they got themselves killed.

Then, that morning, Custer started chasing the survivors. Right there, they went to that camp. That's where we started getting that land.[13] Right there, we were supposed to have gotten some claim money from Washita, payment from the government for what Custer did. Now we are having a hard time getting any claim. Now you young men, listen. Now. Let it be clear, one way or the other, so we can get this claim settled, get the money right away. What I am telling you, my grandfather, Whirlwind Coming, wasn't a councilman or anything, but the government listened to him. He got what he wanted. My grandfather got what he wanted from them white men, a lot of money. He gave all that money away. He didn't use it right. We just spent it all. We were supposed to have got rich off of that money, but nobody did. Instead, we just lost it. And us Indians, we don't know how to use the money wisely. And the white man, he just knows how to handle the money. And even there, some of them, they spend their money foolishly, like we did. They drink it up and use it foolishly. Buy some houses, some homes. Now your folks have sold a lot of their lands and made you poor. Now you are always getting into arguments and misunderstandings over things. Right now, you guys need to pity one another. Help each other. That's all I wanted to tell you. That's what God, Our Creator, told us. "Love one another. Help each other. That's why I gave you life." And that's why we're living today. Now try to follow this way of life, all of you of all ages, young to old, all of you follow this good road of life. Now that's why I am talking to you guys that way. That's why I told you Black Kettle's story. Now they died in a pitiful way, our people. There isn't a person living that was involved there, but we are still seeking just payment for what happened. All those who were killed, your grandparents, great-grandparents, whomever, now we, their descendants, are trying to fix up the papers to get a settlement. That's where we will get whatever amount we will get. That's how the government will comfort us for the loss of our loved ones, our homes, our tipis, all the things we had that were lost right there.

That's where we lost all these people. We cannot see them anymore. We cannot show them love. We cannot love them. From here on out, you guys love one another. Help each other. From here on out. Now that's why I am telling you this kind of talk, a good respectable Chief's talk, that's what I am using now, trying to help our people. Now, I always think about all of you, all of my tribe, all ages, all walks of life, everybody. I always pray for you, pray for all of you. Now I am getting old. I am not such a young person. Now, you men, you fellow Chiefs, listen to me now. Love one another. Pity one another. Help one another. Love and respect one another. Don't follow this no-good road of the white man. Follow this good road of life. Think good. Always think right, and be glad I am talking to you. I am just reminding you of these nice things. I am just telling you Black Kettle's story in a good way, so you will know. Now that's why I am telling you children. All I have left now is this talk. I am qualified, as a Chief, to make this kind of talk. Now, that's where I am at now, at this age. I've come this far, and I pray for you guys, all of you, me, at this age. Now, I am at the old man stage. My fellow Chiefs, listen to me. Love one another. Help each other. Don't be mad at each other. Follow this path that was given to us Cheyennes. Now, follow it in a good way. That's it. I am telling Black Kettle's story and my father's story in a good way, in the best way, that's it.

1　Cheyenne tradition holds that Custer was taken captive by Cheyenne men at the Battle of the Little Bighorn and handed over to Cheyenne women to be killed because of his broken promise, and because of Custer's and his soldiers' cruelty to women, which included even killing pregnant women and mutilating their genitals. The women first poked holes in his ears with awls so that in the afterlife he might be able to "listen" better than he did in life. He is said to have begged for his life and cried "like a woman." Then the women killed him with their knives and retaliated in kind by taking body parts for trophies in a scalp dance. This is why today in traditional Cheyenne dress women wear knives in leather sheaths attached to their belts and a string of silver conchos hanging down in front from their belts to represent Custer's sabre. Some women were always with the men in battle—Cheyenne Women Warriors. Other tribes have this tradition as well. The women cooked and cared for the warriors but also stepped into battle if necessary, or if they felt compelled to do so to intervene for a male relative or to avenge him. It is possible that another tradition, that of the Warrior Societies' (Bow String, Kit Fox, Dog Soldier, Hoof Rattlers, and Red Shield) adopting a sister—which continues to this day for the Bow String and Hoof Rattlers—grows out of the tradition of these women warriors. Society sisters are supposed to be reputable young women, virgins, when they are taken as sisters by these Warrior Societies and are supposed to conduct themselves in a good way, not drinking, taking drugs, or consorting around with men. If these young women misbehave there are negative consequences in the form of bad luck for the men in the Societies that adopted them. Perhaps this led to the tradition's ending in some Societies, to avoid bad luck in light of cultural change. It is also possible that the tradition of the Pow Wow Princess grows out of these traditions, as those selected are supposed to conduct themselves in this good way for young women as well, in an orderly manner.

2   Bird Chief's warriors were among these Tsis-tsis-tas who were camped a little way away from Black Kettle's group and came to their aid. This account is told by Andrew Bird Chief who witnessed his father's deeds and brave death but he was also told the story repeatedly later by older people, as he was too young to understand much of what he saw at the time.

3   Monasetah, a Cheyenne woman, was among these captured. A newspaper story on indybay.org says: "Eddie Rickenbacker's is a bar in San Francisco's Financial District. While the bar has received good reviews, even by supposedly progressive newspapers, it is home to one of the most offensive and racially insensitive displays one can find in the city. Along with displays of guns used in the wars of extermination against the Native American population, there are what is claimed to be the teeth of Monasetah. A sign above the teeth claims that they were 'knocked out of her mouth in a jealous pique' By General George Armstrong Custer. It has been claimed that, following the Battle of Washita, Custer invited officers 'desiring to avail themselves of the services of a captured squaw to come to the squaw Round Up Corral, and select one.' Custer took first choice, Monasetah, and lived with her during the winter and spring of 1868 and 1869. The display has been around for years with little complaint. If the display is real, then it could be in violation of the Native American Graves Protection and Repatriation Act. If it is not real and is merely intended to add atmosphere, it shows acceptance by the bar's owners and patrons of a form of racism and misogyny that would never be allowed if the remains were claimed to be a person from any other ethnic group. The bar's owner, when questioned about why he has a Native woman's teeth on display, replied that concern for cultural sensitivity was 'not living in reality.' "

4   His father was the kind of Chief, a real Chief, a man Chief, who had earned that honor the old way, by being willing to lay down his life for his people in battle, to fight even to the death if necessary to allow his men to get away.

5 Cheyenne people count kinship in their traditional way. A man and all of his brothers would be "father" to all of their children collectively; a mother's sisters would also be "mothers." So it is unclear whether the "father" initiated into Chieftainship was an uncle or his biological father, just as it is unclear whether the Bird Chief who dies in the following story was his father or one of his uncles. Andrew Bird Chief and his relatives would have been given the last name Bird Chief during enrollment because they were descendants or relatives of the Bird Chief who earned the Warrior Chieftainship.

6 The Tsis-tsis-tas, today's Cheyenne located largely in Oklahoma, are a separate group from the Suhtai, located largely today in Montana, the Northern Cheyenne. They almost met in battle in the early 1800s, but heard each other speaking a similar language and decided not to fight. Instead, they talked and began camping together on occasion. At the time of the massacre at Washita, Black Kettle's people, many of whom had been slaughtered at Sand Creek, were few; this is likely why so many of those camping with him were Suhtai. It is also possible that one of his wives might have been Suhtai, therefore encouraging her people to camp with them.

7 Just as with the way fatherhood is counted, a grandfather might be a biological grandfather or a grandfather's brother. The term "grandfather" may also be used as a term of respect, as well, for an older man. Also, adoptive relationships between individuals within the tribe and from outside the tribe were taken at that time as they are now. This makes these terms fairly ambiguous in mainstream interpretation, but the relationships within the culture are all treated with the same degree of seriousness, affection, and respect, making the terms truly interchangeable for a traditional Cheyenne.

8 When the forty-four Chiefs gather, the four principal Chiefs sit at the rear of the tipi in the honor seats. The others, twenty on each side, sit to the south and the north sides.

9 In other words, bad things happen to someone who breaks a vow or an oath. If someone promised to be willing to give up even their wife if someone asked, and then didn't, bad luck would surely follow.

10 Even though the original Bird Chief earned the right to be a Warrior Chief for his male family members during the massacre at Washita by defending his people against Custer's soldiers and laying down his life for his people, his family members weren't initiated until nearly thirty years later. It is possible that they had to wait to save up the things needed for a proper giveaway, hence causing the commentary that follows.

11 Killing another Cheyenne is one of the worse things a Cheyenne can do. Traditionally, murderers, Cheyennes who killed another Cheyenne, were sent away from the tribe for four years. Their skin was believed to turn dark and their breath would begin to stink. Today, as they were expected to in the past, they are supposed to stay away from all ceremonial gatherings for the rest of their lives. Ceremonial people (or medicine people, in common terms) and Cheyenne Chiefs should never smoke or eat with a murderer.

12 They wanted supplies from the fort. Bird Chief here implies that they were "hanging around the fort Indians" and caused their own death.

13 This is the beginning of land being assigned for the reservation. The survivors and other Cheyennes were camped in this area.

NICARAGUA:

"WHAT'S WARD CHURCHILL GOT AGAINST YOU?"

DAVID SEALS

BY 1984 I was a veteran of thirteen years in the criminal underworld of revolutionists, not the least of which, of whom I have not spoken, was my own family on the Arizona and Quebec reservations; a reserve not often exhibited among natives who usually have little else to claim or talk about, for our families and tribes are usually the primary trait or indicator of our nativeness (whether we're Irish or Aymaran), and we feel more tied together by many of our interrelated bonds and "Bands," and are proud of it. I have neglected this cultural credential intentionally, and elusively, for safety reasons, because of the insidious dangers to any of our movements by the covert intelligence operatives who like to hurt the helpless ones. Cowards: they like nothing better than to put us in jail or murder us.

The aim of all our efforts, simply stated, is the breakup of nations back into ethno-units of families and tribes as we were for many thousands of years, before these artificial superstates with imperial monotheisms destroyed the successful, natural balance of power. Indigenous ethnogroups, often tiny in numbers, threaten absurd giants like China and Russia and the USA even more than they threaten each other. One-God ideas like Islam, Christianity, and Judaism are just as absurdly threatened by a small band of Kashmiri rebels, Uighurs in Xingjian, or miserable Misurasatas in Nicaragua infinitely more than they threaten each other through thermonuclear war or global terrorism, and they know it, which is why they are always desperately trying to crush Chechens or Incans ("Sendero Luminoso" in Peru) or Aborigines. We are made of a more truthful, social spirit than they are, in our existence as Celts or Lebu Berbers or Cheyennes.

It was with this sublime and beautiful plan we fought against the otherwise hopeless odds, and which was further proved by the massive COINTEL (COINTEL is shorthand for FBI counterintelligence programs to repress political dissent in the United States) efforts against us by the unreasonable, unspeakable police. Why did they bother if we were only a handful of ethnic separatists? Why should so many FBI people care if two of their own number were killed on June 26, 1975, at Pine Ridge? The number was insignificant. America was in no danger of losing the war—if it was defined in conventional terms. Why should Porfirio Diaz have cared about a few starving *campesionos* in his own 9/11 in 1911 when he had all the money and guns in the world? Why should the mighty Soviet Union, with its thousands of atomic bombs, have worried about a few scruffy mujahideen, Pashtun tribesmen, in the mountains of Afghanistan in the 1980s? Yes, they wanted a geopolitical Al Quaida base closer to the oil fields of the Persian Gulf, but from the first, the quasi-divine Lenin was greatly, disproportionately, concerned about recalcitrant, petulant Kazhaks and Kyrgyzs and Siberian Evenks. Why was Ayatollah Khomeini's Islamist revolution in Iran so important to President Regan that he had to sell them some missiles, in his twisted Hollywood logic, to pay for the anticommunist contras slaughtering a few lousy thirty thousand Indios in Nicaragua? Why did the COINTEL snoops have to infiltrate our pathetic ethnocentric liberation movement when all we were trying to do, in their eyes, was redefine the national boundaries based on our silly-assed tribal quests for self-identity in grassroots alignments? George Orwell had even written a masterpiece of a book, *1984*, in which he made perfect sense of The State's program and purported that Big Brother was a good guy who didn't need to convince us of the error and futility of our petty, personal feelings. Doctor Zhivago was right to care about his love for his family and Russia herself in the embodiment of Lara the goddess (based on Tolstoy's Natasha), but the police apparatchik secretly protected the authors in the guise of their sympathetic KGB half brothers, so that Lenin's dictatorship was really serving the greater, common good against the old conservative, reactionary tsar. Mother Russia was building dams and a proletarian infrastructure that Napoleon would have been proud of—that would transform the wilderness of the steppes into a viable industrial economy—and it would do it without the sociopathic crutch of religion.

"I always wondered how double agents could do it," a newspaper reporter commented while he was interviewing me in 2005 about the publicity around Ward Churchill that was finally starting to expose the poseur, "you know, work against the ideas he was espousing, I mean."

"Good question. I don't know."

Of course this was a mainstream journalist who'd never waded across the Rio Grande with us pathetic, anarchic wetbacks, so he was ignorant, uncomprehending, of the concept of Churchill as a cop. When I said, "I am sorry you don't believe me," he got defensive.

"I didn't say I don't believe you."

He certainly knew there were covert agencies in his government, just as other competent journalists like Bob Woodward of the *Washington Post* knew there was a "veil" of the CIA behind which unscrupulous politicians routinely espoused ideas and policies they didn't care about or believe in. Charlie Brennan, of the daily *Rocky Mountain News* in Denver, certainly understood the possible parameters of the story I was giving him when I compared it to Woodward's and Bernstein's Watergate exposé, but he just couldn't cross that metaphor between belief and knowledge. He didn't have the handy dandy facts his editors wanted to edit the story, because it was too *grande* for the nationalistic outrage they were feeling about Churchill's "treasonous" inflammatory statements (about cheering the 9/11 terrorist hijackers, or at least sneering at the hapless stockbrokers in the WTC leaping from the frying pan into the fire of their own making). The reporter just wanted a convenient angle about how bad this guy Churchill was and how he wasn't really an Indian at all. This reporter couldn't go into the depths of Gorky and Solzhenitsyn's gulag, not here, not now. All they cared about in Colorado was the Denver Broncos and the skiing depths at another kind of Vail and the drainage in acre-feet of the Colorado River irrigating Phoenix and Los Angeles downstream in the mainstream.

He couldn't see my family.

"It feels like a swamp to me," he said in his friendly, businesslike voice on the telephone.

"That's just what it is," I replied in my little kitchen, sitting on the little stool my kids used to stand on to reach the Apple Jacks or pretzels in the cupboards above.

"You mention Wounded Knee and Leonard Peltier, but those were at different times?"

"1973 and '75, yes."

"And you were there?"

"I'm still here. Are you *from* Denver?"

"No, I didn't move here until the mid-80s."

He knew nothing about Indians or the West and wanted me to explain it all to him in a neat package as it related to his stories about Ward Churchill, who was the shibboleth of the hour in the mainstream's craw, in which, in whom, lo, Indian issues began to relate to them for the first time since they escaped the toxic clouds of New York and LA to go white-water rafting on the Colorado and elk hunting in the Sangre de Cristos and golfing in Boulder and Aspen, because Churchill had dared to explain the 9/11 attacks on the anything-but-innocent playbabies. My point about taking another leap forward in the cultural paradigm was way, way, way too much for the reporter to handle, to leap from the establishmentarist outrage and hurt feelings that anyone wouldn't love their pain to denunciation, to angry criticism. To link their ideological pain to something self-inflicted by their own secret police suicide bombers was way beyond comprehension, about like the Trail of Tears as an episode of their history from which they have managed to survive as a nation than as a living pain that the Cherokees are still living. ("We've gone through some terrible times in our history," liberal Supreme Court Justice Stephen Breyer said on C-Span the other day, as if the Trail of Tears was his very own personal pain, "but we've survived them as a nation.") Comfortable, rich judges in Greek marble temples have a blind man's sense of the imbalance of the scales and about the same amount of impartiality. Their ignorance is no excuse for their indifference, and their indifference is no excuse for immorality.

The news reporter sensed my ethical reticence about him, about my own friendly and businesslike tone in our digital, wireless, and dial-tone-less world. "Chronic remorse," Aldous Huxley wrote in *Brave New World*, "as all the moralists are agreed, is a most undesirable sentiment. On no account brood over your wrong-doing."

"To summarize Lurch," (as we called the six-feet five-inch Churchill) I said, "is a complex plot of thirty years of running into the guy, and him in turn backing up and running over us like Joe McCarthy going in reverse. You know what I mean?"

"Reverse McCarthyism?"

"Right-wingers posing as left-wingers, double agents in an Ian Fleming yarn, spies and traitors loyal to nothing. How can a fascist pose as a communist?" I asked him. "You've got to be kidding."

"Yeah, I guess you're right . . . I see the point . . ." he answered.

"What was it Aleksandr Solzhenitsyn said? 'Today the thinking Russian can be free only in jail.' "

"Getting back to AIM and . . ." He wanted me to relate half a century of life into an hour-long phone call for an article he never wrote, with no quotes or acknowledgements from me, that made me feel like a Russian zek photocopying my poems in the underground samizdat in the full glare of Amerikan zeks reversing the prisoner-guard relationship; that is, with all the printing presses and e-books in the world now, less of the truth is being digested because these self-righteous zeks in their sports coats are pretending they aren't being controlled by advertisers spamming all over our faces. The proof is that Lurch is *still* getting away with it. He's getting rich on his tenured professorship

($114,000 a year salary as chairman of the ethnic studies department) and the notoriety of his badly written books, which are probably selling like hell, and he has many speaking engagements now on the free speech circuit at five grand a pop. My point to Charlie that I'm also a writer writers are blacklisting imperviously unimpressed him, about like my rave review of *Sweet Medicine* in the Sunday *New York Times* book review section in 1992.

"Yawn," the media explained.

"To plunge underground," Solzhenitsyn replied to their yawn, "to make it your concern not to win the world's recognition—Heaven forbid!—but on the contrary to shun it: this variant of the writer's lot is peculiarly our own, purely Russian, Russian and Soviet."

"And then he won the Nobel Prize."

"And then he won the Nobel Prize, instant fame and fortune.

So much for the honor of infamy. In the Amerikan samizdat, Charlie, you get your byline every day and your paycheck every week. So how could you possibly understand self-rhetoric?"

"Self-irony in Orwell and Huxley."

"Maybe. The point is, applying the subtle laws of censorship developed in the mutually assured construction of the Cold War—"

"The Cold War?"

"The benefits. The perks. Aleksandr Isaevich was an anticommunist, so he was okay to the West—and I don't mean the cowboy-and-Indian West—just as Leo Tolstoy *wasn't* okay because he believed in freeing the serfs. In that he was a left-winger like Napoleon, who rampaged across Europe pissing off the conservatives because he freed the slaves and serfs and brought the "Enlightenment" of the French Revolution into the darkness of totalitarian England and Prussia. You know that Republicans see the human species cynically, the Democrats naively. Conservatives have a lock on God versus the godless liberals. A double agent is the ultimate cynic, the original man without a country because he has all the faith in the world. He has cowboy delusions of taking control of his life by raising a cattle herd to go on a drive to Texas, while all the time blanking out the real religion of the buffalo that were already there and could have fed everybody free forever—self-sufficient, self-perpetuating food. A COINTEL operative doesn't give a thought to that because he is like John Wayne in *Red River*, shooting people dead and then reading the Good Book over their graves. The buffalo don't exist. They never existed. All that exists is his pain, his strength, his desire to do something powerful in his life."

"Power. All right."

"I don't want to get psychological, but you asked."

"So you think Churchill was an FBI agent?"

"I know he was. He still is. There is no separation of Churchill and State."

The human ape's ability to lie, and the inability to do anything about it, segues into the naiveté of liberals who don't care if progressive speeches have substance behind them, or meat on the bones. Their naiveté is therefore just as cynical as the Rwandan machete-hackers hacking the world in the cyberspace of spoiled computer geeks who think they can find a story with data and who want to go to MIT. *After* they've matured past their youthful, irreverent, rebellious years of smoking marijuana and burning illegal CDs of Snoop Doggy Dawg and Tupac—hip-hop hippies cutting their natty hair and 'getting a job.' Reverse zeks in designer Italian shoes."

"What're you saying?"

"The hips and the hops never cared about God's Plan, they were just hopping to the barley and Bob Marley. The Nation of Islam may be social liberals and religious conservatives but how can they Rap the Rap and still maintain the revolutionary hop, until it all results in the same methamphetamine-ing the family to death!"

"It's a leap in time, from Nicaragua to now."

"Not all that much, dude. A quarter-century ain't much."

I lost Charlie (I said postmodernist literature alone would lose him). I knew the moment I opened my mouth indiscreetly about Intel Ad. Until then I was gonna get published. To back up to the hiatus, postmodernist jive—Tom Wolfe and Norman Mailer instead of Thomas Wolfe and Ernest Hemingway—I had to leave the novel approach to nonfiction and stop lying under cover of my book covers and as an unas-similated chickenshit who needs cover like a COINTEL pig even in the best of times, in war—(Stonewall's brigade lying behind the crest of the hilltop at Manassas, back in the trees)—even at their most courageous when it comes to killing men: hunting Hunter Thompson in the glossy pages of Mick Jagger's and Bob Dylan's *Rolling Stone* with a magazine of metaphorical ammunition, quick clips of wit and words like M16 clips, Richard Pryor verbally on fire. No wonder I couldn't talk to Char-lie in the DMZ, and he couldn't hear me.

John Trudell could hear it back in the old days from his shadows in the basement where he lurked (like I still do) back at the Peltier house, in his strong Midwestern twang. "The earth is a spirit and we are an extension of that spirit. We are spirit. We are power."

The problem is Lurch wasn't there. He was never once anywhere in AIM, although I ran into him almost from the beginning—but never in a good way, not once. John Trudell was there, and oh boy, was he; the native-rapper as the antithesis of the policeman's thesis, and I heard noth-ing but negative reports of Lurch. John may have lurked in the dark but he didn't lurch toward a music career too much. I last saw him last year in the federal courthouse testifying under oath for the state against Arlo Looking Cloud in the Anna Mae Aquash murder case. Arlo said to me, swearing another kind of oath in jail, "John looked like he was coming down from the morning's high."

It was the effect of the monster-spirit in the Hills, the evil archipel-ago of advertisements on billboards popping up like spam right in the middle of an online article of faith, hope, and charity; the ditch weeds so many of the bros were pushing up like daisies. Pushers trying to do pull-ups on the monkey bars, but they couldn't quite make it to that cos-mic buzz Ray Charles needed with some sugar smack, Eric Clapton on lead syringe, and all the others in the other world musicians admired so much, lyrically, interactively fingering the frets on the Nintendo and Play Station-2 controls of ninjas slamming millions of Orcs and Harry Pot-ters passively.

Our kids played together while we shepherded the remnants of the

flock that Lurch left bleeding in the pastures of plenty and that Charlie fertilized with more good chemical insecticides and water impuri-
fiers impolitically infecting our boys and girls. We went to D.C. in the
spring of '83 to lobby for Leonard Peltier, but all we got for it was an
amicus curiae brief that was like our own local contra-Iran catch-22
about illiberal slogans redistributing the wealth among the PACs,
conservationist slogans ignoring treaties nonproliferating "West" (as
Occidentals called it [accidental Orientals, we?]) but not quite east of
Eden. Okay, we lobbied Congress, now what? Peter Matthiessen published a book and Nixon resigned and Reagan got shot and Tripoli was
bombed.

I went to jail.

GRAMMA THUNDERSHIELD proudly watched her three sons Sundancing
in the night in a thunderstorm flashing wild, white bursts of lightning
all around all of us all night, and I proudly sat on the hot, dry dirt watching her in her plastic lawn chair and the central Tree framed in the flashes
behind her, towering with red capes of cheap cloth tied to the branches
by long strings of tobacco ties in offerings to the thunderbirds exploding.

Yeah, I was back in South Dakota, but it could have been in the geographical Central of America, on the battle site where the cops and
Coeur d'Alene warriors named Joe had been wasted in T. S. Eliot's
wasteland like W. C.'s over-footnoted, anal academic speciousness—
"What are the roots that clutch, what branches grow out of this stony
rubbish?" We laid a plot to trap the pigs that night on the same graveyard plot of ground where Lurch and his ilk were working to kill us,
and nothing less.

"The motive ain't hard to see, or far off, Charlie. He wants to kill us."

"That simple?"

"What's simple about that?"

Gramma watched the dance in the storm and I laid myself out as bait
for a warthog like those good boys, good friends of mine, Paul, Willard,
and Dallas Thundershield, pinned to the pine trees of Pine Ridge like
bait, like Prometheus or Jesus John nailed to his rock-tree waiting to

draw in Satan's vulture to eat his liver and thereby grabbing the scavenger even as he picked our meat, and not letting go. They'd been pierced by sharp sticks on their breast muscles. Dallas had already been killed trying to escape from Lompoc Prison in California with Leonard Peltier, set up for the assassination, and his family was dancing in his honor at Oglala like he was there with them. So the least I could do as part of the bloody sacrifice was to sacrifice myself, too, and fast along with them, and go to jail to suck in the traitor in our midst, like Zeus betraying his Father Sky and Mother Earth by nailing Forethought to a holy mountain to be devoured forever by the vultures. It wasn't a pine tree I was pining for, of course, in the course of the cottonwood ceremonies, but it was still a damn good way to grab a passing demon. Fools Crow often said the thunderbirds laid eggs in the holy land at the point where lightning bolts struck, and he (and I) had just such of these stony eggs tied to our medicine bags like umbilical cords of tobacco offerings in the Tree to work oracular miracles. They were light little stones that felt hollow, with crystal chicks ready to hatch inside. They move on their own, I swear to Goddess, when tied to pendulum guts, like baby gods wiggling around inside.

This was only one part of the ceremony that was anything but simple.

Michael Taylor had taken my son's umbilical cord and buried it in an elaborate ceremony. He had first mentioned Lurch's unspeakable name to me back in the seventies as someone in Boulder who was in AIM who would probably want to help me in the production of my play, *Two Men*, at the Steamboat Springs Repertory Theatre, but Mike didn't want to help me. "I know more than you do about Indians," he actually said to me, as we drove around town and he adopted his parent-child attitude. Only I wasn't the child anymore. I was striking out on my own as a parent into the ceremonial twinness of my mystical play that was very much like the Hunkpapa dance of the Standing Rock Thundershields, and he wasn't the authoritative, academic advisor anymore; out of his element outside of the city and neither he nor his fellow educator bothered to drive the hundred miles into my advancing mountains not tied at all to Ski Areas, to see the play. None of his old clique in Denver came to the show, including Kendall, who worked for Marvin Sonofsky a few years later in Washington and introduced me around. "Get in touch with Ward Churchill," they said, and in saying that I was cast out of the clique lorded over by Tough Shit Eliot and his intellectual mafia down at the schoolhouses and the pioneer museums. (Mike had even directed me in Eliot's *Murder in the Cathedral* back in the halcyon optimism of 1971). I didn't play the game and they didn't want an adult-adult footing with an artist like sundancer playing footsy with their hustle. My play got the cover of the "Roundup" arts section of the Sunday *Denver Post* and they went undercover.

"Yawn," academia lectured.

The one and only time I ever spoke to Lurch was in Russell Means' office down the hall where I worked as editor of the *Black Hills Alliance* monthly rag and I said, "Oh, you know Mike Taylor?"

He grinned contemptuously, his long legs splayed out casually and proprietarily behind Rascal (Russell) at his desk like a daddy longlegs. *"Winktay,"* he said

Homosexual.

"Yeah," I tried to smile, although I wouldn't be too sure of that until Mike died of AIDS in 1988, and his anti-Castro Miami Cuban wife confirmed it for me. I didn't want to talk to the guy. I didn't want to ask him why he never returned our phone calls or letters asking for his advice or support of the radical play about hostiles who hated Amerika (and which of course bombed in Party-Ski town), or where he was when we needed help throughout decades on the front lines. He was never there. I never saw him help anyone, nor did I ever hear of one person say he'd helped anyone but himself, helping himself to the banquet in the universities that were instituting ethnic studies departments because so many warriors were dying on the nightly news to bring attention to the Four Horsemen of the Apocalypse. Camp followers rushed in to pick the bones of the fallen heroes, claiming to be fallen angels themselves, I guess. Those theoretical analysts in the children's prisons, indoctrination center, the First Amendment balance of the bodily constitution growing in African-Americanism, relativism versus absolutism, ad nauseam, doctorates doctoring the budgets of the foundations in good fellowships, tenurous, pompous, philosopher-kings. He had nothing to teach me. Uninspired himself, he didn't inspire the songs Dallas Thundershield sang that his Granny heard that night, and which I heard her hearing as she died the next morning.

In the Rapid City emergency room Steve Robideau burned sweetgrass, setting off oxygen alarms of fire, and nurses came running, but we didn't care about their form of caregiving, not technically. We circled the old woman on her cold gurney and Steve laid the eagle feather on her face, praying. "She died happy, with all her sons around her, returning to their traditions. *Wakan Tanka, Tunkasila, pilamaya wastelo.*"

"Hau!"

Uninspiration is the surest sign a writer isn't breathing. Bad words prove a teacher is a liar. Ronald Reagan's worst crime was that he was a bad actor.

Her young grandsons were thinking, "What did we do wrong?" The Sundance had stopped at dawn when the matriarch fell over dead from her lawn chair at my feet, at the foot of the Tree. It was a stunning reversal of the sun as it rose in the heavens after the rain clouds (that never rained) cleared at dawn, promising another scorching day of struggling for your breath. But not to Gramma. It was the finest death I ever saw, and John T. played the drum in his tipi and no one blamed her boys for an inappropriate sacrifice and when I told Leonard about it when he called from Leavenworth he said, *"Lela waken."*

Holy.

Steve's smoke in the ER scared the nurses that we were going to blow up the hospital behind the white curtains in Gramma's cubicle, and I had to go outside and think.

On Columbus Day 1983, we all got busted at the Peltier house (which Leonard would describe it in his book *My Life Is a Sundance*). Gramma was in her grave and the FBI was in its office and I sat in the Pennington County jail like living death, bait, waiting to draw the jackal to me by my scent. Fear and anxiety sent off a stink to the ivory tower, I guess, because Steve called me up not long afterward from the Hereafter and asked, "What's Ward Churchill got against you?"

"What? Nothing that I know of. Why?"

"He is calling up everybody and saying you're a Fed."

"What!"

Steve laughed it off. "Sounds like a provocateur somewhere. Yeah. Bill Wahpepah in San Francisco, me and Jimmy here in Seattle . . ." We'd all skipped town after our lawyers got us out—Steve to Seattle, me to Denver, John to LA,, and Gramma to the Happy Hunting Grounds. My bank-robbing spree and forgery days had finally caught up to me, and for good measure The Sting snatched Steve for child custody on the same day, and John for what I don't know. When I confessed to all but one of my crimes against inhumanity, which I'd used to pay rent and take care of my family, the Feds sniffed the pork chops and took the bait. Not even the lawyer or the local sheriffs knew about the one felonious omission I booby-trapped for the unknown, unwary Sneak, but Lurch did. He referred vaguely to my omission of guilty pleas, that I said to my associates in AIM security, "Only a cop didn't know; and probably a Fed, since the local and state oinkers didn't know anything about it."

"You didn't confess to this one job?"

"No. No one knew about it but me."

"But Ward Churchill knows it?"

"Yeah."

The interrogation lasted all day, at an undisclosed location, and I don't mind telling you I was sweating bloody dingle berries as the hardest asses of the hardcores were grilling me like a pheasant about to be served up for dinner. One ex-Lurp had an especially large bowie knife I'd seen him use with great skill on poached deer up at Yellow Thunder Camp, which was not, unfortunately, at an undisclosed location in the H'e Sapa (Black Hills); unfortunately, I say, because drunken retards liked to snowmobile out there and take potshots at old women and children down below the cliffs, by the tipis next to the creek and the pretty little pond. I mentioned this as the only clue I will provide from these aforementioned classified proceedings appertaining to my banditry. A young warrior we'll call Catch-the-Bear blew away one of those fuck-ers named Clyde Tollefson in a celebrated incident early in the eight-ies, and went to prison. But the redneck went to hell. More than a few of us nodded conditional approval and disapproval of the imbalanced scales of justice, blindly regarding this incident as one of only many such incidents of outlawry, murder, and mayhem, uninvestigated in the fron-tier and unreported.

"Then how would Churchill know it? How could a cop know it?"

"Because he's watching the Peltier house, duh, for criminals or even just frame-ups. Because it was a celebrated, unsolved mystery. It was very well known by one and all, but I, the unlikely perpetrator, the unsus-pected innocent like Philbert in the middle of it all, the fair-haired boy who'd only been in jail a few times for a few minor drunken brawls and reckless driving sprees, was suddenly a prominent author, however self-published, threatening the Ivy Leagues of literature. Murder is nothing, but good writing is serious. Not only am I a helluva good guy . . . well, let's admit it, a jolly good fellow, but I can also write circles around any of those anal-retentive school teachers! Cry Havoc! Get the Organizer, the guy who can type, the culprit with a car! The thief of Baghdad!"

Well, needless to say, they didn't accept any of that bullshit, but they didn't have any evidence to murder me on a one-way dark road to Nowhere either. I skipped by a nose hair over that light fantastic lie to safe havens on the far shore, and AIM security shrugged it off in my bed of roses. I think it was because I was learning how to do my own pri-vate sundances, tiptoeing through the tulips, outsmarting myself like Iktomi the trickster contrary, until my authoritative career was stillborn before it had a chance to breathe on its own and I knew the McCarthyite blacklist forward and backward, reversing my own self-McCarthyism in what successful second-rate hacks have called my "self-destruction" in an Ivy League of its own. Yup. Destitute, a beggar monk, a mooch of the month, I stopped feeling sorry for myself when I was glad to learn the identity of the mastermind who was killing thou-sands of Grammas and Dallas Thundershields in all kinds of Central Americas: putting the pig in the pokey.

During the Somoza era an indigenous organization called Alliance for Progress of Miskutu and Sumu (ALPROMISU) was initiated by a Moravian pastor concerned about commercial opportunities for the Indians. ALPROMISU continued up until the time of the insurrection and was never considered a serious threat by the Somoza regime.

After the victory the people wanted to retain ALPROMISU but the FSLN was concerned that it would not fully cooperate with plans to finally integrate the Atlantic coast with the rest of the country. This caused some friction, but it was finally agreed to change the organization's name to Misurasata (Miskitu, Sumu, Rama, and Sandinistas Together). Steadman Fagoth, a young Miskitu from the Rio Coco area who had studied at the university in Managua, was elected head of Misurasata. The organization operated freely for over a year, growing rapidly in size and influence among the people, and Fagoth became Misurasata's representative on the council of state.

Certain tensions between the Sandinistas and Misurasata emerged, however, stemming from the FSLN's tendency to analyze problems from a class perspective and view ethnic distinctions as being possibly separatist in orientation, and Misurasata's view that certain government programs and policies were assimilationist in character. For example, the government saw education as a priority, and in 1980 the council of state passed a law authorizing bilingual education (English-Spanish and Miskitu-Spanish) in Creole and Miskitu communities. Misurasata expressed concern that the rural school through its methods, program, and language was outside the people's cultural reality and looked to change the children into a type of Mestizo without definition or personality.

—THE NICARAGUA READER (49)

Now, put Lurch in there, as he put himself and his hireling Rascal (Russell Means) in there, and you have the Unstated Department fucking up the incontinent from Yellow Thunder to the Zapatistas today. Take note, Bobby Woodward and LBJ aka Deep Throat:

In his own way—private, personal, idiosyncratic—[CIA Director William] Casey found the roots of espionage idealistic. There was something, in this case the United States, which was worth fighting, even fighting hard and dirty. Winston Churchill had a notepad headed "Action Today." That was what Casey wanted.

The next day, Sunday, Casey was alerted to an Associated Press wire report that disclosed a CIA guerrilla warfare training manual advising the Nicaraguan contras on "selective use of violence" to "neutralize carefully selected and planned targets such as court judges, police and state security officials, etc." By Wednesday the *New York Times* had the story on the front page: "CIA Primer Tells Nicaraguan Rebels How to Kill." It was difficult to avoid the logic that "neutralize" meant "assassination." The ninety-page manual also urged the contras to "kidnap all officials or agents of the Sandinista government. . . ."

"Psychological Operations in Guerrilla Warfare" had been drawn up and given limited distribution to the contras a year earlier, after Casey's trip to Central America. Under "Shock Troops" he read: "These men should be equipped with weapons (knives, razors, chains, clubs, bludgeons) and should march slightly behind the innocent and gullible participants."

The word neutralize appeared under the heading "Selective Use of Violence for Propagandistic Effects." After a Sandinista official had been selected, the manual said, "It is absolutely necessary to gather together the population affected, so that they will be present, take part in the act, and formulate accusations against the oppressor." One sentence had been edited out of some editions of the manual, but unfortunately not all. It said, "If possible, professional criminals will be hired to carry out selective 'jobs.' " This was embarrassingly reminiscent of the CIA's hiring of John Roselli, a member of the Mafia, to assassinate Castro in the early sixties.

Assassination was like no other subject in the American psyche, Casey knew. No subject so challenged the national self-image and moral credibility. Assassination was the Scarlet *A* of American politics. The use of the word neutralize was probably worse than the use of the word assassination because it suggested the shadowy, plausible deniability that was supposed to be the bread and butter of CIA operations. In that concealed world, the agency never said what it meant, anyway.

The nature of guerrilla warfare revealed itself in the manual. The goal was to crush the constituted government.

—BOB WOODARD, *VEIL* (50)

Rascal and Lurch went down to Honduras and sucked up to Reagan's contras, and the Indios got wise to them immediately and shot Russell. He showed me the scar in his gut. They knew how to deal with Elliot Abrams' boys in the under-secretariat at the U.S. State Department, sucking up to suckasses in Washington, D.C., themselves, but to no avail in the swamps of his mind that Charlie talked about, in the jungles of Folger's Coffee and United Fruitcakes where the CIA's Brooklyn Rivera passed himself off to the happy cameras from Bud McFarlane's and Colonel Oliver North's patriotic "Defense Department" like a tribal chairman who looked like Panama's dictator Manuel Noriega pockmarked with a lifetime of lies.

"Yeah, they fucked 'em up," the Marxists told me in Denver. "We have no use for Churchill, either. He just comes in here to our meetings and turns everybody against each other."

Reagan won reelection in a landslide in forty-nine states and Puerto Rico. We all rallied around Leonard Peltier in North Dakota, and went to spend the night under the stars at Yellow Thunder Camp before supporting Dennis Banks in nearby Custer, South Dakota, for his sentencing hearing about the '73 riots. Steve and I were temporarily out of jail, but Dennis and Leonard were not, so we stopped off to see them. Then we went on to Denver in a great caravan of about twenty cars, and about a hundred Warriors stayed in the big house we were renting in the black downtown ghetto of Five Points.

Luella Gansworth (upper left) and friends, posing in front of a backdrop at a Niagara Falls tourist attraction, New York, circa 1943.

Victor Sakiestewa
in band attire,
Tuba City, Arizona,
circa 1960s.

Inside a classroom of Sherman Institute, an Indigenous boarding school in Riverside, California, circa 1907.

An outside view of Sherman
Institute, an Indigenous boarding
school in Riverside, California,
circa 1907.

Dud, Piper, Ivan: Burnham family children, circa 1910.

Sharpnose, Northern Arapaho war leader, 1871.

Little Chief, A.K.A. Dickens Nor, son of Sharpnose, 1881.

Scott Dewey, age 46, Fort Collins, Colorado, 1941.

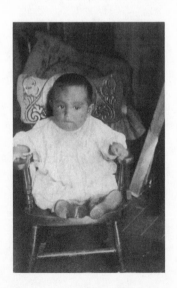

Earl Timothy Burnham, 1914.

Rocky Boy Cree female from the Denny family, Montana, circa 1920. Photo courtesy of the author.

Rocky Boy Cree male from the Denny family, Montana, circa 1920. Photo courtesy of the author.

Joseph Youngman (Cree) and family, East Glacier Park, Montana, circa 1949. Photo courtesy of the author.

Edward Boushie family, Rocky Boy Indian Reservation, Montana, circa 1924. Photo courtesy of the author.

William "Pe-ya-ches" Boushie, wife Susan, and family at Rocky Boy Indian Reservation, Montana, circa 1917. Photo courtesy of the author.

4

MATRIARCHY:

WHERE WERE/ARE THE WOMEN IN ALL OF THIS?

JUST ONE DRESS
TO WALK 800 MILES

PAMELA J. KINGFISHER

HOLOCAUST: *On December 9, 1948, in the shadow of the Nazi Holocaust, the United Nations approved the Convention on the Prevention and Punishment of the Crime of Genocide. This convention establishes genocide" as an international crime, which signatory nations "undertake to prevent and punish." It defines genocide:*

[G]enocide means any of the following acts committed with intent to destroy, in whole or in part, a national, ethnical, racial or religious group, as such:

a. Killing members of the group;

b. Causing serious bodily or mental harm to members of the group;

c. Deliberately inflicting on the group conditions of life calculated to bring about its physical destruction in whole or in part;

d. Imposing measures intended to prevent births within the group;

e. Forcibly transferring children of the group to another group.

THERE ARE arguments concerning our use of the word *holocaust* but, for me, one culture cannot own that word or that experience. I have spent my life pulling the threads of my people into something I could see and understand. My life's path has been to find the women in my family— all those grandmothers I never met. I wanted to discover my history through their stories, to hear their voices. I have found many threads and whispers, mostly in government documents, and I have spent a lot of time in our woods, as well as in historical and sacred sites, imagining what they felt.

The Cherokee holocaust was a long, slow process. From our first visitors in the 1520s, through the wars and land claims, we have stood in the path of a conquering world wanting what was ours. To commemorate other travesties there are shrines and museums, like the Vietnam Veteran's Wall of Names and the Jewish Holocaust Museum's pile of empty shoes, but what do we have to tell the story for the Cherokees and all Native Americans? We have a few native museums, but there is such a political correctness to them—steering away from the more horrific "American" truths—that they make me wonder what would our symbol be? be. It can't just be the four hundred plus names from the Trail of Tears; there were so many more murdered over the centuries, many whose names will never be known.

If I were the curator of the Cherokee Holocaust Museum, what would I choose as the symbol of all those lost souls? Would I choose boxes of pearls and temples of corn from 1542; a chunk of gold from 1826 representing the greedy theft of our lands; would I go back to 1836 and the wagons of dead trailed by women with just one dress to walk 800 miles; or would I jump to 1932 and a small box of braids representing all the Indian boarding schools serving up assimilation when annihilation didn't work? For now, I choose the voices of the women who lived and died throughout our Cherokee Holocaust, and the hope of those who live on as the mothers of our nation today.

Death by Contact: South Carolina, 1545

THEY CAME through like a swarm of vile creatures—just two visits and we were all dying. My aunt was smart enough to flee ahead of them, but I was excited! I was so young and arrogant; I wanted to meet these foreign men. I accepted their pleas for help and met them with dignity, and then I gave them all we had to share. They wanted gold, but they took our pearls and our corn. And me—stealing me like some slave girl. They know I am the niece of the Queen, but they had no fear and no shame. DeSoto was amazed by the amount of corn we had stored in our large temples. His group of 900 men would camp in the surrounding, abandoned villages. We showed them our stores of corn, so they ate as much of it as they could, and then they took the rest for their journey. In this way they endangered our people to starvation as well as the diseases spread by the men and the swine they left behind.

—SENORA OF COFACHIQUI AND XUALAI

1736

MY DAUGHTER, Nanyehi, was born into the worst smallpox outbreak ever to strike our people. It was said to come from a slave ship that unloaded its cargo in Charles Town harbor in March of that year. A few slaves ran away, carrying the disease and eventually coming into a Cherokee middle town with some hunters. Soon everyone was sick and any messengers who had left the town had carried the disease all the way to the capital of Chota and the other overhill towns in Tennessee.

It was a very hot spring and it was dry. The usual rainy season did not come as it should have and the creeks were running thin and slow. Almost everyone was sick that summer. The center of Chota was choked with thick smoke so it was hard to see or breathe. There was a constant fire on the east side where the bodies were being burned. As you walked in on the main path, you could see that every hut had smoke coming from the hot houses and there were fires outside of the houses for cooking and constant water boiling. The few women who were not sick were washing, gardening, and nursing full-time.

People were gripped with a hard fever, chills, sweating, and painful muscles. There was lots of coughing, and the Medicine Priest came and told us to use the hot houses. As the people got sicker, the diarrhea and vomiting began to smell very bad and everything just got worse. Our Medicine Priests threw away their most sacred items, sending word to other Priests from the overhill and middle towns—fearing the disease as a violation of ancient law. The great eagle-wing and redstone pipes that had been handed down from father to son for six generations were destroyed—broken, burned, and buried.[2]

Then in the late summer a new trader arrived in town with two barrels of rum to trade for deer hides. He stayed on the outskirts of town, knowing to stay away from our diseased state. That evening a few men went out to his tent and traded a few hides for the rum and began to drink in their anger and fear. They were so unhappy they just kept drinking. By the third night, some of our bravest warriors were moved to take their spirit in the most tortuous of ways: shooting, stabbing, and even dancing into the fire and burning themselves alive rather than live with the scars and the public shame of their scorn by Creator.[3]

—TAME DOE MOYTOY

Death from War: 1755

MOST OF the smaller coastal tribes have all died or been killed by settlers now. Cherokee warriors had dwindled to about 2,600 when the French and Indian war began to rage. There is another smallpox outbreak and a group of chiefs were murdered in Charleston, South Carolina. That same year Nanyehi's husband, Kingfisher, was killed in one of the last big wars with the Creek Nation. There were very few years between then and our removal in 1836 when we were not at war with someone: the French, the English, the settlers, and other Indians. Nanyehi, a mother of two young children, became Blooded in the Battle of Taliwa after Kingfisher was killed. Her war cries and violent attack inspired the almost defeated warriors to beat the Creek and claim the northern lands in Georgia.[4]

Nanyehi (Nancy Ward, 1736–1824) was one of the younger women to be esteemed as Beloved Woman by our people. She came from a family of Chiefs and Clan Mothers in the White Peace Town of Chota, spending her lifetime in council and negotiations with settlers and their governments. One of the Beloved Woman's duties was to act as peace negotiator, and it is through this role that Nanyehi became known to the settlers as "friendly." Nanyehi learned diplomacy from her uncles and became a shrewd negotiator. She had grown up during a time when continued white settlement on Cherokee lands, in violation of the Royal Proclamation of 1763 in which the British Empire had recognized the rights of native people, created constant tension in Indian-white relations. Nanyehi, like many other Cherokee women, married a white Scots trader, named Bryant Ward, in 1758. This began the dilution of our Indian blood in our children. We didn't know they would change the face of our nation forever, more readily accepting the ways of our white neighbors. Nanyehi's daughter Betsy married a white man who worked for the government, but soldiers eventually murdered her. At the same time, soldiers, including Colonel Montgomery, were busy burning all the Cherokee lower towns, killing many Cherokee. The next spring he destroyed fifteen more towns, including all of our fields, orchards, and granaries. People ran to the hills to live in caves and were forced to kill their horses for food.

Taking the Land with Paper

IN 1775 at Sycamore Shoals Cherokee leaders sold the settlers over 20 million acres for 2,000 pounds of sterling and goods worth 8,000 pounds. This was the biggest corporate real estate transaction in U.S. history. Over 1,200 Cherokees attended the purchase. In July 1781 Nanyehi entered into peace talks with Tennessee politician and soldier John Sevier at the Little Pigeon River in present-day Tennessee:

"You know that women are always looked upon as nothing: but we are your mothers, you are our sons. Our cry is all for peace; let it continue. This peace must last forever. Let your women's sons be ours, our sons be yours. Let your women hear our words."[5]

It would never occur to Nanyehi or other Cherokees that English women did not decide matters of war and peace. At the end of the Revolutionary War lands in Virginia, North and South Carolina, and Georgia were given to the soldiers in military reservations and the states began to form within these ceded Indian lands.

November 28, 1785

THE TREATY of Hopewell was the first treaty negotiation between the Cherokee and the new government of the Untied States. Signed by thirty-six chiefs and attended by a thousand Cherokee people, the meeting began November 18. Here the Cherokee acknowledged the supremacy of the United States for the first time. Nanyehi spoke in council again at the Hopewell Treaty Conference. She was forty-eight years old. This was the first federal and Indian conference, and new boundaries in which the Cherokees could stay were drawn up. Before signing the treaty, Old Tassel requested that the Woman of Chota talk to the commissioners. Nanyehi offered the following:

I am glad there is now peace. I take you by the hand in real friendship. I have a pipe and a little tobacco to give the commissioners to smoke in friendship. I look on you and the red people as my children. Your having determined on peace is most pleasant for me, for I have seen much trouble during the late war. I am old, but I hope yet to bear children who will grow up and people our Nation, as we are now under the protection of Congress and shall have no more disturbances. The talk I have given you is from the young warriors I have raised in my town, as well as myself. They rejoice that we have peace, and hope the chain of friendship will never more be broken.

She gave them two strings of wampum, a pipe, and some tobacco.[6]

June 15, 1789

"AS THE settlements of the whites shall approach near to the Indian boundaries established by the treaties, the game will be diminished, and the lands being valuable to the Indians only as hunting grounds, they will be willing to sell further tracts for smaller consideration," Secretary of War Henry Knox wrote to President George Washington (American State papers, Indian Affairs). Knox follows up with a letter to James Robertson: ". . . the average price paid for Indian lands in various parts of the United States within the past four years does not amount to one cent per acre." In the fall of 1790 President Washington sent 1,900 troops to destroy our towns once again. After intense fighting off and on for one year, only five hundred troops went back. Cherokees knew at that point they were fighting for all of their lands.

Nanyehi was the last woman leader in the original matriarchy. She was our tribe's Beloved Woman and Head Clan Mother when the U.S. government forced us to outlaw the matriarchy in 1808. They *knew* they had to get the land out of the hands of the women. Ironically, Nanyehi applied for reservation land but was refused. Even after her death her children could not get land. So it was that Cherokee women lost their traditional political power and ownership of their lands when the ancient Cherokee law of matrilineage was overturned in 1808. A council of headmen (there is no evidence of women participating) established a national police force to safeguard a person's holdings during life and to give protection to children as heirs to their father's property, and to the widow's share, thereby changing inheritance patterns and officially recognizing the patriarchal family as the norm.

That same year the Women's Council, with Nanyehi at its head, made a statement to the Cherokee people urging them to sell no more land.[7] But the illegally signed cessions were enforced anyway. Between 1721 and 1819, over 90 percent of our traditional territories had been ceded over to the settlers. Thomas Jefferson knew he wanted to create a new Indian Territory within the new Louisiana Purchase, and planned to move them there. Jefferson warned John Adams in a letter that despite the progress of some Indian nations, such as the Cherokee, to adopt representative government, many Native Americans "will relapse into barbarism & misery, lose numbers by war & want, and we shall be obliged to drive them with the beasts of the forest into the Stony mountains." In a previous August 28, 1807, letter to his secretary of war, Henry Dearborn, Jefferson stated, "if ever we are constrained to lift the hatchet against any tribe, we will never lay it down till that tribe is exterminated, or driven beyond the Mississippi."

Illegal Removal

IN 1830 the U.S. government passed the Indian Removal Act. Almost simultaneously, *GOLD* was discovered in our homelands in Georgia, in a mountainous northern county of mostly full-blood families. These people were driven off their lands and never really compensated for neither the land nor the gold. Georgia immediately held lotteries to give the land and mineral rights to white men and stopped all Cherokee government functions. The settlers and soldiers moved in quickly. This event sped up the efforts to take all of the homelands and remove the Cherokee people from the whole region. The Cherokee Nation filed a lawsuit against Georgia in the Supreme Court and won. But when President Jackson heard of it he said, "John Marshall has made his decision; let him enforce it now if he can."

Over the strong protest of more than 15,000 Cherokees, the U.S. Senate ratified the Removal Treaty, or the Treaty of New Echota, on May 23, 1836, by just one vote. Our mixed-blood progeny were responsible for changing the face of Cherokee society, and their descendants negotiated the treaty of cession with the U.S. commissioners. The U.S. government sought out these few who agreed with removal and dealt only with them.

Of the twenty signers at New Echota on December 29, 1835, there were twelve Georgians, four Tennesseans, four Alabamans, no North Carolinians—and very few full-blood Cherokees. A few months later in Washington, D.C., only nine of the original signers and nine new signers came to sign the final treaty. Of the additional nine, seven of them were from Georgia. There was not one major chief who agreed to this sale of all Cherokee territory east of the Mississippi for $5 million and new land in Indian Territory, and there were only three hundred to five hundred Cherokee citizens attending.[8]

Concentration Camps

IN 1836 the U. S. government built 29 removal stockades in four states. In May 1838 over 6,500 federal troops and state regulators were called into service to move the remaining Cherokee. There were still an estimated 8,000 Cherokees in the state of Georgia alone. The soldiers and volunteers swept through the land and took people as they found them. Children ran to the woods and were lost to mothers. Women out visiting were seized and children dragged off with strangers. All of their belongings and money that weren't on their backs were lost. The settlers were standing ready to seize it all for themselves.

Prodded by bayonets, whipped and exposed, our people were herded like cattle to the camps. Most women had only one dress to walk 800 miles, and many were without shoes. They carried babies, trembling with cold and their lips blue—alongside old blind men and ancient women who were completely worn out by the travel—to the stockades, everyone brokenhearted. In two or three days everyone was poor, homeless, and captive.

By that summer three groups had left from Chattanooga, but there were still over 15,000 captives in the camps. There were over five hundred people fenced in small, wet, muddy pens for days—which turned to months for many. At Red Clay—the stockade in Tennessee—there were 8,000 Cherokees, many getting sick. The chief pressed for delay in removal and that the people remove themselves. Delay was granted but the people remained prisoners. The Cherokee refused the money the government offered them, saying they were prisoners, not volunteers. They took only food from the soldiers but no money or clothes, saying the authorities of the nation did not make the treaty, so they would not take the money. The missionaries were even selling our lands, claiming it as theirs, getting paid by the government, and driving off in new buggies.

The volunteers raped the women and girls at night, even at Brainerd, the mission stockade. When the women's camp called out for help, the volunteers cursed them and called them liars. The murders were all committed on Saturday night after much liquor. The night woods were filled with drunks, both white and Cherokee. No one could sleep on Saturday nights. Everyone was sick. At Calhoun, Georgia, from four to ten people died every day in the camps. There were no toilets or privacy and much dysentery and bloody flux. The people had to lie on the bare ground, exposed to rain and wind. One of the doctors was accused by Cherokees of killing Cherokee patients. He admitted he was only a dentist. By July there were twenty deaths a day in the camps. Then the suicides started.

During the roundups at least half of the babies under one year and most of the elders over age sixty were killed, and at least one-quarter of the rest were sick until the move. Reverend Buttrick at Brainerd Mission was reported as saying that this was a very expensive and painful way of killing people. The Cherokees were not removed from Brainerd until September.

In 1838 there were many claims from women for their land, but those women were mostly mixed bloods. There is evidence of Cherokee lands being taken by settlers long before this. Sallie Hughes was a wealthy ferry operator in Georgia. She was paid for her home before removal but lost her lands. A land speculator saw her thriving ferry business so he went down the main road a half mile and built a new ferry there, thus stealing her business and shutting her down. He then claimed all of her lands, saying she had abandoned them.[9]

Nancy Callahan Dollar hid with her family in an Alabama cave for two years during and after the removal. She had to hunt for food at night to feed the family while their father was in Florida. They lost everything on their small farm. Later in life she dressed as a man and drove a supply wagon from Atlanta, Georgia, to Alabama and sold to stores along the way, all the while carrying a rifle and smoking a pipe. She managed to survive to be 108 in Alabama, living with her dog and roosters and many memories of Cherokee life before the white settlers came.[10]

Elizabeth Pack and her mother, Elizabeth (Peggy Shorey) Lowry, who were my relatives, both ran ferries and owned a lot of land and stock in Tennessee. In 1839 they paid attorneys to fight fraudulent claims to their lands in Tennessee. After removal to Oklahoma Elizabeth was paid with one check for $2,569.75 and her mother received $6,820 for her 650 acres on Battle Creek and her house, barns, stock, and ferry. They also received $1,170.00 for another ninety-five acres on Battle Creek with five houses and a corncrib. They rode their horses to the bank and continued to quietly farm their new land in rural Oklahoma.[11]

The Death Marches

DURING A cold November 12, groups of a thousand people began walking west toward this new Indian Territory.

> "Long time we travel on way to new land. People feel bad when they leave Old Nation. Womens cry and make sad wails. Children cry and many men cry ... but they say nothing and just put heads down and keep on go towards West. Many days pass and people die very much."

Sometimes they went two or three days without food. Most of the troops drank and gambled. The soldiers would force the women to drink liquor and then keep them out all night. They would drag the women around by the arm or hair after they were drunk. After making one woman drunk, they tied her dress over her head and left her in the street that way to shame her. They also taught the women to be prostitutes. One old grandmother tried to save her daughter during a rape and had to fight two soldiers who had knives. Babies were born on the side of the roads with the help of the few grandmothers surviving. They would quickly tie the baby on the mother's back in order to catch up with the group. No one was allowed to rest from sickness or childbirth. They were driven on as long as they could walk and then thrown in the wagons. At Lafayette a woman fainted and fell in the road; the soldiers drove over her. When the people died the bodies were left on the side of the road; sometimes family members could bury them if they knew about the death. Wagon masters recorded in their logs how many babies died in their wagons each day. Families would carry sick women on litters after they died until they could bury them. One woman in childbirth fell at the river, so a soldier stabbed her with his bayonet, killing her and her baby.

On the four different Trails of Tears, over 16,000 Cherokees were force-marched. No one can really know how many died during roundup and captivity, but there was an estimate by one missionary, Dr. Butler, that over 4,000 died along the way. That would be about one-fifth of the nation—mostly elders and babies.[12]

Surviving and Thriving: Oklahoma

I HAVE worked hard to trace the women of my blood and land from Tennessee to Teresita, Oklahoma. In 1918 Grandma Louella Kingfisher Duffield died from the swine flu epidemic when my mother, Floy, was two years old. Mose Shankle and his daddy drove their wagon up the holler where my grandma lived, delivering milk and eggs, and they picked up the dead. Mose picked up Grandma Louella and carried her down to the Teresita cemetery and buried her by a cedar tree. In 1932 Grandpa George Duffield was murdered in Long John Holler and buried at Moody, ending the family at Teresita. Uncle Roy moved in with Grandma Duffield and Nancy moved in with Grandpa and Grandma Kingfisher, but Moma wanted to go to school, so she went to Chillocco Indian School, way out past Tulsa. She was twelve years old and watched as "they cut our hair and threw our braids in a big box." She worked in the kitchen, laundry, and the infirmary. This work prepared her to run a home but not the many businesses she later bought and operated.

By 2004 I could touch those precious papers deeding land to my grandmother Louella. It was time to plant some corn and bloodroot. It was time to prepare for my granddaughter. I remember . . . it was Wednesday, a hot July day in northeast Oklahoma. My people pray by "going to the water," so I drove down to the river to give thanks. Along the way, I found one more turtle shell in the road, for my shakers, which I wear when I dance at Cherokee ceremonies handed down for generations. Then I was ready. It was a momentous event for me. This was the end of a thirty-year odyssey of loving this land, waiting for this original allotment of 160 acres to pass on to my name, land that has never been listed in the name of a man, never been bought or sold by a white man.

To an outsider, that day in the Oklahoma Cherokee County Courthouse would have seemed ho-hum. The lady at the county register's office wrote the transaction in a huge book and asked me for $19. She gave me a receipt and looked at me as if to say, "Well, what are you waiting for? Get out of here." I landed on the sidewalk in two minutes, stunned and giddy. This was one of the last original Cherokee allotment sections! Still in one piece and still in the hands of the same family! I wanted to shout and cry and hug someone. I wanted to dance around crazy and yell to the whole town. But it was just another small act at the courthouse. One more piece of land moved around between names.

I got in my truck and headed north in a state of elation and heightened awareness. I drove the twenty miles to the gate leading into our land, realizing I had driven this road to my work at the hospital for so many years but that it all felt different now. I got out and walked to the creek bed, dropping my clothes along the way, thinking of those Cherokee women of long ago with just one dress to walk 800 miles. Saying a prayer for them, I realized this creek, where ceremonies had been performed for generations, was even more sacred now. I dove straight into the deepest pool of water, shocking my breath and body with the icy waters.

This is what it's all about. Water and land, in the hands of women, being taken care of by women. And now it is my turn, my responsibility to protect this land in the name of all the Kingfisher women, all the women of my DNA. That day signaled a personal revival of the matriarchy for me; it's a continuum of Cherokee women as keepers of the land. It's also the spirits of my mother and grandmothers all touching me. This land was always in the hands of women. We created corn and we knew how to feed our people. We maintained the town's fields and ensured nurturing and health of our people. That is still our role today; we have survived and our population is growing.

So the holocaust of invasion, colonialism, annihilation, assimilation, and absorption put upon us has not been so effective. America's shameful past will be known and healed, because we are alive, because our children are learning the Cherokee language, and because our women are keeping the land. *Wado.*

1 Garcilaso de la Vega, *The Florida of the Inca,* rev. ed. (1723, repr., University of Texas Press, translated 1951).

2 James Mooney, *Myths of the Cherokees and Sacred Formulas of the Cherokees* (Nashville, TN, 1982).

3 David E. Stannard, "Disease and Infertility: A New Look at the Demographic Collapse of Native Populations in the Wake of Western Contact." *Journal of American Studies,* 24 (1990), pp. 3, 325–350.

4 Pat Alderman, *Nancy Ward, Cherokee Chieftainess* (Johnson City, TN: Overmountain Press, 1978).

5 Charles J. Kappler, "Indian Treaties, Indian Affairs: Laws and Treaties," Senate Document No. 319, Washington, D.C., US Printing Office, 1904.

6 John Haywood *The Civil and Political History of Tennessee from the Earliest Settlement up to the Year 1796* (Knoxville, TN).

7 Marion L. Starkey, "The Cherokee Nation," New York, 1946, pp. 6,7. The message from the delegation of women, dated June 30, 1818, is preserved in the Papers of the American Board of Commissioners for Foreign Missions, Houghton Library, Harvard University, Cambridge, MA.

8 Don Shadburn, *Cherokee Planters in Georgia 1832–1838* (Cumming, GA, 1989).

9 Ibid.

10 Marjorie Ferguson, *The Legend of Granny Dollar* (Fort Payne, AL, 1992).

11 Maybelle Chase, "1842 Cherokee Claims," Flint District, vol. 1, 1991.

12 *The Journal of Rev. Daniel S. Butrick, Cherokee Removal* (Park Hill, OK, 1998).

FIRE

LINDA HOGAN

Hidden Fire

IN A Cree story Wolverine, an animal known for its intelligence and cunning, tells the other animals to hide their inner fires by closing their eyes, so that the jealous humans will be unable to find and kill them. The humans, it seems, envy the animals their grace and power, their radiance and life. The animals have a grace we believe we humans lack.

The closing of the eyes may have saved the animals from the people but it also meant that they could not see; so were they safe? Perhaps Wolverine tricked them. Perhaps he was hungry that day. I do not know the ending of this story. But I do know that for us, to open our eyes, to see with our inner fire and light, is what saves us. Even if it makes us vulnerable. Opening the eyes is the job of storytellers, witnesses, and the keepers of accounts. The stories we know and tell are reservoirs of light and fire that brighten and illuminate the darkness of human night, the unseen. They throw down a certain slant of light across the floor each morning and they throw down, also, its shadow.

Because of this shadow, I never know if I should let our lives sit in silence, undisturbed, disappearing, or if I should shake them, search them,

and speak them so they are not lost, our lives not passing without meaning or without telling. Nor do I know which of the stories of the past are
true, but there are photographs in my father's family that tell a story.

In those of my father's family there are men clowning around with
pistols, looking dangerous and careless, wild men in fur chaps, Stetson
hats sometimes on their heads, spurs on their boots. They were reckless young men. In one photograph, my grandfather, the man I had only
known in his poverty, looks dapper in a greatcoat, walking through the
streets of Ardmore, Oklahoma, like a businessman, my uncle and father
hurrying along at his side, all of them looking like they had a good handle on the world. My grandfather was the same man who, years later,
would hitch a ride to the streets of Ardmore to drink with the other
Indian men, to sleep there some nights on the street. As a child I feared
him. As a woman I think I understand him and how he fell into that
world and that life.

Indian Territory

MY LOVED one told me that, almost asleep one night in that twilight state
where we hover between sleep and waking, I said, "There are eight people in this bed." It's true. Many fates dwell inside a single human being.
We sleep with all those whose blood or lives we share, inheriting their
histories.

Like everyone, I fell into the fire of all those other lives—my mother's,
my father's, my grandmother's, my husband's, even those of the children
I adopted to love and raise. In this I became the meeting place of forces
not my own. I must have known that there is something about the com-
mingling of lives and spirits in all their randomness that makes for a spark
of life that, like fire, creates change.

ONE YEAR my father and I went back to our homeland in Oklahoma.
We were together in search of our world, our histories. We wanted to
visit with some of the Chickasaw elders. As individuals and as tribal

people my father and I were searching for ourselves. The American Indian Movement had gathered strength, and we, in turn were strengthened by it. My father's own transformation was great, as if he'd held inside himself generations of anger and hurt that now found expression. At the time, we both received *Akwesasne Notes*, a native newspaper in which we read about the occupation at Wounded Knee and the people who were there in the early 1970s surrounded by the United States military, the FBI, and the nontraditional members of the tribe who had the cooperation of the federal government on their behalf.

That we had not, as Indian people, given up was a force of our returning strength. We still held the spark of ourselves, our histories, our future. Up until then, for many of us, it was as if we were beneath something, in a darkness sometimes lacking hope. The poverty rate was high. Large numbers of native women had been forcibly "sterilized," especially in Oklahoma and South Dakota, and children were lost from communities. A nurse at the Indian Health Service hospital at Pine Ridge said that, one year, all the infant children were taken from their mothers.

At the time of the occupation I was myself just beginning a life, just waking up. I'd been married, divorced, gone to adult education to learn to read better, and enrolled in school with the unfocused hope that I would one day be able to offer something to my own people.

AND SO we went, my father and I, on a journey to Oklahoma, the place of my interior. It was not my birthplace, but it was my home, the place of my heart, my inner world, the place where I lived before I was born. Oklahoma was the place that shaped me with its loving people, beauty, and heat. It was where, always, I encountered kindness.

When we arrived, I was struck as always by the silence and stillness of our homeland. I have always felt it—a physical line crossed where suddenly everything is changed, as if I'm an animal recognizing territory. The air is heavier than in other places, containing the sensuous stillness of land, the rich, heavy odor of nut trees, the heat and the way it rises from the fields nearby. There were fireflies and the rich smell of red earth and leaf mold. It is an ancient place, with plant fossils along the ground and mountains so old they are underground, covered by what came later—depression sandstorms, washes of clay.

Along with many other tribal people, we were just beginning to rest in our pasts, to look toward them as something most significant. Only now was it safe to return to the interrupted journeys our ancestors began, to look history in the newly opened eye.

Before then, like the animals whose eyes Wolverine closed, we could not see. Now we remembered. We came from the mound builders, the brilliant calculators of time who stretched their hands in reverence toward the new moon and who touched the trunks and leaves of trees—their old friends—with grief to say farewell when the were removed along the Trail of Tears to Oklahoma, some in wagons, some walking. My ancestors were followed by thieves and the military and they would later be charged $720,000 by the United States for their own removal from their own homeland. The Chickasaws owed money for food and supplies that never arrived to those who coldly forced us away. Unable to leave their pets, they traveled with cats and dogs and the famous Chickasaw ponies that were a special breed. These beloved horses were stolen by thieves who followed along as the people walked west and were bred with others, became lost, or so they say, in the recorded history of horses.

As an adult, going back to school, I remember finding a reference by Faulkner. He commented on a Chickasaw woman, just before removal, looking like royalty, he thought, in her purple turban. Even though we were the tribe that had never lost a battle, by the end of the removal we seemed lost.

We are from the Colbert family, of mixed blood, some of us in history good people, but not all. My grandmother, and maybe my grandfather, was the descendant of tribal leader Winchester Colbert. She was born in 1883 and lived through times that were filled with injustice and horror; the 1890 Massacre at Wounded Knee had its roots in the fear of a very young federal government agent assigned to watch over an ancient, intelligent people who were despairing at the sharp edge of history. They called him Young Man Afraid of His Indians. It was the time of deliberate policies of starvation and wars, with the multiple losses of people, animals, and land. The buffalo bones were heaped up by then, mighty animals killed only to subtract life from the world, an act none of us have ever comprehended, even yet. Grasslands were set on fire to drive Indian people from their lands, and by then the waters were already polluted by pathogens from Europeans and their animals, pigs, and cattle. The new diseases killed the majority of tribal nations and those who survived were forced to fight or move away. By then, too, wagons had eroded enormous ruts into the land. And last there was the banning of Indian religions, religions that had kept the world in balance with song, prayer, and reverence.

THE STORIES of suffering that befell other tribes were continent-wide and traveled into Oklahoma. The United States government planned to place all Indians inside this seemingly insignificant place they named Indian Territory and then build a wall around it.

It was a dangerous thing to be Indian. My grandparents witnessed what some called the end of our nations. They survived through treaty-breaking times, gunpowder times, and finally the whirling sands of a deforested Oklahoma where even their trees were stolen by white men looking to sell hardwood for gunstocks. My father tells about leaving for the day, taking the wagon into town, and returning to find their trees gone. It was a time when it seemed that even hope itself was killed. And so hiding our light became a daily necessity. Survival depended on it.

MY FATHER and I, on our journey to Indian Territory, visited a man named Pud Bean. Like everyone else in the county, he was nicknamed by my grandfather. We sat on his porch in Mannsville, Oklahoma, and listened to him and the insects. He had recognized my father and he talked to us about my great-grandfather. Although a recent article had said my great-grandfather, Granville Walker Young, was a Canadian métis, he was listed on the Chickasaw rolls as white. My father seemed to already know the story of his grandfather, but no one had ever stated it so forthrightly as this elderly man. Granville Walker Young was ambitious and dangerous. He was enrolled as a white intermarried Chickasaw citizen. As it turned out, he was a thief, or so they say, of Indian lands, and according to some a hirer of killers. Yet he has always been upheld by history as a good man, held up just enough to throw us into doubt. Perched on the edge, we can't say for sure which side he fell into, the good man written about in history books or the man who had a cold streak. Or, as happens in so many histories and stories, as is frightening about our species, he might have been a combination of the two.

AT THIS same time, my mother's grandfather wrote in his journal about killing buffalo and how he saw Indians and they seemed peaceful. When I think of these parallel worlds, it's with the realization that I contain blood of both victim and victimizer. But I also hold that there are forces deeper than blood. It is to these that I look, to the roots of tradition and their growth from age-old human integrity and knowledge of the world.

MY GRANDMOTHER and her sisters were disowned by G. W., as he is still called. It is said that he had wanted them to marry white men, but they chose Chickasaws. My grandfather and his brother-in-law, an attorney, spent a great deal of time and most of their money contesting the will. G. W. had left all of his money to his son. A few years ago, G. W.'s grandson, a man I knew only from our family reunions, was killed, along with his wife, by their own child. The son drove home in his truck one Sunday morning and met them as they returned from church and shot them outside their home. And it was to everyone's grief, for they were good people with a rare kindness. But also with a son who had also inherited the blood of two sides.

Bloomfield Academy: Grandmother

Like the lives of all the other Chickasaw girls, my grandmother's life was influenced in part by missionaries in Indian Territory. Their purpose was to Americanize the girls. She and her sisters went to the Bloomfield Academy, a Chickasaw girls' school. I once found her graduation exercises in *The Chronicles of Oklahoma*. She played a piano solo at commencement. Her sister recited "The Lotus-Eaters," by Tennyson. The Reverend Burris, an Indian orator, delivered the invocation in Chickasaw. It was a mixture of traditions and worlds. The girls were educated as if they were white, but leaving school upon graduation they returned to their Indian world. They ended up, like most other Chickasaws in that time, in rural poverty, without water, lights, or plumbing. They lived at this burned place where I stood, where my grandmother once lived, looking out on the man-made pond where cattle drank. As a girl, I had fished here and caught a turtle larger than the circle my arms could make.

MY GRANDMOTHER had been the light of all our lives. She was a quiet, tender woman. I loved and was loved by her. I admired her and longed to become like her, wanting all my life to become a grandmother. It was my goal. Even as a young girl I thought ahead to my later years when I would cook for grandchildren, create stacks of toast and platters of eggs like the ones she had served to all us cousins, uncles, and aunts in the mornings.

Like most of the Chickasaw women, she was an active churchgoer, practicing the outward shape of Christianity while retaining, I believe, the depth of Indian tradition, a reverence for life, a way of being in the world, a certain calm and clarity. Yet the double knot of America was tied about her and inescapable. She lived outside the confines of the white world within an older order, holding the fragments of an Indian way. She was the face of survival, the face of history and spirit in a place where even women were forced to take up arms to protect themselves. At death, she made a statement of resistance, a rejection of the American ways. Her gravestone reads, as does my grandfather's, "Born and Died in Berwyn Indian Territory."

ACCORDING TO my father, his mother was never sick a day in her life. Her only visit to the hospital was when she was burned by hot grease, which spilled onto her stomach and legs from a kettle on the stove. Now, with pain of my own, I sometimes think of her suffering, the burning of skin, the most painful of injuries, the tissue of flesh growing over, and I grieve for her pain, all of it, the history and grief of the times.

My grandmother was the woman who spoke to the turtles and they listened, the woman who wore aprons and cleaned fish. She was the woman with never-cut hair, and I loved to rise up early in the mornings and help her brush it. She was patient with all of us running around her legs and feet. She used lye and ash to turn corn into white, tender hominy, cooking *pashofa*, a Chickasaw dish, in a large black kettle on the woodstove she still used into the 1960s. There were Oklahoma nights full of my remembered fears, wet heavy air, and fireflies, the smell of pecan trees, a land with tarantulas and rattlesnakes, the numerous and silencing sounds of gunshots in the night. The lightning flashes that revealed my grandpa coming home, sometimes drunk. This must be a widely told experience or story, for more than one of my friends tells the same story about her grandfather. Including the part about how his horse stood by waiting for him to come around the next morning.

She was a woman, forced into English, who used snuff and healed her children with herbs, home remedies, and the sometimes help of a black Chickasaw freedwoman named Aunt Rachel, a root-worker who lived nearby and came from the slaves once held by upper-class Chickasaws before the Trail of Tears.

When I was young, in truth, I knew almost nothing of her except that she was loving and kind. Somehow that was always enough. It was nearly all I would need in my life.

ON OUR trip to Indian Territory my father and I stood near my grandmother's house, which was now burned down. We stood beneath the remembered tree and looked at the ruins. There were broken dishes I remembered, lying on the ground alongside other discarded, burned, or otherwise broken goods. An instant iced tea jar still contained brown crystals of tea. I picked up a chip from one of the dishes and put it in my pocket along with the plant fossils from the "tanque," our name for the man-made waterhole. I carried away mementos not only for the memory and connection but also as if these things would prove my life, my tribe, my worth.

This is the sometimes dilemma of the mixed-blood person. We come from people who lived in a time when dances, with their central fire, were outlawed, gatherings suspect, languages forbidden. But, however broken or burned to the ground they were, many of us have risen out of the forbidden ways. It is the same way a frog wakes up beneath mud, smells water, feels rain, and digs out of the safe depths toward life and daylight, its internal fire still burning, its heart moving. I am one of the children who lived inside my grandmother and was carried, cell, gene, and spirit, within mourners along the Trail of Tears.

As my father and I stood there I saw the world with my grandmother's eyes. Oklahoma as a word means red earth, red people. It is a term of connection. I always feel a certain love coming from the land itself, and that day I did; my grandmother's world remembered us. My father and I listened to the deep sounds of bullfrogs behind us, and I recalled the still Oklahoma nights of fireflies and bullfrogs, locusts and cicadas, and running through the darkness with my cousins.

I remembered then reading a story about a man who tried to warm himself in the light of fireflies; he succeeded, I believe, because it was beauty that warmed him, not fire.

AS WE stood at the old house, my father's face looked sad with memories. I looked at him a long time, seeing it all there. This world, for my father, was superimposed on his life and on a better world. And it showed on his face. Beneath his cowboy hat, suddenly he was tired, almost gray. I had the good fortune to be young; I did not possess the memories that inhabited my father. While I was sad for what was lost, because it was so much, I also felt a calm happiness that here, even in a burned place, at least a part of my life was held and remained. I had this, if little else, I told myself. It was important to me, a child born for relationship, one that would spend her life addressing the past and how it had become the present blaze of life all around her, how it could move into the future. This place was my foundation, even burned, even ash. Yet I grew up from it and came as if from mystery to honor, love, and care for all the alive earth.

LIKE MOST other Chickasaws we became landless. We lost nearly everything. The Ardmore airpark was now on our land. My father told me what the old land had looked like, and from within myself, standing there with him in the heat and the smell of black walnut trees, I could see it beneath the airport. I could, with my mind's world, my open eyes, see what had been beautiful. Creek. Pasture. Pond. Valley.

After the Depression and dust bowl, after frauds and con men living off other people's misfortunes, the changes in his world had been unbearable for my grandfather. He was the son of a white banker and a Chickasaw woman. He'd been a rancher. He went to school at Harley Institute, a Chickasaw Choctaw boarding school. He was intelligent at algebra and years later, after my father brought him a battery-powered radio—for even in the sixties they had no electricity—he knows every baseball player, who they played for, and their averages. An odd thing, I thought, for a man who had been so hurt by his losses.

Impoverished, the young men in those photos with guns and chaps and Stetsons, my uncles and father, went into the CCC and traveled the country. They received a small payment and the government sent the rest of their checks home to their mother. My father worked on man-made Lake Murray outside of Ardmore, Oklahoma. He went on to learn stonemasonry and then the art of grafting trees, so that an apple tree would give birth to peaches, a peach tree would grow plums.

BY THE time of this visit with my father to Oklahoma I had adopted my two daughters. The older was ten, almost eleven, when we adopted her. The younger was five. They shared the same birth mother. Adoption, like fire, was a life-changing event. It was not as easy as being a grafted tree. My father had learned to create trees that bore two kinds of fruit and would heal two together into one, and this is what I believed adoption would be, old trees bound with newly grafted limbs, bearing blossoms and fruits. With humans, it isn't as easy as trees.

After they moved in, and their story unfolded, I thought it was more than Wolverine who'd stolen my daughters' fire. Sometimes a person closes their eyes to keep fire in, unstolen. But it doesn't always work. The girls, too, had interior worlds inherited from others, a history dwelling inside them. Sometimes the thieves of fire are the closest people to you. You live in their house. It is by proximity, after all, that fire burns. And pain, in all its incarnations, physical, emotional, historical, is like fire a thief who changes lives and people irrevocably, a verb disguised as a noun.

With my own mother, she and I come from vastly different times and cultures. While we were related by blood, my heart came from some other place, from a tie to this continent. In her time as a younger mother she mended underwear and darned socks, ironed and kept the house tidy. She had a mother's duties. She was disappointed in the adoption of my daughters. While I considered it a gain, a hoped-for tripling of love, she thought of it as the loss of a bloodline. I saw it as the strengthening of tribes, the future of our Indian children, back in their right place, open-eyed and knowing who they are. But the people of my mother's generation think differently from ours.

I was a proud mother, but she wanted our "own," the word that stands for possession, the small word with big meanings that had already damaged my daughters. Over time, though, worlds and people change. She has grown now, in all these years, beyond those words into a kind of love and a joy in her great-grandchildren.

I ONCE believed that love was a steady glow that would light the house of life. The hearts of children would open. So would the hearts of parents. I had room for love, so much to give, as if it is an *eternal* fire, like the ones my ancestors carried over the Trail Where People Cried. And always, when confronted with smallness, what I wanted to have count was my own capacity to love. Like my father, I had survived history, survived even myself. All of it. History. Mental hospitals. Alcohol. An American education. I look back now on the history of a life; mine was one of a drunken young woman who once went so far as to drink a bottle of peroxide and a bottle of cough syrup together. Now it seems that young woman is gone, transformed, as by the fire of life.

One day not long ago, at my parents' house as I cleaned my grand-daughter's face, my mother looked at me and said, "You love them all, don't you?"

And I said, "Yes, every last life." Every last thing. Every last creature.

AS TIME has passed, things in me have been burned away and I see my life more clearly, more cleanly, than I had ever seen it before. And in that vision of my past, my history, my body, I also saw there was something inside me that had survived, and not merely survived but had done so whole and nearly intact. The hurt child raises itself and doesn't just walk but swims and flies. This child sees that life may never be easy but that it may be beautiful, as the story of the man who warmed himself by the beauty of the fireflies.

Fire, like pain, like love, is a power we do not know. Yet from the ashes of each, something will grow. No one knows if it will be something beautiful and strong. But in our lives it is sometimes the broken vessel, as writer Andre Dubus calls it, that spills light.

ONE WOMAN CAN MAKE A GRAND DIFFERENCE

LELA NORTHCROSS WAKELY

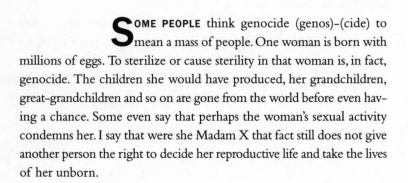

SOME PEOPLE think genocide (genos)-(cide) to mean a mass of people. One woman is born with millions of eggs. To sterilize or cause sterility in that woman is, in fact, genocide. The children she would have produced, her grandchildren, great-grandchildren and so on are gone from the world before even having a chance. Some even say that perhaps the woman's sexual activity condemns her. I say that were she Madam X that fact still does not give another person the right to decide her reproductive life and take the lives of her unborn.

GOOD GENES
Prison walls enclose the damned
Evildoers judged unfit to live among us good folks

Razor wire cuts the fine line of
right from wrong, good from bad

Some say damned from the start, bad blood
Born criminals, better not to have been born at all

So the unborn are judged, never given a chance
Lines drawn, cut and never to be crossed

Sowed in secret, evil deeds go undetected where razor
Wire makes an effective prison of the dysgenic uterus

Inmates damned from the start, never live to tell their side of the story
Justifiable genocide to genetically alter a bad woman's birthright

Who decides?
Who defines good from bad?

To the Dr.: she was bad for being unwed, bad for being poor
bad for being Indian

The Pt.: he is bad for showing his hate, bad for using his knowledge
to try to conquer her power

They say knowledge is power, pen mightier than the sword
I know what was done, I know why he did it, I know what I can do

Write Tell
Confront Heal

I was removed from my family when I was fifteen and sent briefly to foster care, then to state-run facilities. I didn't know the meaning of the word *abuse* until I was sent to the diagnostic and evaluation center. I didn't know the meaning of the word *rape* until I was placed in state-run homes.

At twenty years of age I was just a young girl. I didn't know what was wrong with me. I can ignore pain up to a point but, after I fainted for the first time in my life, friends took me to the emergency room of a small-town hospital. I was asked if I was pregnant.

I had no idea that I was, or that it was an entopic pregnancy about six weeks along that was causing internal bleeding and the pain I had been ignoring.

I was admitted and taken to a room where I continued to bleed internally. A doctor on call came to examine me. I was in the beginning stages of shock from loss of blood. This doctor took the time to tell me what he thought of me. He told me I wasn't fit for decent society. He told me I was just like all those other unwed girls who have children and go on welfare to leech off the good folks who work for a living. He told me I didn't deserve to have children. He said he wasn't going to lie for me and was disgusted to have to tell my parents of my shameful diagnosis. He said he would take care of me only because of the oath he had taken as a doctor. "But I'll take care of you. I'll take care of you."

I'll take care of you were the last words I heard him speak to me before my operation.

Six years later and in a different town with different doctors, I had surgery to determine the cause of my infertility. The assisting surgeon later came to talk with my husband and me about the results. She apologized for the great length of time it had taken and explained, "There was all that wire we had to remove." I was never told wire had been used to suture my reproductive system or even my abdomen. The doctor just passed it off by saying, "Well, some doctors tried wire as suture material back then. Don't worry about it."

I dismissed it from my mind, but the following years of heartbreaking disappointment left me wondering: Why?

In 1993, after my seventh and last miscarriage, I started researching on my own. In the university medical library are documents that show just what can happen if wire is used as suture material in the reproductive system. Crying, shaking, at last I found the reason why.

The continued pain I complained of, the low-grade fever, and the slightly elevated white-cell count after my first surgery now made perfect sense: my body was rejecting all that wire that was in me, poisoning my body, poisoning my reproductive system. The doctor kept telling me to "Ignore it. It will go away." Months later, I was admitted with a massive pelvic infection and finally treated with antibiotics by a different doctor.

Wire sutures run as a continuous coil, winding around and around, very much like the razor wire used on top of prison walls. Even after it is removed the wire leaves scars that interfere with an embryo implanting properly. At least prison inmates have their day in court. My unborn were never given a chance to speak for themselves, just sentenced to die without trial, without just cause, without justice. Who would be a jury of their peers? Or of mine? My birthright to have children was taken from me and can never be replaced.

Although it may make no difference to the first doctor, I'd just like to tell him that I have never been on welfare, that I wouldn't change my ethnic identity even if I could, and that being poor is less about how much money you have in your pocket and more about how much love you have in your heart.

WINYAN WAKAN (SACRED WOMAN)

MARY BLACK BONNET

WHEN THOSE around you treat you as sacred you cannot see yourself as anything but. In traditional Lakota culture, a *wincincala* (girl) was seen as sacred. When she was born, her umbilical cord was placed in a beaded turtle pouch, usually made by the mother or aunt, and hung over the cradleboard to provide health and help through her young years. As she grew in body and spirit those around her incorporated her sacredness into her everyday life; it was never a question, rather a fact. When she had her first moon, an *isanti*, the sacred puberty ceremony would be held for her. This ceremony marked the close of her childhood and her entrance into adulthood. She would now be taught the responsibility of the immense power she held. She was no longer allowed to play with her male cousins and her interactions with her father, brothers, and uncles changed and became ones of respectful distance. She would learn that her moon gift was so powerful she must not touch food, be around medicine or go visiting other people in case they were taking medicine. She was told to use this time to take care of and nourish herself, physically, mentally, and spiritually. Her moon time was powerful and beautiful, something she should embrace fully with gratitude.

How the Lakota people raised their daughters was a way of life. *Winc-incala ki* (girls) grew up with the belief instilled in them that they were sacred. As a result, they internalized this belief and it affected the way they interacted with the world. Once grown, they became strong, confident members of the tribe. But the world changed, and for good or bad the Lakota women changed with it.

After Europeans invaded our lands Lakota children were forcibly removed from their families to boarding schools, where they were stripped of anything remotely Indian. While not all boarding schools were bad, they all stole a vital part of Lakota children and their formative years. When the female children returned from these schools they were armed with skills that would get them far in the white world, but the important lessons about how to be a *winyan wakan* (sacred woman) were foreign. Unfortunately, this also included how to be a Lakota parent.

In a normal traditional setting, Lakota *wincinkala ki* would have experienced loving parenting from their mothers, aunts, and grandmas. They would have been raised in a home where there was no corporal punishment. In Lakota society, an adult needed only to look at children to let them know they needed to change their behavior. One could see this all the time when *uncis* (grandmothers) were tending to their *tako-jas* (grandchildren). There was no physical punishment for naughty Lakota children, as Lakota people believed that children should live life on life's terms, thus they learned by living. A mother would warn her child not to do something and if the child did not listen, he or she would experience the consequences firsthand, a lesson to be kept for life. But in boarding schools, young Lakota *wincinkala ki* saw and experienced corporal punishment. When they became parents, they had only their experiences from which to draw. So, rather than coming from a place of love and gentleness when correcting their children, they came from a place of anger and bodily punishment. Rather than guide their children, they began trying to control them, like the way they were raised and corrected when they were in the boarding schools. Children learn what they live, and as adults the cycle continues.

Lakota women have been polarized throughout history. They were either beautiful brown-skinned, long-haired princesses who made nice accessories to the milk-white-skinned men by their sides, or they were savages who deserved nothing better than to be treated less than human and called such degrading names as "squaw." Abuse was never a Lakota tradition. While I could spend time tracing the roots of how violence was forced upon our culture, I would rather educate by sharing.

The state of our Lakota women today makes me ill. There are many strong Lakota women, of course, but there are many more cowering under the rule of men (Indian and non) who hit them, degrade them, or rape them. I was not always a strong Lakota woman. I have had my share of beatings—physical, mental, and emotional—both by my white adoptive father and by teenage boyfriends. For me, this was a family tradition. I grew up watching my mother being mentally and emotionally abused and seeing my sister come home from her boyfriend's house beaten and bloody. But nothing was ever said about how to change this; nothing was ever said about how wrong this was. So when I started dating I didn't realize that having men treat me as a possession and over-power me so they could have their way with my body was not how life was supposed to be. How sad. How disgusting.

It is because of these experiences that I know why my Lakota women friends stay in the muddy quagmire of abusive, empty relationships. But knowing why doesn't make it OK. It still pisses me off and I still spend time trying to tell them that life can be different. But if someone had tried to convince me that I had a choice when I was in my teen years and early twenties, would I have believed it? Probably not. When you have been beaten down and isolated so much that you don't care how you get love and attention as long as you get it, you are willing to put up with anything.

I know a woman who is beautiful, smart and innovative, and could have the world if she put her mind to it. But she is trapped in a horrible relationship where there is no respect and no sense of sacredness. She is a married woman, but for all intents and purposes she is a single mother of three children. She didn't just wake up one day and say,

"Hmm, I think I want to walk on the wild side and start dating jerks."
The man who raised her taught her that she had no self-attained value
and was only worth what value a man placed on her. She has always been
in some kind of abusive relationship. I prayed that when she had her children she would see her own sacredness through theirs. But she didn't,
she only continued to allow herself to be seen through the eyes of the
men she dated and by extension her children have suffered. They don't
know what real love is, because the only love they have experienced has
always had conditions attached to it. I have tried to get her to understand that, no matter how old she is, every day she wakes up is a new
day; one that she can decide she wants to change and begin to truly
believe her own beauty and worth. But I have yet to see this happen.
She says she wants to change, to be strong, but she doesn't know how
or she just doesn't have the determination. I know that I cannot make
anyone do anything that they don't want to, so I try to be an example.

I love my life now and would not change it for anything. I got to this
point with a lot of work and fortitude. One day I realized that in a few
months I was going to have my twenty-third birthday and had nothing
to show for it. I didn't want to be in my thirties, still miserable, unhappy,
and in a terrible life. So I figured out what I could do to stop feeling
bad about myself all the time and to start believing that I was worth
something. I knew that it was going to have to come from within,
because I had tried to make myself feel better by using outside
influences—other people, grand accomplishments, but these never
worked. Consequently I decided that if I was going to believe in myself
I was truly going to have to be the one to do the believing. It took a
while, but I got better over time. I left abusive relationships behind and
went into relationships with the mantra of "I had a life before you, I'll
have one with you, and I'll have one after you." I didn't want to be
defined by the man I was with; I wanted to have my own life and be
my own person. As a result, I kicked many men to the curb, but I had
dated my share of jerks and I thought that part of my life was over. When
I told people my mantra they laughed and said it was a little cold; but
it kept me from getting sucked into a situation that I didn't want to be

in and it kept me from doing something I didn't feel right about. But we don't ever know how strong we are until we are put to the test.

I started dating a man with whom I fell madly in love, and gave of myself more than I had ever given to anyone. For a while I actually was happy, then slowly things began to fall apart when he began drinking, lying, and eventually cheating. One night he came home from work drunk, and we fought. He pulled back to hit me, but I stood my ground, knowing that if he hit me I was going down but that when I got up I was gone. He glared at me and I stared back at him, scared horribly on the inside but knowing I had to stand up to him. He didn't hit me, but stormed out the door. I left him the next day. My heart was broken but I knew I could not stay in a relationship that was sick, no matter how much I loved him. I tried to talk to him a few days later to see if there was anything in our relationship worth saving, but he was still drunk and tried to rape me. I left and never looked back. I was sad that the man I cared for had fallen apart, but I was not willing to put up with the garbage just to enjoy the occasional good parts.

My Lakota aunt played a big role in my growth as a person. She was a strong woman who didn't take any crap from anyone and she helped me learn to do the same. I loved her dearly; she was my role model. When I was feeling down I drew strength from her. She gave me so much and never doubted that I could be and do whatever I wanted. To her, accomplishments were not goals; they were a part of life. I recently lost her, and my world nearly fell apart, as I was horribly depressed and could not get myself to get out of bed. I didn't want to write anymore, or dance, or even wake up in the morning. I would sob, deep gut-wrenching sobs. Because my loss was so great, I didn't think I would ever be the same, and I didn't think I could go on without her. As I cried and mourned her, I felt her presence by me. She came to me in dreams, telling me I was going to be OK and that I needed to take all the things she had taught me and put them into application. Now was the real test. She was gone. Had I really been listening? Would I truly implement the things she taught me? Over time I stopped crying so much and was able to get out of bed, pick up my pen, and write. I knew that I was not left dangling in this life without her. She was still with me, and she had given me so much, I needed to take the strength I had and move on. I was a proud, strong *winyan wakan*, her niece, and I needed to step back into the world as such.

Today I am married and my husband tells me how wonderful I am, how beautiful I am. He doesn't just mean my outside appearance, he means the total me, and that is such a blessing. Because, even as great as my life is, I still have days when I feel low, but he helps me. However, he does not define me: I am still my own separate person. Ten years ago I would not have been able to stand in such a healthy relationship. I'd have sat up, begged, and rolled over for any scrap of attention someone would have given me. I know now that because I am a *winyan wakan*, I make the rules about my life, myself, and where I'm going. When I have a daughter I will teach her the same things, help her realize that she defines who she is, what she will do in life, and never to forget that she is a winyan wakan.

If all women could internalize this age-old indigenous belief, I think the abuse and degradation would lessen and eventually end because women would not take it anymore. As the world evolves more of our Lakota parents are choosing to include some of the traditional practices of our culture; this will no doubt educate them to a gentler way of teaching their children. As women embrace their cultural traditions and practices, hopefully they will learn of their own sacredness and allow themselves to embrace the power they each have as a *winyan wakan*. They will know that the residue that remains from the wrong teachings of the boarding schools, as well as from the generations of trauma, can be healed as we return to traditional Lakota beliefs.

FROM WASOUK TO SHOAH AND BACK:

A MI'KMAQ HONOR SONG

ALICE M. AZURE

AMONG MY favorite places in southeastern Connecticut is the Arrival of the People Gallery at the
Mashantucket Pequot Museum and Research Center. There, fantastic
pieces of art depict the creation stories of various native nations. Raven
captures Sun; Grandmother Spider protects one of the heavenly twins.
Panther, Crawdad, Wind, and Bird form clans to guide the People. Nan-
abozho and the animals regally sit in a big canoe, saved from the Great
Flood by Muskrat's diving prowess. Sky Woman falls through a starry
black cosmos. Whale becomes land. White and Yellow Corn dance upon
a background filled with luminous, mysterious silhouettes of petro-
glyphs. Sometimes, in the semidarkness of that gallery designed to be a
time before the ice age, I become so absorbed in these dramas that I can
feel the urgency and intensity with which these mythic intercessors are
carrying out their Herculean tasks. How hard they are at work on
behalf of our native nations! I believe they still help us, with lots of assistance from principled men and women.

My own Mi'kmaq Nation had its origins in Wasouk (Sky World,
Place of Happiness, Paradise, Heaven). We are northland people, primarily from what are now New Brunswick, Quebec, Nova Scotia,

Prince Edward Island, and Newfoundland. In their joyful account, *On the Trail of Elder Brother*, the Mi'kmaq authors Michael B. Running Wolf and Patricia Clark Smith say that our great teacher, Glooscap, was sent down from Sky World by Kesoulk (Kitchi Manitou, Nigsgam, or God) to help make the new earth habitable for all creatures. Moreover, Glooscap taught all creatures how to live with one another. When his work was done, he left in a stone canoe—like a great island—from Cape Blomiden, promising to return someday when he was needed.

Daniel Paul, a Mi'kmaq human rights activist and author, estimates there were a minimum of 200,000 native people in the Atlantic maritimes before John Cabot arrived in 1497 (*We Were Not the Savages*, p. 45). By 1600 that number had declined to around 50,000 (p. 56) and by 1840 to just 1,425 starving people (p. 188). Today, according to the Department of Indian Affairs and Northern Development, there are over 27,000 registered Mi'kmaq people, including the five hundred members of the Aroostook Band in Presque Isle, Maine. If one includes the substantial number of Mi'kmaq métis spread throughout the northeastern coast from Quebec down to New York, this number would be well over 30,000.

My father always asserted that he was of Mi'kmaq ancestry, as did his mother, Eliza Boudreau, and his grandmother, Celestine Portier. On the few opportunities I had to press him on this subject he never backed away from or doubted this assertion. In fact, toward the end of his life, he was known to citizens band radio enthusiasts in northeastern Maine as "Nova Scotia Micmac."

Joseph Alfred Hatfield was born in 1913 in Yarmouth, Nova Scotia, and spent the first eighteen years of his life in various lumber camps of northern Maine and New Hampshire. It was a rough, often brutal life for a little child. One is reminded about a cruel situation in this far northeastern part of our country: an Indian seen hitch-hiking with his or her possessions in a paper bag or gunnysack was said to be "micmacing." Like my late husband, my father was a gifted harmonica player. How I loved to hear his rendition of "Donkey Serenade!" When one considers the whole of my father's life—as well as the historical legacy of genocide that continued in those early years of the twentieth century against New England Indians and other groups so well described in Joseph Bruchac's writings, especially *Bowman's Store* and *Roots of Survival*—is it any wonder that he and his family conveniently lost the ability or desire to keep track of ancestors? What is a wonder is that he remained proud of his native ancestry!

This was pretty much the way things remained until my second year of graduate studies at the University of Iowa's School of Urban and Regional Planning. In the fall of 1973 an interim professor joined our faculty. His name then was John Salter, a sociologist and community organizer. He has since assumed the family name of his Mohawk ancestors and goes by Hunter Gray. In fact, later I learned that he was the Mustard Man of the Jackson, Mississippi, Woolworth lunch counter sit-in of 1963. Astoundingly, he was Mi'kmaq as well as St. Francis Abenaki and St. Regis Mohawk. What could have been more serendipitous than two Mi'kmaq people winding up in—of all places—Iowa City?

Right after his introductory lecture I went up to welcome him. Before I could say another word, he looked directly at me and asked, "What is your tribe?" Taken off guard, I mumbled something like, "I'm not sure. There's so much we don't know." Shortly after this startling introduction he challenged me to claim my Mi'kmaq ancestry. I accepted his challenge, totally ignorant of the difficult journey before me.

After graduating from the university I resolved to do two things—to seek out some members of the Intertribal League of American Indians in the Quad-Cities (Moline, Illinois, and Davenport, Iowa) and to contact as many Mi'kmaq reserves and officials as possible in a personal quest to identify my Mi'kmaq relatives.

In August of 1974 I convinced my husband to go to Nova Scotia. Imagine. I had no Mi'kmaq contacts. I didn't know the location of the reserves. I had no knowledge of St. Ann's Procession around the end of July when Mi'kmaq people gathered at Chapel Island to honor her and to enjoy each other—much like today's powwows. What I did was head for Yarmouth, knocking on as many doors as possible that bore the name Boudreau or Portier. Meanwhile, my husband slouched way down in our little yellow Pinto.

I'll never forget one tall middle-aged lady's reaction to my chipper questions about my grandmother and great-grandmother. She took a few steps back, straightened her back and managed to regain her composure, momentarily lost at the shear audacity of my questions. Looking down at me over her glasses, she assured me in no uncertain way that there was no Indian blood in the Boudreau name, an assertion that has been repeated over and over again. I can't remember how many doors I knocked on that afternoon but when we finally headed for Halifax, my husband's surly mood disappeared.

Shortly after we arrived back home in Moline, Illinois, I was able to secure a list of twenty-seven Mi'kmaq reserve addresses from George Mitchell, then the commissioner of Indian Affairs for the State of Maine. I wrote a letter to every chief on the list. Several individuals sent back kind responses, especially Peter J. Barlow and Ellen Robinson. It was Mrs. Robinson's sister-in-law, Viola Robinson, who suggested that my search for Mi'kmaq relatives was going to be very difficult as native women lost their status if they married a white man. Upon such a marriage, all records pertaining to her status as a First Nations person were expunged, as the Canadian government considered her dutifully enfranchised. This practice was repealed in 1985.

As mentioned, I also joined the Inter-Tribal League of American Indians. Because of the presence of John Deere International, Oscar Mayer Meat Packing Company, Harvester International, and other manufacturing companies, the Quad-Cites in the 1960s and 1970s were a powerhouse of wonderful jobs, so there were a number of native people in the area—Mesquakie, Red Lake Chippewa, Sioux, Yaqui, Oneida, Kickapoo, and Ho-Chunk, to name a few.

As Hunter Gray had worked amongst this group, primarily with a jail visitation program to native prisoners at the Fort Madison penitentiary in southeastern Iowa, he was able to give me the names of the organization's leaders, then Patrick (Chippewa) and Iva (Mesquakie) Roy. I visited them at their Bettendorf home. After telling them a little bit about myself and offering to assist in the work of the league, they welcomed me to join. Hesitant at first, I slowly began to participate in some of the activities. There was a small CETA (a federal jobs initiative during the

1970s) program, enhanced by a partnership with Chicago's American Indian Business Association (AIBA), thanks again to Hunter Gray's association with the Chicago Indian community. Through its status as sole Indian CETA agent for Illinois Native Americans, the AIBA was able to give our little organization enough money to set up an office and to hire an executive director.

One of my best memories is the time when a Mi'kmaq family from Nova Scotia found their way to our part of the country. Composed of a husband and wife and two children aged around eleven and fifteen years, this family was in need of medicine, housing, food, and services for the older boy, who was mentally retarded. We weren't able to get any help from the Illinois Department of Children and Family Services (DCFS). I somehow knew of Pine Tree Legal Aid in Maine. So we asked that organization for advice. Their first words were that this family came under the provisions of the Jay Treaty of 1794. They offered us legal guidance, which we accepted.

I drew up a memo, about which I had to give my boss, Bob Garrison, a heads-up, as United Way of the Quad Cities, where I was now employed, and DCFS sometimes collaborated together on behalf of the area's low-income people. Bob gave me his blessing but wouldn't allow the memo to go out under United Way's stationery. So the league designed its own letterhead and logo and sent the memo, dated April 11, 1980. Viola! In a few weeks the family received medicine, food, and a small stipend. What I will never forget is the outpouring of help. Robert Lee, director of public housing in East Moline was the first to respond. At the request of my husband, whose architectural firm had some building contracts with the East Moline's housing authority, Bob found a nice apartment for the family by "jumping" over many others on the waiting list. Members of the league donated all the furniture, linens, books, and other household items needed to equip a new home.

Thus began the time, from 1975 to 1980, of my education about Indian Country. I traveled a lot with Darlene Sanchez to Sisseton Wahpeton Sioux Reservation in South Dakota. Florence Child invited us to meet her relatives in Minneapolis and Red Lake Reservation.

Ethelbert and Al Caswell's relatives from White Earth, Red Lake, Leland, Michigan and elsewhere visited them in Moline, where they owned a small home. I was always invited over to meet everyone. Many of the friends of those years have lasted to this day.

One family in particular eventually became my relatives in more ways than one. Alec (Turtle Mountain Chippewa) and Joan (Mesquakie and sister to Iva Roy) Azure maintained a large home in Davenport, Iowa, where any number of their children or nieces, nephews, and grandchildren hung out. Each had been married a few times, so their blended family taxed my ability to remember names and relationships. Joan and I became particularly close. She taught me to bead my newly designed Mi'kmaq regalia. It was Joan and her aunt, Annie Lasley, who bestowed upon me my Indian name of *Ka MiYa Nu Sa'qua,* Walking in the Rain.

In 1987, at age sixty, Joan Azure passed on. As I had divorced and moved to Washington, D.C., I missed her letters and phone calls. When I did manage trips back to the Quad-Cities to visit with my family and friends, I always tried to see Alec and his children. Early in 1990 the tables turned! Alec started to visit me in Springfield, Virginia. Within six months, after an old-fashioned courtship, he asked me to marry him. How could I refuse, after all the nice things Joan used to say about him while she was teaching me to bead! Happily, I said yes. So we were married and then moved across the country to start a new home in Evanston, Illinois, close to my job at a small accredited college for American Indians but not too far from his children and grandchildren in Davenport, Iowa.

Whenever I could, I continued a vigorous search for Mi'kmaq relatives, writing to officials in Toronto, hiring genealogists, traveling to Presque Isle in northern Maine, and talking to various Mi'kmaq acquaintances. I could not scale the great walls of silence. Nothing developed. I began to feel vulnerable, with the growing criticism in Indian Country about wannabes." After all, the rock-bottom criteria of being Indian appeared to be some knowledge of one's family. Yet, I remained unable to name the native relatives of my ancestry. A few times I came close to giving up the search and started to give my things away. To my brother Fred, I gave my Mi'kmaq pipe, with its distinctive ridge under the bowl. It was at a time like this that I believed the Spirit World intervened. Like when Alec Azure came into my life.

The history of Alec's nation, the Turtle Mountain Band of Chippewa Indians of North Dakota, is fully reflected in his large and diverse family. My primary source for this history is *Aun nish e naubay*, or Patrick Gourneau. In his *History of the Turtle Mountain Band of Chippewa Indians* he carefully explains that, although the main group of the tribe evolved from woodland-based Ojibway nations, other nations are parts that come from "a little bit of Cree, a little bit of Ottawa and also a little bit of Assiniboin and Sioux" (Gourneau, p. 5). Over a hundred years or more, from 1790 to 1890, after coming from the various woodlands east and north, this mixture of people changed and evolved into a Plains culture. An identifiable band in 1849 (Gourneau, p. 12), the Turtle Mountain Reservation was established by the Federal Government in 1884 and today numbers around 29,161 enrolled members (according to the North Dakota Indian Affairs Commission). The people of the tribe are referred to as Plains-Ojibway in culture and outlook.

Alec Azure was born in 1923 in a tent, place unknown other than somewhere around Turtle Mountain. Until he was around seven years old, his only language was Mechif, which he learned from his paternal grandmother, Adelia Belgarde. Mechif, says Gourneau, is a jargon

> . . . *involving a unique mixture of French, Cree, Plains-Ojibwa, and English. French and Cree Indian words dominate the jargon, and with the addition of Plains-Ojibway and English words, the size of the vocabulary was greatly increased. The whole mixture of words was termed "Cree," but it differs greatly from the real Cree. Inclusion of much more Cree than Plains-Ojibway words indicate there was much closer association between the 'Mechifs' and Cree than there was between them and the Plains-Ojibway at the time the jargon was in its adoption stage.* (pp. 9, 10)

Alec's mother, Theresa Gunville Azure, died after her sixth child was born. Eventually, Joseph Azure, Alec's father, remarried and moved the family down to Cheyenne River Sioux Reservation in South Dakota where his new wife Irene Robertson and her children were enrolled. It was at the Moreau River Day School on this reservation that Alec was forbidden to speak Mechif. Alec obviously grew into a diversity of cultures and experiences. At Cheyenne River, he became baptized into the Episcopalian Church on the reservation. My short life with him reminded me that the Christian tradition was not always so divorced from that of the Native Americans.

Although it was said that the Turtle Mountain métis kept somewhat aloof from traditionalists (Gourneau, p. 12), this was not true of Alec. He participated as fully as possible in tribal life at Tama and Chicago. He exhibited great tolerance for people of mixed heritage. Words like "wannabe," "step-child," "step-mother," and "prairie nigger" were never a part of his vocabulary. We attended weekly community gatherings at the Chicago Indian Center on Wilson Avenue. He had a good eye for excellence of work with regard to crafted regalia.

Above all things, Alec was a musician, as were many of his relatives. He played guitar, fiddle, harmonica, and a form of lute. At a 1991 family gathering of his family at Turtle Mountain I was able to record over ninety minutes of his wonderful impromptu fiddle playing accompanied by his brother Isadore on the guitar. When Alec passed on in early 1993 that tape comforted me for over a year.

Many times I have felt supported and energized by Alec's spirit. In particular, I began to experience a series of visitations from Old Grandmother Spider, whose essence and character is best described in Paula Gunn Allen's astounding work, *The Sacred Hoop: Recovering the Feminine in American Indian Traditions* (Beacon Press, 1986):

> *This spirit, this power of intelligence, has many names and many emblems. She appears on the plains, in the forests, in the great canyons, on the mesa, beneath the seas. To her we owe our very breath, and to her our prayers are sent blown on pollen, on corn meal, planted into the earth on feather sticks, spit onto the water, burned and sent to her on the wind. Her variety and multiplicity testify to her complexity; she is the true creatrix for she is thought itself, from which all else is born. (pp. 13, 14)*

Now as I try to gain a little perspective of those visits, I believe they pointed to new directions in my life—writing and a beginning association with Wordcraft Circle of Native Writers and Storytellers. Its logo is a spiderweb! Its mission, which I helped compose, is to ensure that the voices of native writers and storytellers—past, present, and future—are heard throughout the world.

My initial intent in writing this essay was to demonstrate the action in my own life of beneficent spirit beings and people who, despite my continual inability to identity specific Mi'kmaq ancestors, led me on a journey to reclaim that part of my ancestry which is native. It didn't take me long to understand that this journey required a familiarity and understanding of five hundred or more years of an unending, deliberate policy of extermination of native peoples and their cultures.

It is hard to fully face this Gorgonian specter of genocide. At times, my personal belief in a spirit world palls next to realities represented by the Boston Shoah (Holocaust) Memorial, next to Quincy Market. Incised on six glass towers from top to bottom are the serial numbers of six million Jews who perished in Europe's concentration camps. In total, we know there were twelve million souls lost during this Shoah.

It is encouraging to know there is an emerging scholarship focused on worldwide genocide, such as Samantha Power's *A Problem from Hell: America and the Age of Genocide* (*New York Times Book Review*, June 5, 2005, p. 32). Powers is among a growing school of scholars spearheading a demand that America abandon its great silence on the issue of world genocide and begin to "live up to its ideals."

Here's a dream from March of 2001: I'm looking for my family at a park alongside the Mississippi River in Moline, Illinois. I come upon a red-bark pine tree that must have been gigantic at one time. The top of its central trunk had been violently snapped off. I thought it was dead. Then I noticed one lone remaining branch, the lowest to the ground. I am astounded to see that this branch is still alive! It is sturdy and many green needles protrude along its length, which is about seventy-five feet. For some reason I begin to talk to this ancient, wounded tree. Under the branch are hundreds of little evergreen shoots, upon which I am careful not to trample.

In this dream, the miracle was the red pine's one live branch. I gave little attention to the ugly, jagged splinters where once its growing top had been. Daniel Paul's passionate and forceful *We Were Not the Savages* broadened my initial approach to this essay. In the fullest sense of the meaning behind the words genocide and holocaust (Shoah), I have been compelled to own the specific experiences of my own ancestors, Mi'k-maq and Acadian, represented by the repulsive, splintered treetop. What Daniel Paul has done is to give a voice to people—oppressed as well as oppressors—who lived through four hundred years of unimaginable horror and injustice.

After the Treaty of Utrecht in 1713 the English laid out a series of policies and treaties, including three scalp bounty proclamations, which cemented a foundation of hatred, humiliation, and debasement of Mi'kmaq and Acadian people. Paul says that his research came directly from meticulous notes and minutes left by the British (p. 81). To read excerpts of these source documents is to understand how deeply racism and hatred perpetrated a horrific legacy that permeates to this day the families and societies of Mi'kmaq and Acadian people. This may sound strange, but all of a sudden it was not a holocaust of Chero-kee, Chiricahua Apache, Lakota, Taino, Mashantucket Pequot, or Chickahominy and countless other nations; it was part and parcel of my own heritage.

Where have I been not to recognize this, one may ask? It's a fair ques-tion. But, until Daniel Paul's book was published in 2000, I had no con-cise history of my own nation from the point of view of a Mi'kmaq author, nor of the Acadians, such as John Mack Faragher's *A Great and Noble Scheme: the Tragic Story of the Expulsion of the French Acadians from Their American Homeland*. Thanks to Catherine Martin, a filmmaker from the Halifax area, I was able to secure and read Dan Paul's work.

Our family's experiences today cannot be compared to that of our ancestors. All I claim is a newfound realization that the great walls of silence I have experienced in searching for my own ancestors' records is part of the tail end of deliberate policies of genocide set in motion after the Treaty of Utrecht in 1713. In April of this year I heard some wonderful words from my grandchildren that, in my mind, are one small example of the ultimate failure of those policies: "Farmor," they quietly asked, eyes expectant, "will you teach us to Indian dance?"

Through my sister, Joan Hatfield King, I have found out that many of our family's ancestors may now be documented through the Nova Scotia Confederacy of Métis, which has headquarters in the areas where our father, grandmother, and great-grandmother were born—Yarmouth and Digby Counties. Small as this victory is, I wouldn't have prevailed way back in 1974 without the help of certain spirit beings and of good people like Hunter and Eldri Gray, Alec and Joan Azure, and many, many other native friends in Chicago and Washington, D.C. For all of them, I wish to add my gratitude to the beautiful, haunting prayer-song of George Paul's "Micmac Honour Song," the English translation given in the *Song of Rita Joe: Autobiography of a Mi'kmaq Poet*:

Let us highly respect our people
My dear friends let us come together
Let us highly respect our origin
My dear friends let us help one another
Let us help one another according to the Creator's intentions
As to why he placed us here. (pp. 184, 185)

IN EACH TRACE OF FOOTSTEP:

THE CONSTANT SONG OF SPIRITMEMORY
(FOR MY MOM, JANICE HERNÁNDEZ)

INÉS HERNÁNDEZ-ÁVILA

Grandpa Tom and Grandma Alice, the summer of 1964

WHENEVER I see my family members, in person or in my heart's eye, I am filled with an abiding love at the sight of each one. My love for family is enduring, compassionate, and rooted in the generations. This is my inheritance from my mother and father. My parents truly love(d) and cherish(ed) their own parents and siblings and each other's parents and siblings.[1] It is a love that spirals inward to the center of the self and outward, moving from the beginning of time to the future generations, in ancient, lasting, ongoing expression. It is a love that encompasses personal and collective history, honoring and singing with constancy the legacy of spiritmemory.

For indigenous peoples, the story of genocide, of holocaust, is present in every cell and fiber of our beings, in every step we take as we walk this remembering earth. But it is a story within the larger story of who we are as original peoples of this hemisphere. This larger story resounds in the eternal search for justice that is in our hearts, in the cherishing of truth that nourishes our spirits, in the practice of or the yearning for the ancient teachings that, for some of us, sometimes seem just out of reach. For me, in spite of the history of annihilation and horror, the trust in those teachings persists in my mother's face, in the lilt of her voice, in the sound of what one of my dear friends calls her "girlish laughter," in her intentionally resilient ways. She will not be moved from her love, and she will not surrender who she is as a Nez Perce woman.

In Indian Country, walking down the street, discovering another Indian in a store, at a concert, or any other public place, after the meeting of the eyes comes the almost simultaneous nod of recognition (the relief that you see each other, that you found each other, that you witness each other's existence). Then, "Where are you from?" On my mother's side, I am from Nespelem, Washington; my family is the Andrews family. We are Nimipu, Nez Perce of Chief Joseph's band, enrolled on the Colville reservation.

Mom and me, Galveston, 1950s

My grandpa was Thomas Andrews, Ukshanat, and my grandma was Alice Andrews, Tomahwahli.[2] My mom is Janice; she is the sister who moved away to Galveston, Texas, in the 1940s to marry my dad, Rudy Hernández. I grew up knowing I am Nez Perce and *mexicana*, or Mexican Indian. My mother told me when I was a child that native people are the First Americans.

She took me back home with her often when I was growing up, so that I would know who I am, so that I would know who she is, as Nez Perce. I remember receiving a gift of Indian-cured buckskin as an adult, and I was struck with memory, my whole being instantly traveling to the doorway of my grandparents' bedroom, where the aroma took me, the smell a guide, my fragrant amulet. Just outside the doorway, in the kitchen, I could see—as I can still see—my grandpa sitting, drumming and singing, and I know that I am at the center of being Nimipu; I know that I am home. This is my mother's will to me, a will to remember who I am, to be brave, to carry myself with dignity. It is the strength she has given us all, my sons, and my grandchildren.

> There are no fairy tales
> that can live up to
> a woman who knows
> her beauty
>
> emergence comes
> not from divine intervention
> or magic wands
> incantations or spells
>
> emergence comes from
> incandescent courage
> grounded rooted deep
> within the womb
> the earth
> herself

Mom in Nespelem, 1940s

The photo of my mom standing by her home in Nespelem has a
wonderful composition. Whoever took the picture had a keen eye. My
mother is framed in the window of the house, she is very comfortable
with herself, her face is beaming, and her beauty shows through good
and strong. The sun is perhaps going down, thus the full presence of
shadow and her double is behind her. This is a woman of daring spirit,
who sought independence, who made a commitment to herself and kept
it, as she would other commitments in her life, to my father, to me, to
her grandsons and great-grandchildren, to her family. When she was
twenty-two, she left the reservation to go to Seattle to find work. My
mom says she was one of the only ones to leave Nespelem to do this.
She got a job at the Boeing Aircraft Factory and became a riveter during World War II. She was "Janice, the Riveter," a job that was arduous
and challenging, a job that allowed her to make friends with women
from different parts of the country. Janice, Jan, or Janie, as her siblings
and friends called her, my sons and grandchildren call her "Gramma Jan."

I love the many photos of my mom from her time as a single young woman, living and working in Seattle, the city she embraced and loves so deeply that the mere image of Mt. Rainier can move her heart to tears. I love knowing that she and her friends, besides working hard, had fun in the big city; they got dressed up, they liked to see themselves poised and posing, they felt their own beauty. This is the city where she met my dad, the strong and tender young man of promise who would become her husband and best friend. As a marine he was stationed on Bremerton Island after he came back from his service in the Philippines. Seattle is where he courted her and proposed to her. In this photo from Seattle, taken in one of those "instant photo galleries," I see how she must have caught his eye. There is a certain fearless serenity to her.

Mom in Seattle, 1940s

She is wearing a dress with white piping on the lapels and on the pockets of the skirt. Once, many years ago, I kept looking at this photo and I was inspired to do a watercolor replica of it. The result was somewhat rudimentary, but I was pleased that her image came through my hands. I showed it to her, and she was surprised, because I painted the dress the exact color it had been. The photo was black and white, so I chose a deep rose for the color of the dress, with the white swirling piping. "How did you do that?" she said. It made me happy to know I reached back and saw her so clearly. Memory is a gift of resonance that vibrates through our beings.

Photos are mysterious. There is so much in the making of each one. The subject being photographed. The photographer. What the photographer sees. What the photographer records or captures. What the subject wants to show. What the camera captures no matter what. What the viewer then and in the future sees. From second-to-second a mirror image can shift, sometimes so slightly, sometimes in startling ways, offering us faces that reveal the generations of pain and love, all on one face. My mother's gaze in almost all of her photos is direct. Her eyes are amazing in their power. She does not see herself in this way but the evidence appears in these captured moments and in her daily reactions with her family and anyone who meets her.

I have one photo of my mom wearing a traditional buckskin dress and moccasins. She is smiling, her hair in braids, two eagle feathers gracing her head. She looks relaxed and beautiful. My mom cherishes traditional dress, the real, old pieces, and the ones that are made with such care they could be centuries old. She wants to see me dressed this way. She was happy when I received a wing dress from my friend and relative, Jeannie Moon, and more recently moccasins. She wants this for me, just as she has always wanted me to know Nez Perce traditions. She cherishes the beadwork that my Grandma Alice did so beautifully, the cornhusk bags and baskets that my great-grandma Hiyum Otway (Old Grizzly Bear Woman) made with her good eyesight. My mom pours over catalogues that she somehow encounters, searching for Nez Perce work. At any opportunity, she is happy to see old work by native people, or recent work that has been done with the same loving care and precision of the ancestors. She thinks I am a good singer, so she has always wanted me to learn the old songs. I have told this story before. I prayed often for the songs to come to me, and they did, thanks to the work of Loran Olsen at Washington State University, who collected all of the Nez Perce songs that he could gather into an eighteen-cassette series.[3] This is my mother's will (and certainly the will and prayers of many Nez Perce people) at work.

The Nez Perce have been described as being of the Dreamer faith, which is actually the Seven Drum religion, according to the late Nez Perce elder, Joe Redthunder.[4] While I am tremendously moved by the Seven Drum religion, my mom did not explain it to me as I was grow-ing up, yet she always encouraged me to pay attention to my dreams. From her I understood that my dreams belong to me; they are for me to interpret, not for me to hand over to someone else to tell me what they mean. My dreams have often taken me precisely to places I will see in the future; they let me know what will happen, or they will give me indications of what is already happening, sometimes quite literally, sometimes symbolically.

the dreaming woman
finds her path lit by song worlds
rich with dance and sound

> *sometimes dreams frighten*
> *the spirit flies to war sites*
> *the heart cannot breathe*

sometimes a father
tells the story of eagle
dreaming a rescue

> *dreamer mother shares*
> *her secrets with her daughter*
> *laughter becomes her*

In the early 1980s, while I was living in Fresno, my mother wrote me to tell me she had gone with my oldest son to the library. She always loved to take me to the library and set me free with all the books; she let me bring armloads home for me to devour, and she would scold me at night because I would be reading under the blankets with a flashlight. On this particular visit to the Galveston library, while my son was doing his research she browsed in the American Indian section, looking for books on the Nez Perce. She found *With One Sky Above Us: Life on an Indian Reservation at the Turn of the Century*, by M. Gidley, and began to leaf through it.[5] The book's focus is on reservation life near the time of Chief Joseph's last years. As she turned the pages, she found her mother, my Grandma Alice (as a young girl, perhaps about eleven or twelve years old), her Aunties Waheupum and Washatonmy (Waheupum was my Auntie Tillie Red Elk's mother; my auntie was an older cousin, like a sister to my mom, and a mentor to me), and other relatives. She wanted me to find a copy of the book for her, which I did, and the quest led me to the University of Washington archives to review the larger collection of photos that appear in the book. One of my aunts helped me review the photos and we picked out many of them to copy for our family.

As the years have passed, more of these old photos are emerging from our family's collections, and at least two of my cousins/sisters have worked, or are working, with the tribal history preservation section at the agency. While the energy in contemporary globalized/ing society is so strong to deny, to forget, to bury, to erase, to build a wall against (particularly indigenous) memory, there is another energy more powerful that will not be denied. This energy is an immense love that seeks answers, that wants the stories, the images, the documents, the songs, the dances, the details—all the details. I am so grateful that these photos hold our treasuries of memory.

My mom enjoys going occasionally to powwows, especially to see the traditional dancers. She has a strict sense of what she wants to see, saying to me every so often, "Things are just not done anymore the way they once were." She is particularly happy to see people dressed and dancing old-style. She is happy when I go out to dance, even as I dance in everyday clothes, but with one of my beautiful shawls. The Veterans' powwows are the most important to her. When she gets to greet men of my father's generation, those who served in World War II, her sobs surface quickly, her tears of pain intermingled with her joy of recognition for all the warriors, especially my dad, her brother, and my uncles.

Once, when we were at a Veterans' powwow at DQ University, a remarkable instance occurred, which I believe was for her. As the head dancer reached the midpoint of the emcee's stage, he paused the dancers behind him, causing them to dance in place for what seemed like several moments of the song. Sitting with my mom on the front row, we had a beautiful view of them, as they all faced our direction. I was moved at the way they all looked together, men, women, young people, children. I thought to myself, *How wonderful! The way they are in formation is as if the lead dancer wants her to see them all together.* At his signal, the dancers began to move again, all of them coming toward us as they completed the quarter circle before turning past us. I like to think this was done as an honoring for my mom, because she was perhaps the oldest of the elders at the event that night. Serendipity is her loving friend.

In September 2004 my youngest son took my mom, my husband, and me, to the opening of the National Museum of the American Indian in Washington, D.C. We marched in the procession with the Yakima Nation, because we had no idea how to find the Colville reservation representatives. We joked with the Yakimas about how we are all related anyway. My mom enjoyed the tour of the museum—so new, so elegant—and the opening events, especially Paul Ortega's performance. She did end up wondering, as she looked carefully at the specific exhibits, "Where are the Nez Perce?" But she was happy to be there with all of us, especially with her grandson.

The highlight of the trip, for her, is our visit to the World War II memorial, even though she believes passionately that this memorial should have been built long ago. She takes in everything, the fountains, the beauty of the space, the way each state is honored for the men and women who served their country, the stars that represent those who lost their lives, the way the two fronts are distinguished. As we walk along the path where the bronze vignettes portray scenes from the war, as well as scenes on the home front, we suddenly come upon the image of women riveters working at an aircraft factory. As I see her face, I realize this moment is one of the major reasons we have made the trip. We take photos of her by this image and we take photos of her next to the message engraved in stone that honors the women who did their own heroic part for the war effort at home. My mom wanted to go to the memorial for my father's sake. What she found was herself represented with him as the equals they were throughout their married life. And she finds the confirmation of her own life's decisions as a single young woman in Seattle.

Mom at the World War II memorial,
by the scene honoring the women riveters

As if this were not enough, when we continue on our tour of the memorial we move to the site that represents the war on the Pacific front. We begin to talk to an older man who served in the marines in the Philippines like my father. During the conversation with him and his daughter I ask his name and he answers, "Alvin Josephy." I am stunned. My words fall over each other as I tell him he and I have met at least twice some years before, and that of course, I know his work.[6] I turn and introduce him to my husband, my son, and my mom, and I let her know he is an eminent historian and specialist in Nez Perce history. We take photos together and wish each other well. Once again, I know the good ancestor spirits are with us. They are with my mom, even though she is innocently unaware of their favor.

My mom, who is my best friend, and I

Memory
Sacred in each trace of footstep
Each drop of blood's vibration
Become part of the song of this land
The blood sings deep
The heart of the earth responds
And holds us close

In early October 1998, my husband and I traveled with my mom from Woodland, California, to Nespelem, where we picked up my Uncle Frank, my mother's younger brother, and one of my nephews, Nathan Desautel, so that we could all drive together to Bear Paw, Montana. My mom had always wanted to make this trip to the ceremonies in remembrance of the 1877 flight of the non-treaty Nez Perce from the U.S. military, and Chief Joseph's necessary surrender of the people in the face of ultimately impossible military odds. Living so far away in Texas during most of her married life, it had always been impossible for her to go. But in 1998 she decided to make the journey. This journey is one of the only times she left my father's side during his hard last years of battling heart disease.

The trip to Bear Paw is a long, good drive for us as a family; we talk, laugh, we are happy to be with each other. My uncle is the one in our family who faithfully continues to express his commitment to Nez Perce history. Joseph's band of the Nez Perce who live in Nespelem are not so many in number these days. The Nez Perce Nation in Idaho numbers approximately 3,400.[7] The elders like my uncle are becoming smaller in number. He teaches the Nez Perce language, he takes part in the historic preservation projects, he travels to Bear Paw each year, and as much as he can, to the other sites of resistance, such as Big Hole. Jeannie Moon says he scolds them when they don't take part in these commemorations. She tells me with a smile, "It's good, though, we need the elders to scold us like that."

My mom is seventy-eight years old on this trip. She was born on January 14, 1921, a little more than seventeen years after Joseph died in Nespelem of a broken heart on September 21, 1904. It is like yesterday. January 14 is also the date of Joseph's famous 1879 address to congressmen, cabinet members, and diplomats in Washington, D.C. In his speech, when he says, "Good words do not mean anything unless they amount to something," I think of how my mom demands honesty from us and a love that means what it says.[8] She is quite critical of the current U.S. presidency, not only for the way the administration is handling the war in Iraq, but the crises at home such as the disaster of Hurricane

Katrina. Her voice rises, her indignation cuts to the core of the issues, and she is clear about her distrust of the political expediency of "good words" that amount to nothing. In Joseph's address, when he expresses what it is to be a free man and asks that our people be accorded that right, I also know that my mom carries this inherent principle in her whole being. She has always shown that she is "free to think and talk and act for [her]self."[9] Joseph's words, spoken for his people, lived by my mom, are the heart and spirit of Nez Perce and indigenous autonomy.

My mother's mother's father, Hiyum Kish Kish, Grizzly Bear Standing, was an eighteen-year-old warrior in the 1877 flight. My uncle has given me many accounts from the oral tradition of the devoted bravery, intelligence, and deep-rooted strength of the people. One hundred and twenty-one years after October 5, 1877, we are standing on the battlefield become sacred with graceful courageous memory, with the powerful intent of the warriors to defend the people from the fateful assault. The blood sings of mourning and continuance in the golden hues of this venerated land. Bear Paw is history, holds history, holds memory close. The earth's witnessed eloquence is strong here; the expanse of yellow fields holds the eye of the heart, as our footsteps humbly meet those of our ancestors. It is cold but it is not bitter with snow as it was in 1877. We are being treated with utmost kindness by the elements.

At one part of the commemoration my mother stands up to see the entry of the horsemen in full traditional dress as they ride around the ceremonial site. She had long ago given me the memory of her grandmother, Hiyum Otway, who used to cry when she would see the riderless horse that is led in these processions, representing the ones who died in battle and the ones who have since passed on. My greatgrandmother, tiny woman, powerful medicine woman, gave this gift of memory to my mom. When one of the men passes us leading the riderless horse, my mother suddenly sits and begins to weep. I lean down to comfort her, touching her shoulder gently, but her sobs become stronger. I call her brother over and he places his hand on her and prays. My mother's tears bless us all that day and we are cleansed with the grief and love of our generations.

It is almost October 5 once again, as I write these words. These days are the ending days of the flight. On September 30, 1877, Joseph's brother, Ollokot, the old chief Toohoolhoolzote, and Poker Joe, and other men, and women and children fall to the aggression of the soldiers of General Miles. On October 1 Miles betrays Joseph by taking him prisoner during a temporary truce. Joseph's hands and feet are bound and he is left outside in the cold. On October 2 Miles agrees to release Joseph in exchange for the release of one of his lieutenants. By October 3 Looking Glass is killed by an Indian sniper. On October 4 General Howard arrives to join General Miles. On October 5, after continuing deliberation with the other Nez Pearce leaders, Joseph prevails and surrenders on behalf of the people.[10] Joseph's words, that he would "fight no more forever," had to do with taking up arms against the United States government. He continued to advocate for the people in every other way up to his death in 1904. It is years before our ancestors are able to return to mountain country, and they are never allowed to return to the Wallowa Valley as Miles had promised Joseph.

As with other indigenous peoples, the whole heart-wrenching, spirit-strengthening story runs deep within us, coursing fervently through our beings, needing to be told so that the healings can reverberate throughout our lives, for ourselves, for those who came before, and for those who come after. The earth who loves us asks this of us. My mother's will is as deep and as ancient as the earth's beginnings. She is our song. She is our spiritmemory. For our family, she is the promise of the Nez Perce generations.

1 My father passed away on December 31, 2000.
2 These are spellings of their Indian names based on how our family hears them. They are not phonetic spellings.
3 See Nez Perce Music Archive, collected by Loran Olsen, Washington State University, 1989. These songs are a rich collection for the Nez Perce people. They do have cultural protocols that attach to them, though, so they cannot simply be taken to sing.
4 There is a chapter titled "The Dreamers," in L. V. McWhorter, *Hear Me, My Chiefs: Nez Perce History and Legend* (Caldwell, Idaho: The Caxton Printers,

LTD, 1986), pp. 83–84. See also, "Park bill honors final resting place of Chief Joseph," The *Spokesman Review*, Spokane, Washington, January 24, 1993, p. B4. Joe Redthunder is featured in this article. Jeannie Moon is Joe Redthunder's daughter.

5 M. Gidley, *With One Sky Above Us: Life on an Indian Reservation at the Turn of the Century* (New York: G.P. Putnam's Sons, 1979). The photographs that form the basis for this book were taken by Dr. Edward H. Latham, who was the U.S. Indian Agency physician at the beginning of the twentieth century. Latham is the doctor who recorded that Chief Joseph died of a broken heart.

6 I didn't recognize Professor Josephy right away because he was much slimmer than when I had seen him last. He told us he was eighty-nine. It is with sadness I note that he passed away on October 16, 2005. He was a great friend to the Nez Perce people, and he will be deeply missed.

7 See Nez Perce Nation Web site, www.nezperce.org, which lists the number at 3,363 as of November 2004. I remember a conversation in Oaxaca with a Zapotec writer friend, Javier Castellanos. He mentioned that the Zapotecs were not large in number, since there were only about 400,000 of them. He was struck when I told him how many Nez Perce there are. I have since seen a map of Mexico, which has a listing of all of the indigenous languages spoken in that nation. The number recorded for Zapotec speakers was approximately 750,000.

8 Alvin M. Josephy, Jr., *The Nez Perce Indians and the Opening of the Northwest*, abridged edition (New Haven: Yale University Press, 1971), p. 621.

9 Ibid., p. 622.

10 Bill and Jan Moeller, *Chief Joseph and the Nez Perces: A Photographic History* (Missoula, MT: Mountain Press Publishing Company, 1995), pp. 62–69.

5

AT THIS MOMENT:
REVIVING THE SPACE BETWEEN
THEN AND WHEN?

AMERICAN HERITAGE

ERIC GANSWORTH

THERE IS no equivalent of the Shoah Foundation in American Indian communities, but even if there were who would we record on videotape—ghosts? We have our survivor stories, having endured the lasting damage from the actual genocide of our ancestors, but they are not first-hand stories of death camps and forced removals. Those stories have long gone to their graves, with the restless bones of the victims who endured them, a good number probably in some East Coast museum at this point or becoming parts of repatriation packages. Either way, those bones are not talking to anyone about the heads of their children being smashed against walls and bayoneted, though period woodcuts tell that story in black and white as vividly as any narrative Steven Spielberg might reconstruct for American cinema.

The stories we have are quieter, less immediate in large scale, but no less damaging in their effect or in their sense of loss. My mother saw the world through her own filters, which had been provided by her parents and grandparents, likely supplemented with the teachings of the reservation Baptist Church and those of Indians who had been shipped off to Carlisle Indian School to make something of themselves. She had framed her life the way they had taught her, as an Indian stuck in a "White Man's World," and she felt it was her duty to perceive and retransmit the world through that mind-set. It took me a long time to discover the damaged nature of the stories. I had naturally been unaware as a child that I was, like most children, a willing recipient of a world-view presented by the first authority figure I had known. Why would I doubt the person who had safely guided me away from the poison of snake-berries and who had taught me how to balance myself over the hole in the outhouse to avoid falling in? When she said it was a White Man's World, I listened.

The last of my mother's siblings, her younger sister, passed away unexpectedly two years ago. My mother and I went to the funeral and, as we drove to the cemetery to see my aunt out of this world, she turned to me and said mysteriously, "I guess I am the cheese." When I, not knowing an appropriate response, said nothing, she clarified by adding, "The cheese stands alone." It had always been her way to offer succinct and obscure observations on the world. Sometimes it was like living with a William Carlos Williams poem or a fortune cookie or a horoscope. At other times, it was like glimpsing another world removed not so far from my own, but a mystery, just the same. She was acknowledging the closing of an era in her abstruse way, offering me a new and subtle warning about the White Man's World; but by then I was an adult and had grown accustomed to keeping her reality filters in mind whenever I listened to her, attributing some of her comments to the nature of her worldview when, in fact, I should have been listening as clearly as I had when I was a child.

She told me of seeing, at the age of eight, that same sister just born, lying on the kitchen table being cleaned off by their older sisters under the bare bulb that hung from the ceiling next to the fly strips, their mother resting on the floor and their father somewhere else, unmentioned. Other times, she told of the way she and her sisters were shipped off every summer they were still in school, from the ages of twelve until they got real jobs, to live with white families as servants, from the day after school ended until the day before the school year began. When they returned, in early September, she said my grandfather held out his hand and they were to pass him their entire summer's pay before he would let them back in the house. He told them he was preparing them for the life of adult Indian women in America, that they would always be subservient to people who considered them inferior. She continued cleaning and serving for wealthy white people until the age of sixty-two and, though I was an adult, she still tried to give me money she didn't have so I would not drop out of college. She was convinced that the only way to escape a life as difficult as hers had been was to master the White Man's World she was convinced she had lived in all her life, totally acknowledging that she was forever on the periphery of said world.

She told me her father built her brother the house across the family lot on the reservation, and that her brother still came home to eat the meals she cooked, long after he had moved out. She told me that her brother used to threaten to kill her if she had not cooked his meal correctly and that their father overlooked these threats. She then added that the first time her brother introduced her children into the threat she beat him with a baseball bat until his eyes would not open. She allowed herself to be subservient only as long as the survival of her children was not a part of the equation, but even our learned subservience was complicated, multilayered.

My family and I are enrolled as members of the Onondaga Nation, but our history, for better or worse, is inextricably tied to the history of the Tuscaroras. When the Tuscaroras eventually settled in western New York, having asked the Haudenosaunee if they could join its confederacy of five nations, Onondaga, Mohawk, Seneca, Cayuga, and Oneida, two Onondaga women left their homeland and traveled with the Tuscaroras to western New York. This settlement occurred some time before 1800, but even this event is not entirely clear and various credible sources offer significantly divergent narratives of the Tuscarora migration to New York and their current place just south of Lewiston, New York, on a five mile by seven mile patch of land. The general consensus of sources suggests that the Tuscaroras became affiliated with the Haudenosaunee sometime between 1722 and 1724, but the source of their removal—contact with aggressive colonists—began approximately ninety years before.

As is the way within Onondaga and Tuscarora matrilineal culture, we had all received our identities from the women of the family. We were Onondagas in Tuscarora territory, which complicated our lives to a considerable degree. My mother, and her mother before her, had married Tuscarora men, and as such always held tenuous relationships with the men in their lives. Growing up, my mother, her sisters, and her mother lived in a dangerously patriarchal house. Her parents, as was the prevailing ideology at Tuscarora, were staunch Christian churchgoers and her mother accepted the Western idea of women's roles for the early twentieth century, pretending to ignore the balanced role women had in other nations within the Haudenosaunee. They pretended on the surface to ignore or forget their roles, but in no way was that true at their cores. They knew they were survivors generations removed, but still survivors of a holocaust.

Holocaust. You could probably not find another word with more specific cultural resonance. When I have mentioned this word in the context of Indians in America I've received puzzled looks. David E. Stannard's examination of contact history, *American Holocaust*, is apparently not as well known in this country as it should be. It seemed that, to much of the American population, the word only belonged to one group of people. Out of curiosity, I pulled down a dictionary to see the "official" definition of the word. It clarified that in the twentieth century we saw the invention of holocaust with a capital *H*, invoking the word as a definition for a specific event. The dictionary ranked this event as the third entry for this word in the entire history of humankind, following variations of mass destruction and disaster. The capital *H* event occurred in the twentieth century in Europe, largely against people of one ethnicity, but including people from a few other groups then deemed socially unacceptable. The horror of this event is undeniable in the scope of human history. Beyond this entry, the dictionary also contained a passage below the actual numbered definitions, under the title "Usage Notes." The paragraph explored the relative merits of using the word, suggesting that though the word has several definitions that are more abstract and do not necessarily denote a particular group of humans killing another particular group of humans; the history of Europe's twentieth century has forever changed popular perception of the word.

This passage suggested that a large percentage of the population would find certain usages in poor taste because they were not ugly enough to warrant the use of the word, despite the fact that the more abstract definition is concerned with destruction on a broad scale. The dictionary included examples of holocaust incidents among groups of people. Beyond the formally named twentieth-century Holocaust of European Jews, Cambodians, Africans, and AIDS victims were listed with varying merits. American Indians were strangely absent from any of these examples. This was, after all, the *American Heritage Dictionary*. How could the editors have overlooked such a key example from within America's own borders?

I began to question my own history. My own history. Was there no American Indian holocaust? There certainly was not one with a capital *H,* in anyone's mind, but perhaps this is because no capital *H* could appear without explicit evidence. There were no photographs from 1700, no radio transmissions, no Leni Riefenstahl, no SS Officers making home movies of bodies being dumped into pits, no quieted furnaces, or empty barracks to visit with solemnity and recognition, as Alain Resnais does in the landmark film, *Night and Fog*. But does the lack of official documentation mean the event did not happen? Sure, there were people like William Bradford and his entourage, even as early as Plymouth Plantation. Bradford claimed in his highly subjective account, the early American literature standard *Of Plymouth Plantation*, that God had obviously meant this land for them, the Pilgrims (with a capital *P*). The evidence he offered up? The "fact" that the beings already living there were godless, and God could not have provided such wondrous land to the godless, making a leap in logic that these people were closer to animals than humans. Bradford's observations are usually cast as the author being "a product of his time," in American literature classes, softening the possibility that Hitler might have gotten a jump-start of inspiration from across the ocean. Isn't the first step in any holocaust the denial of human status to those who are about to be eliminated?

If those perpetrating the demise of my ancestors were not so good at keeping records, my ancestors themselves had an even greater disadvantage. A difficulty present in reconstructing the histories of oral cultures is the fluidity of that history. This is not to say that historians from writing-based cultures are any more truthful in their reporting of past events, but the documents they left behind at least could later be examined for incongruity with other evidence. In an oral culture, once the story changes the old stories are gone for good and those earlier versions live only as long as the last person who remembers them. The history of nearly anything is always up for grabs and self-serving interpretation, and I do not know anyone who has not modified at least one event from the past to suit his or her needs. Doubt and Ambiguity, or perhaps their cousins Faith and Narrative, saturate the arcs of many lives. My story contains two separate strands, Tuscarora and Onondaga, of these historically malleable abstractions.

The sources I have found to document the period of Tuscarora history before the western New York settlement are not easily accessible and are, at best, vague or not reliably traceable. I knew of the migration and the approximate years, but I had never heard these stories in my entire life. The few citations I had found over the years stated briefly that the Tuscarora, after having been nearly wiped out in their homelands in present day North Carolina, made their way north to officially ask if they could join the Haudenosaunee, the league of Five Nations in New York, having originated in the same area. The migration was cast as a homecoming, as it were, the welcoming back of the sixth nation.

One of the documents I recently found suggested a different interpretation of the migration. The narrative, a scholarly discussion from an online source, asserted that the Tuscaroras had constructed wampum belts documenting continued encounters with the white settlers who had first removed them from the places they had lived for a very long period of time. When the Tuscaroras retaliated against this removal they were effectively driven by force. They were then constantly harassed wherever they tried to thrive on the edges of their previous homelands.

In a severely deteriorated state, already removed to Pennsylvania, the Tuscaroras constructed treaty wampum belts asking that their homes not be burned, that they not be captured and sold into slavery, and that they not be killed whenever they left their encampments to hunt or gather wood or haul water. They were not living in a death camp, per se, but instead, the world around their small sanctuaries had become one giant, all-encompassing death camp. In essence, these belts asked simply that they be allowed to survive. The dire pleading nature of the belts moved some Indian witnesses from other nations to act on behalf of the Tuscaroras and they sent the belts to the Haudenosaunee. The Haudenosaunee responded by agreeing to embrace them as members of the confederacy. Is this the true story, or is the homecoming told through the Tuscarora community the true story? Who am I to say?

The Tuscarora Nation is currently a place that is heavily Christian. There are no longhouses within its borders. It has been suggested that missionaries effectively infiltrated the vulnerable community when the members first arrived in western New York, struggling to survive. Present repercussions of this forced ideology even continue to influence the attempts at regaining the nearly eliminated indigenous identity. Now forms of traditional culture are briefly and randomly glimpsed, at times arbitrarily resurrected or changed for political convenience. What is one day a game the next day becomes a ceremony, named as such by people who want to prevent the game from being played because it might reveal political affiliation. Ultimately, who can argue, having such fragmentary knowledge of our own history as we do?

In that light, a history of a homecoming seems suited to a group of people trying to keep some version of their culture alive. And on the other side, some historian's research relying upon documents of the era, well, that has its own problems. It suggests that the person recording the original accounts had no agenda, when in fact the picture of Indian nations in disarray and highly fragile states certainly suited the argument for the elimination of tribal identity and for aggressive programs of assimilation eventually formalized in the Dawes General Allotment Act of 1887, whose sole purpose was the systematic dissolution of separate and specific identities among the indigenous peoples living within the formally recognized borders of the United States.

While the history of the Onondaga Nation is a little more clearly documented in Dean R. Snow's volume, *The Iroquois,* from the nation's concrete and formative involvement in the origin of the Haudenosaunee, to the first contact deaths by smallpox in 1635 and beyond, my own relationship with the official nation has been tangential and peripheral at best. I had asked my mother over the years who we were related to over at Onondaga. I knew all 250 of our close relatives at home, but I had no clue about our genetic affiliations from our official homeland, the Onondaga Nation outside of what is now Syracuse, New York. She consistently gave one of her abstract William Carlos Williams answers.

She said that they used to visit relatives at least once a month when she was a little girl, but they were probably dead now. She seemed to dismiss the obvious—that those people she had known as a child had likely grown to adulthood, at least some of them, anyway, and had children of their own. But I guess she believed reconnecting with them would be relatively fruitless, given our century-and-a-half history at Tuscarora. Conversely, she never wanted us to forget that we were not Tuscarora, that we were Onondaga.

Every year when I was a child, around the fifth of June, we received money from the Onondaga Nation, which was issued to every person on the roll books as part of some treaty agreement. I never knew, and to this day still do not know, what the "June Money" represented, but even when I was as young as three my mother gave me my share and reminded me it was something we were getting because we agreed to lose something else. It was usually somewhere between two and six dollars. This probably doesn't seem like a lot, but we were deadly poor in that period, frequently reduced to lettuce and mayonnaise sandwiches for supper because that was all we could afford. Our dubious suppers didn't matter to my mother, though. She wanted us to understand that this money represented a relationship our nation had with the United States and that a collective memory relies upon individual memories as well as those of the group. And so here I am, a fairly literate and educated Onondaga man from the Tuscarora Nation, harboring only the sketchiest of cultural history. But we go with what we have, and who we are and what we have are the fragmentary voices of the children of the children of the children of the children of the children of the children of the survivors of the American holocaust.

Shortly before my mother's eightieth birthday an idea that had been buzzing around in her head for years moved to the forefront. She insisted I get my tribal ID card from the appropriate place. I had one issued from the Tuscarora Nation, but my family members had been increasingly trading theirs in for cards issued at Onondaga, where we were officially listed on the Nation roll book. I had tried three times in the years before, without much luck, because the person who issues the cards does the work on a volunteer basis and so gets to them as he can. I think my application had been lost all three times but I gave it one last try, not knowing my mother had taken steps to ensure it would not get lost that last time, pulling a convoluted set of strings to be certain my papers would not get misplaced a fourth time. When she turned eighty I had my correct tribal identification. She became "the cheese" standing alone that same year when her last sister left us.

She talked of her siblings rarely after they had left us, or of her history, the older she got. It was almost as if they had not existed. Even when questioned directly she gave fairly perfunctory answers. I think, as I would visit and relentlessly ask her about her youth, trying also to get her to confess to being one of the fewer than ten people fluent in Tuscarora, she knew that I recognized what was happening as her generation left us. We were becoming holocaust survivors one more generation removed, losing yet another piece of our remembered history. As she had with the June Money, she wanted me to always know who I was, officially, in the eyes of the United States, and that to forget the relationship, regardless of what else I might or might not know, could cause serious problems for the official status of any of us. History and memory to her were incidental. National identity was another matter entirely, involving the question of where we were born or any other anomalies that might show up in our official United States lives. She needed to know that I had my documents in order.

On her eighty-first birthday, a Thursday, she and I had made arrangements for Sunday. I'd recently had a new novel published and some colleagues had invited me to participate in a discussion of it, as they had the year before with an earlier novel. I had ingredients to pick up before I got back to my mother's house. She was going to teach me to make fry bread. We had tried this for the previous year's book discussion, but she'd grown impatient with my ineptitude and made me step aside so she could finish it more quickly. I tried explaining to her that it wasn't so much that I had wanted to bring fry bread to the discussion but that I had wanted to learn to make it. She laughed, saying it was a matter of feel and that I was trying to learn too late to ever be as good as she was. It was critical for me to learn, as fry bread is not only official "national Indian food," but every family's fry bread is a little different, has its own signature style, and so the way you find your way home is to taste the particular fry bread you grew up with. I needed to know how to make it and was not sure if anyone else in my family had learned my mother's exact methods. "And besides," she sighed, "why are you feeding this to white people anyway? They're not going to like it. Let me put some sugar in it, make it more interesting for them."

My mother always maintained that the cultures were so different that her fry bread would not cross culinary borders without some modification. She likened me to her fry bread and was confident that I had only completed my education because I was able to remove myself from the reservation influence. She could never understand why anyone ever read anything I wrote and thought that nobody could possibly be interested in the reservation life she had negotiated for so long. I left her house at 9:00 Thursday night, with a plan to be there with a full grocery bag of ingredients by 2:00 on Sunday, which she assured me would be plenty of time to get this lesson over with.

Sometime Friday morning my mother had a massive stroke from which she never awakened. We brought her to rest with her siblings and parents and grandparents and great-grandparents a little over a week later. As we lowered her into the ground I thought of all the things I did not know, and of what little I did. Shortly after she left us, some people from around the reservation gave us photographs they had of her in her youth, pictures I had never seen.

She was vibrant, smiling, a young and beautiful Indian woman who had found some period of time where she was not on her knees, scrubbing someone else's floor. There she was, standing with some other young Indian women, smiling, posing before a backdrop of Niagara Falls, in high fashion for the era. If the young woman's face had not so clearly been hers I would have sworn this was not my mother. She had always been sure to show me the difficult life of Indians in America, convincing me by fear instead of example that I had to learn to thrive in that White Man's World she saw surrounding us and not the subservient one she inhabited the entire time I had been alive. She felt that if her children were to live a life solely within the context of an Indian community we would surely be as exterminated as all those Indians who had come before us.

What holocaust was this? I wondered, closing my *American Heritage* and putting it back on the shelf. At what point does America give us our own capital *H*? Or do we just have to take it for ourselves, rewriting or respeaking history in the way it has been rewritten around us for over five hundred years?

LOOKING TO THE PAST TO FIND THE FUTURE

YUFNA SOLDIER WOLF

I AM Yufna Soldier Wolf. My first name is a description of when the rain is over and the rainbow comes out; another meaning is Mother Nature's Child. I am the youngest daughter of ten children, twenty-four years old, and the only sibling to graduate from the University of Montana. I am now working toward getting my master's degree in public relations with a minor in Native American studies.

My people are the Northern Arapahoe Nation. My branch and the other thirteen branches of Arapahoe call us *Ha-day-none-a-ei,* which means "The Ancient People." Other native people refer to us by the more contemporary name *Hinononei,* which means "Blue Sky People." Still other Plains tribes call us "teachers" because we have been willing to share our ways with them. Virginia Cole Trenholm, in *The Arapahoe, Our People,* has written that we are the "earliest known being the old Algonquin designation Bison Path People." A long time ago we migrated from the area of Minnesota to the High Plains where we now reside in the central part of Wyoming on the Wind River Indian Reservation. We still have stories from the Paleo-Indians that tell of the ice age and various animals that are now extinct. We have names for some of these that our ancestors hunted: the saber-toothed's name in Northern Arapahoe is *ba-ha-hawk* and the giant beaver's is *ha-ba-des-it-hebes.* We also have names for the places where the ancestral Arapahoe traveled, such as *Hen-a-jay-none-ee,* which means "Giant Bison," for the Linden Meier site, which is almost on the Wyoming-Colorado border a few miles from Fort Collins, Colorado.

The area in which the Arapahoe nomadically traveled and inhabited is from Canada to Texas, from the Rockies to Nebraska, Kansas, and on to the headwaters of the Missouri. The Arapahoe have a name for the Gulf of Mexico, *Baa-ex–woo,* which means "The Great Ocean to the South." My nation was once a traveling people because our way of life was sustained by following the roaming buffaloes' migration over the Great Plains. These buffaloes were our source of food, shelter, clothing, home utensils, home décor, and various other items. The pioneering settlers, the United States government, and the railroad wiped out all our sources and way of life by taking our lands and intentionally decimating the population of the buffalo.

In 1869 President Ulysses S. Grant put into effect his "peace policy," whereas pressure was put on all American Indians to live and stay on reservations and to become more "civilized." In 1870 Congress agreed with Grant and allotted to this policy $100,000 for Indian education, which would cause mass cultural genocide. Ancestral lands were taken away from Indians and given to white settlers. During 1877 and 1878 the Arapahoe were placed with our enemies, the Shoshone, on the same reservation. At the time, we were promised our own reservation. The U.S. government has never lived up to this promise.

We Northern Arapahoe still live with the Shoshone on the Wind River Indian Reservation. The Shoshone sued the United States for breach of treaty stipulation by letting the Northern Arapahoe stay on the reservation. The Shoshone were angry because we were considered equal landholders and they did not want to make decisions with the Northern Arapahoe. In 1930 we Arapahoe had to buy our part of the reservation from the Shoshone, and paid them $14 million for it. This was money that came from selling Arapahoe lands in Colorado near the

Platte River where gold and silver mines were abundant and where farmland was wanted. Out of this total the Shoshone received $4,408,404. The Shoshone call this the "Tunnison Money" after George Tunnison, who represented them in court. Where did the rest of the $10 million go? Bureau of Indian Affairs officials at that time seemed to have some corruption and conspiracy going on as they still do today. Nothing has ever been done concerning this shortage, nor will it ever be seriously looked into.

My great-great-grandfather Sharpnose, was one of the Northern Arapahoe war leaders. The authority to be in charge of his people was given him in 1851 by his father, Red Bear, at the Great Council Tree in what is now known as Fort Collins, Colorado. To have Sharpnose and his people settle on reservations was the government's way to suppress and take land from the Northern Arapahoe, as well as from all other American Indians during this so-called taming of the West. The United States government men deemed this land free because, in their opinion, the Indians were not putting the land to good use. So with their superiority complexes and dirty political issues, they took the Indian families to reservations where they were given diseased blankets and where they existed on pitiful food rations, since the American Indian way of hunting food was strictly forbidden.

I now ask you to put yourself in the Indian children's moccasins.

Imagine being a child again. Envision being eleven years old, thinking of your friends and life with ease and being full of nonstop questions. Imagine being a carefree spirit and still having innocence in your life, still loving without reason, and having thoughts of the world as complete in your own eyes. Then imagine that everything that makes you who you are is being attacked. You are told that the way you dress, the way you speak, and everything you were taught about your heritage is evil and wrong. Envision that people want to take everything you hold dear away from you and send you off to a school far, far away from your family and comfortable surroundings. You are sent all the way across the country to a place called Pennsylvania. When you arrive you are stripped of all your beliefs. Your hair is cut. You were raised to believe that hair was cut only when someone close to you has died and so you feel like a part of you is dying. Your comfortable, traditional clothes are taken away and you are made to dress in foreign clothes. You are told the language you speak is wrong. If ever you are caught speaking your language you are punished by one of the following: being hit, slapped, beaten, given hard labor to perform, or put into solitary confinement. Imagine being horribly punished for trying to maintain your essential nature. All of this is hard to envision, isn't it? This and more happened to many native children who were taken to Carlisle School and other boarding schools. Taking children away from their families in Indian Country was a common governmental practice from about 1879 to the 1950s.

My great-great-grandfather Sharpnose was born in 1830. After reaching adulthood he married and had three daughters and three sons. His son Little Chief, who was the eldest child of his family, grew up with his siblings in the time of cultural genocide and assimilation of the American Indian. Remember imagining what life was like when you were eleven? This is the age that Little Chief was sent off to boarding school. He was told that everything he stood for as a human was wrong. He was sent to Carlisle, Pennsylvania, in 1881 and went through the degrading process of his hair being cut, his native clothing being taken away, and being told that if he spoke his own language he would be severely punished. Upon arrival at this military school he was told that his name of Little Chief wasn't acceptable and he was made to take the name of Dickens Nor. The sheer arrogance of the imagined superiority of a white society that would not even let a boy keep his name!

While living at this school he endured long days of not being able to communicate with his family or his childhood friends. He and other native students would cry themselves to sleep at night because they were so terribly homesick. Some of the children died from sheer loneliness and confusion. Little Chief/Dickens endured this life until the age of fourteen, when he died of pneumonia in 1883. The historian of Carlisle, Barbra Landis, e-mailed his obituary to me:

On the 2nd of the month Dickens, one of our Northern Arapahoe boys, died of pneumonia. Dickens was one of the merriest of the company of boys who had quarters by themselves and a matron of them and he will be much missed by the little family. His aptness to learn and his obedient spirit endeared him to his teachers and his death has brought great sadness to our circle. While we mourn our hearts go in sympathy for those at his home who have anticipated his going home to them, their pride and joy. He was the son of Sharpnose, second chief of his tribe and this fact would of given him much influence among his people

Dickens' body was interred at Carlisle, not returned to his home and parents. Along with Dickens, there were nine other Arapahoe children who died at Carlisle and whose bodies were never sent home. Dickens' sister, Minnie, was also sent to Carlisle. She escaped and tried to return home to her people but only made it as far as Bemidji, Minnesota. If an Indian child ran away from a boarding school, he or she was either taken back for a reward or shot. Minnie never made it home. She is buried in Bemidji, Minnesota.

Richard Henry Pratt, captain of the 10th Calvary Buffalo Soldiers, was the founder of Carlisle Indian School. His motto was "Kill the Indian, save the man." In 1875 he escorted seventy-two Indian warriors to prison in Florida and experimented by trying to teach them how to read and write. The process and ways Pratt used to teach would later be labeled as cultural genocide and assimilation. The news that Mr. Pratt was experimenting with these Indians spread; soon afterward, he received permission from the U.S. government to expand his program by establishing the Carlisle Indian School. The school continued into the 1930s, until the administration saw that the promised opportunities for Indian students would not materialize, that they would not become "imitation white men." The Carlisle Web site states that Pratt had a strong desire to see Indians assimilated. In an article from March 18, 1898, the school newspaper, called the *Indian Helper,* embodied Pratt's assimilation philosophy:

I would think it would interest our readers more if at least one of the inside pages contained some interesting stories or would describe the Indian a little better by telling how he is tamed and brought up. The Indian that is shown is dressed in hideous costume of feathers, paint, moccasins, blanket, leggings, and scalp lock, which displays their savagery. It is this nature in our red brother that is better dead than alive, and when we agree with the oft-repeated sentiment that the only good Indian is a dead Indian, Carlisle's mission is to kill this Indian, as we build up the better man. We do not like to keep alive the stories of the past, hence deal more with his present and future.

How were American Indians at this time expected to move on in their lives when the idea of "Kill the Indian, save the man" was being used for their very extinction? Can this be compared to the Nazi war when only blonde hair and blue eyes were acceptable? Of course it can!

All the years of being abused and victims of genocidal assimilation at boarding schools gave many Indian people varying perspectives concerning education. More negative than positive, we still see the ripples from the treatment the students endured. Today, many older grandparents and parents hesitantly send their children off to school. They know that school now is not as harsh as it was for them, but deep inside they still relive those moments of assimilation and mistreatment, and so they no doubt question their children's education. But revitalization of the Arapahoe culture is now going strongly. Thanks to determined leaders in my tribe we have made it this far holding onto our culture, and we benefit from the choices that our past leaders made to keep our tribe and ways of life imperative. These leaders were true visionaries.

My parental grandpa, Scott Dewey, was a survivor of Carlisle's assimilation. Scott, Burdick Addison, Louis Headley, and Jim Large—who were all Northern Arapahoe—attended Carlisle. My grandpa's experiences are relayed through my father, Mark Dewey Soldier Wolf, and also through my grandpa's journals. Scott Dewey was an avid writer and wrote every day about anything and everything. I appreciate his writings today even more, as he has passed on.

My grandpa and his peers, Burdick Addison, Louis Headley, Bill Mint Horn, Louis Towanama, and the well-known teammate Jim Thorpe, were part of the football team at Carlisle. They became renowned after beating West Point when Eisenhower attended school there. Scott had many experiences—good and bad—at Carlisle. The most important is what I call the grey cloud with silver lining. The grey cloud being that of the assimilating and tearing at his culture, but also the silver lining, which was Glenn "Pop" Warner. Pop was the coach at Carlisle and treated the Indian students as equals. Pop's relationships with Scott and other students are what kept some of them from running away. My grandpa also endured some hard times while at Carlisle. His dad died but he was not permitted to leave the school to help his mother. Thanks to Pop, he was able to get through his hard times. The bond he had with these boys was so grand that, when Scott and Burdick finally returned home, Pop shared a tear with them at the train station. After Grandpa had been home for a few years, one day a knock came at the door and he heard Jim Thorpe's voice outside his cabin asking, "A Scott Dewey live here?" Jim had come to ask my grandpa and Burdick if they would go with him to Rawlins for a reception in honor of the football team.

Throughout Scott's life at Carlisle he not only made lasting relationships but also received the education that proved to be essential in helping his people. Scott was oftentimes dealt a hard hand during those days of boarding school, but he coped with it the best he could and came away being a leader for our people. At the age of twenty-eight in 1923 he first served on the Northern Arapahoe Business Council and continued to serve on this council for thirty years, off and on. He was one of four men to persuade the Bureau of Indian Affairs to grant per capita payment of tribal funds to enrolled members of our tribe. Today we still receive this money monthly and a thirteenth payment every Christmas

After a very long time, the U.S. government has tried to amend some wrongful doings to us Indians by passing a federal law called NAG-PRA—the Native American Graves Protection and Repatriation Act—

in 1990. This embodies a process for museums and federal agencies to locate Native American cultural items, human remains, funerary objects, sacred objects, and objects of cultural patrimony, which are then given back to the lineal descendents and affiliated tribes and Native Hawaiian organizations. Also, there is another group called the American Indian Ritual Object and Repatriation Foundation, which mediates and acts as a conduit for both parties. These parties and the people who know the laws and guidance in implementing the process of returning to American Indians the remains of children such as Little Chief, sacred artifacts, and other objects held in high regard can offer a great service to Indian communities. I have documentation of pipes being sent with children to Carlisle and I often wonder whatever happened to these, which would now be considered sacred artifacts.

At Carlisle the first Indian students were the ones who built the administration building, gym, shops, chapel, and the cemetery. In addition to this labor, the Indian children did not have the immune systems to cope with Euro-American diseases. Some students were stricken with TB, small pox, and pneumonia, and others just could not cope with the severe stress of separation from family and tribe. The ones who died were buried there, not sent home. Of all the children buried there, the Apache tribe represents the largest number of deaths.

The remains of our ancestors being sent back to reservations is a very controversial issue in some ways but, in the bigger picture, it is looking to the past to move on with the future. According to NAGPRA, only lineal and federally recognized tribes can ask for human remains and objects. I have been working on having Little Chief's remains returned for three years now. My dad and his father had tried many years ago but at the time there was no NAGPRA or NATHPO, the National Association of Tribal Historic Preservation Officers, which also helps with repatriation. I am writing a grant at present to help with the cost, and am also trying to raise money on my own, which is difficult. So far it has been a long, hard path because Carlisle is a military installation; thus, I have to go through the Department of Defense.

Indian reburial is a contemporary issue that deals with ceremonial practices, as well as help and support of tribal elders, tribal council, and everyone involved. Reburial also has much to do with spiritual and emotional issues that need to be addressed, not only by natives, but also by the "white society" so that we all may move on. I believe the general public should be aware of what the American Indians have endured throughout the past and are still enduring today. This is why it is good to write about these issues and present society with the truth of what has gone on.

The American Indian Holocaust did happen. Perhaps not in the same way the holocaust happened for the Jews, nor for the people in Rwanda, nor for the Puerto Ricans at Carlisle, nor for the Asians at Heart Mountain, nor for all culturally oppressed, assimilated people everywhere in the world. But it did happen and bits and pieces of this oppression are evident in all Indian communities today. That these grave injustices happened to many groups, not just one, and in various ways, should finally be confronted. The general population should come to terms with what happened and, most importantly, be aware so that atrocities like this won't happen again. To learn from history would be grand. To deny this ever happening to American Indians is to become another victim of the genocidal process.

I am reminded of a story I once read in *Reader's Digest*. As the trains that were filled to capacity with crying Jews on their way to be annihilated passed by churches, the servants of God only sang louder to drown out the cries of the victims. Today our cries are continually getting louder. The war did eventually end for the Jews. Will it ever for the American Indians?

RESILIENCE AND RESPONSIBILITY:

SURVIVING THE NEW GENOCIDE

SHAUNNA OTEKA McCOVEY

IT'S NEARLY 10:30 in the morning and I've managed to finagle a boat ride along the Klamath River with the Yurok Tribal Fisheries Program (YTFP). We are going to take a trip approximately twenty-five river miles from the upper part of northern California's Yurok Indian Reservation to the mouth of the river where it empties into the Pacific Ocean. I'm excited because, even though I grew up on the reservation, I've never been on this trip before. There isn't a road that connects the lower and upper reservation, so boat travel is used today much like it was 150 years ago.

As we begin the winding drive from Weitchpec along State Route 169, what we locals refer to as "downriver," I'm very nostalgic. This happens every time I travel this road, every time I go home. My siblings and I grew up here in this remote area without electricity or a telephone, so we spent much of our childhood outdoors. Being outside as much as we were helped foster our special relationship to this place. That, combined with the knowledge that our people have been on this river since time began, makes for a pretty solid connection.

There is something about the way it smells downriver that is unlike any other place I've been. It isn't simply one unique smell, but every time we turn a corner there are subtle changes in the smell. Sometimes it's fresh and clean, with a hint of berries and wildflowers; other times the fragrance is of cool dew and moss. If you're lucky, you can catch a whiff of breakfast being prepared in one of the houses along the way.

We are going to put the boat in at Sregon, an old village site about eighteen miles from the tribal office at Weitchpec. The sun is warming things up on the river bar and the water is calm and glassy.

The sunglass-sporting lad at the helm of our jet boat just happens to be my younger brother, who has been with our fisheries department for nearly six years. His knowledge of the river and its biology is very sound, as is his coworker's, a young woman who can name every creek and riffle along the river. On our trip we will pass by those creeks she ticked off: Pecwan, Tectah, Little Surper, Big Surper, Bear, Ah Pah, and Blue. Farther downriver we will pass McCovey Riffle and Blake's Riffle, then Omagar, McGarvey, and Terwer creeks and finally come to Requa, where the river turns into an estuary and mixes with saltwater. The end of our journey is a place we call "The Lips," where the Klamath passionately kisses the Pacific. It is here that the great runs of salmon enter the river and make their way up to spawn.

The Mouth of the River

At first the mouth of the river was at Omen (Wilson Creek). The Sky-Keeper made an opening and that was the mouth. Now the people were ready and stood on the bar at the mouth of the river with harpoons and eel hooks to catch lamprey eels but they could not see any fish. They said, "How will we live? How shall we eat?" So the Sky-Keeper changed the mouth and made it where it is at Requa. The people stood on the bar there (at Requa) and speared and got many salmon. So they were glad.

—Capitan Spott of Requa
Yurok Myths

You may be wondering what a boatload of Yuroks traversing the mighty Klamath has to do with genocide. The answer is simply—*everything.*

The arrival of whites to this part of the country was not a surprise. We knew that one day the *wogé,* or white beings, would appear. What we didn't know was the destruction they would cause or the havoc they would wreak. The discovery of gold at Sutter's Mill, in California's central valley, meant the end of the Indian world as we had known it for thousands of years. We lost most of our ancestral lands and many aspects of our culture, and our language took a severe beating. In the boarding schools we began to emulate the whites. Our girls learned to sew and set Emily Post's table, while our boys were taught to weed and manicure lawns to prepare for great futures in menial labor. Not long after that, the United States imposed upon us a governing structure that looked nothing like our traditional way of governance.[1]

To say that the Yurok people have suffered as a direct result of U.S. law and policy would be a drastic understatement. It is also an obvious restatement, because the same story can be told on every reservation, in every Alaska Native Village, and in the Native Hawaiian homelands. But this story is not about suffering, it's not about the poor Jedi Indians and what the Evil Empire did to disrupt the Force. This story is about our ultimate survival and what we do day-to-day to ensure that survival. It's about our resilience, the kind that allows us to bend, mold, and adapt, then to somehow create a space for us to remember what is of utmost importance: who we are. It is also about our responsibility and how we define it so that our actions will always reflect what is of utmost importance: *remaining* who we are.

The mountains in this area are steep and rugged, so much so that the river acts as referee to keep them from pummeling one another into the bedrock. The unforgiving terrain has acted as a barrier from the outside world for some time. Let's face it, not a lot of Americans, or Native Americans for that matter, have heard of the Yurok people. Our mountains keep us secluded, and in many ways seclusion has been to our benefit. Our reservation captures some of our traditional territory and this has allowed us, with some interruption, to continue to conduct the ceremonies of our land-based religion. In other words, we dance where we have always danced.

Our people, however, came into the spotlight, though not under the best of circumstances, in the late summer of 2002. The biggest fish kill in Yurok memory thrust the Klamath River and its water crisis into the national media, pitting farmers in the upper Klamath basin against fishermen, Indians, and environmentalists in the lower basin. The loss of salmon, both chinook and coho, was estimated upward of 60,000, and those of us dependent on the salmon runs were completely devastated. What happened is what I refer to as an attempt at cultural genocide. Cultural genocide is just as appalling, if not more so, than physical genocide because its form appears benign. From this standpoint, the perpetrators of these acts can evade responsibility for the demise of a group of people because the people are, in fact, still living and breathing. Remember the old Anglo mantra, "Kill the Indian, save the man?" This tactic has not gone away, only changed its shape over the years. Now it is used under the guise of "scientific findings," "administrative decisions," "legislation," and "statutory interpretation." And we must not forget how our tribal sovereignty is constantly under attack in the courts.

Though the federal government refuses to take responsibility, low water levels in the Klamath reportedly caused the fish kill of 2002. The lower levels delayed migration, thereby causing overcrowding in the estuary (where salmon acclimate to fresh water from salt water). In essence, there were too many fish in too little water. The fish became stressed, which created a higher susceptibility to diseases, including the two they contracted: *Columnaris,* or gill rot, and *Ich,* a white spot disease. Both were fatal.

The United States Bureau of Reclamation (USBR—the federal water agency in charge of dam operations) did not release enough water from the dams along the upper Klamath for the fish to survive. The operating plan for the Klamath heavily favored irrigating farm crops in the upper basin while it completely ignored the needs of the salmon species in the river, particularly the Coho, which is listed as *threatened* under the Endangered Species Act. As a result, the worst fish kill in recent history occurred only one year into Reclamation's ten-year water use plan for the Klamath Basin.

As the Yurok tribe and other affected citizens collected and counted dead salmon carcasses we received no government apology, no compensation, and certainly no claim of responsibility or promise to change the undoubtedly ineffective water use plan.[2] But should we have expected any of these things? Certainly not. We've never been apologized to for the loss of our people during the gold rush, we've never been apologized to for the theft of our land under the General Allotment Act of 1887, we've never been apologized to for the loss of language and the attempted extinction of our culture by the boarding schools, and on and on and on. We cannot trust the federal or state governments to help us protect what is ours, and that is precisely why we are the agents or our survival. We are responsible. The question for us all now is: how will we carry out that responsibility?

We stop at Blue Creek, cold-water refugia for salmon, where the Yurok Fisheries Department team snorkels and does a fish count. They are also using, for the first time, an underwater video camera to help with data collection. It's all very Jacques Cousteau and a clear indication of our adaptability and willingness to be the instruments of our survival. We've come to realize that some things, including technology, must be embraced if we want to have a say in decisions made about our fishery. To mix clichés and make them my own: we've got to learn to talk the talk, while maintaining the ability to walk our own walk.

The Origin of Salmon

It was at Enek that they made salmon. Two women lived there and there were no salmon in the world when Wohpekumeu (the Creator Being) came. As he entered the world he saw the two women. One said to the other, "What shall we eat?" The other replied, "Go wait on the terrace," and she went to retrieve a box with water and salmon inside. All of the time, Wohpekumeu watched her. She took salmon out of the box and they split it, put it on sticks, and broiled it by the fire. Wohpekumeu came to them and put his hand into his carrying case. He said, "I shall eat my salmon." They looked at him and watched him draw it out, but it was really alder bark. They thought, "Where did he get his salmon?" They were the only ones that owned salmon and they concealed it. . . . the women proceeded to cook the salmon and put angelica root in its mouth . . . that they might not have bad luck. Then they said, "Let's go out."

As soon as Wohpekumeu saw that he was alone in the house he went hastily to where he'd seen one of them take the salmon out. He found the box, tipped it over, and ran out. The water flowed and turned into a river, and Wohpekumeu ran upstream with the women pursuing him. They were about to catch him when he found two Tan Oak trees, asked them to split apart, and took refuge in them. The women could not reach him. Then Wohpekumeu said, "Let the river run downstream," and he blew downstream. That is how the river comes to flow. Then Wohpekumeu said to the river, "A great salmon must come up. He will be the salmon leader and they (people) will never catch him in their nets. Only the little ones shall be caught. Every spring, the great salmon has to come first, and all the little ordinary ones follow him upstream.

—STONE OF WEITSPUS (WEITCHPEC)
Yurok Myths

I like to think that I think like a fish. A coho (*Oncorhynchus Kisutch*) or chinook (*Oncorhynchus tshawytscha*) to be more exact. I use the scientific names for these specific salmon only to impress my biologist brother. I can't accurately pronounce the names yet, but in the Yurok language, salmon are called *nay-pooii*. If I think like a fish, then I am better able to understand what is needed for their survival and in essence my own. One thing in particular leaps to mind: clean, fresh water and lots of it. While I acknowledge that the world is full of multiple truths, our truth is salmon. Salmon are such an integral part of our culture that we cannot be Yurok people without them. It's true they are our food, but more than that they are what sustain us, what keep us tied to the river, and we are responsible for their survival as well. If you reread the salmon origin story above, it is clear our role in their survival is respecting the passage of *Nepewo,* or Great Salmon. Doing this brings the promise of healthy salmon runs in the future. That is why the loss of so many chinook and coho as a result the 2002 fish kill was felt so heavily here

along the river. It wasn't just a blow to the food supply or the local economy, but to our existence, our way of life.

To better understand the importance of salmon to our culture, I've
prepared a sample test question for the non-Indian reader, or linear
thinker, much like one you would find on an SAT exam.

Please select which of the following best expresses a relationship similar to that expressed in the capitalized pair:

SALMON : YUROK ::
○ Corn : Hopi
○ Buffalo : Lakota
○ Oil : Bush Administration
○ Liberal : Michael Moore

Difficult? Not really. Not when thought of in terms of necessity and
what is absolutely related not only to physical survival but also to cultural survival.

Cultural genocide is the new genocide. It impacts us in ways we can't
often predict, which makes it more insidious. It we do not learn how
to talk the federal government's talk, so to speak, we will never have a
voice in decisions made about us. This creates a dilemma for some
because there is a fear that exists of becoming too much like white people. This is the struggle: how do we understand their world and still exist
in ours? I think the answer is what it has always been—balance.

Here in northern California, the Yurok, Karuk, and Hupa people
dance to balance the earth, to fix things, to put them back into place.
Our dances are biennial. This year (2005) the Yurok people won't have
our world renewal ceremonies, but the Hupa's will. Next year, in late
summer, we will hold our Deerskin Dance, our Boat Dance, and finally
our Jump Dance. Ten days of dancing and fasting, ten days of rest, then
ten days of dancing and fasting again. What is most unique about our
dances is that they are not just about balancing our Yurok, Karuk, and
Hupa worlds, but about balancing the world for everything that is alive
and in need. We dance for you and we pray for you just as much as we

dance and pray for ourselves. This is a great responsibility, but one we acknowledge as ours. These ceremonies also mean we acknowledge that things fall out of balance and that our life's work is to make them right again. There is even talk of bringing back our Fish Dam Ceremony, a specific dance held in honor of the salmon runs that we have not done in years. If this dance were to take place again it would only strengthen our resolve.

This is who we are: *Poliklah,* the "People from Downriver." This is why what our tribal fisheries program is doing is so important. Learning the science behind salmon migration and reproduction, coupled with our traditional knowledge of salmon origin and its place in our universe, keeps our feet in both worlds. Balance. We have traditional knowledge of our native relationship with the river, but we also know how the federal government and other non-Indians see the river. Balance. Survival often means having to do things on the government's terms, but our new knowledge allows our voices to be heard much louder than they would have been, say, a hundred years ago. We are not static people; we move along a continuum of past, present, and future always striving to achieve some sort of balance.

Future generations of Yurok people depend on us to provide them with a clean river system and a viable salmon fishery. We have a duty and a responsibility to preserve our way of life. Therefore, our survival begins with us.

LIFEBLOOD

It is too much to ask
to see the river as
heart and lungs;
an artery of hydrogen
and oxygen that nourishes
the body of earth,

too much to ask them
to let go of ego and

embrace a worldview
in which the center
of the universe can be
seen, touched.

In their houses they decide
river fate, our fate,
without ever feeling
the lifeblood of the river,
without fully knowing
an Indian's life:

prayers to fix the world,
a natural affinity for
salmon and the sacred,
the intrepid will to
never grow tired,
never give up.

1 For a more explicit account of mass murder with all the gruesome details, one can refer to the book *Genocide in Northwestern California* by Jack Norton.
2 For more information on the lawsuit that followed the 2002 Klamath River fish kill please see www.earthjustice.org.

MAJESTIES LOST

ALFRED YOUNG MAN

ONE OF my earliest childhood memories growing up on the Blackfeet Indian Reservation in Montana was seeing an impish elf one morning just after daybreak. I unexpectedly caught the little character peaking around a blanket my mother had hung over the bedroom door, used as a divider between that room and the next. I was three or four years old, lying in bed, wide-awake, when that little person, less than a foot tall, appeared, flashing a mischievous grin. He had pointed ears, red hair, wore a little green Robin Hood-style hat, had rosy cheeks, an oval face, and big green eyes. I was utterly amused at what I was seeing, never stopping to think for a moment that this little fellow was not supposed to exist. I sat up immediately and he quickly closed the blanket. I slid down from the bed in a flash to get a closer look but he was already gone.

In a second similar incident, I remember sitting on an earthen bank overlooking Highway 2, just outside my grandfather's house. I saw an old Indian man driving by in an orange, dual-wheeled, gravel dump truck (the State of Montana was building a new road through our neck of the woods). Although I didn't think it odd at the time, the steering wheel of that guy's vehicle was on the right side of the cab, on the passenger's side, as in England. The dark-skinned driver was dressed like the Indians of old, even sported an eagle feather in his long black hair that flowed freely in the wind. He wore a brown beaded buckskin vest, had buckskin armbands tied around his bare upper arms, and gave me a happy wave and a wide grinning smile. I remember his pearly white teeth seemed to sparkle and glint in the midday sun. To punctuate his grin, the old Indian driver laughingly made fire shoot out of the smokestacks of his truck, high into the air rising above his cab. Strangely enough, I can't remember any sound to associate with that event; it was like a dream, perhaps imaginary, like it never really happened—but of course it did.

My family lived on a small hill forested with trees of aspen and pine located between Highway 2 and the Great Northern Railroad. We stayed in a small two-room shack outside of the tiny town of East Glacier Park, Montana, the gateway to Glacier National Park. We had no running water, no indoor heating, no indoor toilet, and no modern amenities, not even electricity. We used a kerosene lamp for a nightlight and I wouldn't see something called television for several years. I grew up in a world far removed from the world in which I live today.

The front room of our shack consisted of our dining area, where my visiting aunts, mother, and sisters cooked meals for us. My dad had died of a heart attack when I was two, and I was often told how he hunted for our subsistence, mostly elk, deer, and moose in the backcountry. He was a good shot and an avid hunter and also a respected medicine man. I would give anything now to get the chance to know my father, but then there is so much about life that is unfair and unknowable, and I suppose there always will be. The back room was a bedroom consisting of two beds and a wood-burning stove. My mother and her second husband slept there in one bed, and my little sister and brother and I shared the second bed. My older brothers and sisters stayed with my aunts and uncles, sometimes with my maternal grandfather and paternal grandmother. I still walk through that house in my dreams, always situated as it was, facing the rising sun to the east with the Rocky Mountains and the setting sun in the west, practically in our backyard.

I spent the first five years of my life speaking Cree. On warm summer days I would take Cree sweat baths with my uncles and grandfathers—in that place where the Cree sang songs and sought out the help of the spirits, where they prayed to the Grandfathers for spiritual guidance and assistance in getting through the many challenges of life. If anyone had asked me when I was growing up if I was an Indian, it would've been like asking a fish if it had ever discovered water. I had no idea I was different from others outside the reservation, and I didn't learn to question my identity until I left my home and others began to query who I was.

All that childhood knowledge would be callously taken away from me and my brothers and sisters when we were sent away to stay in the government-run Cut Bank Boarding School, just north of Browning, Montana. I was sent away to this Bureau of Indian Affairs boarding school when I was six. By the time the BIA school had completed its initial two-year duty of "civilizing my mind" into the English language, I was no longer able to understand the Cree language that my grandmother spoke. My life after that was a long series of Indian boarding schools: white education systems where we were treated as savage primitives; where the pedagogy of the age was meant to strip us of every last vestige of our Indian personalities—kill the Indian, save the man. Later, as a young man studying European art and history in London and North American Indian art and history in the U.S., I would learn that the U.S. and Canadian governments systematically tried to eradicate the "Indian" in the man for over seventy years, roughly from the 1890s to the 1960s.

The Ghost Dance, about which much has been written—and much of it erroneous—was performed amongst the Sioux in South Dakota, which led directly to the Massacre at Wounded Knee in 1890. It is well known that the U.S. Army slaughtered over 150 of Chief Big Foot's Miniconjou people on a cold December day in a misguided attempt to eradicate the Ghost Dance. Thereafter, federal law forbade any kind of dancing, vision quests, sweat baths, or powwows throughout the Plains. Montana followed suit when the territorial governor of Montana, J. E. Rickards, issued a proclamation banning the Sun Dance—also known by the people of the time as the Thirst Dance—which was primarily danced to renew the spiritual, mental, and physical health of the individual. My great-grandfather's family became victims of the new law that stated any Indians on the Plains caught performing these rituals or dances would be arrested and locked up. The law remained in force for over a century, until the American Indian Religious Freedom Act of 1978 came into effect for the "protection and preservation of traditional religions of Native Americans." The law in part reads: "On and after August 11, 1978, it shall be the policy of the United States to protect and preserve for American Indians their inherent right of freedom to believe, express, and exercise the traditional religions of the American Indian, Eskimo, Aleut, and Native Hawaiians, including but not limited to access to sites, use and possession of sacred objects, and the freedom to worship through ceremonials and traditional rites."

There is a little-known Sun Dance circle composed of the remains of huge cottonwood trees located just south of Roundup, Montana, where elders say that the Sioux, Blackfeet, Cree, Assiniboine, Crow, Shoshone, and Cheyenne held a Sun Dance long before the white man invaded the Plains. As cottonwood trees can live up to a century and more (there are still cottonwoods alive that lived at the time of the great buffalo herds), some of the Roundup trees are still standing, situated two-by-two in a half-circle. The local white people, of course, have no idea the trees are sacred. My great fear is that some local rancher may decide to cut them down one day, not knowing their significance to Plains Indian history. My elders told me years ago that particular Sun Dance must have been a powerful one since the trees, once they were cut and set in a circle two-by-two, took root, lived, and continued to grow.

The Roundup Sun Dance, I was told, was held to make and honor the peace between the "tribes" on the Plains. With so many tribes aware of each other's existence, they could have had only one ideal in mind with that dance: To live in and honor peace, and share the land, game, and other resources among themselves. The white man's history tells us something else, of course. They came to divide and conquer by making treaties with the various native groups, thereby driving a wedge between the nations. No one knows for certain how many different tribes used the Plains as their breadbasket before the white man arrived and exterminated the buffalo and mega fauna.

The robbing of Indian graves and cultural objects by early army surgeons and social scientists for the purpose of scientific study was all the rage in the 1800s and 1900s. There are many documented cases where Indians were no sooner buried than their graves were dug up and their corpses stolen and sent back East. A letter dated June 27, 1892, which was sent along with fifteen skulls, partial skeletons, and assorted "ornaments," from grave-robber Z. T. Danial at the Blackfeet Indian Agency to Doctor J. S. Billings, Major and Surgeon, U.S.A., Washington, D.C., Army Medical Museum reads:

Dear Doctor:

I have gotten the crania off at last. I shipped them today to Post Surgeon Byrne at Fort Assiniboine, in compliance with your request under date of April 6th. There are fifteen of them. I collected them in a way some-what [sic] unusual: the burial place is in plain sight of many Indian houses and very near frequented roads: I had to visit the Country at night when not even the dogs were stirring. This was usually between 12 P.M. and daylight: . . . the graveyard is two miles from office, so that I have traveled sixty miles on foot to secure them: . . . P.S. The skulls are all genuine Piegan Indians as they were buried Indian fashion: none of them are half-breed or white

Apparently, stealing the remains of Indians and looting their graves was a dangerous business since there were Indian sentries on duty at this place. Today, the robbing of archaeological sites goes undeterred as the rebuilding of the old Boneau Dam by the Bureau of Indian Affairs on the Rocky Boy Indian Reservation continues to unearth remains. Employees take home ancient fossils and bones found at least three hundred feet deep, something that University of Montana archeologists in nearby Havre should be raising holy hell over. It seems that the federal government still cannot respect its own laws or our history.

The Rocky Boy Indian Reservation was created by Executive Order in 1916, signed by President Woodrow Wilson. My great-grandfather, William Boushie *(Pee-ach-eese)* certainly deserves an honored place in that reservation's history. However, politics being what they are, the Rocky Boy tribal councils over the years have failed to recognize or respect that history. Chief Rocky Boy, or Stone Child, from whom the Rocky Boy Reservation takes its name, gets all the credit.

The first location chosen for my people was near what is now Babb, located on the current Blackfeet Indian Reservation. Some 11,000 acres was to be turned over to the Cree and Chippewa. The Great Northern Railway punched its way through Montana in 1887 to connect with those railroads operating in the Pacific Northwest. Railway boxcars moved my grandfathers, grandmothers and their children, and the Chippewa leader Rocky Boy and his Band of followers—more than one hundred people in all—to an area around Saint Mary's Lake, Montana. This was around 1908, in a food-for-allotted-land deal made with the Blackfeet (101 allotments in all). The story of how this betrayal happened is a long one, but basically the people of Montana had tired of trying to chase my family and a Cree Band of Little Bear followers to Canada, so in order to arrive at a workable solution, Montanans asked the U.S. government to negotiate with the Blackfeet for land for these "homeless Cree." As it turned out, the Blackfeet received the food and later the allotted lands as well. I grew up believing that this deal had been approved in Washington, since my mother and her father, and all the other Cree had been led to believe that the land was ours; our elders told us that it was. I believed this until four years ago when an anthropologist friend of mine found a letter of rejection filed away in the deep dark recesses of the Bureau of Indian Affairs filing system in Washington, D.C. This letter clearly stated the deal did not happen. "Charles S. Spencer, Superintendent, Blackfeet Indian Agency" had signed this letter, which included a census of the Rocky Boy Band, on June 27, 1955. Can you imagine the disappointment of being told all of your life that so many square miles of land belonged to your family only to learn that such was not the case? And so we have yet another bald-faced lie, a nine decades-long lie, perpetrated on my family.

The genocidal practice of splitting up Indian nations along individualistic family lines to prevent their ability to organize a strong political movement and resistance is a practice Canada has used for the better part of the last two hundred years on its own Cree people, indeed, on all native people in Canada. Canada has the smallest Indian reserves in all of North America, some being only a few miles square. The site where the last battle between the Cree and the Blackfeet fought around 1869–70, where over three hundred Cree and Blackfeet died, is the very site where the University of Lethbridge campus is currently located. Ironic that I should be teaching in this university. There isn't a day that goes by I am not reminded that the Cree and Blackfeet are traditional enemies. With that in mind, what better way for the U.S. to control the two groups of indigenous people in Montana than to locate them on the same reservation? The U.S. Army's theory was to keep these two groups fighting amongst themselves so they would not have to worry about each of them fighting the U.S. Army. That plan has worked out exceedingly well this past eighty years or so. In fact, we are still fighting amongst ourselves and killing each other.

Several years ago Blackfeet Indian police murdered my younger brother in his jail cell, and with the help of the attorney general of Montana and the Blackfeet Tribe, covered up the atrocious deed. Justice denied is no justice at all. The Blackfeet settled out of court in a wrongful death suit for $20,000 for the three children my brother left behind. The policemen who committed the murder were left free, no doubt to kill again. As far back as 1972 there were over ninety unsolved murders on the reservation. Who knows how many more have happened and gone unreported or unsolved since then? As radio commentator Paul Harvey once remarked on his internationally syndicated broadcast, "If you want to get away with murder, move to the Blackfeet Indian Reservation in Montana!"

Today the Cree people have no federal rights on the Blackfeet

Indian Reservation, no housing, no legal rights. To make matters worse, our own tribal council on the Rocky Boy Indian Reservation refuses to assist us with any kind of housing or educational needs if we live off the reservation, even though this same council is more than happy to include our substantial numbers in their annual census reports to Congress to get more funding. We certainly never get to "enjoy" those benefits. We have become, through acts of sheer racism, greed, and stupidity on the part of U.S. bureaucrats, the academic communities, and many amongs the Cree and Blackfeet, the destitute of the destitute. Subterfuge and lies, political deception, theft of our land and resources from all sides of this equation is the legacy of our history.

Fortunately, even through all that, we Cree still retain the important ingredient of "seeing," our way of viewing the universe. Just as importantly, the governments of the U.S. and Canada can imagine no way in which to exterminate the mystical knowledge within us. My two childhood sightings, along with this inner mystical knowing, is how I know who I am today. This way of seeing, of knowing, is an important part of how we Cree Indians think, what we believe and how we continue to survive today.

Over my lifetime I have often remembered those two "sightings" that at present would be akin to seeing a UFO, Sasquatch, or some other unworldly creature. Cree have always spoken of the little people, sometimes with wonder, sometimes with certain fear. Seeing and experiencing the unusual was part of the everyday world in which we children lived. When we saw such things we weren't told that we were crazy; we weren't told that what we saw didn't really exist, that we were hallucinating, or that these things only existed in our imaginations. To the contrary, our elders accepted what we told them as being the literal truth. They would always share with us a few similar experiences they had when they were growing up. In this way they confirmed and accentuated our recent experiences into time and place as factual events, to be remembered for the rest of our lives. These encounters acted as precursors to the spiritual and visionary happenings we would later undergo in life, of which I have had my share. These happenings were not simply imaginary events, therefore considered to be unimportant as is the case with the way the Western mind handles such occurrences. They had texture, substance, and feeling, were tactile and occupied real time and space. Therefore, they had, and still have, great meaning. Today Western science categorizes these happenings as quantum mechanics or physics. We simply had Indian science.

Fortunately for us, there were no Sigmund Freuds or Carl Jungs hanging around the Indian villages waiting to second-guess what our beliefs were telling us about the world. Being forewarned of the unusual as a child made it easier for me to accept the strange and unfamiliar when it did happen. If one is uncertain about the true nature of the universe and humbled before its mysteries, then the unexpected will come easier, and a person is less prone to believe he is crazy. Native people never had insane asylums. It seems that we were more connected with the mysteries of the universe back then than we are today. But now, if one of my extended family members' children comes to tell me they have seen something odd, I confirm this unusual experience with my own stories and those told by my elders; that is the way it is supposed to be. We are not the manic depressive people that some anthropologists have labeled us, albeit there are still some social scientists that believe we are. Truth be told, we are not the savage, primitive, superstitious Neanderthals of their imaginations and we never were.

The loss of our great men and women, which include my great-grandfathers and great-grandmothers, grandfathers and grandmothers, aunts and uncles, who fought to keep our nations together, who suffered to retain their religious rites, who taught us children the truth, are truly majesties lost. They were a proud and noble people and didn't deserve the treatment they received from the immigrants who came to kill, steal, and take away all that was wonderful.

WHEN THE TRUE ENDING BEGAN

JOSEPH A. DANDURAND

IT'S HARD to start but I will try my best to make sense of where I am and where I am going as a survivor. As a Kwantlen native man, father, fisherman.

A thousand years ago a man, like myself, sat on the shores of the Fraser River, near what is now called Fort Langley, British Columbia, Canada, knocking two stones together creating a knife to cut the fish he was about to catch. They say this man was born from the Sky People and later transformed into ancestral animals and the fish we still to this day take from the Fraser River. That is why we say every day in our lives: "We have always been here...." Since our time began we have been here for 350 generations. We have fished here forever and we will fish here as long as the river provides.

DAY FOUR

lights always going out when you need them the most
true test of a good net mender is if he can do it in the dark
truer test is when you are on the river and you are surrounded by
    darkness
and black clouds and only a sliver of a moon and the tide is changing and
    you know the fish are going to start moving and that last sturgeon has

ripped a hole in your net and you are working frantically to get it
mended and you can't even see your fingers it is so dark.

i remember one time it was so dark that i could hardly tell the river
   from the sky
that sturgeon had ripped a big hole and i was still shaking from pulling
   that 100-pound
monster into my boat
yes
they are monsters
those old sturgeons with their big sucking mouths and their old-man
   whiskers trying to tickle you into that big sucking mouth so they can
   break your bones away and get to your sweet blood and you know if
   you do not grab them right that those bony spines on their backs can
   cut through skin as easy as a razor blade and the last thing you want
   to do is bleed 'cause bleeding only excites them and then they spin
   these big monsters when you begin to pull them up out of the water
they spin and rip your net and they are heavy and your hands begin to
   bleed and those small evil eyes stare at you and you pull their big
   white bellies into your boat and you are left sitting there with your
   bleeding fingers and you are shaking and now you have maybe 10
   minutes to mend your net and you begin with bleeding fingers and
   you can't even see the beginning of the hole but you have to start
   somewhere and it is so quiet that you do not hear that old indian
   woman as she walks down to the river and she doesn't see you as
   you quietly mend your net and then you do notice her and you try
   to see who it is but it is too dark and you keep mending your net
   and your fingers are bleeding all over your torn net and that stur-
   geon in the bottom of your boat just lies there and stares at you as it
   slowly moves its monster gills sucking the cold air from the darkness
   that surrounds all of this.

the woman takes all her clothes off and she places them neatly on the
   river's edge and she places her pretty red boots beside her neatly piled

*clothes and she pins her final words to her clothes and she steps into
the water first touching it with her toes and then she wades into the
darkness and she doesn't even see you as you mend your net and
she is up to her shoulders and then she disappears beneath the water
and she walks further out almost to where you are mending your net
and she finally drops into the 60-foot fishing hole that you have
fished all your life and that your grandfather fished all his life and
she fell to the bottom and she stands there drowning quietly in the
darkness of that hole and the other sturgeon come and they begin to
feed on her sweetness and she is gone as those sucking monster
mouths break her apart and all her pain fades deeper into the
white bellies of these monsters with their old-man whiskers tickling
soft skin.*

Today I watch the smoke rise above the head of a sixty-five-year-old
Kwantlen man as he sits at his set-net hole. His mind is partially
destroyed by decades of pot smoking. The anger within him is there
because he was taken to residential school. His life has been torn from
any sense of family, of history, of a future. He, in a sense—exists.

For me, in life, there are very simple teachings. Have a good mind and
have a good heart when you do anything in your life. Whether it's writing or cooking a meal for your family or starting a fire, have a good mind
and a good heart and the work you are doing will go well, and with that
you are humbled.

We are a humble people, though we went to war with our neighbors
and others who came to conquer and steal from us. We protected ourselves and we were barbaric. Our history is not filled with glorious tales
of passive survival. We lived in harsh times and we fought back, and even
tales of our people having slaves are true. We also took people to be our
slaves as others to be theirs took our people.

Our past is our past. But as we survived we also created sophisticated
laws and spiritual ceremonies. None of what we repeat today can be
found in any book. None of our scared rituals did we just one day make
up. Ritual is repeated and repeated.

Smallpox wiped out 80 percent of our people. Hundreds of families then became perhaps two to three main families. Then the fur traders came and soon realized that furs were not what would make them rich; it was the fish from the rivers that provided the riches they sought. Then this place became a colony. In 1858 the British Government proclaimed our traditional lands a Crown Colony. In 1859 new leaders of this land chose a policy of "benevolent assimilation" for our people; in other words, "they will be gently transformed into Europeans."

What of us, survivors of epidemics? What shall be done with us? Assimilated? Transformed? How can you transform a people who were created from the Sky People? How can you even think of changing legend? Begin to destroy them, weaken them. Take from them that which keeps them: food, language, belief, and of course—their children.

One man, an Indian agent, James Trutch reduced our reservations by 92 percent and he gave us only parcels of past traditional lands. Slivers of good lands, mostly flood plains, became our villages. Then they told us to be farmers—but we were fisherman. Then they said to stop our ceremonies. Then they said speak English so you may understand why we tell you that you must assimilate. Then they took my mother to residential school at the age of six.

My mother to this day denies residential school had any effect on her. Denial is as rampant in our village as it is in all villages. Denial until death sometimes comes too quickly. The effects, though denied by my mother, filtered down to me. Older boys abused me and a priest at a Catholic school my parents sent me to abused me. My parents are not to blame. How could they have known of pedophiles? How could they have known the effects of assimilation?

TWO
2 eagles talk
as we track a song
lost in eroded island
bluffs.

2 old drummers
reminisce about what
it used to be like.

fish jumps looks
around
devours the current
and is away.

2 cats lie in dirt
sleepy eyes barely open
dead mouse beside them
not telling tales of last
night's torture.

unknown truck
goes by our house
not supposed to be here
strangers
in a strange land.

old reserve #6
an island
squa'lets
its old name.
(where waters divide)

2 indian kids play hockey
one shoots
one saves
they are not strangers
nor is this place strange to
them.

old rez #6
an island that
becomes more
of an island
less of an island.

eroded
by the
fraser river.

squa'lets

this old place
not a strange
word anymore.

language is like that:

taken
eroded
returned.

As I live here now on this small island I am not ashamed of the past. I am not burdened by it, either. Yet I teach my daughters about who they are and at the age of seven my older daughter, whose name means *Forever*, knows she is Kwantlen and she knows her culture; she knows the teachings that have been passed on through centuries. Through this we weave our way past the alcohol, past the drugs, past the beatings, the hatred, the lost people who still are drunk and damaged by abuse and drugs, and the yelling and the screams. If you sit still long enough you can hear screams coming from the cedar trees.

It's truly a blessing and a tragedy to be so near Western civilization and to have our past, our culture, our language, and our spirituality. We do not forget who we are and where we come from. We are ancestors of the Sky People. It is tragic that Western civilization and its concrete needs and the destruction of the earth and the destruction of the river remind us how simple life should be and how unfortunately it is not. My family and I and thousands of other Indians accept this and we move on. To stop and look and wonder makes it tragic, it deadens you. I move forward each day, as does my family. From season to season we live our lives to their fullest, never repeating negative situations and always pushing ourselves to be constantly busy.

It's a hard life but a good life.

One of the teachings often repeated is that a life of drugs and alcohol is easy; treating yourself, healing yourself is hard. I find (although not when I was drunk or smoking way too many drugs) humans who drink and do drugs to be selfish. Life is not only about one person; life is not only about me. I chose to live. My ancestors chose to live in order for me to sit here and live a good life, a life much easier than the hardships they endured.

DRUNKS, DRIFTERS, AND FAT ROBINS

he wears his 3-dollar sweater bought from value village
his 2-dollar shoes stolen from a party long ago
as he stumbles up our one road.

this drunken drifter squeezing some life out of his sore eyes
as fat robins feast on big worms nearly pulling their heads off as they
  tear them
from the wet ground.

past the old church that no one uses anymore he makes the sign of the
  cross
and nearly falls and nearly lands on a fat robin that just won't let go of
  a 6-inch worm
they both
the drunk and the robin
look at each other with sore eyes and squawk

their displeasure for the other
regain their balance
and move on.

the church sits quiet
no more prayers or salutes to a false god
a god who preys upon small boys through the skin of men in clergy
   clothes.

the windows are all broken
the pattern of them now reflects some sort of eerie
message that only drunks and robins could comprehend.

shards of prayers follow him as he stumbles forward
never looking back at the old white church
its paint folding and falling away and landing on the ground
this sacred ground where little boys used to be touched and used by men
   in clergy clothes
their rotten breath floats throughout this place causing even the drunk
to stop and choke it out of his already dead body.

then he falls down
spreads out as if catching himself would help
his arms and legs spread
not like jesus on the cross
but like a defenseless worm about to be pulled up out of the warm earth
   below him
he breathes in that rotten breath
and he stays there like the church with its broken windows and falling
   paint.

rain falls as the drunk does not move
robins eat big worms and become too fat to fly so they hop around the
   dead drunk

his sore eyes opened
if only for the
last
time.

How do I survive? I tell myself every day that I am from the Sky People. I tell myself that I am a Kwantlen man, a simple fisherman, a father and a husband. I wake up every day and repeat my ritual of getting myself clean and ready for my work. I sip a cup of coffee and watch the local news, watching the weather. I wake my daughter for school, make her lunch and get her shower ready, and then I get her clothes all set for school and make sure she hurries in the shower, because sometimes when she is really tired she will just sit there and let the hot water put her back to sleep. When she is ready, I drive her to school and wait for her to go inside and start her day. Then I go to work. Every day I repeat this ritual. Every day I am alive because I choose to walk past assimilation and abuse. Every day I am proud of who I am. I know that if I am of a good mind and if I am of a good heart ... then so, too, will my children and my wife have a good life.

They say we are medicine for our family. If we are sick or drunk or high or victimized by our past, so, too, then will be our children.

I am medicine for my family and the song in my head heals my family and me. It is a song repeated over and over—FOREVER.

PERFECTION
the touch of a 5-month-old baby
calms me.

the sound of 1,000
drummers
calms me.

in an old house
upriver they place

bones beneath
cedar benches.

rock thieves
comb the beaches
as old houses
descend back to the
earth
that they
came from.

soft little hands
cradle my old face.

(anger left its mark.)

childhood abuse from
older boys
haunts me to no end.

please
place me
beneath cedar benches
so i can lie still
for a moment.

it is that breath
that
lovely
final
breath
that
i become

perfect.

SO OUR CHILDREN WILL KNOW

CLIFFORD E. TRAFZER

IF **YOU** traveled to Indian Country and spent some time in any Native American community in the Western hemisphere, you would soon learn that among the tribal elders there are people who know the old stories. These special elders are the keepers of the council fires, the keepers of traditions. These men and women are the real historians of American Indians, the people who know the ancient and recent history of the people. Through rich and diverse oral history, spoken in a plethora of languages, tribal storytellers tell of the time when humans interacted with plants, animals, sun, moon, stars, rocks, rivers, lakes, mountains, forests, and much more. Together, they created a drama equal to any known in the world. Storytellers among each tribe, band, village, or family keep the historical traditions for their people, and they know a good deal about the history of other Indian people, particularly those with whom their people interacted. For thousands of years before the arrival of nonnatives, keepers of traditions recorded their histories, sometimes by memory alone and sometimes through material objects or painted and carved accounts on wood, skins, rocks, textiles, basketry, and ivory. Storytellers still keep the traditions, each year adding to the tribal memory that has been preserved and treasured for generations. To know the history of

First Nations people, you must listen and learn from the elders. Their knowledge, wisdom, and memory is vast, and their contributions significant. But they also tell the stories of how European invasion has caused, and continues to cause, much heartache, loss, and humiliation of indigenous peoples.

Mary Jim, a Palouse elder from the village of Tasawicks on Snake River, lived at her traditional village until the 1960s, when the "law" forced her removal to the Yakama Reservation in Washington State.[1] During her life in the early twentieth century, she lived by traveling on horseback to root grounds near Badger Mountain and Soap Lake. She raced horses on the Columbia Plateau, fished Snake River, and gathered berries in the autumn. At the age of ten or eleven, her parents took her to Steptoe Butte, where she had her vision. When her grandfather died, the people cut a dugout canoe in half, inverting the canoe halves to form a coffin. With her family, Mary sang funeral songs all night long and laid her grandfather to rest the next day. She also buried her mother along Snake River and other family and friends. One night an amphibious vehicle traveled up the river to the island where the people had buried her grandfather. Archaeologists from a university dug up the grave and took the canoe burial and remains, never to return. Whenever Mary told of this event, she cried, just as she did when she remembered the story about when the Army Corps of Engineers built Ice Harbor Dam, backing up the water of Lake Sacajewea over her mother's grave. In 1980 Mary still lived on the Yakama Reservation and, while walking near an irrigation ditch, she pointed to the ditch and said, "That is not my Snake River. I am *Naa'hum*, Snake River. I miss my Snake River; it played music to my people." For forty years Mary tried to return to live at Snake River, but she died in 2000, visiting Snake River from time to time and lamenting the loss of her land and the desecration of her mother's grave. Near her old home site she cried and remembered, just as her children continue to do today, keeping the story alive.[2]

Like Mary Jim, governmental agencies have forced many Indian people from their lands or severely limited tribal lands from 1492 to the present. Removal remains an option of national governments and tribes are fully cognizant that the threat always exists, because Indian removal has been a part of American history for a long, long time. The Spanish forced Teninos off their islands to work on other islands, and they pushed native populations in North, South, and Central America to many new locales. The French, Dutch, Russians, Spanish, Portuguese, English—indeed all European nations—practiced forced removal of Native Americans, whether or not the people consented to the move. Before the Indian Removal Act of the United States in 1830, people often labeled the removals as "voluntary." But expansion of nonnative peoples most often contributed to the movement of native populations. Still, during the 1820s and 1830s, the government of the United States began moving Indians in earnest, trying to clear lands east of the Mississippi River for white settlers.[3]

The government forced many diverse tribes into Indian Territory, a place west of the Mississippi River that is roughly contained within the present-day boundaries of Kansas and Oklahoma. Weas, Piankasha, Kaskaskia, Peoria, Ottawa, Sac, Fox, Potawatomi, and many others joined the Cherokee, Choctaw, Chickasaw, Seminole, and Muscogee-Creeks. In addition, the government forced most Wyandots from Ohio and Michigan to Indian Territory. For years, Wyandots had lived along the Sandusky River and its tributaries, farming, hunting, and gathering. The people lived on the Grand Reserve of northwestern Ohio and the Wyandot Reserve near Detroit. Some Wyandots had sided with Tecumseh against the United States, but most followed Tarhe, The Crane, and remained friends of the United States. Yet, the alliance with the United States in the early nineteenth century did not prevent the government from demanding Wyandot removal in the 1840s. In 1842 Wyandots ultimately agreed to cede the Grand Reserve in Ohio and the Wyandot Reserve in Michigan to the United States. A year later, the people prepared to move west.[4]

On July 12, 1843, Wyandots and their friends gathered in the shade of the tall oaks and maples surrounding the Methodist mission at Upper Sandusky, Ohio. The people expressed their strong attachments to the beautiful site, the burial place of many of their people. Several children of Wyandot lay leader Squire Greyeyes had been laid to rest near the church. Their small, carved, stone headstones had a prominent place near the church. In a poetic but sorrowful address, Squire Greyeyes said good-bye to his Ohio home.

> *Adieu to the graves where my fathers now rest!*
> *For I must be going to the far distant West.*
> *I've sold my possessions; my heart fills with woe.*
> *To think I must leave them, Alas! I must go.*
> *Farewell ye tall oaks in whose pleasant green shade*
> *In childhood I sported, in innocence played;*
> *My dog and my hatchet, my arrows and bow,*
> *Are still in remembrance, Alas! I must go.*
> *Adieu ye loved scenes, which bind me like chains,*
> *Where on my gay pony I chased o'er the plains.*
> *The deer and the turkey I tracked in the snow.*
> *But now I must leave them, Alas! I must go.*
> *Adieu to the trails which for many a year*
> *I traveled to spy the turkey and deer,*
> *The hills, trees, and flowers that pleased me so.*
> *I must now leave, Alas! I must go.*
> *Sandusky, Tymochtee, and Brokensword streams,*
> *Nevermore shall I see you except in my dreams,*
> *Adieu to the marshes where the cranberries grow.*
> *O'er the great Mississippi, Alas! I must go.*
> *Adieu to the roads which for many a year*
> *I traveled each Sabbath the gospel to hear,*
> *The news was so joyful and pleased me so,*
> *From hence where I heard it, it grieves me to go.*
> *Farewell my white friends who first taught me to pray*
> *And worship my Savior and Maker each day.*
> *Pray for the poor native whose eyes overflow,*
> *With tears at our parting, Alas! I must go.*[5]

The U.S. government forced Wyandots from the "Land of the Beautiful Waters," just as the administration forced many native people to leave their homes to live in far-off places. During the nineteenth century removal became an official policy of the government in its program to clear the land of its original inhabitants so that nonnatives could make the land "productive." Removal became a part of nearly every tribe's relations with the United States.[6]

The governments of Canada, the United States, Mexico, and others of Latin America made treaty and agreements with native nations, but these governments abided by the agreements only when it was to their advantage to do so, changing the terms of the agreements whenever it suited them by making new agreements time and time again. Word of this kind of action spread quickly in Indian Country, and many Indian people had no taste for negotiating with foreign governments or following their policies. As Wyandot elder Mary Lou Henry once put it, "The government forced Indians to the worst places but said they could have it as long as the grass shall grow and rivers flow."[7] But this changed with new leaders and more settlers who wanted more Indian land. Indians learned that governments wanted to confine them to certain areas so that nonnatives could steal their lands and exploit their resources. Indians soon learned about reservations and the marking of lands to separate native from nonnatives for the convenience and benefit of the latter. Initially, few Indians warmed to the idea of life on a reserve or reservation. The land had always been open where people could hunt, gather, fish, and farm, often in joint-use areas where more than one tribe shared in the bounty of the land. When native people had resources, they had little reason to seek refuge on a reserve controlled by government agents, but once their resources dwindled they had no recourse but to starve or move to a reserve. Government officials knew this, particularly the army, so governments set about to destroy native food sources as a means of forcing the people to designated areas. Nowhere was this plan more apparent than on the northern and southern Great Plains where buffalo herds had flourished for generations, numbering in the millions.

Kiowa elder Old Lady Horse remembered that the United States had a "war between the buffalo and the white men." When the army moved onto the plains, they built forts and "the woolly-headed buffalo soldiers [the Tenth Cavalry of African-American troops] shot the buffalo as fast as they could." The buffalo fought back, so "the white man hired hunters to do nothing but kill the buffalo." Buffalo hunters slaughtered millions of buffalo and "skinners with their wagons" made huge piles of "the hides and bones." Old Lady Horse recalled that at times "there would be a pile of bones as high as a man, stretching a mile along the railroad track."[8]

Lakota Luther Standing Bear recalled hearing from hunters "that the plains were covered with dead bison" and when he went to investigate, he saw "the bodies of hundreds of dead buffalo lying about, just wasting, and the odor was terrible." White people, he reported, were the "wasteful, wanton killers of this noble game animal" and he found the hunters to be "repulsive."[9] Arapaho Artist Carl Sweezy remembered hating "the white men who slaughtered bulls and cows and calves alike and left them to rot on the prairies." As a result, "the herds grew fewer and smaller, and our scouts went farther in search of them." He lamented that "We wanted to believe what we had always believed, that the buffalo came up out of a hole in the ground somewhere out on the western Plains and that if we held our dances and used the buffalo as we had been taught to do, there would always be more. But our medicine was gradually losing its power."[10]

And the Crow chronicler Pretty Shield said that after the white people killed the buffalo, "Sickness came, strange sickness that nobody knew about." She linked the destruction of the buffalo with disease and death among the people, including her own daughters. One got the coughing sickness, or tuberculosis, and died. "I did not believe it," but then "my other daughter died." Pretty Shields was convinced that this "would not have happened if we Crows had been living as we were intended to live." She lamented the loss of her daughters and the buffalo. "Ahh, my heart fell down when I began to see dead buffalo scattered all over our beautiful country, killed and skinned, and left to rot by white men." The entire land "smelled of rotting meat" and the hearts of the people "were like stones." She remarked that not even the Lakota, Cheyenne, Arapaho, or Pecunni "would . . . do such a thing as this."[11] In order to deal with the tragedy, one Kiowa woman had a vision that in the "dawn mist . . . rising from Medicine Creeks" she saw Mount Scott open and a buffalo bull lead "the cows and their calves" into the mountain where "the world was green and fresh, as it had been when she was a small girl." The buffalo disappeared inside the mountain "never to be seen again."[12]

The nonnative destruction of the buffalo did more to harm the Plains Indians than any single factor, but soldiers harassed the people for years. In 1876 Lakota warriors, with the help of Cheyennes and Arapahoes, defeated Colonel George A. Custer at the Greasy Grass. "These *Wasichus* wanted it," warrior Iron Hawk recalled, "and they came to get it, and we gave it to them." In the end, "the soldiers were all rubbed out."[13] However, the Indian victory at the Little Big Horn increased the fighting between the army and the people of the northern plains. Ultimately, the United States created several reservations to confine Lakota people and their neighbors. Some Indians remained off the reservations, fighting the United States, but the destruction of the buffalo made life miserable for the Plains people, and gradually Indians had to seek refuge on reservations where government agents issued food rations. But Indians found difficulties on the reservations, where splits occurred between people who believed that the best policy was to seek cooperation with whites and those adamantly opposed to dealing with whites.[14] Conditions became worse after the Ghost Dance religion spread among the Lakota and when Indian policemen killed Sitting Bull. At Standing Rock Reservation Lakota policeman Lone Man reported that Sitting Bull resisted going to see the agent "so the three head officers laid their hands on him." Outside "the ghost dancers were trying to get close to the Chief . . . trying to protect him" but soon Sitting Bull's "camp was in commotion—women and children crying while the men gathered all around us." In the chaos "Bear That Catches . . . pulled out a gun . . . and fired at Lieutenant Bullhead and wounded him." Bear That Catches tried to shoot Lone Man but the gun misfired, allowing the policemen to knock him down. "It was about this moment that Lieutenant Bullhead fired into Sitting Bull" and "Red Tomahawk followed with another shot which finished the Chief." The policemen started firing at the ghost dancers and some ghost dancers fought back, while most fled.[15]

Big Foot took his Miniconjou band into the Bad Lands where Custer's old unit, the Seventh Cavalry, found him camped along Wounded Knee Creek. Big Foot had pneumonia and ordered his people to surrender before the soldiers killed more people. The chief could see the three Hotchkiss guns pointed at his village. The next day as the soldiers raided tipis women and children cried out as soldiers terrorized them, making matters worse. When an officer tried to disarm Yellow Bird, the gun went off, killing the officer and triggering an ugly episode. Shells from the Hotchkiss guns exploded and soldiers shot men, women, and children. Lakota holy man Black Elk arrived at Wounded Knee immediately after the killings and reported that "soldiers had followed along the gulch, as they ran, and murdered them in there." Women and children died "in heaps because they had huddled together, and some were scattered all along." Black Elk "saw a baby trying to suck its mother, but she was bloody and dead." When Black Elk absorbed the carnage into his brain he "wished that I had died, too, but I was not sorry for the women and children. It was better for them to be happy in the other world, and I wanted to be there, too." When Black Elk was an old man he commented that when he looked back "from this high hill of my old age, I can see the butchered women and children." He believed the "people's dream died there."[16]

During the early twentieth century nonnatives used the destruction of the buffalo and Wounded Knee as metaphors in describing the "Vanishing Indian." Like the buffalo and the Ghost Dance Religion, whites believed that Indian people would disappear, but Native Americans survived, just like the buffalo and the Ghost Dance. In fact, Indian populations grew in the twentieth century and Indian people and tribes asserted themselves in numerous ways. They held onto many elements of their traditional cultures, beliefs, and institutions while living in a changed world. First Nations people lived through the transition into contemporary society, not without pain and struggle, but with the same fight, determination, and humor that had always characterized them. Stories, songs, and dances of many stripes, circles, colors, and styles became the threads that wove the past to the present. And material culture of all sorts made the past come alive in the memories of the elders. Musical instruments, paintings, wooden sculptures, stone implements, masks, moccasins, clothing, and feathers remained the representatives of distinct native nations. Stories told through song and dance continue to bring the people alive, recreating the people again and again. Iroquois use their water drums and hoof rattles when they hold their social dances in the longhouses, and False Face masks appear in the doorway, moving carefully close to the floor, when people become ill and need doctoring.[17] Muscogees still do their stomp dances and sing their songs, just as Palouse raise their voices, praising the Creator for providing salmon, venison, roots, and berries.[18] Among the Hopi, antelope and snake dancers still sing for rain as they conduct ceremony to display their trust in unseen forces.[19] Kumeyaays, Quechans, Cocopas, Mojaves, Cahuillas, Serranos, and others sing their bird songs, telling of creation times when the first peoples moved upon the earth.[20] Chemehuevi and Southern Paiute peoples share their Salt Songs in all-night ceremonies that mark the movement of two women on a grand adventure over a huge portion of Arizona, Nevada, and California.[21] And Indian people of the northern and southern plains, as well as the Great Lakes, still sing their powwow songs, sharing the body of their music with brothers and sisters across Turtle Island where non-Plains people have taken the beating of the drums into their own hearts and cultures, ever expanding the powwow circle.[22]

Throughout the twentieth century Indian people treasured and nurtured their cultural traditions, sometimes sharing their stories with others. Many different tribes have war stories that have been shared throughout the ages. But the Navajos enjoy one of the most unique stories in American history. During World War II they developed a special code that no one ever broke.[23] When the Japanese bombed Pearl

Harbor, many Indian people joined the armed forces to fight for their country while many others left the reservations to work in factories making war materials. Navajos turned out at the agency at Window Rock bearing many different kinds of weapons, but they contributed most to winning the war after twenty-nine young men entered the Marine Corps and developed the Navajo Code based on the Navajo language, but a code that even Navajo speakers could not decode. The meaning of words changed in this dynamic and effective code. In one campaign, the Diné word *Gaagi* (Crow) was used to denote one kind of fighter plane, but in another campaign, the word *Debe* (Sheep) might be used for the same fighter plane. The number of Navajo Code Talkers grew in number throughout the war, and they participated in some of the worst fighting in the South Pacific. When Pima soldier Ira Hayes and the other marines raised the American flag on Mt. Sarabachi the word went off the island to the ships, and from the ships to San Francisco in the Navajo Code. Many marines owed their lives to the Code Talkers who sent and received messages rapidly and effectively. One of the original marines, Teddy Draper, Sr., remembered that after the war he remained in the Marine Corps to work in the occupation force in Japan. There he quickly learned Japanese and met numerous Japanese men who had fought in the South Pacific. They reported to Draper that every time they heard the Navajos speaking they feared for their lives because they knew that something bad was about to happen, but they did not know what to expect.[24]

When men and women returned to their reservations after the war, they were a changed people. Many of them had put their lives on the line for the United States and they refused to be treated as second-class citizens. Some of these individuals became tribal leaders, drawing on their ancient traditions of tribal laws and government to lead the people. They strengthened their tribal governments and fought measures injurious to their people. Lucy Covington of the Colville Reservation was one of these people, a woman of intelligence and ability who refused to allow her people to accept termination, a measure that would have destroyed their reservation.[25] Edward P. Dozier of Santa Clara,

Crow elder Barney Old Coyote, Joe Sando of Jemez Pueblo, Hupa elder Dave Risling, and Ben Reifel of Rosebud Reservation were among the hundreds of people who fought in World War II and became tribal leaders.[26] But women like Serrano elder Martha Chacon worked making war materials in Los Angeles during the war, leaving the San Manuel Reservation near San Bernardino, California, to work against the Axis Powers. After the war, Chacon returned to her reservation, where she worked to bring running water, electricity, and better education to her people. She also continued to teach her language and culture to young people. Chacon became a prominent spokesperson for her tribe and helped create a formalized, written government, drawing on the democratic traditions of the Big House where men and women had always had a voice in tribal affairs. Traditional government guided her vision of contemporary tribal government and she helped her people launch a new government firmly based on past traditions. Chacon was just one of many Native American women on Turtle Island who contributed to the war effort and led her people into the twenty-first century.[27]

Native American men and women continued to fight on behalf of their people throughout the twentieth century, strengthening their own cultures and governments while dealing with federal, state, county, and city officials in a government-to-government relationship. The people had given up a great deal over the years, but they never knowingly surrendered their personal, familial, or tribal sovereignty. In fact, sovereignty helped guide the people into new ventures, but the power of self-determination originated from within native people and communities, particularly from elders. Anishinaabe elder Eddie Benton-Banai once asserted that sovereignty was not "a privilege someone gives you" but "a responsibility within oneself, the same site as wisdom." Hoh elder Leila Fisher pointed out, "Wisdom comes only when you stop looking for it and start truly living the life the Creator intended for you."[28]

For hundreds of generations elders passed along wisdom and knowledge, history and culture through oral traditions. Shinnecock elder Harriett Starleaf Gumbs pointed out that she and her people "only ask to survive so that we can remain who and what we are" and "to pass on our way of life ... to our children and grandchildren."[29] It is through stories that the native cultures have survived and through the oral tradition that generations have learned who they are and where they came from. In the 1890s Serrano elder Dolores Crispeen Manuel told her family:

> Look now, you see that I am telling you this so you can pass it on to your children. Hear me well. See that faint little speck of light way down there from the homes of whites. Some day there will be more and more. I won't see it, but you will and you'll see the changes all around you. But never forget who you are or where you come from. Always remember we were here and they came. Try and live as we always have and maybe things will work out. We don't know.[30]

Since the 1890s the Manuel family has passed down Dolores's statement and held true to the course of remembering who they are and where they come from. For Indian people, words and stories are medicine.[31] Old and new stories come from the hearts, minds, and mouths of storytellers, settling into the presence of their listeners, taking hold like ice from water and slowly melting over time so that listeners can remember and be renewed. With each telling the people, places, plants, and animals of our stories come to life and live again. To know the American Indian past is to know the stories of the people, the stories told by elders who lend their voices so that we might know. Stories are tribal medicines that continue to heal the wounds caused by greed, racism, and worst of all, indifference. We tell stories so that our children will know who they are, where they are from, and where they are going.

1 Mary Jim, in oral interviews by Clifford E. Trafzer and Richard Scheuerman, May 1, 1977, April 2, and November 10, 17, 1979, and April 25, 1980, Yakama Indian Reservation.
2 Ibid.
3 Clifford E. Trafzer, *As Long as the Grass Shall Grow and Rivers Flow* (Fort Worth: Harcourt, 2000), pp. 148–166.

4 Ibid., pp. 166–169. Robert Emmett Smith, Jr., has written an authoritative study, "The Wyandot Indians, 1843–1876," (PhD dissertation, Department of History, Stillwater: Oklahoma State University, 1973).

5 Ibid.

6 Ibid.

7 Ibid., pp. v–vi. My mother, Mary Lou Henry Trafzer, made this statement many times as I was growing up, so I used the phrase as a title of my text on American Indian history.

8 The statements of Old Lady Horse are found in Alic Marriott and Carl K. Rachlin, *American Indian Mythology* (New York: Thomas Y. Crowell, 1968), pp. 169–170.

9 Luther Standing Bear, *My People the Sioux* (Boston: Houghton Mifflin Company, 1928), pp. 67–68.

10 Carl Sweezy's testimony is found in Althea Bass, *The Arapaho Way* (New York: Clarkson N. Potter, 1966), pp. 41–42.

11 Frank B. Linderman, *Pretty-shield, Medicine Woman of the Crows* (Lincoln: University of Nebraska Press, 1972), pp. 248–250.

12 In the 1960s, Old Lady Horse told this story to Alice Marriott and Carl Rachlin, who published the account in *American Indian Mythology*, pp. 169–170.

13 Iron Hawk's testimony is found in John G. Neihardt, *Black Elk Speaks* (Lincoln: University of Nebraska Press, 1961), p. 127.

14 Trafzer, *As Long as the Grass Shall Grow*, pp. 280–284.

15 Lone Man's statement is found in Stanley Vestal, ed., *New Sources of Indian History, 1850–1891* (Norman: University of Oklahoma Press, 1934), pp. 49–55.

16 Neihardt, *Black Elk Speaks*, pp. 265–266, 276.

17 Ross Coates, ed., *Gods Among Us* (San Diego: San Diego State University Publications in American Indian Studies, 1989), pp. 48–51.

18 Charlotte Heth, ed., *Native American Dance* (Washington, D.C.: National Museum of the American Indian, 1992), pp. 13, 29, 177; Clifford E. Trafzer and Richard D. Scheuerman, *Renegade Tribe: The Palouse Indians and the Invasion of the Inland Pacific Northwest* (Pullman: Washington State University Press, 1986), p. 143.

19 In 1977, the author attended a Hopi Snake Dance. The ceremony began without a cloud in the sky, but as the dancing progressed, the clouds gathered, enveloping the entire horizon. It began to rain on Second Mesa by the time the dancers gathered all the snakes and returned them to the four corners of the earth.

20 Paul Apodaca, "Tradition, Myth, and Performance of Bird Songs," (PhD dissertation, Department of Anthropology, Los Angeles: University of California, 1999), pp. 113–160.

21 Clifford E. Trafzer, "Chemehuevi in Nevada and California," in Tom Greave, ed., *Endangered Peoples of North America* (Westport, CT: Greenwood Press, 2002), pp. 9, 15.

22 Heth, *Native American Dance*, pp. 105–134.

23 In 1976–1977, the author studied with Teddy Draper, Sr., and Carl Gorman at Navajo Community College (Diné College) where he learned firsthand from two of the original Code Talkers. See Trafzer, *As Long As The Grass Shall Grow*, pp. 377–383.

24 Ibid.

25 The author learned from Lucy Covington through conservations in Spokane and Pullman, Washington, when he taught at Washington State University. Covington had grandchildren attending the university at the time.

26 Sharon Malinowski, *Notable Native Americans* (Detroit: Gale Research, 1995), pp. 130–135, 296–297, 357–358, 365–366, 384–385.

27 Clifford E. Trafzer, *The People of San Manuel* (Highland, California: San Manuel Band of Mission Indians, 2002), pp. 31–36. The author learned a great deal about the Serrano Indians through several conversations with elders Pauline Ormego Murillo and Ernest Siva.

28 For the wisdom of Eddie Benton-Banai and Leila Fisher, see Harvey Arden and Steve Hall, *Wisdom Keepers* (Portland, Oregon: Beyond Words Publications, 1990), pp. 48–55, 72–75.

29 Ibid., pp. 42–47.

30 Trafzer, *The People of San Manuel*, pp. 36–37.

31 Trafzer, *As Long as the Grass Shall Grow*, pp. 11–13.

6

REMEMBERING AND NEVER FORGETTING:

THE FIRESTORM IN BETWEEN

PERFORMING NATION, PERFORMING IDENTITY:

AMERICAN INDIAN STORYTELLING, POETRY, AND SONG IN PRACTICE (THOUGHTS ON CULTURAL SURVIVAL IN THE WAKE OF THE NEW INDIAN WARS)

CAROLYN DUNN AND CINDI ALVITRE

WHEN WE began writing on the topic of American Indian holocaust and survival, the first idea that came to us was the fact that in spite of overwhelming attempts to exterminate Indigenous peoples religiously, culturally, politically, and economically, native peoples in the Americas have continued to flourish and survive. Our participation in this project is from purely a diasporic perspective: What are the ramifications of several forced migrations of a people from their ancestral homeland, a place which is so clearly culturally identified from traditional stories, songs, poems; from within the body and soul of a people that a connection to the land is what has remained in the memory and hearts of a people who weren't supposed to survive? How can thousands of native peoples, from over five hundred different tribes, nations, and communities come together in a place that itself is full of the storied conquest of native peoples in place names, in film, literature, oral history, and name? When the forced migration occurred from reservations and rural communities starting from Indian Removal and well up into the twentieth century, native people left ancestral and adopted homelands to call urban areas "home." What was the impact of these immigrants upon the many native nations still living in the urban landscapes, facing erasure and extinction in a city that looked nothing like their ancestral villages? It is through ceremonial performativity, that is, the artistic, folkloric, mythological and political relationship native peoples share with the nations of origin that has allowed us to survive together in a place in which we have been erased. We cannot be simply labeled "urban" Indians because we are a diasporic people, dispersed and spread out across the world, far away from home, family, and community.

First, let us identify and unpack our terms. *Webster's* definition of diaspora is as follows: "noun, Greek, meaning dispersion; from *diaspeirien,* to scatter, from *dia* + *speirein* to sow. 2. a: the breaking up and scattering of a people; b: people settled far from their ancestral homelands (e.g., the African diaspora); c: the place where these people live."[1]

Through the breakup of tribal lands, through separation, adoption, boarding schools, relocation, and termination, native peoples in the United States have been separated from ancestral homelands, settled far from those ancestral homelands, and relocated in large populations to urban areas that are far from the nation. Los Angeles then, with the largest urban American Indian population in the nation,[2] is a site of displacement, temporal and spatial, that is an ongoing experiment in cultural survival that continues into the twentieth-first century.

Ceremonial performativity becomes important in this discussion of holocaust, diaspora, and survival. J. L. Austin, the linguistic philosopher, described performativity as the following: "A performative is the semiotic gesture that is being as well as doing. Or, more accurately, it is a doing that constitutes a being; an activity that describes what it creates."[3] As native peoples, the performance of our identity is intimately connected to our stories, songs, and poems, to the landscape we inhabit that informs our being as well as our doing. It is through our ceremonies, our songs, our words, that our rituals are reenacted in daily life. We speak of our creation and connection to each other and to the landscape, and our actions, our dances, our artistic expressions, reify the core of who we are as native peoples.

The result of colonization and government policies of termination

and relocation have resulted in a substantially large, multitribal population of young indigenous peoples existing as second- and third-gener-
ation urban American Indians, some with or without tribal relations
"back home" intact. The role of the traditional and modern storyteller
is the role that forms the subject ancestrally and represents "the call" from
home. The late Lee Francis III wrote about the experience of his son,
Lee IV, as an urban Indian in the essay "We The People: Young American Indians Reclaiming Their Identity":[4]

> My son was born in Fairfax, Virginia. He is an urban. Since
> infancy my spouse and I told our son story. We told a story about
> all of creation, seen and unseen. We told him about the People.
> We told him a story about the People of Fairfax, Virginia. He
> learned about the civil war and the pogroms committed against
> the People. We told him stories that incorporated the values, atti-
> tudes, and beliefs of the People. We told stories about humming-
> bird and coyote and the tree people and the cloud beings. . . . the
> sad reality is that a majority of urban Native students do not have
> a clue about the trials, tribulations, joys, and hopes of the People."[5]

For many young urban American Indians, the concept of the landscape
of home is a faraway image told only in story from those who left it
behind. Home is also problematic in the sense that, as a result of colonization, it is not always the "safe place" in the traditional sense of
"home." It is not "safe" due to cause and effect of colonization, exter-
nalized and internalized oppression.[6] Eduardo Duran and Bonnie Guillory Duran's theories of intergenerational post-traumatic stress disorder
that leads to domestic violence, substance abuse, and suicide are often
located in a trajectory that begins and ends with the sense of home,
home encompassing domestic space, land base, tribal center, language,
literature, and economic struggles. Home also represents environmental and political struggles—the struggle for an ever-decreasing land
base which is still "held in trust" by the American government,[7] land
that is used by others for toxic waste disposal on or near reservation

water and agricultural systems, the desecration of sacred places such as Puvungna (the Tongva place of emergence in Southern California) and Puthidiim (Ajachumen place of emergence at present day San Juan Capistrano Mission.)

Many young Indians have some concept of their tribal identity, yet an outside "other" constructs an alternative "Indian" identity for them. How many of us have been told, "Funny, you don't look Indian," or asked, "How come you don't have black hair?" or "Do you have a tipi in your backyard?" or "I knew you were an Indian; you're so spiritual!" We are constantly barraged by images of the pretend, or the Hollywood Indian. If we don't wear beads, feathers, or turquoise, then the non-Indian "other" does not see us as authentically Indian. The return home then becomes an important aspect to a ritual of remembrance for many young urban American Indians.

The role of story, as Lee Francis states, is the ceremonial performative of modern tribal and clan identity. This return home informs what has become the Native American or American Indian canon: the writings of many contemporary writers, from Mourning Dove on through Dawn Karima Pettigrew[8] reflect this sense of home: a contested space. Story for us then becomes the connection to the landscape, to the nation, to our identity as an American Indian, as a tribal person. It connects us to what Paula Gunn Allen calls "the universe of medicine."[9] It is through the story, through the landscape, that the performative speech of storytelling draws us into the web of creation that calls us home.

It is difficult to imagine the urbanized Southern California landscape replaced with hundreds of Tongva villages and even more brown bodies weaving buff-colored juncus baskets or shaping redwood planks for *ti'atem*, lashed redwood canoes, the earliest form of transportation to and from the southern Channel Islands. But we can—and we do—at least in moments when we have to withdraw from the reality of a sprawling city like Los Angeles, inundated with silicone and spiritual orphans. We feel alienated; even as native we have become immigrants. Even to many relocated Indians, who since the 1950s make Los Angeles their home, we are not real and have no status, federally unrecognized, extinct, not here—go away imagination woman. How can we give them eyes to see our pain?

The white sands, once abundant with life of the ocean, are now scattered with the disposable culture they call "civilization." The sandy shores are inundated with newcomers in g-strings and pseudo-tans, whose ignorance of the sacred ones contribute to the continued destruction of Tongva land. They look at us as if we are the strangers to this land, with our brown skin, assuming we are one of the "illegals" from the south, as if this is truly their land.

I (Cindi) walk across the massive constructed rock barriers, returning to that place where I spent countless hours as a young girl, shrouded like indigenous royalty with seaweed skirts. It was on these rocks that my relatives would speak to me and teach me as I sat watching the sacred ones. I learned of the creations and watched forever as they flew into the skies, as they crawled onto the rocks, and as they freely swam in the tide pools. I learned the gentleness of life in the water as I swam beyond the crashing waves without fear.

The *Torovim,* the dolphin people, forever danced along the ocean horizon, protecting the Tongva. Our elders emphasized that they are the protectors, the ancient ones, and forever the caretakers of the world. It was in the old days they trusted man. Today, the tourist boats chase the dolphin people to catch a glimpse of their silver beauty and seek out the grey whale during the migratory journeys to give birth to future generations. *Moomat,* the ocean, now purifies herself by casting remnants of oil spills onto her shores. No longer does my father dive into the ocean to gather food for his family. The shellfish are contaminated with excrement and chemicals that empty into the bays. I listen and hear the ancient language of the Ocean People as they roar with foamy frustration at the destruction of their own tribes. They tell their story over and over, with the crashing of each wave onto moonlit shores.

Our people have resisted the ways of the intruder for over two hundred years, beginning with the arrival of the Catholic missionaries and Spanish soldiers in 1769. In their quest for world power and wealth, a nation of people violently lost their lives. Within a fifty-year period after the missionaries arrived, our populations, which at one time exceeded 10,000, dwindled to a few hundred survivors. The missions bred disease of the body and of the soul. Sensing the obvious danger many fled inland, finding sanctuary of surrounding tribes. We have carried the stigma of being called "mission Indians," without acknowledgement of the diversity of our people or respect for our individual names.

The destruction continued as we went through oppressive rule by the Mexicans after the secularization of the missions. They say we were given choices to flee the confines of the missions and become ranchers or to find acceptance in newly formed pueblos dominated by the invaders. The reality of the situation was that this "new freedom" was conditional. It meant a Tongva woman could be an obliging domestic or forced into sexual slavery to the oppressors. Hard labor was paid in *aguardiente*, numbing the loss and intoxicating the minds and the will of the people.

The women, in particular, lost their voices upon invasion of our homeland. They were treated like the women of the Spaniards. They were confined, separated from the men, and perceived as whores simply because they were not seen as human, but as Indian. The inquisitors conquered, murdered, and grossly seduced indigenous men into their ways. The emasculation of the men occurred by removing the ceremonies and traditions that made them warriors. Since then, they have attempted to recover their positions by fighting wars that are not ours to fight. This has led to a distortion of masculinity—a twisted manifestation of right and wrong and constant questioning of who they are. Yet even in their absence, in the midst of their abuses, as women we cannot turn our backs. We have to help our sons, our brothers, our fathers, and our lovers to heal. We have now spent generations in a luminal state of decolonization. It is a constant challenge. Yet we, as women, as lifegivers, once again become responsible for bringing new ways of healing to our families and community.

Healing reaches into all spaces. It takes a transformation of space where ceremonial performitivity occurs. There are few who will reach out, outside of the comfort of their Indian circles to look at themselves.

In LA we have them all—Indian scholars, Hollywood Indians, powwow people, Redroad Recovery Indians, aerospace Indians, and even some churchy Indian folk, all seeking something that was lost in their journey to the western edge of the universe.

To step outside means to redeem any communal sanctity and to become a voyeur of sorts. The looking glass reflects a haunting image of what we have become in their culture. We seek our reflection in pools of clear water lit by our grandmother moon, but her illuminated glow is lost somewhere under layers of asphalt and concrete. Out of desperation we look to other tribes to seek validation of our clandestine thoughts and good intentions. We must escape the constant chaos of the city that comes in wave after wave, never allowing us to stand and catch our breath. We frequently travel to gather and harvest healing food to bring home. Some of us go really far . . . as far as overseas. We did, two women, a local and a diasporic homegirl. We dared to look beyond and take our own dreams with us and see if they fit anywhere in the indigenous universe.

The silvery jet roars across the Pacific Ocean to *Aotearoa*, to the land where day begins. After days of packing uncolonized baggage, I anxiously await the opportunity to spill it out onto Maori earth and see if their eyes see it the same way ours do. We are two women from two communities, both native, sharing our differences, embracing our similarities and airing our *dirty laundry* in an international setting. The *silenced knowings* can no longer be contained. We unleash them, and our solutions, to the world. We talk about the space and place we have created to allow our communities, our families and others come to share, to transform, and feel just fine being the trickster in a chaotic world.

The last of ceremonial houses were burned in the 1960s in native Southern California. For generations the ceremonial house, the *wamkish*, was the center of the world. Our spiritual leaders fed the house to assure the balance and nurturance of our community. On the other side of the world, the Maori welcome us into their ceremonial house, the *morae*. In the midst of Maori ceremony the message is clear. We have a ceremonial house in Los Angeles—Mother Bears. It is a space of transformation and healing for the community. It is there we sing and dance, we weep with joy and sadness as we feed the people—all tribes. We have come across the ocean to realize what we do have.

In Janice Norwood and Vera Monk's collection of writings on Southwestern women's art,[10] the landscape's influence upon the myth and imagination of its writers and artists inform the region as well as the psyche of the individual and communal artist, specifically female artists. The landscape is a vehicle from which artists draw inspiration, express social and personal aesthetic ideals, and form communal connections with society, place, community, spirituality, family, and creativity. Landscape provides necessary connections for life; it informs who we are and how we are in a way that sometimes there is no other expression for other than poetry and art. Native peoples in the Southwest, because of our deep ancestral connections to landscape and the mythologies of the living landscape, express connections to the landscape in unique ways. Landscape tells the story of emergence, of history, of religion, and of birth that is indigenous of our native experiences. The connections expressed through ritual and ceremony, through art and music and poetry, celebrate that ritual connection in the everyday. Tribal aesthetics[11] are applied to the landscape, and the aesthetics cannot live without the land.

The indigenous mythology of the landscape reveals a relationship between people and earth that takes shape in very human ways. The difference between disaster fiction and native ecological fiction is that landscape is seen in adversarial ways as opposed to simply the landscape. Like Mary Austin's *American Rhythm,* there is a cadence to the landscape, but there is an understanding of responsibility for the landscape that is missing in both Austin's romantic past and the noirist disaster fiction of West and Macdonald.

Shape-shifting, we move along the street darkened with porcelain bodies, leathered, grunged, and inked with borrowed ancestral symbols. Swiftly we thread our way through bodies quickly inspecting their tribal tattoos and wonder, "What tribe are you? Were your people also annihilated and dispossessed of their land?" Once again we become the trickster, hiding our own identity, never to be found out, only if we choose to. Concrete paths lead us to the storefront of Mother Bears, our community house, and our sacred space—in the midst of chaos. Taking deep breaths, secure in an energy that is familiar, assuring us that there are others who also are in constant negotiation of who they are—here in LA, whether you be Native-native or diaspora, the ceremonial houses have returned.

> *Every poet is aware of this primordial depth in language, whereby particular sensations are invoked by the sounds themselves, and whereby the shape, rhythm, and texture of particular phrases conjure the expressive character of particular phenomenon.*
>
> —DAVID ABRAM, THE SPELL OF THE SENSUOUS

As a young poet growing up in Los Angeles, I (Carolyn) couldn't feel the voice of the landscape as I could in more rural places. David Abram posits that landscape and oral culture are so closely related that the suppression of the landscape affects the ability to speak of place. "If we listen first to the sounds of an oral language," Abram writes, "to its rhythms, tones, inflections that play through the speech of an oral culture, we will likely find these elements are attuned in multiple and subtle ways to the contour and scale of the local landscape, to the depth of its valleys or the open stretch of its distances, to the visual rhythms of the local topography."[12]

In his work with the Western Apache, Keith Basso talked about the concept of "stalking with stories," how landscape and language are intertwined and language reminds the Apache of landscape and vice versa.[13] California's indigenous peoples have similar stories. Driving along the freeway at rush hour, with the city's beautiful people riding along with cell phones attached to cosmetically enhanced ears, riding alongside the city's poor, dispossessed and colored, I wonder if they truly will ever know that we ride with them, under cover of beads, feather, buckskin, and abalone. Out of the cracks in the cement, like the forgotten ancestor they are, sprout broad-leafed California alata, yellow blooms bright against the whitewashed adobe so many now call home. The green tobacco reminds me that the land's voice is strong, even over the roar of traffic, airplanes, oil refineries, and shipping lanes. In the midst of this native diaspora, the tobacco gave me a story:

COYOTE TEARS
Mist of rain
and wild tobacco
dot the earth
in subtle
songs of remembrance
and
longing for
the loss of a language
of harvest
and blessing.
To rule this land
is to subjugate
the center
of the world
by blood,
by living,
by water
and power.
And she knows
the sound
of footprints
upon rain
is a breath
of dying
and decay.
So this land
breathes
barely standing in
the midst

of darkness
and perverse delight.
Oh where
is the song
of survival,
of living
on the
cusp of disaster?
I can see her:
in wild tobacco
in a mist of rain
that sails away
on a whisper
of survival.
I wander
the landscape,
her breasts empty
only for those
who do not
listen.
I picked this earth clean,
and she gave me
wild tobacco,
a mist of blessing rain,
a breath of desire
and she sings
sacred songs
only for those
who listen.
Tears glisten
upon the breath
of ancestors
who cry
what they want

to know
and what will happen
if I begin
to howl a love song
lost to the souls
of decay
and wonder
where is
my voice?
Where is
the red earth
and gifts she honored me
as my tears
land in soft
moon-shaped
puffs of smoke,
turning ash
to clay
and wild tobacco,
singing.

Stalking with stories, the landscape of the Los Angeles American Indian diaspora emerges through the Anglo mythologies in the narrative of its indigenous peoples, reminding us of the role the place played and still plays in the larger city narrative. It also connects us to that universe of medicine, to the ceremonial performativity that reminds us of who we are, where we come from, and where we are going. We just need to listen to the stories, hear the songs, and use them as the roadmap that will send us home, in all parts of the world in which a diasporic people call home. The ceremonial houses, placed upon the now urban landscape, the places where story is shared and relived, is where we find our spaces of remembrance, of renewal, and of regeneration.

1 *The Merriam-Webster Dictionary* (Springfield, MA: Merriam-Webster, 2005).

2 U.S. Census Report on American Indian Population, February 2002.

3 As quoted by Eve Sedgwick and Andrew Parker in *Performance and Performativity: A Reader.*

4 MariJo Moore, ed., *Genocide of the Mind* (New York: Thunder's Mouth Press, 2003).

5 Ibid., pp. 80–81.

6 Native *American Postcolonial Psychology*, pp. 32–35.

7 Suzan Shown Harjo.

8 A mixed-blood Muskogee/Cherokee/Seminole/Chickasaw/African- and Anglo-American, Dawn Karima Pettigrew's first novel/memoir/poetry volume, *The Way We Make Sense*, was one of the first published works in the twenty-first century dealing with issues of the contested home space.

9 *Grandmothers of the Light* (Boston: Beacon Press, 1991).

10 Vera Norwood and Janice Monk, eds., *The Desert Is No Lady* (New Haven: Yale University Press, 1987; [2nd ed. Tucson: University of Arizona Press, 1999).

11 Paula Gunn Allen, *The Sacred Hoop: Rediscovering the Feminine in American Indian Traditions* (Boston: Beacon Press, 1996).

12 Abram, David, *The Spell of the Sensuous* (New York: Vintage Books, 1996), p. 140.

13 Keith H. Basso, *Wisdom Sits In Places* (University of New Mexico Press, 1996).

JUMPING THROUGH THE HOOPS OF HISTORY

(FOR COLUMBUS, CUSTER, SHERIDAN, WAYNE, AND ALL SUCH HEROES OF YESTERYEAR)

SUZAN SHOWN HARJO

(ON THE EVE OF 1992)
10 little, 9 little, 8 little Indians
7 little, sick little, live baby Indians
poor little, me little, you little Indians
the only good Indian's a dead 1

a lot of young Indians got dead in the '80s
*   just like the '70s and the '60s*
*   both 19 and 18 hundreds*
*   and all the other 00s since 1492*
a sucker's #s game over the sale of the centuries
*   with 99-year leases and 1-cent treaties*
*   with disappearing ink on the bottom line*
*   signed by gilt-eyed oddsmakers*
*   whose smart $ bet on 0 redskins by half-time*

in the 4th quarter, when this century turned on us
*   we were down to 250k in the u.s.*

from the 50m who were here
but who just didn't hear about
the lost italian lurching his way from spain
with scurvy-covered sailors and yellow-fevered priests
at least 1,000 points of blight and plague
in 3 wooden boxes marked "india or bust"
and "in gold we trust"

columbus washed up on our shores, praising paradise on earth
and kinder, gentler people
who fixed them dinner, but laughed so hard
at these metal-headed, tiny whitemen
that they fell to their knees
we please them, dear diary, columbus wrote home
they think we're gods
so the knights of the lost boats
spread syphilis and the word of the 1 true gods
and planted 00s of flags of the 1 true kings
and sang their sacred 3-g song
    "a, b, c, d, g, g, g
    "glory, god and gold, gold, gold"
rub-a-dub-dub, a nina tub
rub-a-dub-dub, a pinta tub
rub-a-grub-grub, Native gold and lands
rub-a-chop-chop, Native ears and hands
rub-a-rub-rub Indians out
    8m by 1500, or thereabout

meanwhile, back in the land of wicked queens and fairy tales
serfs were sowing and owing the churches
and paying dues to the papal store
all for the promise of the kingdom of heaven
starving and dying to make it to that pearly door

the inquisition kings reaped peasant blood $, but wanted more
    than those in robes could rob from the poor
    so the captains of invention
    designed the missions to go forth and mine
    with tools of destruction to kill the time

so cristobal colon led the chorus in the same old song
    kyrie, kyrie, kyrie eleison
    a new world beat for average savages
    who didn't change their tune
    and were bound by chains of office
    and staked out to pave the yellow brick road
    at invasion's high noon

and wizards in satin read their rights in latin
    kyrie, kyrie, kyrie requiremento
    and a lot of Indians got dead
    as was, by god, their right
    to the sound of death songs in the night
      kyrie, kyrie, kyrie requiremento

and amerigo begat the beautiful
    and the bibles grew and the bullets flew
and the pilgrims gave thanks
    and carved up turkeys and other peoples' lands
and mrs. Gov. stuyvesant bowled with 10 bloody skulls
    and begat up against the wall streets
    and shopping mauls on 00s of mounds
and the 7th cavalry prayed and passed the ammunition
    and loaded gattling guns 100k times
    and shot off extra special 45/70s
    for any Indians or buffalo
    between europe and manifest destiny

meanwhile, in Indian country
 no one heard about the ironhorse or goldwhores
 or the maggots in the black hills
 with no-trespassing signs
 or what's yours is homestake mine's
 but that's what they called ballin' the jack

then it was 2 late, about a quarter to midnight
 and us without a second hand to tell the times were a
   changin'
so, we jumped through the hoops of history
 on mile-high tightropes without a net
 with no time to look back or back out
 with no time to show off or cry out
  look, ma, no hands
   no hands
   no hands

and the calendar was kept by #s of sand creeks
 and washitas and wounded knees and acoma mesas
 and 00s of army blankets of wool and smallpox
 and a lot of chiefs who made their marks
  no longer able to thumb their way home
  where x marked the spots on their babies
 and pocahantas haunted england
  singing ring-a-ring-a-rosy
  ashes, ashes, all fall dead
 and a lot of fences got built
  around a lot of hungry people
  who posed for a lot of catlins
  who shot their fronts
  and snapped their backs
  just say commodity cheese, please

and a lot of Indians got moved and removed
   relocated and dislocated
   from c to shining c
   from a 2 z
   from spacious skies to fort renos
   from purple mountains to oklahoma
   from vision quests to long walks
   from stronghold tables to forks in the road
   from rocks to hard places
   from high water to hell
   from frying pans to melting pots
   from clear blue streams to coke

and we got beads
   and they got our scalps
and we got horses
   and they got our land
and we got treaties
   and they got to break them
and we got reservations
   and they got to cancel them
and we got christian burials
   and they got to dig us up
and they got america
   and america got us

and they got a home where Indians don't roam
   (now, follow the bouncing cannon ball)
and they got a home where Indians don't roam
and a lot of young Indians got dead
   and those were the glory daze
and we learned the arts of civilization
reciting the great white poets
   (oh, little sioux or japanee

    oh, don't you wish that you were me)
singing the great white songs
    (onward, christian soldiers
    marching as to war
    to save a wretch like me
    amazin' race, amazin' race)
sailing down the mainstream
    (with land o' lakes butter maiden
    and kickapoo joy juice role models
    for good little Indian girls and boys)

and we got chopped meat
    and we got buffaloed
and we got oil-well murders
    and they got black-gold heirs
and they got museums
    and we got in them
and they got us under glass
    and we got to guide them
and they got the kansas city chiefs
    and we got a 14,000-man b.i.a.
and we got pick-up trucks
    and they got our names for campers
and they got rubber tomahawks
    and we got to make them
and they got to take us to lunch
    and we got to eat it

and they got richer
    and we got poorer
and we got stuck in their cities
    and they got to live in our countries
and they got our medicines
    and we got to heal them

and we got sick
  and they got, well, everything

and we got to say please and thank you
and good morning, america
you're welcome, y'all come
and have a nice hemisphere

then, all of a sudden, a new day dawned
  and america yawned
  and the people mumbled
    something about equality and the quality of life
    some new big deal to seal the bargain
    and jack and jill went to the hill
    to fetch some bills to save us
    and the united snakes of america
    spoke in that english-only forked-tongue way
    about cash-on-the-barrelhead, hand-over-fist
    in exchange for Indian homes on the termination list
  and bankers and lawyers and other great white sharks
  made buyers-market killings when more chiefs made their
    marks
  and lots of Indians packed their bags and old-pawn
  for fun with dick and jane and busing with blondes
  for a bleached-out, white-washed american morn
  while we were just trying to live and get born

and a lot of young Indians got dead
  in america's 2 big wars
  and the little ones they tried to hide
    like the my-lais
    and other white lies
  and the millions on the grate-nation's main streets
    with holes in their pockets
    and tombstones for eyes

you see, america was busy lunching
    and punching clocks
    (and each other, don't tell)
    and pushing paper
    (and each other, do tell)
    and loving and leaving cabbage-patch/latch-key kids
    in the middle of the road and nowhere
    (where everything got touched but their hearts
    where $ bought the love they were worth)

and america's daddy and mommy looked
    up from their desks
    out from their ovens
    over their shoulders
    behind the times
    down their noses
        and right before their eyes
        but just out of sight
        behind flashlights in abandoned buildings
        through crack in the walls
        and in the halls of boarding schools
    a lot of young Indians got dead, too
        girls with bullets, booze and lysol for boyfriends
        boys with nooses and razor blades for cold comfort
        and a few grandmas and grandpas
            on their last legs anyway
and we who were left behind
    sang songs for the dead and dying
        for the babies to stop crying
        for the burned-out and turned-out
        for the checked-out and decked-out
   ain't that just like 'em
    we said over cold coffee and hot tears
        for getting themselves dead
        forgetting to tell us goodbye

for giving america no 2-week notice
forgiving america with their bodies
ain't that just their way
to gather us up and put us down
gee, kids really do the darnest things
like get themselves dead
like a lot of them did
just yesterday and today
and a lot of young Indians got dead
faster than they could say
tomorrow

oh, say, can't you see
they learned america's song and dance
from the rocket's red glare
to god shed his light on thee
they read america's history
where they weren't
or were only bad news
they laughed when president rip van reagan
told the russians the u.s.
shouldn't have humored us
they passed when senator slender reed said
find another country or play this hand
they learned the lessons about columbus
in child-proof, ocean-blue rhymes
along with other whiteboy-hero signs of the times
they saw the ships sailing, again
and a future as extras
in movies where Indians don't win
they knew they were about to be discovered, again
in someone else's lost-and-found mind
in an old-world, new-age, snake-oil re-run
as much fun

as the first scent of those sailors
fresh from the hold
exhaling disease, inhaling gold
and a lot of young Indians escaped just in time
to miss the good wishes and cheer
have a happy, have a merry
have a very nice columbus year

10 little, 9 little, 8 little Indians
7 little, sick little, live baby Indians
poor little, me little, you little Indians
the only good Indian's a dead 1

LONG TIME GONE CRADLEBOARD SONG

DAWN KARIMA PETTIGREW

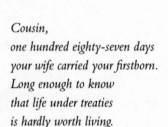

Cousin,
one hundred eighty-seven days
your wife carried your firstborn.
Long enough to know
that life under treaties
is hardly worth living.

She should have chosen California,
Cleveland,
not Chicago,
when the BIA,
with its alarm clocks,
its relocations,
its first month's rent,
sent us to the cities,
called us terminated,
like your baby,
Cousin,
born too soon,
on the slaughterhouse floor.

The pains came as she walked to work,
grew as she slit the throats of chickens,
and haven't stopped yet.

At least your child was born among feathers,
which almost makes up for the absence of drums.

JAPANESE GARDENS

JOEL WATERS

in the Japanese gardens
i wait for the H-Bomb
to drop
i feel like
the little trees
they have cut and trimmed
into a forced bonsai

as fake as the bamboo
house that i sit in
concentrating
like the camps
the U.S. government
put our people in
first Indians

and then Japanese Americans
preserving cultures
by putting up a fence

keeping them safe from us
as though we plan
to hara-kiri
we should be so lucky

stone and cement
lanterns
light the way
of a dim view
as though to say
Hiroshima
was not bombed into ash

like the tree
they have planted
in the garden
where every culture
is perfectly positioned
an origami America
that nobody wants to unfold.

ALL MY ANCESTORS HAVE BLISTERS ON THEIR TOES

SARA SUTLER-COHEN

Pulsing, bloody, every grueling step raised
  heats only on the surface, and not enough
  to warm me that winter.
Baby at my breast, I arch over dead beneath slick horse hooves carrying
  a drooling vigilante—the horse walks over me, shoving my face into
  icy ground
    Ravenous babe
    gnawing loosely at my
    breast for life. A grandmother, not stopping,
    lifts the child whose
    mouth is now filled with my blood and bits
    of nipple.

In this ever-rocky terrain, it's cold and I can't stop
  I'm hungry and filled with terror
  the pungent odor of sweat over grime carries us over miles of barren,
  salty earth
  we held onto one another for warmth
  bit by bit we were torn apart.

Blankets ripped from our bodies
walking in our sleep—dying on our feet

All my ancestors have blisters on their toes
Pus-filled boils on heels—chipping away at his soul—marched over the
frosty forests of Poland.
I was raped and tortured while he watched—seventeen soldiers: perfect
Aryans—robust, blond, steely eyes—then our children, fair of hair
and skin, kidnapped and raised like good Aryans

This is what genocide tastes like. Grit on my tongue, my throat turned
to dusty, swollen glands.

Incinerate the Torah from within—shred the Quaballah before our eyes
—call us dirty, filth, swine, subhuman, der Jude—you brand our
bodies but not our souls
singeing flesh
burnt hair
burnt flesh
scarred and mutilated—starved bellies searching for broth distended and
stretched just so.
They march us for miles until I'm shoved on a train; bodies matted and
greasy, bald heads dried and cracked—dust in the crevices—hol-
lowed-out eyes—deep-set with rage and silence, my baby still fat
from thinned milk, watery and runny—cold—gnawing at my flesh
for nourishment but now I am immune to the pain as I bite my lip
until blood drips away.
we were made unclean
beasts—piles of bodies
shin on shin
bone to bone
cracked skin
bald spots
blisters

on

toes . . .

All my ancestors have blisters on their toes

   The famine-rotten potatoes
     rotting bodies
You walked for miles for a tiny potato with no scourge
on
skin.

This is what genocide feels like. Desperate to the bone, with no options
   to heave on our shoulders.

Our babies with distended bellies
toes red heels hard from trailing behind me—her papa is not her papa
but an English soldier under a policy from the Crown "broke" me in on
   our wedding night to ensure racial purity. Raped in grisly fashion,
   drunk Englishman spat on my breasts, slapping at my clean mouth,
   soiling my innocence with his rough hands and throwing me to the
   cold night to walk for miles back to my husband waiting in terror
   and tremendous guilt.

This is what genocide looks like. Barren eyes set back in a face forgot-
   ten, hands worn and wilting at the knuckle.

All my ancestors have blisters on their toes—
Every one of my ancestors has blisters on their toes—
Everyone but me. I wear my blisters on the inside.

LADY IN TURTLENECK

SHIRLEY BROZZO

Looking to the west with
A certain sadness in her face the
Anishnaabekwe hears for the first
Time the story of Wounded Knee and
Sand Creek. Weighed down by the
Fatigue of her grandmothers and
Their grandmothers she wears, but does not
Feel, the luxury of braided hair or
The commitment to truth.

Only the ancestors hold the truth of
What happened on those snow-filled cliffs and
They only share the knowledge with
Those who have come after, those who
Are strong enough to carry the pain of
Shrieking babies and mutilated women as
Soldiers complete their assigned tasks of
Annihilating the red man and liberating the
Land for colonial expansion causing
Urban sprawl and degradation.

This sad, lonely woman of
Anishinaabe or Lakota descent looks to
The west now and hears the cries from
Fallen warriors, fathers, and brothers, and
Uncles of the slain. This Cheyenne woman with
Blue in her eyes sees the homeland of
Her ancestors, ancestors in unmarked graves in
Final places of unrest and
Cannot sleep at night for
The voices in her head turn to
Blood on her hands because
We all bear the guilt of the truth.

INVISIBILITY LESSONS #1 AND #2

DRUCILLA MIMS WALL

#1

Daughter:
This is the way Indians walk in the woods.
This is the way human beings
walk in the woods.
Your weight on the outer edge of the foot,
like a blade in the earth.
Roll heel to toe,
each step in the print of the last.
Bend the knees; relax the shoulders so.
Eyes follow four directions:
down, ahead, left, right.
Faster now and silent:
down, ahead, left, right;
ears more open than eyes.
You'll know when you get it right
by the deer ignoring you,
and the arrowhead hunters,
with their shovels and sieves,

shouting your obituary
right across your path.

#2
Our sacred towns
are names of rivers.
The one drop rule
bled us white, or black.

Our trickster rabbit
sells breakfast cereal.
Ruckers Airforce Base
covers Grandmother's farm.

Uncle Stuart's parole
leaves him homeless in Dallas.
The New York Times
proclaims us fake.

GIVEAWAY

(IN GRATITUDE FOR ALL OF IT—
THEFT, SMALLPOX, RELOCATION,
AND DENIAL.)
WI-DO.

KIM SHUCK

We need to be stubborn for this work
Stubborn and loving.
The most difficult of lessons for me
Sometimes.
Generous gifts
Are often given
By those who didn't intend to give anything at all.

I call the slave master
Who lost track of my ancestor
A blanket for you
In gratitude.

I call the soldier
With a tired arm
Who didn't cut deeply enough
Into my great-great grandfather's chest to kill clean.
I return your axe head
Oiled and sharpened
Wield it against others with equal skill.

Will the boarding school officer come up?
The one who didn't take my Gram
Because of her crippled leg.
No use as a servant—such a shame with that face . . .

Finally the shopkeeper's wife
Who traded spoiled cans of fruit
For baskets that took a year each to make.
Thank you, Faith, for not poisoning
Quite all
Of my
Family.

Blankets for each of you,
And let no one say
That I am not
Grateful for your care.

I DREAMT THE WORLD WAS ROUND

NAKESHA BRADLEY

I dreamt of a man traveling across vast waters
Only to be lost
He was rescued and fed by our cousins
He told his King he had discovered us
And all our gold
So much for Friendship

I dreamt my people united
Only to be marched into the sunset—The Darkening Lands
I dreamt of all my Aunts, Uncles, and Cousins
Dying in the snow
No one had time to mourn
Their spirits will dwell on that path
Where a thousand tears were cried
I live only to dream of them and all we lost
So much for Unity

I dreamt I was taken from my mother
I was beaten for trying to speak

In the only language I knew
I was taught to speak proper English
So I would not be stupid anymore
So I could sign my name to lies I did not understand
So much for Truth

They took my language
They took my history
They took my home
But they will never take my Spirit
It is all I have left
And mine is stronger than theirs
So much for Genocide

TO TELL OUR SIDE

RITA JOE

I stand before the native children
Baring my soul about our culture.
I stand before them offering my last,
For that golden dream, and the ladder
We try to climb.

The maiden speech,
The dawn of that titled page
To open doors.

I bare my abilities to them
Stating the limits,
The all-important meaning
To tell our side,
The aspirations.

They listen:
A generation of cultural mend is born
I see it in their eyes
The healing art of smouldering interest.

APPRENTICED TO JUSTICE

KIMBERLY BLAESER

The weight of ashes
from burned-out camps.
Lodges smolder in fire,
animal hides wither
their mythic images shrinking
pulling in on themselves,
all incinerated
fragments
of breath bone and basket
rest heavy
sink deep
like wintering frogs.
And no dustbowl wind
can lift
this history
of loss.

Now fertilized by generations—
ashes upon ashes,

this old earth erupts.
Medicine voices rise like mists
white buffalo memories
teeth marks on birch bark
forgotten forms
tremble into wholeness.

And the grey weathered stumps,
trees and treaties
cut down
trampled for wealth.
Flat Potlatch plateaus
of ghost forests
raked by bears
soften rot inward
until tiny arrows of green
sprout
rise erect
rooted
from each crumbling center.

Some will never laugh
as easily.
Will hide knives
silver as fish in their boots,
hoard names
as if they could be stolen
as easily as land,
will paper their walls
with maps and broken promises,
scar their flesh
with this badge
heavy as ashes.

And this is a poem
for those
apprenticed
from birth.
In the womb
of your mother nation
heartbeats
sound like drums
drums like thunder
thunder like twelve thousand
walking
then ten thousand
then eight
walking away
from stolen homes
from burned-out camps
from relatives fallen
as they walked
then crawled
then fell.
This is the woodpecker sound
of an old retreat.
It becomes an echo.
an accounting
to be reconciled.
This is the sound
of trees falling in the woods
when they are heard,
of red nations falling
when they are remembered.
This is the sound
we hear
when fist meets flesh
when bullets pop against chests
when memories rattle hollow in stomachs.

And we turn this sound
over and over again
until it becomes
fertile ground
from which we will build
new nations
upon the ashes of our ancestors.
Until it becomes
the rattle of a new revolution
these fingers
drumming on keys.

FINDING CARRIE:
REAFFIRMING IDENTITY THROUGH BLOOD, BEADS, AND BONES

KATHRYN LUCCI COOPER

PART I: CHOOSING LIFE
And I will weave her story,
With beads pulled tightly
Against the swollen, conjured dreams
Of our continuance

"**D**OCUMENTED" BUT "unenrolled." Removed and moved about with paper and pens, another trail along the Trail of Tears. A quiet form of genocide. An impersonal, personal holocaust. Categorized and counted, we became *free persons of color, mulatto, black, white, and other.* We are not, however, identified by the truth of ourselves, Tsalagi, Renape, Haudenosaunee, Catawba.—

What began with the colonial aggression of deSoto, and his march of "500 Christians" in 1540 extends into the present-day conceptualized assault on indigenous peoples as they struggle for identification, recognition, and sovereignty. The misery and oppression inflicted upon our ancestors during this attempted five-hundred-year-long extermination process have brought about a reshaping of traditional cultural values as they relate to the harmony of the circle and the connectedness of self for the good of the whole. It is what Paula Gunn Allen refers to in the book *Off the Reservation,* when she speaks of "the whole-the tribe-earth-universe-self" for precontact indigenous peoples:

The Native Americans knew the basic law of human universal consciousness was event-ual in nature, and that the event, the use, determined behavior most rationally in terms of human harmony and human development. The Europeans called them savages because they did not bow down to the idea of paper-ownership, or of personal possessiveness, or of ownership of the many by the few, and justified their genocide in these terms. Even as late as 1887, Americans justified the biggest land rip-off since the Mexican War by declaring: The one thing these people (the Cherokee) lack to make them civilized is the virtue of selfishness. ... When the concepts of possessiveness or proprietorship disappear as being meaningful in our lives, the haunting sense of separation from the universe will be lessened because possessiveness requires selfishness, and selfishness is separation.[1]

Paula Gunn Allen concludes her essay, "Notes Toward a Human Revolution," in this way:

[They] studied the Bible assiduously; and cultivated the companionship of literate and important non-Cherokees. Many married white women, some took black people as slaves, and by Cherokee Nation law they divested Cherokee women of political rights. In other words, they took up all the mechanisms of power that they believed would enable them to live as a sovereign nation, a republic on this continent, ally to the United States. They read the laws of the United States, obeyed what they read, and activated all due processes in their fight to retain ownership of their homelands. Imagine their amazement to find themselves walking, destitute, sick, and dying, eight hundred miles from their ancient and beloved home.... They were called "civilized" by whites, but they were powerless to change their fate.[2]

These were the words I carried with me as we—my mom, my uncle, and my three sisters—traveled by van along the mountain roads of southern West Virginia. My oldest sister Vicki had just been told that the breast cancer she thought she conquered seven years before had regained its strength and was once again battling for possession of her body. We gathered that morning offering tobacco to the spirits along with our acceptance that this disease would do with our sister what it willed. This acceptance of "fate" was not fatalistic in nature to us. We knew and understood that in principle there would, there could be no true death, only an elevation of the soul.

So we began our journey that morning in harmony, confident in our identities. We were practitioners of our culture; excluded as we were from the generic paper definitions of who is and who is not, *the whole, the tribe* . . . but rather traveling over the dominant society's definition of civilization, and into the "mythic nature of tradition."[3]

It was Vicki's desire to stand upon the soil that had once been our Grandmother Carrie's sod home. It was my sister who felt drawn to place her bare feet upon the stone stairway our grandfather had placed there by hand, a stairway that could still be seen beneath the new sweet growth of that year's honeysuckle vines. And all of us felt the need to reclaim and honor the grandparents who, when offered the choice between ownership and life, chose life.

These were the grandparents we knew only through winter nights of storytelling, midwifery, and the delicate needlework passed on to us from one generation of women to the other.

PART II: "EXILE IS A LONG AVENUE WHERE ONLY SADNESS WALKS."
—ROQUE DALTON

My needle will pierce the breast
Of her red memory,
And follow the deep greens
Of her resistance

OUR GRANDMOTHER Carrie was born a Cherokee around 1849, one of seventeen children. No one is really sure of the exact year of her birth. She and her siblings (seven older than herself and nine younger) spent their childhoods in constant motion as they traveled about with seem-ingly no regard for politically designed state boundaries. A century and a half later, my sisters and I would find them arranged, numbered, and cataloged on the pages of governmental documents. In these large ledgers we would see them, first here, and then there, as they were processed through the great changes of their times. Beginning in west-ern North Carolina, then moving upward into Virginia and Kentucky, these books traced their movements and kept an accounting of their material losses. They sought refuge for a time in Kansas and finally set-tled into various, small, obscure mountain communities along the rivers and creek beds of West Virginia.

They were sometimes declared "Indian," other times, "free persons of color," and by the time of my mother's birth a little over a half a cen-tury later, our family was simply listed as "white." It was the perfect paper genocide.

PART III: "[THERE ARE] EXTREMES OF SUFFERING INFLICTED UPON THE POOREST OF THE POOR THAT EVEN PIERCES THE HEART OF GOD."
—Julia Esquivel

My beads will follow the lines
Of her blue anger
And sing out the yellows
Of her poverty, her hunger, her grief

THERE WERE never any family birth certificates for us, no paper mar-riages, no ownership of property, no "Last Will and Testaments," only story-names and family histories given to us by our relatives, then later recounted on the pages of large books and copied from the dusty ledgers of local libraries and government offices. Our personal account-ing statement of forced assimilation. Our cultural debit column of war. War upon the Wolves (1700), Small Pox Wars (1738), War upon the Mountain Panthers (1748), War upon the Bald Eagles (1800), Wars of Displacement (1838), Wars upon Race, Ethnicity, Identity (Reservation

Rolls, Emigration Rolls, Henderson Rolls, Mullay Rolls, Siler Rolls, Old Settler Rolls, Chapman Rolls, Drennen Rolls, Swetland Rolls, Hester Rolls, Dawes Rolls, Churchhill Rolls, Guion Miller Rolls, Baker Rolls . . .). *"A listing of those who desiring a 640 acre tract of land in the east, in lieu of removing to Arkansas. Upon the death of the reservee, or the abandonment of the property, title is to revert to the state."* [4] Numbered, named, and claimed.

By 1820 the population of the United States had grown to ten million, the white population surrounding the Cherokee totaled almost one million, while their own population was just thirteen thousand.[5]

She was there, our Grandmother Carrie, as we sat in dark rooms scrolling through faded films listing the names of those who would be stamped with the seal of governmental approval. Columns of names declared as Cherokee beside those who would be forever abandoned. Her name would reach out to us from these pages, along with the names of her brothers and sisters. Pages of ancestral spirits forced to participate in an obscene version of *Cirque du Soleil*. Pulled upon the governmental stage and painted with the names of characters from their history books: Carolina, Christopher Columbus, George Washington, Benjamin Franklin, and so on and sow on and sow on as they planted their seeds for our acculturation one false identity at a time. Names sprinkled upon them in a conformational baptism of dispiteous salvation.

We would find them in the North Carolina census sometimes listed as servants in households unfamiliar to us, or on farms as laborers. They would be in Cherokee County, Ashe or Allegheny Counties, and Surry County. We followed them as they moved yet again during the Civil War—when she met our grandfather, a Cherokee mixed-blood from the Herrin family line—and they journeyed to Kansas together and then sometime later back to the East again. There is no way for us to know the true reasons for their journeys. We know only that my grandfather had at this time two wives, only one of which managed the journey home again.

It was reported . . . (from fifteen hundred to two thousand others, also in the main women and children, and claiming . . . protection) made their way to a point on the Cherokee neutral lands, about twelve miles south of Fort Scott, Kansas. Malnutrition, overcrowding, and bad hygienic conditions generally offered fertile soil for disease. Smallpox alone carried the refugees off by the hundreds. At this time J. T. Cox, special agent for the Cherokee Indian Territory, pleaded for medical aid as "indispensably necessary" but it was not provided. . . . [T]he Cherokee nation continued in a terrible condition and suffered severe population losses. Men died in battle or from sickness and exposure; women and children surely fared worse, since they were more exposed to sickness and death than the men.[6]

The Indian agent at Leavenworth, Kansas reported: "Their condition is the most pitiable imaginable. They were, only a few years ago, the most powerful, wealthy, and intelligent Indians in the United States, and were pleased of their power, wealth, and intelligence. They are now reduced to a third-rate power among Indians, and their wealth all gone. They fully understand their position, and are humbled."[7]

After the Civil War, there was a census taken of the Western Cherokee. The losses were great. Of those counted, the population survey showed that over a three-year period the Cherokee population dropped from 21,000 to a mere 14,000. This decrease is in addition to the estimated 4,000 deaths attributed to the Trail of Tears only a few years before.

PART IV: OUR ENEMIES HAVE ONLY HUNGER FOR PERSONAL GAIN—WE HUNGER FOR LIFE.
—SECUNDINO RAMIRES

They will sustain the Black
Humor of her rabbit trickster stories
And anchor me in their swaying dance
Of Orange admissions

My beads will reconcile
The deep Purples of her bruises
Making the belt stronger
As they merge with the Browns
Of her burdens

They will weave
The patterns of her anguish
Transformed—
By the Cheyenne Pinks
Of her laughter

MY THREE sisters and I would listen to stories as we sat on pillows and our grandmothers and aunties moved our tiny fingers through the patterns created by needles weaving threads, needles weaving wool, and needles weaving tiny glass beads. There were old Civil War stories. Stories of brothers wounded and lost in the prisons of faraway places like Elmira. Stories of loss from hunger, loss from strong winter snows, whooping cough, measles, childbed fever, influenza, and consumption. There were stories of suicide (the uncle who slit his own throat), those who died from too much drink and the fights that would sometimes follow their drunkenness, and the cousins who were hanged having been accused of horse stealing.

And there were humorous stories of bedbugs so large they would dance at night with our Grandfather Levi's most valued possession, a pair of glasses gifted to him when repeated childhood fevers, hunger, and malnutrition took away some of his vision.

There were traditional trickster stories, with veiled warnings attached so that we would know how to exist with the animals, with each other, and with ourselves.

We were gifted by these stories. Our story relatives walked among us every day. We were transformed by them into "Mythic cycles,"[8] where the past blended into the present of our everyday lives. They were, and remain, an oral history written not with pen and paper, but with needle, thread, and beads. They are the narratives of our place in this world and the next, conveyed with authority by *our* elders and affirmed by the ceremony of their retelling.

"What this implies is that the supernatural involvement in human affairs is key to the mythic nature of traditional indigenous narrative.... The mythic cycle is not actually a story cycle, nor is it a ritual cycle as present scholarship currently holds. A mythic narrative is a report on some particular person's journey, her experience in Mythic Time, a place as real as the mundane we moderns believe is all there is. Mythic Time is a space; it is a place *between* places. . . ."[9]

PART V: "YOU PROFANE THE SACRED BONES. YOU POUR CONCRETE ON THE LIVING."
—MARILOU AWIAKTA

My beads will awaken
The gray shadows of her existence
And she will move my fingers
Along the counted rows
Of those who came before me.
And I will find the design
For my own image
In the ivory white color
Of her bones[10]

IT WAS eighteen years ago when my father told me about the man who lived near the railroad switching station in the small community of Handley, West Virginia. "He collects Indian bones," my father said over his cup of morning coffee. "He has the head of what looks like a young child, and it still has the stone arrowhead lodged in the bones that form its skull." I remember feeling a deep sense of outrage as my father continued the conversation by telling me how the man proudly took him on a tour of the many ancestral bones he had collected and paid for over the years from various sources throughout the Southeast. I was nursing my youngest son Patrick at the time of this telling, and was not surprised later when he spit up the whole of his meal as he moved about the kitchen in his tiny red walker. Under normal conditions, I would not have allowed such talk concerning the dead while nursing an infant. The ability to call "restless" spirits in and contaminate a mother's breast milk was something I had been taught and avoided by making sure my thoughts were always where they should be when offering nourishment to one of my children.

But on this day I was caught off guard by my father's concern over what he had experienced while trying to seek the man's advice about a possible car buy. My father had been led into a room of this man's home, devoted only to the display of what he proudly declared were authentic, "Indian artifacts." My father was granted a tour of this room, filled with skulls, pottery, and even complete skeletons taken from what the *owner* sarcastically referred to as the "happy hunting grounds" of over-plowed river bottom land.

My father had not spoken with my mother or anyone about the incident, fearing that it might be too much for our mom to bear as she struggled with my sister Vicki's recent diagnosis of breast cancer. He had waited for my visit because he hoped that I would know what to do with the information. Actually, I didn't. I was a young mother in her early thirties with four small children. My activist momentum was directed toward providing a balanced education for my children, not Native American repatriations. I knew there was a problem. I had been to museums and parks where stolen burial objects and bones lay open on display for a price. But this conversation predated the 1990 passage of NAGPRA (Native American Graves Protection and Repatriation Act), which now provides a governing law for such exploitative acts.

My concerns for this man and his room filled with the skeletal remains of tiny children and sacred objects were not from a political activist framework; they were instead feelings pulled from a more personal place. They were the emotions of a mother, a sister, a daughter, a granddaughter. My father and I never spoke of this sorrow again. We left it on the ground that day. But sometimes I wonder if the man and his room are still there, and if the spirits of the bones he paid to possess walk through his home leading tours for other dissatisfied spirits seeking to view the living face of a fool.

BECAUSE HE was the only one who could remember which mountain path led to where our grandparent's house once stood, my uncle drove us that day. So many things had changed over the years; my mother could find none of the landmarks she once used to guide her. Highway 79 curled its way through mountainsides and along the creek beds of what once had been home to the panther and the bear.

My uncle brushed away the vines from the only thing left that reflected human measure, the stone steps. They were buried so perfectly along the edge of the mountainside that at first glance one would have thought they were merely natural rock formations exposed by years of runoff from some underground spring. And yet they weren't. They were there by the hands of our family, our people, building as they could between the river and the mountains.

We stood there as one family. My sister Vicki in her bare feet feeling the cool breath released from those mountain stones. The rest of us feeling the breath of comfort that comes only from belonging.

My uncle broke our silence as he dusted his hands on his pants and motioned for us to walk with him over the hillside to where he thought he could see the lines of the cemetery. There was a cemetery there, but not the way he remembered it. This one was pristine, with stone-carved headstones and small buildings filled with landscaping equipment and storefront offices for funeral arrangements.

He was at first confused. He had not remembered the town as being only minutes from the original home site. But it had been over fifty-years since he had walked these paths. The town had expanded. The highway had brought so many people and things to this mountain area. It was not a tiny community where harvesting pine timbers for tar and railroad ties supplied the income necessary for next year's seeds. It was now a burgeoning community, a suburb of the larger city.

We could not reach the buildings or the cemetery from where we stood. Fences now guarded the open paths. We would need to go back down the mountainside and into our van in order to make the half hour drive along the new highway to the same spot that would have taken us only minutes to reach by walking over the mountain.

Once there, we were greeted by a solemn man from one of the offices who offered us a printed map of the cemetery grounds. My uncle could not find his way around this piece of printed paper where the dead were sectioned off into communities named for various types of flowers. "This is our Rose Garden section and as you can see by the map over to the southeast is our Lilies of the Field section. If you could just give me the first and last names of your loved ones, I may be able to pull them up on our computer and tell you where they rest," he told us in a very businesslike way.

My mother gave him the names of her grandparents and we waited patiently as he sifted through the lists dating back to the turn of the century. Our Grandmother Carrie had died sometime after 1910. We hoped she would be among those listed.

My uncle excused himself to go outside to smoke and I followed him while my sisters and my mother sorted through the lists. Once outside, my uncle and I didn't speak to each other. I knew what he was doing and he knew I would know.

After several minutes, my family emerged from the office with the director, who informed my mother that he could point out to her where the "colored" cemetery section was located. "It is pretty much overgrown," he told us. "No one really looks after it. You might want to watch out for snakes this time of the year. You may not even be able to make it up the path. We had a flood several years back and that section pretty much washed away. After the highway came through here and cleared out most of the trees, the ground just keeps slipping way. It can't seem to find anything to hold onto. There's no real markers left up there anymore. That section is so old most of the caskets have rotted away. They say when it flooded it unearthed some of the bodies and most of the bones are all mixed up together now."

My uncle put out his cigarette, placed the butt in his pocket, and walked to the van. We drove away from the cemetery with its pretty gray and clay colored headstones, past the small road signs with their painted flowers, and out of the fenced-in community of their dead. We stopped at the foot of a small overgrown area just around the mountain from where we had spent our morning. My uncle got out of the van and stood looking up at the mountain, his hands in his pockets, his eyes squinting from the sun. This was the place where our journey had led us, an overgrown area, where no path was left for us to follow. A place where the bones of our grandparents lay mixed with the bones of so many others. My uncle placed tobacco at the foot of the mountain and climbed back into the van. He gently patted the leg of my sister Vicki who sat in the seat next to him and gave her his best smile as we drove away in silence.

1 Paula Gunn Allen, *Off the Reservation*, (Boston: Beacon Press, 1998), p. 19.
2 Ibid., p. 21.
3 Paula Gunn Allen, *Pocahontas,* (San Francisco: Harper Collins, 2004), p. 117.
4 Bob Blankenship, *Cherokee Roots*, Vol. 2 (Cherokee: Cherokee Roots Publication, 1992), p. 9.
5 Russell Thornton, *The Cherokees: a Population History* (Lincoln: University of Nebraska Press, 1990), p. 48.
6 Ibid., p. 91.
7 Ibid., p. 93.
8 Allen, *Pocahontas*, p. 177.
9 Ibid.
10 Kathryn Cooper, from the poem "Choosing Life" © November 2005.

CONTRIBUTORS

PAULA GUNN ALLEN, **Laguna/Métis**, PhD, Professor Emerita, UCLA, has written numerous anthologies of critical studies and American Indian fiction, which include *Studies in American Indian Literature* (1983), *Spider Woman's Granddaughters: Traditional Tales and Contemporary Writing by American Indian Women* (1989), and *Voice of the Turtle: American Indian Literature*; two collections of her essays, *The Sacred Hoop: Recovering the Feminine in American Indian Traditions* (1986) and *Off the Reservation: Reflections on Boundary-Busting, Border-Crossing, Loose Cannons* (1998); several poetry books including *Skins and Bones* (1990) and *Life is a Fatal Disease* (1998), and a novel, *The Woman Who Owned the Shadows* (1982).

CINDI MOAR ALVITRE is the mother of four children and grandmother of two. She is a weaver, writer, storyteller, and traditional singer. She is a **Tongva** descendant of the Moompetam (Salt Water) Clan, the original people of Los Angeles and the southern Channel Islands. She has been Director of Ti'at Society, the Tongva maritime organization, since its inception in the late 1980s. As the cofounder of Mother Earth Clan, she has been a cultural/environmental educator and activist for nearly three decades. She completed her BA in Anthropology, with an emphasis in California Indian Studies, and went on to compete her master's in history/museology at the University of California in Riverside. Her thesis focused on the preservation and protection of Mockingbird Canyon, a significant solstice site within Southern California. She is currently pursuing her PhD at UCLA in the Department of World Arts and Cultures with an emphasis in folklore, traditional medicine, California Indians, and Native American museum studies. Her dissertation will focus on "The Revitalization of Southern California Indian Basketry as a Healing Tradition."

ALICE AZURE'S poems and short fiction have appeared in *Shenandoah,* the *Cream City Review, Native Chicago,* and *Skins: Drumbeats from City Streets.* She is finishing up twenty-five years of service in the United Way system, having administered program grants and community studies in such places as Rock Island, Illinois; Alexandria, Virginia; Green Bay, Wisconsin; and Gales Ferry, Connecticut. In all those cities, she enjoyed powwow dancing, tribal social gatherings, and many friendships. She is of **Mi'kmaq**, **French**, and **Norwegian** ancestry.

DON L. BIRCHFIELD is a member of the **Choctaw** Nation of Oklahoma and a graduate of the University of Oklahoma College of Law. He is associate professor of Native American studies at the University of Lethbridge in Alberta and has taught American Indian studies at Cornell University, the University of New Mexico, and the University of Wisconsin at Green Bay. He was general editor of the eleven-volume *Encyclopedia of North American Indians* (New York: Marshall Cavendish, 1997) and is a former editor of *Camp Crier* at the Oklahoma City Native American Center. His essay collection, *The Oklahoma Basic Intelligence Test* (New York: Greenfield Review Press, 1998), won the First Book Award for Prose from the Native Writers' Circle of the Americas at the University of Oklahoma. His first novel, *Field of Honor* (University of Oklahoma Press, 2004), won the Spur Award for Best First Novel from Western Writers of America. His second novel, *Black Silk Handkerchief* (the first volume in his Hom-Astubby Mystery Series), will be released by the University of Oklahoma Press in spring of 2006. He is presently at work on a legal history of the Choctaws, forthcoming from the University of New Mexico Press.

MARY BLACK BONNET, an enrolled member of the **Sicangu Lakota** Nation, has been writing much of her conscious life. She grew up writing poetry and fiction and won a young authors award when she was in seventh grade for a fiction story. As she grew older, writing became her tool for expression in an oppressive household. When she began college she began writing nonfiction and ethnohistoric essays. She still writes poetry and is sending her book of poetry to publishers. She hopes to get back to fiction one day, but feels that the pressing matters of real life need to be addressed. Her poetry has been published in *Nagi Ho Journal*, *Tribal College Journal*, *Potomac Review*, and *The Native Law and Policy Textbook: Native Women Surviving Violence*. Her essays have been published in *Frontiers: A Journal in Women's Studies* and *Genocide of the Mind: New Native Writing*. She will graduate from the University of South Dakota in May 2006, with a double major in English and American Indian studies.

EUGENE BLACKBEAR, SR., was born in Watonga, Oklahoma, in 1930 to Paul and Minnie Blackbear. He is the oldest living **Cheyenne** Sun Dance Priest, an Arrow Priest, a Fasting Priest, a Sweat Lodge Priest, and a Native American Church Roadman. He played the role of Chief Spotted Elk in *Last of the Dogmen*, with Tom Berenger and Barbara Hershey. He is the father of four sons and seven daughters and has numerous grandchildren and great-grandchildren. He resides in his hometown of Watonga.

KIMBERLY BLAESER, **Anishinaabe**, a Professor at the University of Wisconsin—Milwaukee, is an enrolled member of the Minnesota Chippewa Tribe who grew up on the White Earth Reservation. Her publications include *Gerald Vizenor: Writing in the Oral Tradition* and two collections of poetry: *Trailing You,* winner of the first book award from the Native Writers' Circle of the Americas, and *Absentee Indians and Other Poems.* Blaeser's poetry, short fiction, essays, and critical works have been widely anthologized and she served as editor for *Stories Migrating Home: A Collection of Anishinaabe Prose* and the forthcoming *Traces in Blood, Bone, and Stone: Contemporary Ojibwe Poetry.* She lives with her husband and two young children in rural Lyons Township in Wisconsin.

NAKESHA BRADLEY, **Eastern Cherokee**, was born and raised on the Qualla Boundary in Cherokee, North Carolina, and still resides there. Her works have appeared in *Feeding the Ancient Fires: A Collection of Writings by NC American Indians,* edited by MariJo Moore; *Night is Gone Day is Still Coming: Stories and Poems by American Indian Teens and Young Adults,* edited by Annette Pina, Ochoa and Traci L. Gourdine, and *Shifting Winds Volumes 1 & 2,* a literary and arts publication of Cherokee High School. She draws her inspiration from home, family, and history.

SHIRLEY BROZZO is a member of the Keweenaw Bay Tribe of **Chippewa** Indians and works as the assistant director of diversity student services at Northern Michigan University (NMU). She is also an adjunct instructor for the Center for Native American Studies and an MFA candidate who will graduate in May 2006. Her poems and short stories have been published in over twenty-five anthologies. She has three adult children and loves to knit and crochet in her spare time.

KATHRYN LUCCI COOPER is a writer, poet, and substance abuse counselor/case manager at Summit House-Alternative Housing for Women and Their Children in Raleigh, North Carolina. Her essays and poetry have appeared most recently in *Genocide of the Mind, Frontiers: Special Indigenous Women's Issue, Red Ink,* and the *Raleigh News and Observer.* She is an outspoken, politically active Indigenous Inmate Religious Rights Advocate for death row inmates as well as those incarcerated in the general populations of North Carolina and West Virginia prisons. Kathryn is of **Cherokee/Sicilian** ancestry.

JOSEPH A. DANDURAND is a **Kwantlen** Indian from Kwantlen First Nation in British Columbia. He is a poet, playwright, fisherman, researcher, archaeologist, and, most important, the proud father of two beautiful girls, Danessa and Marlysse. Joseph received a diploma in performing arts from Algonquin College and studied theatre and direction at the University of Ottawa. His produced plays include *Crackers and Soup* (1994), *No Totem for My Story* (1995), *Where Two Rivers Meet* (1995), and *Please Do Not Touch the Indians* (1998) for the Red Path Theater in Chicago, (1999) for the Algonquin Theater in Connecticut, (2000) for the Debajemejig Theater in Ontario

(2001), and at the Autry Theater in Los Angeles California (2004). Joseph has also authored a radio script, *St Mary,* which was produced by CBC Radio in 1999. His poems have appeared in numerous journals and anthologies and are collected in *Upside Down Raven, I Touched the Coyote's Tongue,* and *burning for the dead and scratching for the poor, looking into the eyes of my forgotten dreams,* and *SHAKE. Please Do Not Touch the Indians* was published in 2004 by Renegade Planets Publishing.

VINE DELORIA, JR., **Standing Rock Sioux**, worked for over thirty-five years to create a body of literature that enlightens non-Indians who have not heard the true Indian story, and empowers Indians by outlining where we are vulnerable and how we can counter the anti-Indian movements. Deloria, considered an internationally prominent spokesperson for the rights and concerns of indigenous people, was chosen by *Time* magazine as one of eleven greatest religious thinkers of the twentiety century. His published works include *Custer Died For Your Sins; God Is Red: A Native View of Religion; For This Land;* and *Evolution, Creationism, and Other Modern Myths.* A retired lawyer and history professor, he resided in Golden, Colorado. He passed to Spirit during the winter of 2005.

LAURA DONALDSON is **Cherokee** and a professor of English, religious studies, and American Indian studies at Cornell University, where she is also director of graduate studies for the American Indian program. Her current book-length projects include *American Samson: Haunting the Native-Christian Encounter* and a critical memoir of Catharine Brown.

CAROLYN DUNN is a wife, mother, daughter, journalist, teacher, poet, and fiction writer born in Southern California. She is of **Cherokee**, **Muskogee Creek**, **Seminole**, and **Choctaw** freedman ancestry on her father's side, and Cajun and French Creole on her mother's. Her fiction and poetry have appeared in numerous anthologies, including *The Color of Resistance, Reinventing the Enemy's Language, Through the Eye of the Deer, Spirit Songs, The Greenman and Other Tales of the Mythic Forest,* and *Sing With the Heart of A Bear: Fusions of Native and American Poetry.* Her poetry has been collected in *Outfoxing Coyote* and *Hidden Creek Journal* and her non-fiction has appeared in journals in the U.S., Canada, and Germany. In addition, she is the coeditor of two anthologies of contemporary Native American writing: *Through the Eye of the Deer* (with Carol Comfort) and *Hozho:Walking in Beauty* (with Paula Gunn Allen). After completing her master's in American Indian studies with an emphasis in American Indian literature, folklore, and mythology, Carolyn taught at Humboldt State University and became the founding director (with Tina Toledo Rizzo) of the American Indian Theatre Collective. Currently pursuing a PhD in the Department of American Studies at the University of Southern California, her fields of study include American Indian folklore, mythology, performance, and literature. Her book of poetry, *Echo Location,* was published in 2005. She lives with her husband and three children in Los Angeles.

JACK D. FORBES is professor emeritus and former chair of Native American studies at the University of California at Davis, where he has served since 1969. He is of **Powhatan-Renape**, **Delaware-Lenape**, and other background. Forbes is the author of numerous books, monographs, and articles, including *Red Blood: A Novel* (1997, Theytus), *Columbus and Other Cannibals* (1992, Autonomedia), *Apache, Navaho and Spaniard* (1960, 1994, Oklahoma), and *Africans and Native Americans* (1993, Illinois). Other books in print include *Native Americans of California and Nevada*, *Native American Higher Education: The Struggle for the Creation of D-Q University*, and *Proposition 209: Racist Trick or Radical Equalizer*. He is also a poet, a writer of fiction, and a guest lecturer in Russia, Japan, Britain, Netherlands, Germany, Italy, France, Canada, Belgium, Switzerland, Norway, Mexico, and elsewhere. Professor Forbes has served as a visiting Fulbright professor at the University of Warwick, England, as the Tinbergen Chair at the Erasmus University of Rotterdam, as a visiting scholar at the Institute of Social Anthropology and Linacre College of Oxford University, and as a visiting professor in literature at the University of Essex, England. He is the recipient of the Before Columbus Foundation's American Book Award for Lifetime Achievement for 1997, and has been a Guggenheim Fellow.

EDUARDO GALEANO is a world-renowned **Uruguayan** journalist and author of the acclaimed trilogy *Memory of Fire, Open Veins of Latin America: Five Centuries of the Pillage of a Continent, Days of Love and War, Book of Embraces, Soccer in Sun and Shadows,* and *Upside Down*. Galeano lived in exile in Argentina and Spain for many years before returning to his homeland. One of Latin America's most distinguished writers, journalists, and historians, Galeano defies easy categorization as an author. His works transcend orthodox genres and combine documentary, fiction, journalism, political analysis, and history. The author himself has denied that he is a historian: "I'm a writer obsessed with remembering, with remembering the past of America above all, and above all that of Latin America, intimate land condemned to amnesia."

ERIC GANSWORTH (**Onondaga**) was born and raised at the Tuscarora Nation in western New York and is professor of English and Lowery Writer-in-Residence at Canisius College in Buffalo, New York. He is the author of the novel, *Mending Skins, Smoke Dancing,* and *Indian Summers* and the collection of poems and paintings *Nickel Eclipse: Iroquois Moon*.

MATTHEW T. SAKIESTEWA GILBERT is a PhD candidate in Native American history at the University of California, Riverside. Gilbert is a member of the **Hopi** Tribe from the Village of Upper Moencopi, Arizona. He is currently writing a dissertation titled "Education Beyond the Mesas: Hopi Student Involvement at Sherman Institute, 1902–1929." His other degrees include an MA in history from the University of California, Riverside, an MA in theology from Biola University, and a BA in history from the Master's College.

SUZAN SHOWN HARJO (**Cheyenne** and **Hodulgee Muscogee**) is the mother of Adriane Shown Harjo and Duke Ray Harjo II. She is a poet, writer, lecturer, curator, and policy advocate who has helped native peoples recover more than one million acres of land and numerous sacred places. She has developed key federal Indian law since 1975, including the most important national policy advances in the modern era for the protection of Native American cultures and arts: *1996 Executive Order on Indian Sacred Sites*; *1990 Native American Graves Protection and Repatriation Act*; *1989 National Museum of the American Indian Act*; and *1978 American Indian Religious Freedom Act*. Ms. Harjo is president and executive director of the Morning Star Institute, a national native rights organization founded in 1984 for native peoples' traditional and cultural advocacy, arts promotion and research. A founding trustee of the National Museum of the American Indian (1990–1996), she worked from 1967 to 1990 to gain repatriation policy and to establish the NMAI and was a trustee of its predecessor museum and collection in New York City throughout the 1980s. She serves on NMAI's Advisory Committee on Seminars & Symposiums.

INÉS HERNÁNDEZ-ÁVILA is a poet and professor of Native American studies at the University of California, Davis, where she also directs the Chicana/Latina Research Center. She is **Nez Perce** from Chief Joseph's band, enrolled on the Colville reservation, on her mother's side and **Tejana** on her father's side. She edited the recent publication, *Reading Native American Women: Critical/Creative Representations* (Altamira, 2005).

LINDA HOGAN (**Chickasaw**) was born in Denver, Colorado, and grew up in Oklahoma. She obtained a MA degree from the University of Colorado at Boulder in 1978. Hogan has played a prominent role in the development of contemporary Native American poetry, particularly in its relationship to environmental and antinuclear issues. She often incorporates a feminist perspective in her verse through description of women's lives and feelings. She is a poet, short story writer, novelist, playwright, and essayist. She taught at the University of Minnesota and at the University of Colorado in Boulder. Her many awards include the Five Civilized Tribes Playwriting Award, 1984; the Guggenheim Award; and Wordcraft Circle Writer of the Year (Prose-Fiction) award in 1997 for her novel *Mean Spirit*.

RITA JOE is like a Beloved Woman in the land of the **Mi'kmaq**. At seventy-three years of age, she is working on her eighth book of poems. The selection in this volume, "To Tell Our Side," came from *Song of Rita Joe: Autobiography of a Mi'kmaq Poet*, first published in Canada by Ragweed Press, then subsequently by the University of Nebraska Press in 1996. Other volumes include *Lnu and Indians We're Called, Poems of Rita Joe* and *Song of Eskasoni: More Poems of Rita Joe*. "I know now that the basic reason for my writing and speaking is to bring honor to my people," she says. Everyone who reads her poetry and numerous essays is inspired by her ability to describe harsh truths about some aspects of native life and history, yet still be moved by her great compassion and unending forgiveness. In 1990 she received the Order of Canada from Governor General Ray Hnatyshyn. She resides in Eskasoni, Nova Scotia.

PAMELA J. KINGFISHER, Cherokee, is former board president and community organizer of Native Americans for a Clean Environment in Tahlequah, Oklahoma; she was instrumental in keeping the health of the people at the forefront of their environmental battle. Their efforts eventually stopped the production of 23 percent of the world's uranium supply at the notoriously contaminated Kerr-McGee plant in Gore, Oklahoma. She has been awarded the U.S. Surgeon General's Award for Outstanding Performance (1990) for creative solutions over fourteen years in the Indian Health Service Hospital in Tahlequah, Oklahoma, and the Ingrid Washinawatok El-Issa Award for Community Activism (2003) for her volunteer work in cultural revitalization projects, women's health, and environmental issues. She recently served as the executive director of the Indigenous Women's Network for three years and continues her community work through her consulting company. She currently lives in Austin, Texas, but is returning to her grandmother's Indian Allotment land in Oklahoma, where she directs a project and botanical preserve.

SHAUNNA OTEKA McCOVEY was born and raised on the **Yurok** Indian Reservation in northern California. She holds degrees from Humboldt State University, Arizona State University, and Vermont Law School. Her poems have appeared in *News from Native California*; *Through the Eye of the Deer* (Aunte Lute Books, 1999); *The Dirt is Red Here* (Heyday Books, 2002); and her chapbook, *Swim You Every River* (Coytesse Books, 2003). Heyday Books published her first full book of poetry, *The Smokehouse Boys*, in the fall of 2005.

MARIJO MOORE (Cherokee/Irish/Dutch) is an author, poet, essayist, journalist, novelist, editor, artist, and publisher. The recipient of numerous literary awards, she resides in the mountains of western North Carolina. For more information, please see "About The Editor" in this anthology.

OHIYESA (CHARLES ALEXANDER EASTMAN), who was **Santee Sioux**, was born in 1858. He received his undergraduate degree from Dartmouth and obtained his medical degree at Boston College before returning to the Pine Ridge reservation in South Dakota as a physician. He spent the majority of his life working to help native people and promoting a better understanding of the American Indian culture. He published eleven books from 1902 until 1918.

DAWN KARIMA PETTIGREW,Creek/Cherokee/Seminole/Chickasaw/ African, and **Anglo-American**, is the author of the novel *The Way We Make Sense* (San Francisco: Aunt Lute, 2002) and the coauthor of *Children Learn What They Read* (Cleveland: UCC), a book about multiculturalism and spirituality in children's literature. Another novel, *The Marriage of Saints*, is forthcoming. Widely published as a poet and fiction writer, she is also an accomplished journalist who is a regular contributor to *News from Indian Country, Indian Life,* and *Whispering Wind.* Norton's *Twenty-Five and Under Fiction,* Aunt Lute's *Through the Eye of the Deer: An Anthology of Native American Women Writers,* St. Martin's *The Year's Best Fantasy and Horror: Fourteenth Annual Collection,* Theytus Books' *Gatherings VII and IX, Glimmer Train,* American Indian Culture and Research Journal, *Red Ink,* Rattlecat Press's *Coloring Book,* and *Hozho: Walking in Beauty: Short Stories by American Indian Writers* are some of the anthologies and periodicals where her creative works have appeared. A former Ms. Native American Worldwide Achievement, she has a BA from Harvard University and an MFA from Ohio State University. Miss Pettigrew is a member of the Native Writers' Circle of the Americas, Wordcraft Circle of Native Writers and Storytellers, National Indian Education Association, and the Native American Journalists' Association.

CARTER REVARD is **Osage** on his father's side and was born in Pawhuska, Oklahoma, in 1931. Given his Osage name in 1952, he grew up on the Osage Reservation and graduated from a one-room community school in Buck Creek and went on to Bartlesville College High, the University of Tulsa, Oklahoma, and Oxford University and received his PhD from Yale University. He has worked in hay and wheat fields, cornfields, and as a greyhound trainer. He has taught English (medieval, linguistics, and American Indian literature) at Amherst College and Washington University at St. Louis. Now retired and professor emeritus of English, he travels worldwide to present lectures and readings. His published works include *Ponca War Dancers, Cowboys and Indians, Christmas Shopping, An Eagle Nation, Family Matters, Tribal Affairs,* and *Winning the Dust Bowl.* He resides in St. Louis, Missouri.

KIMBERLY "EARLY MORNING KILLER WOMAN" ROPPOLO, of **Cherokee, Choctaw,** and **Creek** descent, took her PhD from Baylor University, specializing in Native American literature, in May 2002. She is an assistant professor in the Native American studies department at the University of Lethbridge and is the associate national director of Wordcraft Circle of Native Writers and Storytellers. Her recent publications include "Morning Star Song" in *Studies in American Indian Literatures* 16.4; "Symbolic Racism, History, and Reality: The Real Problem with Indian Mascots," in editor MariJo Moore's *Genocide of the Mind: New Native Writings;* and "The Real Americana," in editors Gloria E. Anzalda and AnaLouise Keating's *This Bridge We Call Home: Radical Visions for Transformation.* She received the Native Writers Circle of the Americas First Book Award for Prose for 2004 for her manuscript *Back to the Blanket: Reading, Writing, and Resistance for American Indian Literary Critics.* She resides in Lethbridge, Alberta, with her husband and the two youngest of her three children. She is currently working on a biography of Eugene Blackbear, Sr.

STEVE RUSSELL is a citizen of the **Cherokee** Nation, a high school dropout, a retired Texas trial court judge, and currently associate professor of criminal justice, Indiana University, Bloomington. A member of the Wordcraft Circle of Native and

Storytellers and Storytellers and Native Writers Circle of the Americas, he has a plethora of published works, which include: "Sovereign Decisions: A Plan for Defeating Federal Review of Tribal Law Applications." *Wicazo Sa Review* 93–108 (2005); "Since September 11, All Roads Lead to Rome." *Critical Criminology* 37–53 (2005); "In Search of the Meritocracy." *American Indian Quarterly* 400–411 (2004; "Honor, Lone Wolf, and Talking to the Wind." *Tulsa Law Review* 147–157 (2002); "Social Control of Transnational Corporations in the Age of Marketocracy." (with Michael J. Gilbert) *International Journal of the Sociology of Law* 33–50 (2002); "Levande Indianer" and "Döda Indianer" in *De Kallar Oss Indianer* 93–117 (Annika Banfield, ed., 2004); and "Apples are the Color of Blood," in *Race and Ethnicity Across Time, Space and Discipline* 19–30 (Rodney D. Coates, ed., 2004).

DAVID SEALS is of **Huron** and **Welsh** ancestry. His books include *Pow Wow Highway* and *Sweet Medicine*. David's next book *The Real AIM: 1971–2006* will be out in the fall of 2006 from Nation Books. He lives on the edge of the Black Hills in South Dakota with many members of his family and tribe all around him.

KIM SHUCK is a mixed **Tsalagi**, **Sauk/Fox**, and **Polish** educator, writer, and weaver. She is self-described as having a short attention span, which makes describing her life path somewhat difficult. Shuck has had myriad jobs, which include writing math curricula, frothing cappuccino, teaching at the university level, and being the mom of three kids who are now entering teenhood. She has attended way too much school, one product of which is an MFA. Her poetry has been published nationally and internationally. These publications include *Shenandoah, Cream City Review,* and the *En'owken Journal.* Her manuscript *Smuggling Cherokee* won the 2005 first book award from the Native Writer's Circle of the Americas and was published by Greenfield Press in 2005.

YUFNA SOLDIER WOLF is a member of the **Northern Arapahoe** tribe of the Wind River Indian Reservation in Wyoming. She was taught to know who she is, so she knows where she is going in her life. She was also taught to believe in her traditional beliefs. She believes tribal preservation of language, arts, and all aspects of the Arapahoe culture are vital to her future, as well as the future of her nation. She is a graduate of Montana State University.

JAMES ARONHIOTAS STEVENS is the author of five books of poetry, *Tokinish* (First Intensity Press, 1994) *Combing the Snakes from His Hair* (Michigan State University Press, 2002), *The Mutual Life* (Cambridge Conference on Contemporary Poetry Translation Series, 2005), *dis (Orient)* (Palmpress, 2005) and *Mohawk/Samoa: Transmigrations* (Subpress, 2005). He is a member of the **Akwesasne Mohawk** tribe, holds an MFA from Brown University, and is a 2000 Whiting Award recipient. He has published in over thirty journals and presented readings from Stirling, Scotland, and Cambridge, England, to Puerto Vallarta, Mexico. He is associate professor of English and director of Native American studies at the State University of New York at Fredonia.

SARA SUTLER-COHEN, of **Tsalagi, Irish**, and **Polish-Jewish** descent received her PhD in Sociology from the University of California at Santa Cruz and teaches part time at Marylhurst University in the human studies department. She is editor-in-chief for *Native Realities,* the online journal for Wordcraft Circle of Native Writers and Storytellers, and is the Native American/Indigenous Studies Area Chair for the Popular Culture and American Culture Association's SW/Texas Regional Conferences. Her poetry can also be found at http://www.unlikelystories.org. She lives in Portland, Oregon, with her partner and their eleven-year-old son. More information on Dr. Sutler-Cohen can be found at http://www.sarasutlercohen.com.

CLIFFORD E. TRAFZER, of **Wyandot** and **German** descent, is professor of American Indian history at the University of California, Riverside, where he is also director of public history and graduate studies in history. His most recent books include *Death Stalks the Yakama, Chemehuevi People of the Coachella Valley, The People of San Manuel,* and *The Native Universe,* with Gerald McMaster for the National Museum of the American Indian, which won an award from the American Association of Museums. Trafzer has served as a member of the California Native American Heritage Commission since 1988 and is actively involved in historical and cultural preservation, particularly through the Native American Land Conservancy as a founding member and on the board of directors.

JAY HANSFORD C. VEST, an enrolled member of the **Monacan** Indian Nation, (BA, University of Washington; MA, MIS, PhD, University of Montana) is an associate professor of American Indian studies at the University of North Carolina at Pembroke. He is a direct descendant of **Pamunkey-Powhatan** leader Opechancanough and his daughter Cockacoeske, Ann, Queen of Pamunkey, as well as, "Robin, ye king of ye Nansemond." Born in Lexington and raised in nearby Buena Vista, he is descended from the **Saponi-Monacan** nation as it devolved from Fort Christanna into Rockbridge and Amherst counties, Virginia. A 1992–1993 Fulbright professor in Bamburg, Germany, he has taught American Indian studies at universities in Montana, Washington, Arizona, Alberta, Minnesota, New York, and North Carolina. His published works include eight monographs, nearly fifty referred journal articles or book selections, and over eighty formal presentations and sponsored lectures, as well as consultations with several tribal nations and scholarly journals.

LELA NORTHCROSS WAKELY (**Potawatomi/Kickapoo**) is a Member of Wordcraft Circle of Native Writers and Storytellers, a pediatric home-care nurse, certified massage therapist, wife, sister, aunt, great aunt, and great-great aunt. Her writings have appeared in various journals. She and her husband live in Chandler, Oklahoma.

DRUCILLA MIMS WALL is **Alabama Creek (Muscogee)**. Her poetry appears in journals such as *Cream City Review*, *Kalliope*, and *Red River Review* and in anthologies, including *The People Who Stayed: Southeastern Indian Writing After Removal*, and *Times of Sorrow/Times of Grace: Writing by Women of the Great Plains/High Plains*. Her essays appear in *Eighteenth Century Life* and *True West: Authenticity and the American West*. She lives in St. Louis, Missouri, with her husband and two children and teaches writing and literature at the University of Missouri, St. Louis Honors College. Her work speaks from her Alabama Creek (Muscogee) Indian, Irish, and Jewish heritage.

JOEL WATERS, **Oglala Sioux**, is an English major attending the University of South Dakota. His poetry has appeared in *Red Ink, The Vermillion Literary Project*, and *Survivorship Quarterly*; his essay "Indians in the Attic" was in *Genocide of the Mind: New Native Writing*.

ALFRED YOUNG MAN, PhD (Eagle Chief), is **Cree** and professor and chair of Native American studies at the University of Lethbridge, Lethbridge, Alberta, Canada. He was born in Browning, Montana, on the Blackfeet Indian Reservation in 1948. Major published works include *Networking*, (ed.) 1987; *Visions of Power: Contemporary Art by First Nations, Inuit and Japanese Canadians* (1991); "The Metaphysics of North American Indian Art" in *Indigena: Contemporary Native Perspectives* (Vancouver/Toronto: Douglas & McIntyre, 1992); *Kiskayetum: Allen Sapp, a Retrospective* (Regina: The Mackenzie Art Gallery, 1994); "First Nations Art," Canada, and the "CIA: A Short Nonfiction Story" in *Studies In Critical Practices,* (Calgary: Canadian/Communications Research Group, University of Calgary 1994); "Native Arts in Canada: the State, Academia, and the Cultural Establishment" in *Beyond Quebec: Taking Stock of Canada* (Montreal: McGill–Queen's University Press 1995 (in second printing)); "Lawrence Abbot Interview with Alfred Young Man," coauthored and published by the *Canadian Journal of Native Studies* (Brandon, Manitoba, Spring 1997); *North American Indian Art: It's a Question of Integrity* (Kamloops Art Gallery, Kamloops, British Columbia 1998); *Indian Reality Today: Contemporary Indian Art of North America* (Westphalian State Museum of Natural History, Muenster, Germany, 1999), and "Indians as Mascots: Perpetuating the Stereotype" in *Genocide of the Mind: New Native American Writing* (Thunder's Mouth Press/Nation Books, New York, 2003). His latest manuscript is entitled *You Are In Indian Country: A Native Perspective on Native Art/Politics,* which is a critique of the issues and problems faced by native artists today in North America, to be published by the Banff Press in 2006.

ABOUT THE EDITOR

PHOTO BY JACK BOGDANOVICH.

MARIJO MOORE, Cherokee/Irish/ **Dutch**, is the recipient of several literary, editing, and publishing awards. Her work has appeared in numerous magazines, journals, newspapers, and anthologies. Her most recent books include *The Diamond Doorknob*, a novel, and *Confessions of a Madwoman*, poetry. She edited *Genocide of the Mind: New Native American Writing*, for which the Wordcraft Circle of Native Writers and Storytellers chose her as 2003 Wordcrafter of the Year. She was honored with the prestigious award of North Carolina's Distinguished Woman of the Year in the Arts in 1998. She was chosen by *Native Peoples/Indian Artists* magazine as one of the top five American Indian writers of the new century (June/July 2000).

Ms. Moore is a member of the editorial board of *Points of Entry: Cross-Currents in Storytelling*, has served on the New York State Council on the Arts Literature panel, the board of the North Carolina Humanities Council, the National Caucus of Wordcraft Circle of Native Writers and Storytellers, the board of the North Carolina Writers' Network, and the Speakers' Bureau for the North Carolina Humanities Council. In the past fourteen years Ms. Moore has presented more than four hundred literary readings, lectures, and creative writing workshops at numerous literary gatherings and educational institutions. In 2004 she was invited to the Library of Congress's National Book Festival to read from her novel, *The Diamond Doorknob*. She is the founder of Renegade Planets Publishing: Books by Indigenous Authors, and resides in the mountains of western North Carolina near her son Lance, his wife Katie, and their two daughters, Zoey Makayla and Emma Kate. http://www.marijo moore.com.

INDEX

Aaron, Daniel, 42
"Aborigines of America"
(Morris), 37
Abram, David, 339
Acevedo Díaz, Eduardo, 12
Adams, David Wallace, 83
Adams, John Quincy, 39–40
"Adieu to the Graves" (Squire
Greyeyes), 318
adoption experience, 225–26
Afghanistan, 183
African-Americans, 109, 158–59
AIM (American Indian Move-
ment), 122–23, 189, 217–18
Alcedo, Antonio de, 36
alcohol, xiv–xv, 174, 204, 210,
226–27, 310, 336
Algonquian Chikahominies,
147, 153
Allen, Paula Gunn, 245, 334,
374–75
Alliance for Progress of Miskutu
and Sumu, 196
"All My Ancestors Have Blisters
On Their Toes" (Sutler-
Cohen), 358–60
allotment process, 53–56,
139–40, 274, 291
All Pueblo Council, 57
Alvitre, Cindi, 335
American Heritage Dictionary,
270–71
American History (Current, et. al),
42
American holocaust. See
genocide of American Indians
American Holocausts Museum,
108–9
American Holocaust (Stannard),
270

American Indian Business
Association, 242
American Indian Movement
(AIM), 122–23, 189, 217–18
American Indian Religious
Freedom Act (1978), 299
American Indian Ritual Object
and Repatriation Foundation,
285
American Indians. See also
native cultures; specific Indian
nations
awareness of self, 182, 240,
310–13, 326–27
in denial, xiii–xiv, 308, 365–66
in early history books, 36–41
historical perspective of, xiv–xv
as immigrants, 334–35
imposition of agriculture,
53–54, 308
as instruments of their own
survival, 289, 290–95
joy at meeting each other, 250
pride in remembering, 71–73
in prisons, 74–77
record keeping, 272, 315–16
removal as constant threat to,
316–17
and renewal of America, 30–31
resilience of, 325
as threat to monotheisms,
182–83
tribal governments, 58–60,
285–86, 289, 301, 303, 324–25
American Literature (Bode, et. al), 43
American Pageant, The (Bailey),
42–43
American Race, The (Brinton), 38
American Rhythm (Austin), 338
Americans (Boorstin), 43

Anglo-Americans. See also
allotment process; racialization
of America
America as entire hemisphere,
35–37, 40, 44
as "chosen people," 146
historical perspective of, 17–22,
41–48, 140–42, 148–49, 152
Indians' perspective, xiv–xv,
344–53
naming of America, 35–36,
130–31
need for legends and denial,
22–23, 61–62, 107–8
Puritans, 16–18, 19, 24
robbery of artifacts and
graves, 300–301, 381–83
southern states, 114, 123,
160–62
takeover of the name
"Americans," 39, 41–46
Anglo culture
ability to lie, 188
American society is of
European origin, 40–41
ceremony versus defining
one's existence, 101
dark skin indicates less than
American, 45–46
fear of losing possessions, 62
inability to grok law and
culture, 52–56
life based on trade, 66–67
loneliness as solitude as virtue,
23–28
private property as essential, 54
unmarried pregnant Indians
deserve to be sterilized,
229–31
Anishinaabe Nation, 325, 389

apartheid in Virginia and the South, 161–64
Apologética Historia (Las Casas), 151
"Apprenticed to Justice" (Blaeser), 370–73
Arapahoe Nation, 55, 176, 281–84, 320, 395
Argentina, 12
Aristotle's Theory of Natural Slavery, 150
Arizona, 78–79, 90–93, 93n3
Arrival of the People Gallery (Conn.), 238
artifact robbery, 300–301, 381–83
assassinate versus neutralize, 197–98
assimilation policy, 282–83. See also genocide of American Indians
Astorpilco, Chief, 9
Austin, J. L., 332
Austin, Mary, 338
autonomy, 32–33
Aztecs, 6–8
Azure, Alec, 243, 244–45
Azure, Alice M., 238–44, 246–48
Azure, Joan, 242–43

Bacon, Nathaniel, 155
Bacon's Rebellion, 155, 159
Bagú, Sergio, 8
Bailey, Thomas A., 42–43
balance, 100, 101, 293–95
Bancroft, Hubert H., 37
Bannon, John Francis, 39
Barbados, slave trade with, 161
Basso, Keith, 339
Bear Paw, Mont., 260, 261–62
Bear That Catches, 321–22
Benton-Banai, Eddie, 325
Beto, Cruz v., 75
Bird Chief, 172, 176, 179n2
Bird Chief, Andrew
on being a Chief, 171–75, 178, 180n10
on Washita massacre, 175–78
Black Bonnet, Mary, 234–37
Black Elk, 322
Blackfeet Indian Reservation, 296, 301–3
Black Kettle, 170–71, 175, 176
Blaeser, Kimberly, 370–73
Blood Law of the Cherokee, 136
"Blood Quantum" (Russell), 135
boarding schools. See also genocide of American Indians
and allotment process, 55
Christian agenda, 82–85, 90, 92

Christianity in, 79–80, 85–89, 90–92
corporal punishment, 233–34
cultural depravation in, 27, 41, 71, 267–68, 289
denial of effect, 308
"I Dreamt the World Was Round," 367–68
Sherman Institute, 78–88, 90–93, 92n3
visualization of experience, 280–81
Boat Dance, 293–94
Boca del Tigre, 12
Bode, Carl, 43
Bolivia, 10–11
Boorstin, Daniel J., 43
"Bosque Redondo" (Russell), 143–45
Boston News Letter, 168n59
Boston Shoah Memorial, 246
Boston University, 76
Bradford, William, 17, 271
Bradley, Nakesha, 367–68
Brandon, William, 25
Brant, Joseph (Thayendanegea), 68, 69–71
Brave New World (Huxley), 186
Brazil, 13
Brennan, Charlie, 184, 185–88
Breyer, Stephen, 186
Brinton, Daniel G., 38
British, 40–41, 43, 68–69, 308
Broken Hand, 175–76
Brozzo, Shirley, 361–62
buffalo slaughter, 219–20, 279, 319–23
Buffon, Count de, 5
Bureau of Indian Affairs (BIA)
and Choctaw, 123
dishonest agents, 55–56, 60–61, 279–80, 301–2
payment of tribal funds, 284
rebuilding Boneau Dam, 300–301
support for white settlers, 35, 52
Bush, George W., 110

California
discovery of gold, 289
Los Angeles, 325, 332, 334–35, 337–38, 339–42
Sherman Institute, 78–88, 90–93, 92n3
Canada
Kwantlens, 305, 307–8, 310–11, 313, 389–90
Six Nations Reserve, 70–71
white supremacy in, 45, 302, 319

Capoche, Luis, 3, 4
Cara Nation (Nicaragua), 12
Carlisle Indian School, 267–68, 281–82, 283–85
Carolinas, North and South, 160–61, 162, 168n59, 202–3, 272
Casey, William, 197
Catawba Nation, 166n30
Catholicism in America, 45, 70, 80, 149–50, 308, 312, 345–46
Cayuga. See Haudenosaunee Nation
celebrations, 257. See also ceremonies
Center for Anthropological Studies, 6
Central America, 2–6, 8
Central Oklahoma Correctional Facility for Women, 74–77
ceremonial performativity, 332, 334, 336–37, 342
ceremonies. See also spiritual beliefs and practices
Anglo outlawing of, 76, 224, 322–23, 336
Deerskin Dance, Boat Dance, Jump Dance, 293–94
Fish Dam Ceremony, 294
Ghost Dance, 298, 322–23
Hopi Snake Dance, 327n19
Katsinam dance, 97–100, 101–3
meaning of, 100, 323
murderers forbidden to attend, 180n11
Nez Perce songs, 254–55, 262n3
Osage Naming Ceremony, 110–11
Pawnee Hako, 110
reburial, 285–86
returning to the homeland, 376
Sun Dance, 190–91, 298–300
Cerro Rico mines, Potosí, 3–4, 8, 11
Chacon, Martha, 325
Charles Town, W. Va., 160, 203
Cherokee Holocaust Museum, 202
Cherokee Nation, 389, 390, 393–95
and Civil War, 138–39
intermarriage, 134–35
Nanyehi, 204–8
paper genocide of, 376–79
prosperity of, 132, 136, 138, 379
South Atlantic Coast and, 18
stories, 100–101, 132–34, 204–8, 383–85

Supreme Court ruling in favor of, 119
treaties, 114, 136, 205–7
United States treaties with, 113–15
Chesapeake Bay, 152
Cheyenne Nation, 55, 170–75, 178, 180n10–11, 388, 392
Cheyenne Women Warriors, 178n1
Chickasaw Nation, 392, 393–94
in Oklahoma, 218–19, 220–25
United States treaties with, 112, 113–15, 125–26n9
War of 1812 and, 18
Chief, on being a, 171–75, 178, 180n10
Chikahominies, 147, 153
Chillocco Indian School, 213
Chippewa Nation, 244–45, 389
"Chitto Harjo" (Russell), 139–40
Choctaw Nation, 388, 394
about, 112–13
as military ally of U.S., 115–17
in Oklahoma, 121–24
on Trail of Tears, 115, 117–18
treaties, 112, 113–15, 117–24, 125–26n9
War of 1812 and, 115–17
"Choosing Life" (Cooper), 374, 376, 377, 379–80, 381
Christianity. See also boarding schools; Catholicism in America
beliefs about Indians, 5–6, 182–83
Catholicism, 45, 70, 80, 149–50, 308, 312, 345–46
and Cherokee, 134, 210
and Chickasaw, 221–22
choice of slavery or, 159
Christians versus, 65–66
Columbus on Indians' lack of, 148–49
diseases spread by missionaries, 335–36
doctrine of discovery, 112, 124n2
and Hopis, 78, 80–82, 83, 85–89, 90–92
with Indian traditions, 222
and Maya-Quichés, 14–15
and Mohawk, 70–71
and Powhatan, 153
support from coca sales, 11
and Tuscarora, 273
YMCA and YWCA, 87–89
Churchill, Ward "Lurch," 184–88, 191–92, 194–95, 196, 198

CIA manual for Nicaraguan contras, 197
Civil War, 138–39
Clemmer, Richard O., 46–47
Clinton, James, 68–70, 73
Code Talkers, Navajo, in World War II, 323–24
COINTEL (FBI counterintelligence programs), 183–84, 187–89
Cold War as source of censorship, 187
Collier, John, 57–59
Columbus, Christopher, 148–49, 159
communism, 25–26
community. See also native cultures
as America's greatest need, 28–30
Cheyenne tradition, 180n5, 180n7
indigenous peoples' valuing of, 24–25, 139
Nature as part of, 66–67
women as keepers of, 25, 336
Compilation of the Laws of the Indies, 3–4
concentration camps, 209–11
Concolorcorvo, 4
Conoy Nation, xvii
Conquest, meaning of, 164n6. See also genocide of American Indians
Conser, Frank, 90–91
Convention on the Prevention and Punishment of the Crime of Genocide, 201
Cooper, Kathryn Lucci, 374, 375–76, 377, 379–85
Covington, Lucy, 324
"Coyote Tears" (Dunn), 340–42
Crane, Vernon, 160
creation stories, 238–39, 323
Creek (Muscogee) Nation, 139–40, 323, 390, 392, 393–94, 397
Cree Nation, 216, 298–304, 397
Crow Nation, 320–21
Crow Old Man, 176
Cruz v. Beto, 75
cultural genocide, 290, 292–93, 308, 336. See also boarding schools; genocide of American Indians; native cultures
culturally-appropriate programming in prisons, 74–77
culture: value, worth, and reality of, 61–62
Current, Richard N., 42

Custer, George, 175–78, 178n1, 179n3, 321
Cut Bank Boarding School (Mont.), 298

Dandurand, Joseph A., 305–7, 308–10, 310–14
Danial, Z. T., 300
Davis, Jefferson, 61
Dawes, Henry, 54, 139
Dawes General Allotment Act (1887), 53–56, 139–40, 274, 291
"Day Four" (Dandurand), 305–7
deaths from diseases
in British Columbia, 308
in California, 336
as cover for genocide strategies, 148
in Mississippi, 112–13
in South Carolina, 202–3
in Southeast, 132
in Tennessee, 203–4
in Virginia, 152
Deerskin Dance, 293–94
De Paw, Abbé, 5
de Soto, Hernando, 113, 132, 203, 374
Dewey, Scott, 283–84
diaspora, meaning of, 332
diasporic people, urban Indian as, 331–32, 339–42
Dionysus and Apollo, 26
disease. See deaths from diseases
doctrine of discovery, 112, 124n2
documentation of survivors, 376–79
Dollar, Nancy Callahan, 211
Dominican Republic, genocide on, 151
Dozier, Edward P., 324–25
Drake, Samuel Adams, 34–35
Dreamer faith of Nez Perce, 255
"Drunks, Drifters, and Fat Robins" (Dandurand), 311–13
Duffield, Louella Kingfisher, 212
Dumont, René, 13
Dunn, Carolyn, 339–42
Duran, Bonnie Guillory, 333
Duran, Eduardo, 333

earth. See Mother Earth
Eddie Rickenbacker's bar (San Francisco), 179n3
Education for Extinction (Adams), 83
encomiendas, 5–6
Española, 151, 159
ethnicity, meaning of, 129
ethnocentric liberation movements, 182–84

Fagoth, Steadman, 196
family. See community
Faragher, John Mack, 247
Faulkner, William, 219
FBI COINTEL, 183–84, 187–89
Ferdinand, King, 150
First Americans. See American Indians; specific Indian nations
First Mesa (Ariz.), 96–100, 101–3
fish and fishing, 290, 291–93, 305–7, 308
Fish Dam Ceremony, 294
Fisher, Leila, 325
fish kill on Klamath River, 290–91
Five Nations. See Iroquois Nation
Flesche, Francis La, 110–11
Fort Christanna Reservation, 157, 158, 166n30
Fowler, Loretta, 171
Francis, Lee, III, 333, 334
freedom, 24–26, 29, 30–31
Freidel, Frank, 42
French and Indian War (1755), 204–5
fry bread, 276

Gansworth, Eric, 269, 271, 274–77
Garceia, Father Gregorio, 5
General Allotment Act (1887), 54–56, 60–61, 274, 291
genocide, U.N. definition of, 201
genocide of American Indians. See also boarding schools; deaths from diseases; Trail of Tears
  accepting reality of, 246–48
  "Apprenticed to Justice," 370–73
  banning ceremonies, 76, 224, 322–23, 336
  banning religion, 220
  buffalo slaughter, 219–20, 279, 319–23
  cultural, 290, 292–93, 308, 336
  effect of, 267
  evidence of, 270–71, 376–79
  historic whitewashing of, xv–xvi, 22–23, 107–11, 129
  holocausts, in general, 107–11, 270–71, 271–72
  justification for, 23–28, 34–35, 53–55, 149–50, 162–63, 375
  "Lady in Turtleneck," 361–62
  in Latin America, 2–6, 8, 10–15, 151
  paper genocide, 376–77

remembering, xvi–xvii, 250, 291
Sand Creek Massacre, 170, 361–62
scorched earth campaign, 68–73
slavery, 1–6, 8, 10–13, 150, 158, 159–61, 168n59, 336
splitting up family units, 24–28, 209, 302
sterilization, 218, 228–31
systematic nature of, 136, 148–51, 204–12, 302
in Virginia and West Virginia, 151–57
Washita Massacre, 170–71, 175–78, 179n3
Wounded Knee Massacre, 219–20, 298, 322, 361–62
Georgia, 119–20, 121, 129, 208–9
Georgia, Worcester v., 119–20, 121, 129
Ghost Dance and Ghost Dance Religion, 298, 321, 322–23
Gidley, M., 256
Ginés de Sepúlveda, Juan, 5
"Giveaway" (Shuck), 365–66
God (Great Spirit). See also ceremonies; spiritual beliefs and practices
  acknowledging without understanding, 103–4
  as connection of all beings, xvii, 98–99, 100
  Cree connection with, 303–4
  in Mi'kmaq creation story, 239
  Wohpekumeu, 290–91
gold, discovery of, 11–12, 13, 119–20, 121, 129, 159, 208–9, 289
Gourneau, Patrick, 244
government. See also laws; treaties
  allotment process, 53–56, 139–40, 274, 291
  Christian agenda at boarding schools, 82–85, 90, 92
  credibility gap, 53
  indigenous peoples as threat to, 182–83
  as separator of human beings, 24–28, 209, 302
  southern states ignore treaties of, 114
  tribal, 58–60, 285–86, 289, 301, 303, 324–25
grandfather, meaning of, 180n7
Grant, Ulysses S., 279
grave robbing, 300–301, 381–83

Great and Noble Scheme, A (Faragher), 247
Great Debate at Valladolid (1550–51), 150
Great Plains, 319–20
Great Republic by the Master Historians, The, 36–38
Guatemala, 14
Gumbs, Harriett Starleaf, 325–26

Haiti, genocide on, 151
Hallowell, Irving, 159
Hanke, Lewis, 149, 150
Harjo, Chitto, 139–40
Harjo, Suzan Shown, 344–53
Harsha, William Justin, 61
Harvey, Paul, 302
Hatfield, John Alfred, 239–40
Haudenosaunee (Iroquois) Nation
  along Virginia borders, 147
  attack on Catawba people, 166n30
  ceremonies of, 323
  and European power struggle, 18
  Mohawks, 70–73, 240, 395–96
  Oneidas, 46
  Onondagas, 270, 274–75, 391
  raids on Tuteloes, 155
  scorched earth campaign against, 68–73
  Ta-ha-yu-ta's speech, 18–19
  treaties, 155, 157–58
  and Tuscaroras, 269–70, 272–73
Hawaiian natives imprisoned in Oklahoma, 74–77
Hegel, 5
Henry, Mary Lou, 319
Her Majesty's Chapel of the Mohawks, 71
Hernández-Ávila, Inés
  at Bear Paw, Mont., 260, 261–62
  Dreamer faith, 255
  happiness with family, 249–50
  mother of, 251–55, 257, 260–61
  Nez Perce songs, 254–55, 262n3
  at World War II memorial, 257–59
Hicks, John D., 41
Hidalgo, Miguel, 9–10
History of the Americas (Bannon), 39
History of the Turtle Mountain Band of Chippewa Indians (Gourneau), 244
Hofstadter, Richard, 42

Hogan, Linda Colbert, 219–20, 221, 223–27
Hoh Nation, 325
Holocaust Museum for Jews, 108
holocausts, in general, 107–11, 270–71, 271–72, 286. See also genocide of American Indians
Hopi Nation, 46–47, 78, 93n2, 96–98, 101, 323, 391
    and Sherman Institute, 78–88, 90–93, 92n3
Hopi Snake Dance, 327n19
Howard, Leon, 43
Howard, Oliver O., 262
Howard of Effingham, Lord, 155
"How the Plants Gave Us Medicine" (Cherokee story), 100–101
"How to Succeed as an Indian Poet" (Russell), 131–32
Huancavelica mercury mines, 2–3
Hughes, Sallie, 210
Huguenots, 156–57
Humboldt, Alexander von, 9
Hunter Gray, 240, 241–42
Huron Nation, 395
Huxley, Aldous, 186

"I Dreamt the World Was Round" (Bradley), 367–68
Inca empire, 6–7, 8–9
"Indian America" (Russell), 130
Indian and His Problem, The (Leupp), 56–57
Indian Removal Act (1830), 115–20, 208–9, 317
Indian Reorganization Act (IRA–1934), 58
Indian Self-Determination and Educational Assistance Act (1975), 122–23
Indian speak, xvi
intergenerational post-traumatic stress disorder, 333
intermarriage, 134–35
Intertribal League of American Indians, 240, 241–42
"Invisibility Lessons #1 and #2" (Wall), 363–64
Iowa Nation, 54–55
Iroquois. See Haudenosaunee Nation
Iroquois, The (Snow), 274
Islam, 182–83

Jackson, Andrew, 24, 114, 116, 119, 129, 136, 208
James, Harry C., 80
"Japanese Gardens" (Waters), 356–57

Jay Treaty (1794), 242
Jefferson, Thomas, 22, 158, 208
Jim, Mary, 316
Joe, Rita, 369
Joseph, Chief, 260–61
Josephy, Alvin, 259, 263n6
Joyce, Barry Alan, 46
Juan de Solórzano, Governor, 2–3
Judaism, 33–34, 45, 182–83, 201, 286, 358–60
Jump Dance, 293–94
"Jumping Through the Hoops of History" (Harjo), 344–53

Kant, Immanuel, 38–39
Kappler, Charles J., 124n1
Katsinam Nation, 97–100, 101–3
Kennewick Man, 48
Khomeini, Ayatollah, 183
Kingfisher, Pamela, 201–2, 211, 212–14
Kiowa Nation, 320, 321
Klamath River (Oregon), 287–88, 290–91
Knox, Henry, 207
Kwantlen Nation, 305, 307–8, 310–11, 313, 389–90

"Lady in Turtleneck" (Brozzo), 361–62
Lakota Nation, 232–37, 320, 388
language and landscapes, 339–42
Las Casas, Bartolomé de, 5, 151
Last of the Americans, The (Brandon), 25
Latham, Edward H., 263n5
Latin America, 1–6, 8, 10–13, 159. See also Spaniards
laws. See also treaties
    benefits of living with, 123–24
    Blood Law of the Cherokee, 136
    and culture, 52, 61–62
    deceptive use of, 118–19, 122, 207–8
    doctrine of discovery, 112, 124n2
    protectorate for Choctaw, 113–14, 123–24
    southern, 162
    Supreme Court, 57–58, 119–20, 121–22, 124n2
    U.S., pertaining to Indians, 58, 115–20, 122–23, 208–9, 284–85, 317, 382
Lea, Luke, 35
Lessee v. William M'Intosh, 124n2
Leupp, Francis E., 56–57, 83–84, 88
"Lifeblood" (McCovey), 294–95

Liñán y Cisneros, Archbishop, 2
Little Big Horn, 321
Little Chief, 281–82, 285
Lone Wolf v. Hitchcock, 121
"Long Time Gone Cradleboard Song" (Pettigrew), 354–55
Los Angeles, Calif., 325, 332, 334–35, 337–38, 339–42
Lowry, Elizabeth (Peggy Shorey), 211

Makers of the American Mind (Whittemore), 44
Making of the Great West, The (Drake), 34–35
Mannahock Nation, 146–47, 155–58, 166n30, 168n63, 396
Manuel, Delores Crispeen, 326
Massacre at Wounded Knee (1890), 219–20, 298, 322, 361–62
masturbation pamphlet (YMCA), 87
matriarchal cultures
    Cherokee, 139, 204–8
    intermarriage with patriarchal, 270, 274
    Kingfisher's renewal of, 214
    Lakota, 232–33, 237
    replacing with patriarchy, 134, 139, 207, 270, 336
Matthews, Maurice, 159–60
Maya–Quichés, 14–15
Mayas, 6–7
McCovey, Shaunna Oteka, 287–88, 292–95
Me and Mine (Udall), 80
Means, Russell "Rascal," 196, 198
Medicine Lodge Creek Treaty (1867), 170
Mennonites, 81–82
mercury mines, 2–3, 4, 8
Mexicans, 24, 336
Mexico, 2–6, 12
Michel, Francis Louis, 156–57
Michigan, 317
"Micmac Honour Song" (Paul), 248
Mi'kmaq Nation, 238–39, 247, 387–88, 392–93. See also Azure, Alice M.
Miles, Josephine, 16, 20–22, 26, 28, 29
Miles, Nelson A., 262
Miller, William, 42
Miniconjou Nation, 298. See also Wounded Knee Massacre
missionaries. See Christianity
Mississippi, 112–15

Misurasta, 196
Mohawk Institute (Brantford, Ontario), 71
Mohawk Nation, 70–73, 240, 395–96
Monacan Nation, 146–47, 155–58, 166n30, 168n63, 396
Monasetah, 179n3
money, Indians' inability to handle, 177
Monk, Vera, 338
Montana, 13, 75, 260, 261–62, 298–300
Moon, Jennie, 260
Mooney, James, 155, 158, 166n29
Moore, James, 160
Morelos, José María, 9, 10
Mormons, 47, 80
Morris, Charles, 37
Mother Bears (Los Angeles, Calif.), 339
Mother Earth
    Americans' amnesia and, 22–23
    Anglos' destruction of, 28, 62, 68–73, 101, 220, 333–34
    caring for, 335
    "Coyote Tears," 340–42
    Indian teachings about, 66–67, 100–101
    landscape art, 338, 339–42
Muscogee (Creek) Nation, 139–40, 323, 390, 392, 393–94, 397
Museum of the American Holocausts, 110

Nahyssans. See Monacan Nation
Nanyehi, 204–8
Napoleon, 187
National Association of Tribal Historic Preservation Officers, 285
National Museum of the American Indian, 109
Native American Graves Protection and Repatriation Act (1990), 284–85, 382
Native Americans. See American Indians; specific Indian nations
native cultures. See also ceremonies; community; matriarchal cultures; spiritual beliefs and practices
    assimilation policy, 282–83
    capping government at level of city or community, 32–33
    ceremonial performativity as lifeblood of, 332, 334, 336–37, 342

importance of wisdom and family, 24–25, 315–16, 325–26
    lack of apology for, 291
    in U.S. prisons, 74–77
    white man's perception of, 53
Navajo Nation, 323–24
Nazi Holocaust, 201, 286, 358–60
Nespelem, Wash., 250, 252, 260
neutralize versus assassinate, 197–98
New England Company, The, 71
New York Times, 109
Nez Perce Nation, 250–51, 260, 263n7, 392. See also Hernández-Ávila, Inés
Nicaragua, 12, 197
1984 (Orwell), 183–84
Northern Arapaho Nation, 278–79
Norwood, Janice, 338
"Notes Toward a Human Revolution" (Allen), 375
No Turning Back (Qoyawayma), 91–92

oaths, 171, 173–74, 178n1, 180n9
Off the Reservation (Allen), 374–75
Of Plymouth Plantation (Bradford), 271
Ohio, 317–18
oil, discovery of, 122, 136–38, 140
Oklahoma, 121–24, 129–32, 217–20
Old Coyote, Barney, 324–25
Old Grandmother Spider, 245–46
Old Lady Horse, 320, 327n12
Oneida Nation, 46
Onondaga Nation, 270, 274–75, 391
"On the Origin of the Americans" (Bancroft), 37
On the Trail of Elder Brother (Running Wolf and Smith), 239
Oraibi Split, 78, 93n2
Oraibi village (Hopi), 78, 90–93
Oregon, 287–88, 290–91
"Original American, The" (1831 schoolbook), 39
Orwell, George, 183–84
Osage Nation, 110–11, 394

Pack, Elizabeth, 211
Pages From Hopi History (James), 80
Palouse Nation, 316, 323
Paquinquineo (Don Luis deVelasco), 152–53
Paraguay, 6

patriarchal cultures, 134, 139, 207, 270, 336
Paul, Daniel, 239, 247
Paul, George, 248
Paul III, Pope, 5
Pawnee Nation, 110
pedophiles, 308, 312
Peltier, Leonard, 190, 193, 198
"Perfection" (Dandurand), 313–14
Peru, 10–11
Pettigrew, Dawn Karima, 343n8, 354–55
Phillip II, 1
photographs, 254, 256
Pine Ridge Indian Reservation (South Dakota), 56, 183
Plecker, W. A., 162, 163
politics, summary of, 187–88
Potosí mita, Cerro Rico mines, 3–4, 8, 11
Power, Samantha, 246
Powhatan and the foreigners, 146–47
Powhatan Nation, 148, 152–53, 154, 391, 396
Pratt, Richard Henry, 282
Pretty Shield, 320
Problem from Hell (Power), 246
"Psychological Operations in Guerrilla Warfare" (CIA), 197
Pud Bean, 220–21
Pueblo Nation, 57–58
Puritans, 18, 19
Pushmataha, 116–17, 126n14

Qoyawayma, Polingaysi, 81, 88, 91–92

racialization of America. See also Anglo-Americans
    apartheid, 161–64
    and Civil War, 138–39
    emergence of North America, 39–40
    Europeans in America, 34–36
    examples of, 33–34
    as life out of balance, 101
    in prisons, 75
    significance of naming the land, 32–33
    white supremacist takeover, 45–48, 302, 319
rape, 210, 229–31, 234–36, 359–60
Reader's Digest, 286
Reagan, Ronald, 193, 198
Real People. See Powhatan Nation
Red on Red (Womack), 171
Reifel, Ben, 324–25

religious prejudice, 124n2, 298–300. See also boarding schools; Christianity
repatriation of dead ancestors, 284–86
Rethinking Hopi Ethnography (Whiteley), 81
Ribeiro, Darcy, 8
Rilke, Rainer Maria, 103
Risling, Dave, 324–25
Rivera, Fructuoso (José), 12
Roads in the Sky (Clemmer), 46–47
Roanoke, Virginia, 153
Robideau, Steve, 193
Roblee, William W., 87
Rocky Boy Indian Reservation, 300–301, 303
Rodrigo de Loaysa, Fray, 3
Ross, John, 136
Roundup Sun Dance, 299–300
Rountree, Helen, 163
Roy, Patrick and Iva, 241
Royce, Charles, 161
Rumsey, C. E., 87
Running Wolf, Michael B., 239

Sachowengsie, Effie, 90–91
Sacred Hoop, The (Allen), 245
Sale, Kirkpatrick, 151
Salt Songs, 323
Sand Creek Massacre, 170, 361–62
Sando, Joe, 324–25
Satz, Ronald N., 125n6
"Savages, The" (Miles), 16, 20–22, 26, 28, 29
Schiller, Friedrich, 109
schools. See boarding schools
Seals, David, 182–83, 194–95
Sealth (Seattle), 21, 27
Seneca. See Haudenosaunee Nation
September 11, 2001, terrorist attacks, 184–85
Serrano Nation, 325
Seven Drum religion, 255
Shakespeare, relevance of, 109–10
Shaping of American Ethnography, The (Joyce), 46
Sharpnose, 280, 281
Shawnee Nation, 158
Sheridan, Philip H., 170–71
Sherman Bulletin, 85
Sherman Institute (Riverside, Calif.), 78–88, 90–93, 92n3
"Sherman Project, The," 93
Shinnecock Nation, 325
Short History of American Democracy, A (Hicks), 41
Shuck, Kim, 365–66

"Singing the Calumet" Pawnee ceremony of the Hako, 110
Siouan tribes of the East, 158, 159, 161, 166n29
Sioux Nation, 390, 393, 397
Sitting Bull, death of, 321–22
Six Nations Reserve (Canada), 70–71
Sky People, 305, 308, 310–11, 313
slavery, 1–6, 8, 10–13, 150, 158, 159–61, 168n59, 336
Smith, Chad, 142
Smith, Patricia Clark, 239
Snake River, 316
Snow, Dean R., 274
society. See Anglo culture; community; native cultures
Soldier Wolf, Yufna, 278, 285, 286
Solzhenitsyn, Aleksandr, 186, 187
sovereignty, meaning of, 32
Soviet Union, 183, 184
Spaniards
    America as entire hemisphere, 36, 39–40
    brutality of, 149, 151, 336
    de Soto, 113, 132, 203, 374
    exclusion from American history books, 43
    Hopi hatred for, 80
    savagism dogma as justification for Conquest, 149–50, 375
    and slavery, 1–6, 8, 11
Spell of the Sensuous, The (Abram), 339
spiritual beliefs and practices. See also ceremonies; God; Mother Earth; native cultures; storytellers; truth
    ancestral spirits as part of, 99–100
    death is elevation of the soul, 375–76
    dream interpretation, 246–47, 255
    of Hawaiians, 74–75
    inner knowing, xiv–xv, 303–4
    landscape art, 338, 339–42
    legal right to, 75–77
    many fates inside a human being, 217
    music and dance, 98–99, 256–57, 323
    Old Grandmother Spider, 245–46
    spiritmemory, 250, 254, 262
    symbolism and interconnection, xvii, 99–100, 332

visions, 296–97, 303–4, 321
Yurok myths, 288, 291–92
spiritual healing, xv, 100–103, 262, 311, 336–38. See also storytellers
Spotswood, Alexander, 157
Squire Greyeyes, 318
Standing Bear, Luther, 41, 320
Standing Rock Reservation, 321–22
Stannard, David E., 270
state laws' extension over Indians, 118–22
stories. See also specific poems
    Cherokee, 100–101, 132–34, 204–8, 380–81, 383–85
    Cheyenne, 171–78, 178n1
    of creation, 238–39, 323
    Cree, 216–17
    of Sky People, 305, 308, 310–11, 313
    Yurok, 288, 292–93
storytellers
    association for promoting, 246
    native culture's dependence on, 326
    role of, 216, 315–16, 326, 333–34
    and symbolism, 99
    for urban American Indians, 333
Suhtai, 179n2, 180n6. See also Cheyenne Nation
Sun Chief (Talayesva), 82
Sun Dance, 190–91, 298–300
Sun Dance circle (Roundup, Mont.), 299–300
Supreme Court, 57–58, 119–20, 121–22, 124n2
Sutler-Cohen, Sara, 358–60
Sweezy, Carl, 320
symbolism, importance of, 99–100

Ta-ha-yu-ta (Logan), 18–19
Talas, Louise, 91
Talayesva, Don C., 82, 86, 89
Taylor, Michael, 191, 192
Tecumseh, 116, 126n14, 317
Tennessee, 203–4
Tenochtitlán, 7–8
Thoreau, 20
Thorpe, Jim, 284
Thundershield, Dallas, 190–91
Thundershield, Gramma, 190, 193
tobacco, 340–42
Tocqueville, Alexis de, 40–41
Tongva Nation, 334–36, 387
Torovim, the dolphin people, 335–36

"To Tell Our Side" (Joe), 369
Trail of Tears
  Cherokee on, 119–20, 129, 209–11, 211–12
  Chickasaw on, 219
  Choctaw on, 115, 117–18
  and concentration camps, 209–11
  "I Dreamt the World Was Round," 367–68
  vision of Cherokee woman, 128–29
  white man's acceptance of, 185–86
treaties
  canons of construction, 125n6
  with Cherokee, 112, 113–15, 125–26n9, 205, 206–7
  with Chickasaw, 112, 113–15, 125–26n9
  Medicine Lodge Creek Treaty, 170–71
  with Mohawks, 72–73
  white man's lack of integrity, 65, 118–19, 122, 319
treaties with Choctaw (1786, 1801–66)
  overview, 112, 113–15, 125–26n9
  removal treaties, 117–18, 119–24
Treaty of New Echota, 136, 208–9
Treaty of Utrecht (1713), 247
tribal fisheries program, 288, 291–95
tribal governments, 58–60, 285–86, 289, 301, 303, 324–25
Tribal Sovereignty and the Historical Imagination (Fowler), 171
Trudell, John, 189
truth
  of Chief Joseph, 260–61
  native museums without, 202
  need for, xiii–xiv, xvi–xvii, 216–17
  oaths, 171, 173–74, 178n1, 180n9
  social spirit of indigenous peoples as, 183
  whitewashing of, xv–xvi, 22–23, 107–8, 129
Tsalagi Nation, 395, 396
Tsis–tsis–tas, 179n2, 180n6
Túpac Amaru, 8–9
Turtle Island, 323
Tuscaroras, 269–70, 272–, 272–73
Tuteloes, 155, 157–58
"Two" (Dandurand), 308–10
Two Men (Seals), 191–92

Udall, Louise, 80
United Nations, 201
United States, 22–23, 48, 101, 207. See also Anglo-Americans; treaties
United States, Experiment in Democracy, The (Craven and Johnson), 41–42
United States Bureau of Reclamation (USBR), 290–91
United States (Hofstadter, et. al), 42
University of Nebraska Press catalog, 46
urban Indians as diasporic people, 331–32, 339–42
Uruguay, 12

Vásquez de Ayllón, Lucas, 159
Vega, Garcilaso de la, 11
Verazzano, Giovanni da, 152
Virginia and West Virginia, 146–47, 151–57, 161–62
Virginia Racial Integrity Law (1924–1969), 162, 163
Voltaire, 5
Voth, Heinrich R., 81–82

Wahpepah, Bill, 194
Wall, Drucilla Mims, 363–64
Wampanoag Nation, 16–17
Warner, Glenn "Pop," 284
War of 1812, Choctaw involvement in, 116–17
War on Poverty, 59
Warrior Societies, 178–79n1
Washington, D.C., xvii
Washington, George, 68–70, 72
Washita Massacre, 170–71, 175–78, 179n3
Waters, Joel, 356–57
Way We Make Sense, The (Pettigrew), 343n8
Webster's New Collegiate Dictionary, 39
Werner Encyclopedia (c. 1875), 36
West Indies, 159
West Indies, Indian slaves sold to, 160–61
West Virginia and Virginia, 146–47, 151–57, 161–62
"We The People" (Francis), 333
We Were Not the Savages (Paul), 239
"What I Learned and Didn't Learn" (Russell), 140–42
"What Indians Want" (Russell), 133–34
Whirlwind Coming, 175, 177
Whiteley, Peter, 81

white supremacy, 45–48, 302, 319
Whittemore, Robert Clifton, 44
William M'Intosh, Lessee v., 124n2
Williams, T. Harry, 42
Wind River Indian Reservation, 279
Winthrop, John, 43
wisdom, 24–25, 315–16, 325–26. See also storytellers
With One Sky Above Us (Gidley), 256
Wohpekumeu (Creator Being), 290–91
Wolverine (Cree story), 216
Womack, Craig, 171
women
  Cheyenne Women Warriors, 178n1
  honoring from birth, 232–33
  as keepers of community, 25, 336
  Kingfisher's search for grandmothers, 201–2, 212–13
  Nanyehi, 204–8
  rape of, 210, 229–31, 234–36, 359–60
  as slaves, 3, 336
  social equality of, 139
  spiritual needs in prisons, 74–77
  subservience of, 267–69
  and Trail of Tears, 210–11
  warfare against, 19, 170–71, 175–76
Woodward, Bob, 184, 197–98
Worcester v. Georgia, 119–20, 121, 129
Wordcraft Circle of Native Writers and Storytellers, 246
World War II Navajo Code Talkers, 323–24
Wounded Knee (1973), 60, 185, 218
Wounded Knee Massacre (1890), 219–20, 298, 322, 361–62
Wright, Louis B., 43
Wyandot Nation, 317–18, 396

Yakima Reservation, 316
Yaqui Nation (Mexico), 12
"Year They Drilled for Oil, The" (Russell), 136–38
YMCA and YWCA, 87–89
Young, Granville Walker "G.W.", 220–21
Young Man, Alfred, 296–98
Yucatán, 12
Yurok Nation, 288, 289–95, 393
Yurok Tribal Fisheries Program, 287